Tourette's Syndrome

Finding Answers and Getting Help

C1

Tourette's Syndrome

Finding Answers and Getting Help

Mitzi Waltz

Beijing • Cambridge • Farnham • Köln • Paris • Sebastopol • Taipei • Tokyo

Tourette's Syndrome: Finding Answers and Getting Help
by Mitzi Waltz

Copyright © 2001 Mitzi Waltz All rights reserved.
Printed in the United States of America.

Published by O'Reilly & Associates, Inc., 101 Morris Street, Sebastopol, CA 95472.

Editor: Nancy Keene

Production Editor: Tom Dorsaneo

Cover Designer: Kristen Throop

Printing History:

       June 2001: First Edition

Library of Congress Cataloging-in-Publication Data:

Waltz, Mitzi
    Tourette's syndrome: finding answers and getting help / Mitzi Waltz.
        p. cm.—(Patient-centered guides)
    Includes bibliographical references and index.
    ISBN 0-596-50007-6
    1. Tourette syndrome--Popular works. I. Title. II. Series.

RC375.W35 2001
616.8'3—dc21   2001018507

[M]

For Jackie and the Sunrise Tourette family

Table of Contents

Preface

WHEN YOUR CHILD is diagnosed with a medical problem, no matter what it is, it turns your world upside down. There are so many questions you want to ask, and so few minutes available to talk openly with your child's doctor about your concerns and fears.

As the parent of a 10-year-old son with Tourette's syndrome (TS), I remember well how it felt to be in that position. It all began in kindergarten, with a simple eye-blink. And then another, and another, and another, in rapid succession, several times each hour. Then his nose began to twitch. He started licking his upper lip so often that the skin became chapped and red.

He has other health challenges in addition to tics, but these strange, repetitive movements were so noticeable—and so distressing to him, to his teachers, and to me—that I couldn't help but worry.

Getting an actual diagnosis took several months. The delay was partly because his pediatrician wasn't sure what she was seeing, and partly because even in the hands of an expert, the official diagnostic criteria for TS call for a wait of many months. As I waited, however, I learned more about Tourette's. It helped me understand some things my son did that had been mysterious before, like the odd shrieks he often emitted for no obvious reason, and the way he seemed to get "stuck" on repeating certain behaviors.

In a way, the doctor's final pronouncement that my child had Tourette's syndrome was a profound relief. His symptoms now had a name, a description, and a set of treatments. I could let go of my secret worry that these odd movements were actually signs of some terrible disease, or that they were caused by an inner anxiety that I could not soothe.

I'm happy to report that my worries about my son's tics were largely misplaced. I've learned that the greatest problems experienced by people with Tourette's syndrome are usually not the tics themselves, but learning to live with them, and coping with how others react to them.

I can't say that either of these tasks has been easy to master. My husband and I are still kicking ourselves for all the times we hissed "stop it!" at our son for repeating an odd or annoying behavior.

As for other people's reactions…well, that one's a bit more difficult. I try hard to accept that other people's stares and rude remarks are outside of my control, but I still do a slow burn when adults who should know better are unnecessarily critical. I've also learned when to give in to my protective instincts, advocating for my child in public and in school when I can.

For his part, my son takes ticcing in stride unless someone else points it out in an unpleasant way. It's simply something he does, often without even noticing, although when a particularly obvious tic pops up he may become self-conscious. He has learned to joke about it, a skill that should help him cope well in the future. He has met other children with TS, and that has actually helped quite a bit.

With my son's permission, and his doctor's agreement, I have decided not to be aggressive with medical treatments aimed at covering up or eliminating tics. Instead, I have concentrated on helping him increase his self-awareness so he understands when his noises or movements have crossed the line of social acceptability, and helping him come up with creative solutions for handling those times when offense to others could occur. His teachers, his father, and I also focus on building up his self-esteem, letting him know that tics are just a minor part of who he is, and not something that can stand in the way of his dreams.

Indeed, it seems heretical to say so, but as I've gotten to know more people with Tourette's syndrome through support groups, I sometimes think the condition might just be a blessing a disguise.

While it's true that people with severe tics can experience physical and mental discomfort beyond what anyone should endure, almost everyone with TS that I've met also has certain gifts. Foremost among these is a sense of humor that makes their company exciting and fun.

In today's business parlance, they're "out-of-the-box thinkers," creative, sharp individuals whose sense of adventure and playfulness may come from the same lack of inhibition that allows their uncontrolled movements. They're the kind of people who take up skydiving, or neurosurgery, and give it their all.

The world needs more people like that, I think.

That's not to say that Tourette's syndrome can't be difficult to deal with. Many people need and want to control their tics with medication, which is currently the only proven treatment. Children with TS usually need a little extra help with school—not with academics so much as with maintaining focus, staying organized, and handling social pressures. And a large proportion of people with Tourette's, including my son, have other neurological disorders that can combine with TS to create increased personal difficulties.

The good news is that there is a wealth of helpful information available. This book is intended to bring together all of the basic facts needed by the parents of a child or teenager diagnosed with Tourette's syndrome, and by adults with TS. Teachers, therapists, counselors, and other professionals who work with people who have TS or their families should also find it useful.

But in many ways, this book is just a starting point. It will direct you to national resources, like the Tourette Syndrome Association, and to sources of information and support closer to home. I hope that it will prove to be a worthy companion on your journey to diagnosis, through treatment, and beyond, into handling TS in everyday life.

A few notes about the text

The first two chapters of this book provide a broad overview of Tourette's syndrome, explaining the medical facts about TS and how it is diagnosed. The chapters that follow cover personal and family coping strategies, medical and alternative treatment options, school issues, and dealing with insurance problems and the healthcare system. Appendix A, *Resources*, lists books, web sites, organizations, special diagnostic and treatment centers, and more to help you find the assistance you need.

I've done my best to provide accurate information about resources in the English-speaking world, including North America, the UK, the Republic of Ireland, Australia, and New Zealand. Tourette's syndrome is a universal phenomenon, however, and occurs in all races and nationalities. Readers in other parts of the world may be able to find local resources and current information in languages other than English on the World Wide Web; some of the web sites and email discussion groups listed in Appendix A can point you toward resources in your part of the world. Simply because this book was written in the US, some information may be skewed toward American readers. Most, however, will be useful to all.

Throughout the text I discuss findings from the latest medical research. This information is not intended as medical advice. Please consult your physician before starting, stopping, or changing any medical treatment. Some of the health information provided comes from small studies, or is experimental or controversial in nature.

Readers should carefully examine any claims made by healthcare facilities, pharmaceutical firms, therapists, supplement manufacturers, and others before implementing new treatments.

Although Tourette's syndrome is more common in boys and men, it also occurs in girls and women, so I've tried to alternate between pronouns when talking about patients.

You will find the words of people with Tourette's syndrome or their parents throughout this book. Their quotes are offset from the rest of the text and presented in italics. In many cases, names and other identifying details have been changed at the person's request.

Acknowledgments

Many teenagers and adults with TS, and over thirty parents of children with TS, took the time to answer my questions about their personal experiences. Their stories helped me make the information presented in this book as comprehensive as possible. They deserve much of the credit for this book, as their replies guided its structure, contents, and focus. No one understands the impact of TS better than people who have lived with it, in all its manifestations.

Special thanks go out to all those who helped with advice, ideas, and their own stories, including Barbara A. Boodhan, Dvora Hersh, Carol and Steve Sordoni, Cathie Coppedge, Cheri Slattery, Deb and Alex Jerison, Grace Deakin, Keith Jarrett, Joyce S., Keith P. Adney, Jennifer Koehler, Kerry, Mary T. Hood, Vicki Hill Riedel, Andrea Krapf Betts, Gabrielle Tindall, Jen and Paul, Len Dalman, Dr. Maria Pugliese Hieble, and many others.

A draft of the manuscript was reviewed by Colleen Wang, RN, medical liaison for the Tourette Spectrum Disorder Association; Dr. Ruth Bruun, prominent TS clinician and researcher; Jackie Aron, RN, an adult with TS and moderator of the Sunrise Tourette mailing list; Chantal Trahan, in-service provider and Resource Unit Coordinator on behalf of the Tourette Syndrome Foundation of Canada, who is also a teacher, an adult with TS, and the parent a child with TS; parent Deborah Smith; attorneys Mark Weissburg of David A. Bryant & Associates and John R. Heard of Heard & Smith, both experts in disability benefits law; and Sandi Bravman, parent of a child with TS and a former corporate health insurance administrator. Their comments, corrections, and criticisms were invaluable, and much appreciated.

Sue Levi-Pearl, director of medical and scientific programs for the Tourette Syndrome Association (TSA) and her colleague Milton Sutton have also been particularly helpful. TSA is a wonderful source of accurate, up-to-date information for families and patients. It has state and local chapters throughout the US, and can help you contact others in your area who are coping with the challenges of TS. In Canada, the Tourette Syndrome Foundation is an equally valuable organization.

Contacts made through Sunrise Tourette, a mailing list moderated by Jackie Aron, have also been essential to this project. I thank everyone who shared their experiences and concerns with me over the years, and particularly the many individuals who patiently told their stories to me once again, answered my latest questions, and cheered me on while I worked on the book.

Nancy Keene, Linda Lamb, Shawnde Paull, Sarah Jane Shangraw, Edie Freedman, and all of the extraordinarily professional editorial staff at O'Reilly & Associates have my utmost respect and admiration, as does my literary agent, Karen Nazor.

Despite the inspiration and contributions of so many, any errors, omissions, misstatements, or flaws are entirely my own.

—Mitzi Waltz
June 2001

If you would like to comment on this book or offer suggestions for future editions, please send e-mail to *guides@oreilly.com,* or write to O'Reilly and Associates Inc. at 101 Morris St., Sebastopol, CA 95472.

CHAPTER 1

Introduction to Tourette's Syndrome

TOURETTE'S SYNDROME (TS) is a neurological condition that can be embarrassing, painful, even disabling. It is characterized by uncontrollable movements called tics that last for over a year, sometimes disappearing temporarily. Physical tics can be as basic as rhythmic eye-blinking, or as involved as twirling eight times and shouting each time you pass through a doorway.

This chapter introduces the common symptoms associated with Tourette's syndrome and explains what's known about the causes of this nervous system disorder. It begins by discussing how common TS is and briefly recounting the history of the disorder.

The following section describes the most frequently reported symptoms of TS, and lists many common physical (motor) and vocal tics. The chapter includes discussions about the many things that can cause tics, and a few things that definitely don't. It concludes with a general discussion about facing Tourette's syndrome.

Tics and Tourette's syndrome

Tics are actually quite common—about 12 in every 100 children will have a tic at some time during childhood—but normally they disappear after a few months or years.[1] When this happens, the child is not diagnosed with Tourette's syndrome. If any label is applied (usually one is not), it's "transient tics of childhood," indicating that the behaviors are relatively unimportant blips in an otherwise normal youth. If no new tics develop, and if the tic itself isn't self-injurious or terribly embarrassing, most doctors feel that the best treatment is no treatment. The tic should simply be ignored until it naturally disappears.

Likewise, some children have motor tics that persist for years, but never have a single vocal tic—or vice versa. Technically, the correct diagnosis for ongoing tics of only one type is "chronic multiple tic disorder." This is an area of some controversy among clinicians diagnosing and treating Tourette's, however. All tics, even those that include sounds, are caused by physical movements. Some clinicians feel that any person who has more than one tic for a long period of time should be diagnosed with TS, while others disagree.

No one is sure how many people have Tourette's syndrome, but the most reliable estimate of prevalence seems to be 1 in every 200 to 300 people. It is four times more common in males than in females.[2]

Surprisingly, it's not unusual for a child with Tourette's to be misdiagnosed for a long time, or to never be diagnosed at all. Often the first diagnosis is Attention Deficit Hyperactivity Disorder (ADHD), which frequently occurs with TS but may also be a convenient explanation for the behavior of a child who is always in motion. Another common error is blaming the behaviors on allergies.

Andrea, mother of 17-year-old Robbie, explains:

> He was 4 years old when we first noticed his behaviors, which included throat-clearing and clucking his tongue, but we didn't know these were tics until he was diagnosed with Tourette's syndrome at about 8. Robbie was tested for allergies twice and had his adenoids out (which evidently he needed to have done anyway) in an attempt to understand why he was constantly clearing his throat.

Tourette's syndrome normally emerges before the age of 18, usually around age 6 or 7. It's often complicated by additional challenges, particularly obsessive-compulsive disorder (OCD), ADHD, problems with anger control, specific learning disabilities, and sleep disorders.

The history of Tourette's syndrome

Tourette's syndrome was first described as a medical condition in the 19th century, although many older accounts describe tics, twitches, and odd behaviors that probably indicate the presence of TS. These behaviors were often ignored, sometimes ridiculed, and occasionally blamed on possession by evil spirits or demons.

In 1885, French neurologist Georges Gilles de la Tourette published a two-part article, "Study of a Nervous Affliction," that summarized his clinical observations of patients with tics. Although he wasn't the first physician to describe tic disorders, Gilles de la Tourette's paper was so interesting and influential that for many decades no one questioned what he had said about the condition named in his honor. Unfortunately, some of his beliefs about tic disorders were not entirely accurate. For example, he believed that TS always gets worse over time, and that a progression toward the symptom known as coprolalia—unwanted cursing—was inevitable.

There was no effective treatment for TS in the 19th century, nor were the causes of the disorder known. Some early researchers suspected that it was caused by brain infection, but they lacked the means to explore this theory. Others noted that the disorder appeared to run in families.

Unfortunately, both ideas were thrown aside in the early 20th century, replaced by notions based on the work of psychiatrist Sigmund Freud and his disciples. These individuals floated strange theories about tics as evidence of either compulsive masturbation or as a replacement for the urge to masturbate, and blamed both the patient and the patient's family for the condition. Some even claimed that tics were evidence of sexual child abuse. Treatment through long-term psychological analysis was suggested, and "success stories" were published that today's doctors recognize as simply reflecting the waxing and waning nature of TS symptoms.

The first challenges to these theories came around 1959, with the advent of psychiatric medications like Thorazine and Haldol. Doctors discovered that administering these strong drugs usually reduced or eliminated tics.

Today, researchers have proven that Tourette's syndrome is a neurological condition, and much better treatments have been designed. Researchers are working hard to learn more about the disorder and its causes. Unfortunately, some doctors do not recognize TS when they see it, and some still do not understand that it is not a psychological problem. Others don't know that symptoms like severe motor tics or coprolalia are not required to make a diagnosis of TS.

Signs and symptoms

Although each person with Tourette's syndrome is unique, the one thing all people with TS have in common is tics.

Most tics involve simple physical movements known as motor tics. These movements can involve any muscle group in the body, including those used for speech.

When the mouth or throat is involved, the result can be vocal tics: sounds, words, even phrases that erupt for no reason. These are also sometimes called phonic tics.

Simple tics involve just one movement, such as shrugging a shoulder or blinking an eye; complex tics combine at least two movements and/or sounds.

Some tics are easy to recognize; some aren't. And because they wax, wane, and change their form, it's easy to dismiss many tics as "nervous habits," the effects of stress or allergies, or simply bad behavior.

Most people with TS have certain long-lasting tics, others that come and go, and occasional tics that appear only once in a lifetime and last just a short while.

It's incredible, but as the Afterword to this book illustrates, it's not unusual for a person with Tourette's syndrome to remain undiagnosed for many years or even decades.

Jen, mother of 6-year-old Paul, says it took a long time to recognize his tics:

> My son Paul started blinking his eyes repeatedly when he was 4 years old. I thought it was just a nervous habit. I suffer from allergies, so I thought maybe his eyes were itchy like mine. Pinching his penis—don't all boys do that? Tugging his shirt at the shoulders. He had just started kindergarten then, and I thought his shirts were bugging him because they were a little big. Nail picking—don't all kids do that, and a lot of adults too? After a cold he had a lingering cough. I even looked that up in a medical book for children. It said many times children cough out of habit after a cold, so I just ignored it.
>
> I didn't tell his doctor for two years. The tics could all be explained away. They were mild. There was only one at a time. Maybe if they all happened at the same time or he did it all day I would have questioned it more.

Some tics are very common, some less so, and many people with Tourette's syndrome have a few tics that are quite unique. Probably the easiest tics to spot, and the most frequently noticed and reported, involve that most expressive of body parts: the face. Common motor tics include:

- Eye-blinking
- Eye-rolling
- Wrinkling or twitching the nose
- Poking or picking the nose
- Facial grimaces
- Spitting
- Flipping or twirling hair
- Rolling the head around on the neck

- Shrugging or jerking the shoulders
- Stretching or twisting the torso
- "Cracking" the back, knuckles, or other body parts
- Tapping fingers or feet (often a certain number of times or in a specific rhythm)
- Straightening clothes
- Moving body parts, such as the feet, so that they are in line with each other
- Picking at the skin
- Licking or kissing oneself
- Grabbing or touching the genital area
- Thrusting pelvic movements
- Thrusting arm or leg movements
- Compulsively touching objects
- Compulsively touching, licking, kissing, or hugging other people
- Bending or jumping
- Twirling around
- Performing movements a certain number of times, or at certain intervals (for example, twirling after every fifth step)
- Pulling out hair from the head or body (known as trichotillomania, this behavior is not usually considered a tic if it occurs alone)

Common vocal tics include:

- Throat-clearing
- Tongue-clicking
- Sounds made by blowing out or sucking in air
- Snorts and other nasal sounds
- "Bronx cheers"/"raspberries"
- Whistling
- Grunting
- Shrieks or similar high-pitched sounds
- Humming
- Hoots

- Howls

- Burps or belches

- Animal noises (meows, barks, etc.)

- Repetition of one's own words (palilalia)

- Repetition of other people's words (echolalia)

- Imitation of accents or cartoon voices

- Repetition of words or phrases out of context

Palilalia and echolalia also occur in some people with autism or schizophrenia, which can lead to diagnostic confusion.

These symptoms can also lead to other types of confusion. For example, if you ask a person who is echolalic "Would you like ice cream, or cake?" his first response may be "cake"—or perhaps "cake, cake, cake"—even if he really wants ice cream. A person with palilalia may repeat words or phrases many times in succession, and might seem to have a stutter instead of a tic.

The physical version of echolalia is called echopraxia: copying the movements of others. A child with echopraxia might put his hand in the air whenever the classmate to his right does, or unconsciously mimic the facial expressions of others. Many people with TS seem quite skillful mimics, despite the unintentional nature of the act.

It is much more common for vocal tics to be sounds rather than words, and more common for them to be words rather than entire phrases. When a person with TS does repeat phrases, the repeated phrases are usually inappropriate to the conversation at hand—but contrary to the common image of TS, not necessarily obscene. Many kids with TS have vocal tics that involve repeating snippets of dialog from cartoons, movies, or advertisements.

Linda, mother of 10-year-old William, tells about some of her son's tics:

> Will's first tic was an eye twitch, which showed up when he was in kindergarten. We took him to the pediatrician to see if he might have an eye infection or something, but she said he was fine. Next he started twitching his nose, then picking it compulsively. We yelled at him a lot for that one, I'm sorry to say. Then he started blinking both eyes over and over, and pursing up his mouth. At this point, a bell went off and we realized something was going on. It's like his facial expressions were always in motion, he was ticcing so much.

> *Over the years we have seen a lot of different tics, involving more than just his face. Some have been worse than others; some are actually kind of cute, although even those can get on your nerves. I remember when he saw Robin Williams in "Flubber" and for months afterward he was stuck on repeating a phrase from the movie, "Shake your little flubber booty," during all sorts of inappropriate moments.*
>
> *You have to develop the ability to accept ticcing, and even to laugh with your kid about it. That's not easy if the tic involves something like picking his nose or, worse yet, his behind. It's a little easier to get used to a twitching nose. But once you realize the kid can't help it, you find ways to handle it and to help him cope.*

Less than 15 percent of people with TS ever experience the most notorious tic of all: coprolalia, the uncontrollable use of swear words or derogatory terms, such as racial or sexual epithets. Of that 15 percent, most have coprolalia for only a while.[3] Like other tics, it tends to come and go over time. However, a somewhat larger group of people with TS experience what might be called "silent coprolalia": an urge to shout out inappropriate words that requires an exhaustive amount of energy to fight.

There is also a physical version of coprolalia, known as copropraxia. People with this symptom make obscene gestures rather than saying obscene or insulting words.

A person with TS may also feel compelled to repeat acts a specific number of times, or to perform behaviors in a certain sequence or pattern. These tics most resemble behaviors associated with OCD. It can be just about impossible to tease the two apart, especially since many people with TS have OCD as well. The main difference is that the urge to tic "feels" physical, while OCD rituals are usually connected to alleviating anxious feelings, as when a person feels she must tap things three times to ward off harm.

Some tics are self-injurious, such as biting or hitting oneself; others cause pain and discomfort inadvertently, such as muscle strains caused by repeated shrugging movements. However, most people with Tourette's agree that the greatest pain connected with this disorder comes from the misguided reactions of observers—condemnation, teasing, and social exclusion.

Rindy, mother of 14-year-old Shawn, says he has experienced social exclusion due to TS-linked behaviors, and has not coped well with it:

> *In general, the teasing from other kids is the hardest thing for Shawn to handle. He has difficulty coping when other kids give him a hard time.*

His social circle is limited—he's at the age where being different is a reason to be exploited and ostracized, so he gets disappointed and frustrated over and over again because of the cruelty of same-age kids in the neighborhood and at school. Most of the teasing probably is occurring because of his reactionary nature rather than the tics.

He rages when a compulsion is interrupted or when he feels physically threatened. His anger is always extreme; he has a concrete sense of right/ wrong and justice, and cannot understand how others could disagree with or not see something so obvious and logical. He reacts in an extreme manner over excessive noise, sensory input, demands upon him, or excessive activity that is not within his control. His first impulse is to run away, curl into a ball under a bush, or go up a tree or inside a heating duct where no one can get to him, but he will react if unable to escape.

Causes of tics

Like every kind of body movement, tics begin in the brain. The mechanism isn't fully understood. As the list of common tics earlier in this chapter illustrates, most are variations on unconscious, automatic behaviors that people routinely perform, such as blinking your eyes when they feel dry, or absent-mindedly brushing your hair out of your face.

Under normal conditions, if there is a sense of discomfort somewhere, the nerves nearby perceive it and send a message to the brain, and the brain responds with a command for a movement that addresses the problem. In people with TS, the genesis of a tic might come from the brain making a misstep at any point in that process— researchers just don't know where. It could be that the nerves are sending the brain erroneous messages. More likely, the brain is responding to perfectly normal messages from the nerves with the wrong command, and then repeating that command; instead of sending the signal for a single eye-blink, it sends out a signal for ten in a row.

What doctors know for sure is that people do not tic on purpose. You can resist the urge to tic temporarily, but eventually you must give in or experience great discomfort. The term many people prefer is *unvoluntary*, meaning not absolutely automatic and unpreventable, but unwanted and extremely hard to resist.

The distinction between involuntary and unvoluntary is subtle. If something is completely involuntary, you don't know it's coming, and you can't stop it. Good examples are the automatic knee reflex your doctor tests for with a little rubber hammer, or the way your eyes automatically blink several times each minute to stay moist. With a movement that's unvoluntary, on the other hand, you might know it's coming, you might even be able to use all your mental and physical strength to hold it back, but eventually it will break through your defenses. For example, everyone has experienced the urge to sneeze in an inappropriate situation, like during a symphony concert. The urge is strong and hard to resist. Perhaps by focusing your will on not sneezing you can beat back the urge or at least delay the sneeze until you can leave the room. But if the urge to sneeze becomes strong enough, there's just no stopping it. That's what a tic feels like to a person with TS.

Various tics "feel" different before they occur and while they're occurring, according to people with TS. Some of them, especially simple tics like eye-blinks and nose-twitches, tend to be rapid, occur in groups, and are just about unstoppable because they come with little or no advance warning. Young children are especially unlikely to notice the early warning signs of an upcoming tic. The more complex a tic, the more likely a person will have a little bit of a warning. There may or may not be enough time to prevent the movement or to leave the room, however.

When Jen's son Paul was 5, he did a great job of explaining how tics feel from a child's perspective:

> One night his head began to jerk to one side and he would tuck his chin into his neck. It scared me greatly because it distorted his face so much. I did not react to the tic, but after he was all tucked into bed and we did our ritual goodnight stuff, I asked him "Why were you turning your head like that?" He was scared, and said "My body makes me do that, I can't stop it." I could tell it bothered him. Then he asked about another tic he had. He describes it as "clicking" the back of his neck with the bottom of his skull. He would bend his head back a little and twist it. He said he was afraid he was going to hurt himself doing that but he could not stop. So here this poor kid had been having these feelings and hid them and his tics.

> That's when I started to research TS. When I read the material I found on the Internet, I sat in my chair and cried. There on the list of symptoms were many things Paul had done. When I read that tics come and go and change, it clicked—I knew he had TS. It explained so much of his behavior…why he put marks in his hand from digging the nails from his other hand into them, and why he said "I can't stop, my body makes me do it" when his fingers were bleeding from picking them so much.

If you have many and frequent tics, the constant effort of trying to prevent or disguise these movements and sounds is stressful and absolutely exhausting. Worse yet, it seems that the harder you try to suppress the unwanted behaviors, the stronger they get. You may manage to hold back a bout of upcoming tics throughout a short appointment, only to have a terrible, jolting, and far worse episode of ticcing as soon as you are safely out of the room.

Inside the brain

If you could look inside the brain of a person with Tourette's syndrome, you wouldn't see anything grossly abnormal. Nothing would be missing, and any observable differences would be quite subtle.

It's how the brain works that's different in TS. Advanced brain-scanning technologies have recently allowed researchers to literally watch circuits misfiring inside the brains of people with TS, but even before brain scans, neurologists already knew that the kinds of automatic behaviors involved in most common tics begin with signals sent by the basal ganglia.

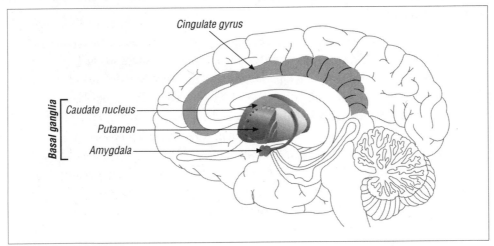

Figure 1-1. Parts of the human brain thought to be involved in Tourette's syndrome

Also known as the striatum, the basal ganglia are tiny structures grouped together deep inside the brain's center. These structures include the putamen, the caudate nucleus, and the amygdala, all of which have jobs whose importance is all out of proportion to their size. They're in charge of controlling built-in, practically unconscious movements, such as raising your hands to fend off an oncoming object. They also control impulsiveness and inhibition. The amygdala is specifically involved in controlling fear and rage.

Brain scans are not used to diagnose TS, but they are helping researchers understand what happens when people tic. Using techniques like transcranial magnetic stimulation (TMS) and functional magnetic resonance imaging (fMRI), researchers have found that the neurons of people with TS appear to be more active and less inhibited.[4] There is a different pattern of blood flow in the brain in TS, indicating unusual activity,[5] and there also are subtle differences in the size of structures within TS-affected basal ganglia[6,7] and those involved in the closely related disorder OCD.[8]

Neurotransmitter differences

All parts of the brain are made up of cells called neurons and glial cells. The glial cells don't seem to play a role in TS, but neurons do. Neurons are the brain's internal communication centers, but they don't trade messages directly. Instead, they rely on a complicated sequence of electrical and chemical messengers.

Neurons have a central cell body with long "arms" called *axons,* and smaller tentacle-like structures called *dendrites.* (See Figure 1-2, "The structure of a neuron.") All of the messages within a neuron are sent via electrical impulses. Where two neurons meet to swap information, however, a small space between them remains. This space is called a synapse. Their electrical impulses have to be translated into chemicals called neurotransmitters to cross the synapse, after which the chemical messages are re-translated into electrical signals on the other side. (See Figure 1-3, "Neurotransmitters crossing the synaptic cleft.")

Most people have heard of the chemicals known as hormones. These chemicals, which include estrogen and testosterone, are special neurotransmitters that carry information about reproduction-related development and activity between the brain and the body. Many of these compounds have multiple effects on the body; for example, estrogen affects such diverse functions as ovulation, mood, and water retention.

Dozens of similar chemicals relay information between the central nervous system (CNS) and other parts of the body, such as the gastrointestinal system. They're all site-specific chemicals, which means they can pass on their commands only to certain cells, and only at certain spots. This ensures that the right kinds of messages get through. When neurons fire off commands unnecessarily, they may send out error messages that cause movements directly, and they may also send out error messages that affect neurotransmitter production and use.

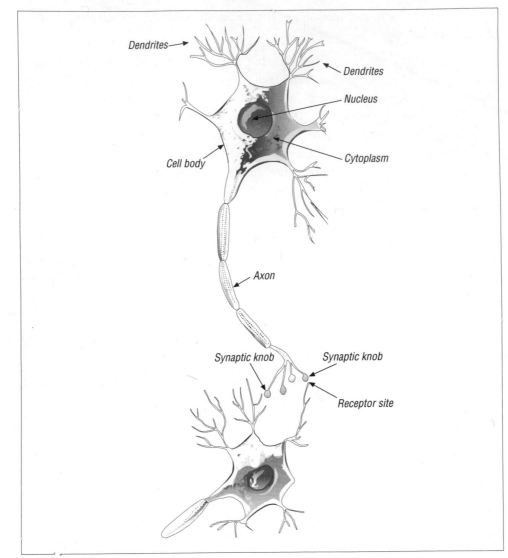

Figure 1-2. The structure of a neuron

Dopamine (DA) appears to be the main neurotransmitter involved in Tourette's syndrome. Dopamine helps control body movements and thought patterns—some doctors refer to it as the body's chemical braking system. It also helps regulate the release of other neurotransmitters and some hormones. Dopamine plays a prominent role in other movement disorders, such as Parkinson's disease, as well as in TS.

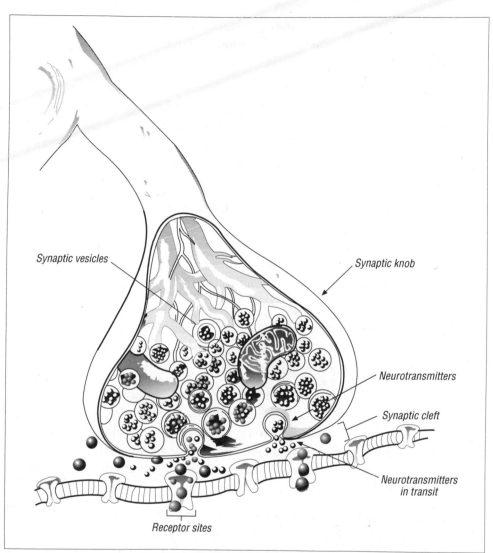

Figure 1-3. *Neurotransmitters crossing the synaptic cleft*

Two other neurotransmitters, norepinephrine and serotonin (5-HT), are also involved in TS somehow, perhaps influenced by differences in dopamine production or use. Norepinephrine regulates blood pressure, and is involved with the body's "fight or flight" response to perceived danger. *Serotonin* controls sleep, mood, some types of sensory perception, and appetite; it helps the body regulate its temperature, influences the release of certain hormones and neurotransmitters (including dopamine), and responds (and sometimes over-responds) to inflammation in both the gastrointestinal tract and the brain.

Medications that change how much of certain hormones and neurotransmitters are produced, or how these chemicals are absorbed in the brain, can produce changes in the symptoms experienced by people with TS, including making tics more or less frequent. All of the effective medications for treating TS affect dopamine levels; some also affect norepinephrine and/or serotonin. Medications used to treat TS are covered in Chapter 6, *Medical Care*.

Exercise, diet, vitamins, and herbal supplements can also affect neurotransmitter production and function. This is one of the reasons that parents and professionals need to be as careful about choosing complementary treatments as they would be about choosing prescription drugs. For more information about nonpharmaceutical treatments for TS, see Chapter 7, *Other Interventions*.

Immune system differences

Immune system differences are a hot topic in Tourette's syndrome research today, as they may be at the root of at least some cases of TS.

One thing that still divides "mental" illness from "physical" illness in the minds of both patients and doctors is that diagnosing mental illness is a very subjective process. You can take a blood test for hepatitis, and you can get a biopsy for cancer, but diagnosing mental illness requires observing symptoms and making a judgment call. Imagine the excitement that swept the medical research community when the first biological marker for a mental illness was discovered in late 1996!

Dr. Susan Swedo and a team of doctors working with the National Institutes for Mental Health, a Federal research facility, evaluated children who developed unusual movements and/or obsessive-compulsive symptoms after an illness known as rheumatic fever. Rheumatic fever is a serious complication of infection with group A beta-hemolytic streptococcus (GABHS) bacteria, the same bacteria that causes strep throat and many childhood ear infections. Children who have had rheumatic fever often develop a movement disorder called Sydenham's chorea, which is characterized by twisting, writhing movements of the hands and legs, facial grimaces, obsessions, over-emotional behavior, anxiety, and compulsions.

These unusual symptoms have been known for well over 100 years, and were the topic of much debate and research around the end of the 19th century. Unfortunately, early psychologists did much to sweep the link between infectious illness and mood or behavior changes under the rug because it conflicted with their theories. Even in cases of Tourette's where the person was known to have had rheumatic fever or encephalitis before the tics emerged, these psychologists either set aside infectious causes, or declared that they were only a contributing factor.[9]

Luckily, Dr. Swedo's team took a closer look, and found an unusual protein, m protein, and B-lymphocyte antigen D8/17 in the blood of most rheumatic fever patients who developed these extra symptoms. Then the team took a look at a group of children with OCD and/or Tourette's syndrome.

Parents had been telling doctors for years that their child with OCD and/or Tourette's had a sudden onset of the illness, or that their symptoms took a noticeable turn for the worse not long after a bout with strep throat. They had also wondered aloud why some children with these disorders (and, it should be noted, some children with ADD/ADHD or autistic spectrum disorders) suffered from so many more serious ear infections than their siblings or other children the same age.

Brenda, grandmother of 10-year-old Charisse, relates a typical story:

> Charisse suffered from tonsillitis and ear infections every few months
> as a young child. We finally pushed for removal of tonsils, and she also
> had her adenoids removed and ear tubes inserted. The family doctor
> seemed to dismiss what we were talking about, in terms of behaviors that
> were worrisome, from about age 3 on. He made my daughter feel very
> uncomfortable and almost incompetent as she described the behaviors.
> At age 5-and-a-half, when the behaviors were being noticed by others
> and the school, it took six months to get a diagnosis of ADHD and TS
> because we had to push to consult a specialist.

These parents' questions went unanswered until Dr. Swedo's team announced its preliminary findings: 85 percent of children with OCD or Tourette's syndrome who seemed to have new or more symptoms following strep infection also had the same blood protein and D8/17 marker as children who developed Sydenham's chorea after getting rheumatic fever.[10] Another study of children with OCD and/or tics found that 100 percent had the D8/17 marker.[11] (It should be noted that Dr. Swedo's work built on research started by Dr. Louise Kiessling at Brown University.)

Swedo's groundbreaking study indicated a strong relationship between immune function and at least some cases of TS and OCD. According to Swedo, the bodies of children who have the D8/17 marker create antibodies to the strep bacteria, just as they should, but those antibodies attack the basal ganglia in the brain as well. It's that attack on the body's own tissue—an autoimmune reaction—that causes the unusual movements in children with Sydenham's chorea and the tics and obsessive-compulsive symptoms seen in this subgroup of children with OCD and/or Tourette's syndrome.[12]

Much more research needs to be done, but one thing is certain: there is a link between a malfunctioning immune system in some—but not all—patients and the appearance and severity of their TS and/or obsessive-compulsive symptoms. Dr. Swedo has named this disorder "pediatric autoimmune neurological disorders associated with strep" (PANDAS).

Strep and autoimmunity may be involved in other neurological disorders as well. A large, formal study has not yet been done in children with ADD/ADHD, but one small study of children with autism identified the D8/17 blood marker in 78 percent of the patients tested, and found that the severity of their symptoms correlated strongly to the marker's presence.[13]

Currently, there's no commercial version of the blood test that Dr. Swedo's team used in its study.

Some children with tics who had a sudden onset after a strep infection or repeated flares in response to strep have been diagnosed with PANDAS simply by observation, and given treatments that seem to help. Chapter 6, *Medical Care,* has more information about these new treatment ideas.

Interestingly, an autoimmune reaction to strep may not be the only infectious link to TS. A link between tics and actual brain infection (encephalitis), as opposed to the inflammatory autoimmune reaction seen in PANDAS, has been known since at least the 1930s.[14] Encephalitis can be caused by a number of different viruses, including cytomegalovirus and several others in the human herpes virus family, the tick-borne virus that causes Lyme disease, and HIV.[15] Bacteria and fungal organisms can also affect the brain under some conditions. If a bacteria, virus, or fungal organism manages to cross the blood-brain barrier, a dividing line that keeps out most organisms, it could easily cause inflammation or damage (lesions) in the basal ganglia. Although no large-scale research has yet been done on non-streptococcal infections and TS, individual case studies have implicated the Lyme disease virus, human herpes virus, and other agents.[16,17]

Genetic differences

Genetic differences underlie the chemical and functional patterns that characterize Tourette's syndrome. These differences may affect brain structure, neurotransmitter production or use, the immune system, and even metabolism—or any combination of these and other factors. They may cause TS directly, or simply make a person more susceptible to developing TS in response to environmental factors such as infectious disease.

Normally, humans inherit 46 chromosomes: 22 pairs of non-sex chromosomes and two sex chromosomes (two X chromosomes for women; an X and a Y for men.) Each chromosome is made of deoxyribonucleic acid (DNA) molecules arranged in a structure that looks like a twisted ladder. The chromosome contains bits of code called genes. Your genes "program" everything about how you will develop, from the curliness of your hair to your vulnerability to ragweed allergies.

Some genes are dominant, which means you need to inherit only one copy of the gene to express the trait it codes for. For example, the gene that codes for brown eyes is dominant. Other genes are recessive, and so you need two copies of the gene to express the trait it codes for. Certain genes or combinations of genes follow even more complicated patterns of inheritance and expression.

As of this writing, scientists around the world are working feverishly to decode the mysteries of the human genetic code. The Human Genome Project is an ongoing effort to make a "map" of the whole human genotype. Although this effort won't identify the precise purpose of the genes mapped, the map itself will allow researchers to pinpoint genetic differences more clearly. For now, researchers are slowly cracking the genetic code by studying what happens when a gene is missing (deleted), changed (mutated), or duplicated. Geneticists know that TS is not going to be an easy puzzle to solve. It's definitely not caused by a single, dominant gene because a difference that easy to spot would have been found early in the genetic research process. It's almost surely what's called a multigenic or polygenic disorder: a problem caused by several genes working together. Some of these genes may be recessive, some dominant. Slightly different combinations of genes may cause TS, including variations specific to men and to women. Studying people with genetic disorders closely related to TS provides clues, as does new knowledge about some rare, genetic disorders that feature similar symptoms.

Some geneticists think that TS is an autosomal dominant disorder. Autosomal dominant genes are not on the X or Y chromosomes, so they can be carried by either parent and passed on to both male and female offspring. Even those researchers who do not support the autosomal dominant disorder theory think that TS genetics involves varying patterns of penetrance: that whether the primary TS gene or genes are actually expressed, and how they are expressed, depends on whether the person who inherits them also has one or more other genetic differences.

Researchers have theorized that this as-yet-unidentified autosomal dominant gene or genes occurs in about 1 or 2 in 100 people—about the same rate as the prevalence of adult OCD—but the combination of other genes that allows it to be expressed as Tourette's is probably more rare. These researchers believe OCD may be an alternative expression of the same basic genotype.[18]

The wild card when it comes to expression and severity is environmental factors, such as traumatic life experiences that could cause a tic-exacerbating chemical reaction, and infections. These seem to govern the severity of Tourette's syndrome symptoms in at least some cases.[19] Environmental factors may also make a difference in expression. This means that the primary gene for Tourette's syndrome may be passed on from generation to generation without being fully expressed as TS—perhaps it will be expressed as OCD, or as transient tics, or not at all.[20]

Researchers working on TS genetic studies are especially interested in families with more than one member who has the disorder. Participating usually requires nothing more than providing a blood sample or two and having a diagnostic workup. There is no charge to participants, and in some cases housing, meals, and transportation to the study site are provided. You can contact the Tourette Syndrome Association (see Appendix A, *Resources*) for more information about studies in your area.

Some genes suspected of involvement in TS have been identified, and research continues. Some possibilities may eventually be ruled out. Genes that may be linked to TS are shown in chart form in Appendix B, *Tourette's Syndrome Genetics*.

People with TS often want to know if their children will also have Tourette's syndrome, and parents with one child who has TS may wonder if subsequent children will have it as well. It's known that there's an increased likelihood of TS in siblings of children who have tics or OCD, and that parents with tics or OCD are more likely to have a child with TS. There is no way to predict whether the disorder will occur in a particular child, however. Families that are concerned about this issue can contact a genetic counselor for information and advice. Reputable, experienced genetic counselors are often available through major hospitals, and can help families assess risk and weigh their options.

Genetic studies may provide answers in the future, but for families struggling with TS today, they have not yet borne fruit. There is no genetic test to diagnose Tourette's syndrome.

What doesn't cause tics

Although parents pass on chromosomes to their children and chromosomes have lately been implicated in TS, parents can no more control this part of their genetic contribution than they can control the hair color of their offspring. There's no reason to feel guilty about it. There are even some who argue that the genes for TS probably carry some powerful benefits as well—perhaps the genes for wit and inspired wackiness, if there are such things, are also part of this genetic package.

Although stress can make tics worse, even the most rotten, mean, and downright abusive parents can't cause a child to have TS. Many older adults with TS went through years of painful psychoanalysis as children, back when Tourette's syndrome was blamed on everything from overprotective mothers to childhood conflicts over sex. Psychologists variously theorized that tics were caused by repressed urges to masturbate or that they were the result of excessive masturbation, that children deliberately ticced to get attention or to make others' lives miserable, or that tics were evidence of serious mental illness that would only get worse with time. Outrageous "treatments" were suggested—and perpetrated on suffering children and adults—including lobotomy and other types of brain surgery, restraint devices, electroconvulsive shock therapy, carbon dioxide inhalation, hypnosis, strong sedatives, and more. Until modern psychiatric drugs arrived on the scene, nothing really worked, although many practitioners falsely claimed to have cured tic disorders, preventing other researchers from following up on more promising leads.[21]

In sum, bad parenting can't cause TS—but there probably isn't a parent of a child with Tourette's syndrome who isn't carrying around a lot of guilt. If it's not misguided guilt over having caused the disorder itself, it's guilt about not recognizing it early on, perhaps even for having punished the child for ticcing. But unless you already know Tourette's is present elsewhere in your family and watch carefully for it, it's very difficult to figure out the diagnosis immediately.

Grace, mother of 17-year-old Keith, waited for years to get a diagnosis and help for her son, now a young adult:

> It took us until he was in his mid-teens to get his Tourette's actually confirmed and officially diagnosed, also to get his learning difficulties properly assessed as significant to severe. In the meantime, every kind of suggestion was made, from fragile X syndrome, to "manipulative naughty boy," to inadequate parenting or abuse.

All the time he was in school he was highly stressed, and we were too,
just waiting for the phone to ring about another incident, the next
stressful discussion with staff, or the next stage of the fight with the
education authority to get appropriate provision. Once we took him out
of school altogether, everything became simple. All the energies we had
been directing toward "putting out fires" now went directly toward helping
Keith. I wish I had done it right from the start of his school years, but I
did not know then that I had the option, nor would I at that stage have
had the confidence.

If you are the parent of a teenager with TS and you've been struggling all these years in ways that don't mesh with the current advice, don't feel badly—you didn't cause the disorder by making mistakes, and it's never too late to make positive changes. Like every other parent in this situation, you've been coping as best as you can. Hopefully this book will help you turn the situation around, bringing relief to your child and lowering your own stress level. (See Chapter 4, *Growing Up with Tourette's Syndrome*, for more information about parenting problems and solutions for families coping with TS.)

Another thing that doesn't cause TS is trauma—but children with a tendency to tic may respond to anxiety by ticcing more. The first time tics get bad enough to notice, and occasionally the first time they're seen at all, may be right after a frightening event such as an earthquake or car accident.

Rindy, mother of 14-year-old Shawn, says that his tics first became noticeable when he was under stress:

Shawn's tics were first noticed when he was in fourth grade, following
a traumatic series of events where he was harassed and bullied by two
other children for several months. He spent much time under his desk
during class before it was brought to my attention; getting him out of the
class into one where he was more protected was very difficult because
the teacher kept insisting she had everything under control and the
principal was uncooperative. The first tics we noticed were head and neck
tics; throat clearing had been happening at bedtime for months but we
never figured out why. Skin-picking and nail-biting were well established.
He started by lifting the eyes up so that his eyebrows were raised into his
forehead, and he added hand and foot tics to his routine later on as he
attempted to redirect painful neck tics. Behavior had been a problem for
quite some time before tics were noticed.

Facing Tourette's syndrome

Since it's such a common problem, it's surprising how little the average person knows about TS. Most people know it only from overblown portrayals in the media, like Rob Schneider's hapless Tourettic date in the movie "Deuce Bigalow: Male Gigolo," or severe cases paraded before talk-show audiences. These stereotypes, along with some of the older literature that you may find while researching immediately after a diagnosis, can make you worry about the future. They can also frighten children into thinking that their symptoms will only get worse, and give bullies and bigots extra ammunition for teasing people who tic.

Jen, mother of 6-year-old Paul, says having involuntary movements is scary enough without adding shame and fear to the mix:

> When we told Paul he had TS, he was a bit scared. His biggest fear was that everyone would make fun of him. When we told him there was medication he could take, he literally jumped up and down, and said he would use his Christmas money to buy it.

In truth, the tics experienced by most people with Tourette's syndrome are mild to moderate, and even the most severe cases can usually be successfully treated. While it's not always possible (or desirable) to make all of a person's tics disappear, they can usually be brought down to a manageable level.

Medication is the primary treatment for TS, but it isn't always needed. In the absence of self-injurious or severely disruptive tics, many people choose to focus on living well despite the disorder. Special education strategies, talk therapy, and developing coping skills all help, with or without medication. These strategies will be discussed in detail in Chapter 4, *Growing Up with Tourette's Syndrome,* Chapter 5, *Living with Tourette's Syndrome,* and Chapter 8, *School Issues.* Only when TS symptoms begin to interfere with normal daily life does medication become a desirable choice.

Paul seems to be developing a positive attitude early in life, despite his earlier worries. His mother relates their most recent conversation about Tourette's:

> This morning Paul comes up to me and says, "Mom, I don't mean to be mean, but I am better than you. I have tics, and people with tics are rare." So I guess we are not experiencing any self-esteem problems in this home with TS. I can just picture him on the playground at school: "Yeah? Well, I have Tourette's, and you don't! Na na na na na!"

CHAPTER 2

Diagnosis

FINDING A DOCTOR who recognizes Tourette's syndrome (TS) is not always easy, and making your way toward a diagnosis can be time-consuming and confusing. Some tics are easily recognized, but others can be mistaken for symptoms of other disorders. True TS experts are few, so you may find yourself educating your physician during the diagnostic process. This chapter discusses choosing a doctor and getting a diagnosis. It begins by walking you through the process—locating an expert, preparing for the diagnostic process, and knowing what to expect from the medical professionals you encounter.

It then outlines the current diagnostic criteria for Tourette's syndrome. It explains the concept of differential diagnosis—telling TS from other movement disorders—and defines the movement disorders and additional conditions your doctor may want to consider before she's sure it's Tourette's.

When the diagnosis is complicated by the presence of other conditions—particularly ADHD or obsessive-compulsive disorder—that can make a difference. Chapter 3, *Related Conditions,* provides basic information on these medical diagnoses and how they impact treatment for TS.

Getting started

If you're worried about your child's behavior and health, or your own, you probably just want to find an expert who can tell you exactly what's wrong and how to fix it. Unfortunately, that's not an easy task when it comes to neurological problems. The brain is a complex organ that affects every aspect of a person's ability to function. When something goes wrong, people who aren't medical professionals are often at a loss to recognize the problem for what it really is, and even experienced doctors sometimes find themselves groping in the dark.

Len, father of 14-year-old David, explains:

> *David's teachers were complaining to us about his behavior, although we didn't perceive any problem. He behaved very differently at home, partly because he was comfortable and felt safe, and partly because school put a lot of demands on him. The school psychologists suggested that he was guilty of willful misbehavior, and wouldn't accept that a neurological disorder was a possibility. Tics observed included hand- and foot-waving, grimacing, growling, and pacing. When he was 7, a diagnosis was finally made at a TS clinic by a neuropsychiatrist, psychiatric nurse, occupational therapist, and education consultant, all working as a team.*

If you feel certain that you or your child have tics, it's best to seek evaluation by a doctor who has expertise in diagnosing and treating TS and has worked with children in your child's age group or with adults, as needed. For some people, this may mean traveling to the nearest large city, but it will be worth it if you find the right person.

Your very best bet is a board-certified psychiatrist or neurologist who has a working relationship with a good hospital, preferably one affiliated with a university medical school. A board-certified doctor has completed a very rigorous training program, has already practiced for some years, and meets the highest qualifications in the field as set by an official board of his or her peers. Of course, the best doctors are also the busiest. Make sure you have a second choice in the wings, just in case.

You can reach the American Board of Psychiatry and Neurology at (847) 945-7900. You can also check a doctor's certification status with the American Board of Medical Specialties at (800) 776-CERT or on the Web at *http://www.certifieddoctor.org*.

Finding an expert

Many individuals and families coping with Tourette's wish they had spent more time finding the best possible doctor. Having an expert on your side from the beginning can help you get a quick diagnosis and information about state-of-the-art treatment options.

Cheri, mother of two daughters with Tourette's syndrome and OCD, explains:

> *Not knowing what we were dealing with and how to treat it in the beginning was the most stressful thing. Both girls have contamination*

fears as well as tics. In the very beginning we saw a child psychologist
for our 8-year-old—not a very good one, I might add—who was all over
the map with what might be wrong. After twelve or so sessions, she said,
"Well, I think she must have been sexually abused at some point." I knew
then we were getting nowhere. I was a stay-at-home mom and my
daughter never left my side. There was a lot I did not know, but that
was one thing I did know!

Then when our 3-year-old started to show signs of tics, I brought this to
the attention of our new pediatrician. He then suspected Tourette's in both
girls, and sent us to a neurologist.

Starting points for identifying a physician who is knowledgeable about TS include:

- The national Tourette Syndrome Association and its state and local chapters, or similar organizations in your area. The TSA does not endorse or recommend physicians, but it does maintain a list of doctors with expertise in this area. Members of your local TSA chapter will know much more, and can usually offer specific suggestions about doctors in your area.

- Specialty clinics for Tourette's syndrome. Although they are few in number, the professionals at these centers can help you get or rule out a TS diagnosis better than any others. They can also prepare a detailed report about the diagnosis, including a list of current symptoms and concrete suggestions for how to help. Even if you can't come back to the center for medication management and other ongoing assistance, this report can help you get what you need from a local practitioner.

- Specialty clinics that treat OCD, anxiety disorders, or movement disorders. While less likely to be at the cutting edge of TS diagnosis and treatment, these centers should have the essential knowledge base you need.

- The psychiatry or neurology department of a nearby medical school. Many medical schools have excellent clinics staffed by both experienced doctors and residents who are learning the ropes. Some of the foremost experts in TS are affiliated with university programs. These doctors are usually aware of the latest research findings and treatments.

- Internet discussion groups like Sunrise Tourette and alt.tourette. Chapter 4, *Growing Up With Tourette's Syndrome,* and Chapter 5, *Living With Tourette's Syndrome,* have more information about the value of support groups, both traditional and online, but it's best to make first contact with these groups when you are still in search of a diagnosis and help. You can save time and prevent heartache by tapping into these resources right away. Even if it turns out that the problems you're seeing are due to another condition, you'll be glad to have found out so quickly. However, local, in-person support groups like those sponsored by TSA are usually a better resource for locating local resources than are online options.

Appendix A, *Resources,* contains a list of TS organizations and clinics, as well as several university-affiliated programs with research doctors who have special expertise in TS. If you don't see a nearby facility listed, call any large hospitals or medical schools in your area. They should be able to point you toward a qualified professional, but be sure to talk to this doctor before making an appointment.

As Len's story earlier in this chapter indicated, a team approach is often useful when dealing with Tourette's syndrome, especially for children. Usually, a neurologist, psychiatrist, or psychologist leads a Tourette's diagnostic team. Other team members may include a child development specialist or developmental pediatrician, occupational therapist, speech therapist, education consultant, family social worker, and so on.

Each member of a team brings specific skills and knowledge that can not only make the diagnosis more certain, but also result in specific recommendations about what to do. For example, while a psychiatrist can recommend medication and therapy, an occupational therapist can suggest specific ways to deal with muscle fatigue or handwriting problems, and an educational specialist can help design a program for school success.

Once you have identified an expert or team that you want to consult, call to make sure they are currently taking new patients. Ask specifically if the doctor or team sees TS patients who are in the same age group as you or your child. You may also want to ask if the office has worked with your health plan or HMO before.

Insurance regulations, or the rules of your national health plan, usually govern just how you go about accessing a specialist. Problems that frequently occur and ideas for dealing with them are covered in Chapter 9, *Healthcare and Insurance.*

The following section, "Accessing an expert," covers a typical process for getting a referral to an expert through a US managed care organization. If you have another type of health insurance, or if you will be choosing your healthcare providers directly, you can skip this intermediate step.

Accessing an expert

Now that you know whom you should eventually see, you'll probably have to go back to square one to get there. If you are insured by a managed care organization, you must put the diagnostic process in motion by requesting a consultation appointment with your child's pediatrician, your primary care physician, or a general practitioner. This kind of appointment is a little different from the typical "height check, weight check, immunization booster, your throat looks fine" visit. In fact, it may take place in a meeting room or office rather than in an examination room. It should also be longer in length: half an hour at least, or perhaps longer.

Accurate, detailed records are the most important thing parents or adult patients can contribute at this appointment. For children, these should include the usual "baby book" milestones (first step, first word, etc.) as well as notes about anything unusual that parents have observed. Areas that a physician is likely to ask about include patient and family medical history, the child's relationships with family members and peers, and the child's play patterns and interests. The doctor will use this information to screen your child for developmental disorders and other health conditions that can mimic TS, increase your child's likelihood to have TS, and complicate TS.

Rindy, mother of 14-year-old Shawn, found an immediate ally in her pediatrician:

> I had been talking to the pediatrician about how extreme his behavior
> was, such curling up under the desk at school, and how oppositional he
> had become in spite of being on clonidine for ADD. As an afterthought,
> I imitated his head-rolling and asked if it was significant. She asked me
> about other potential tics (sniffing, blinking, snorting, throat clearing)
> and made the diagnosis on the spot, then had him come in to confirm.

If your child has seen other doctors, you should sign releases to have her medical records transferred to the pediatrician before the consultation appointment, and to the expert later on. After submitting a signed release, you can also have helpful school records transferred.

If you are an adult, you may not have immediate access to your own childhood medical records. If you know who your healthcare providers were before age 18, you may be able to have applicable medical records sent to you or directly to your current physician by signing a transfer authorization form.

You might be charged per-page for copies of both school and medical records.

Record transfers always seem to take longer than you would expect, so get releases taken care of early, and make sure the records were actually sent and received. Alternatively, if you have your own copies of medical or school records, you may photocopy and deliver them yourself.

Your doctor will want to know a lot of details about your family's mental health history. Take the time to ask older relatives what they know. In years past, most people with TS were never officially diagnosed, but may be described by those who remember them as twitchy or anxious, as having "nervous habits," or as secretive, ill tempered, odd, or explosive. You may get some surprises at this stage of the game, such as tales of a grandparent's secret trips to the hospital or sanitarium.

Be sure to ask about obsessive-compulsive behaviors as well as odd movements or obvious tics—TS and OCD are closely related. Often (but not always), female relatives of people with Tourette's have obsessive-compulsive traits, while male relatives are more likely to have physical tics.

You may need to check family medical records or talk with doctors who knew older family members well. Physicians are duty-bound not to give you personal information about living persons, but they are generally more forthcoming about the deceased. Once you have this family history in hand, you might want to put it in very simple "family tree" form for your physician.

If you can, use a calendar, personal diaries, medical notes, notes and checkmarks from school report cards, and your own recollections to create a rough chart of your or your child's behaviors over the past year or so.

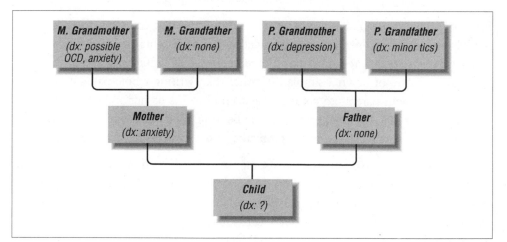

Figure 2-1. Sample family tree

Keeping a daily diary is also an excellent way to prepare for the consultation appointment. Many people with TS and their family members learn a great deal during this process. Use your diary to record activities, diet, symptoms of physical illness, and behaviors each day for a period of two weeks or more, with the time and duration of activities and behaviors noted. Not only can this diary provide a very complete picture of you or your child to a professional, it can also help to identify patterns. Some people have identified food allergies this way, or obtained data they needed to create the most beneficial daily routine for themselves or their child.

If an article or book does a better job of describing what you're worried about, don't hesitate to bring it along. You would be surprised at how many people have "diagnosed" themselves or a loved one by reading something in a popular magazine.

Joyce, age 53, was undiagnosed until her son developed TS symptoms:

> I didn't see a physician about tics until I was about 46. I doubt that even if I had seen someone when I was a child, I would have received a TS diagnosis then, as any symptoms were so mild.
>
> When I approached my general practitioner as an adult, he referred me first to one neurologist who told me I didn't have TS and was just overanxious and needed to relax. I was extremely upset at his ignorance and asked my doctor for a referral to someone else. He then referred me to a second who saw my tics, asked about my history, and diagnosed me with moderately severe TS. He also referred me for an EEG and MRI, and sent me to see a geneticist. The geneticist was mostly interested in my family history of tics, and completed a sort of map of inheritance.

Parents and adult patients may also want to summarize their concerns in writing. The records already mentioned can help you gather your thoughts and jog your memory about previous events. You don't have to be an eloquent writer to express what worries you. You can jot down a simple list rather than writing whole paragraphs if you prefer. It may help parents to compare their child to his or her siblings, or to other children in the day-care center or school. Be sure to include specific information about unusual movements, behavior problems, and obsessive-compulsive traits.

Be sure to list any particularly worrisome behaviors, such as suicide threats or attempts, aggressive or potentially criminal behaviors, self-mutilation, anxiety or panic attacks, or substance abuse that you want to make sure your doctor knows about. Some people send their summary of concerns to the doctor in advance; others prefer to use it as an agenda for discussion during the consultation.

If possible, the complete medical file and any supporting information should be available to the doctor at least a week before the consultation appointment. Be sure that the doctor's staff understands that this will be a discussion appointment so you can be scheduled for more than the usual fifteen-minute slot.

You might also want to talk to a nurse or physician's assistant who works most closely with your doctor. In large medical practices and HMOs, nurses and assistants are important parts of the organization. They can be allies for people who need referrals to specialists, or even just good listeners. If you are lucky enough to find a knowledgeable and sympathetic nurse, his or her input can help greatly.

When you arrive for the consultation, bring any additional records you have gathered, copies of your earlier letter (just in case it never reached the doctor), your summary of concerns, and any questions that you want to ask. You might benefit from bringing a small notebook or tape recorder as well, so you can keep a record of the discussion. Parents whose children are difficult to manage during a long appointment should bring a bag of toys or books to help keep them occupied.

Remember, the goal of this visit is not to get a diagnosis, but to obtain a referral to an expert who has the knowledge to accurately diagnose TS. Your documentation should help you make a case for this referral. The doctor's notes from this meeting will also be placed in your file, and should help the expert get a head start on diagnosis.

Unfortunately, getting a referral is sometimes difficult, especially in those HMOs that financially punish participating doctors for referring patients to experts. If your doctor seems reluctant to write a referral and instead suggests a "wait and see" approach, use your best judgment. Possible strategies include:

- Agree to observe your symptoms for a specific period of time (six weeks, for example), and make an appointment to return then with further notes.

- Attempt to persuade your doctor to approve the referral. This is where your documentation is most useful for reiterating the reasons this referral is needed.

- Ask your doctor for a written refusal to refer. This ploy may get you the referral itself, and if not, it will give you a document you can use in an appeal.

- Appeal your doctor's decision not to refer to an appeals board through your HMO or insurance company. The appeals process is covered in Chapter 9.

- Seek a second opinion from another primary care provider. Most HMOs have a special procedure you must follow to do so for the price of a typical co-pay; call your benefits office for details.

- Make an appointment with the expert you want to see. You will probably have to pay for this appointment yourself. However, if you or your child is then diagnosed with Tourette's syndrome, you can seek reimbursement from the appeals board of your HMO or insurance company.

Under no circumstances should you agree to wait for an undefined period of time if symptoms are causing significant distress.

Your primary care doctor may feel comfortable making the diagnosis herself, and perhaps even want to oversee treatment. This is not usually an ideal situation because the medications and other interventions that are effective for TS are sometimes difficult to manage. However, in some circumstances it is a welcome option.

Jen, whose military family is stationed overseas in an area with few medical services, feels lucky that her pediatrician was willing to take on this responsibility:

> The pediatrician relied entirely on my description of Paul's tics. I had a
> lot of guilt about that. I felt like I was diagnosing my son, and I know I
> am untrained. I thought, "What if I make a mistake and he really does
> not have it, but because I told the doctor he does these things, I have given
> the diagnosis?" The doctor said there were no tests for Tourette's. Even
> MRIs can't show TS. So that was it.
>
> My other son was having a routine physical for school one day. I asked
> the doctor prior to the appointment to watch Paul to see if he could see
> any of the tics. At that time, Paul was cupping his right hand and it
> looked like he was attempting to touch his fingertips to the inside of his
> forearm. Then he would brush the top side of his hand on a table or
> his leg or shirt. Sure enough, the doctor was able to see Paul do this and
> other tics. Paul was unaware, so it worked out well

Jen's comments bring up an important point about diagnosis, whether the prospective patient is a child or an adult: people with tics tend to suppress them when they feel they're under scrutiny or when they are anxious. This is a major reason that physicians sometimes miss the diagnosis. The longer the appointment is, the more likely it is that you or your child will have a visible tic.

The less pressure involved, the more likely tics will be visible. Some experts have installed two-way windows in their waiting room, allowing them to take a look at movements that occur when their patients are not worried about looking odd. Others encourage the use of minor subterfuge, like Jen's plan to bring her son along for his brother's appointment. Because her son with TS didn't feel he was being watched, he didn't suppress his tics.

Videotape can also provide important information, as can written or verbal descriptions of tics you have observed, like the ones Jen told her son's pediatrician about.

Meeting an expert

With any luck, your consultation appointment will result in a referral to the TS expert you have chosen in advance, or to one whom your doctor suggests. Once you get a referral to an expert, bring copies of the records you have collected to your appointment. This is, hopefully, where the actual diagnosis will be made.

Every doctor has a different way of going about things, but you'll probably need to fill out some standardized questionnaires about tics and related behaviors when you arrive. You or your child may need to have some psychiatric, neurological, and/or IQ testing done. The physician will also do an extensive patient and parent interview.

Many experienced physicians screen all patients presenting with tics for ADHD, OCD, and/or anxiety disorders, simply because these conditions are so much more common in people with tic disorders. Appendix C, *Diagnostic Tests for Tourette's Syndrome and Related Disorders,* lists diagnostic tests and measurement tools for both tic disorders and related issues.

Your supporting documentation will prove invaluable in moving this process along, especially if you can get your expert to look it over in advance of your meeting. After the evaluation is over, you should get a diagnosis, information about your or your child's specific challenges and needs, and advice on how to address them.

Often, physicians are leery of diagnosing preschool children with TS. As every parent of a toddler knows, repetitive (and often annoying) behaviors are common in this age group, and most of them don't qualify as tics. However, if you are seeing both vocal and motor tics, or severe motor tics that are obviously not purposeful behaviors, it's probably worth getting a thorough evaluation. This is particularly true if you have a family history of TS or related disorders.

Maria, mother of 4-year-old Jesse, spotted his TS at a very early age:

> *Our pediatric neurologist was already involved in the treatment of our older daughter for ADHD and OCD. We brought Jesse to him at the age of 9 months. I noticed that he hummed from the second week of life, but*

at the time I did not know that could be a tic. When I told the neurologist he was having motor tics, he said our son had benign tic disorder of childhood and to ignore it. Of course, when I brought my son back at 18 months, after 12 months of continuous motor and vocal ticcing, he gave Jesse a diagnosis of TS.

Now he brags about us. He says that when he gives talks to pediatricians and they ask when do parents bring their child in for a tic evaluation, he tells them that parents generally bring their child in between ages 6 and 7, or if they have already had a child with TS at 4 or 5, but he has one couple who are "astutely observant and who brought their son in at 18 months."

The next several sections of this chapter explain how experts get and use the information they need to diagnose TS.

Defining Tourette's syndrome

Doctors use a combination of symptom checklists, parent and patient interviews, and patient histories to diagnose Tourette's syndrome, and to rate the severity of a patient's TS symptoms. Direct observation and first-person reports from patients and family members are the key, but standardized questionnaires about tics are often useful to help bring extra information to light. Once enough data has been gathered, your doctor will probably make sure that it meets the official diagnostic criteria before passing judgment.

The *DSM-IV*

In the US, the standardized classification system for mental and most neurological disorders is published in a book called the *Diagnostic and Statistical Manual of Mental Disorders,* better known as the *DSM*. Written by committees chosen by the American Psychiatric Association, the *DSM* contains hundreds of descriptions of conditions that range from the purely psychological to the purely neurological.

About once per decade, the American Psychiatric Association's *DSM* committees revise the book to reflect the latest information about various conditions. As of this writing in Spring 2001, the current version is the *DSM-R,* a lightly revised version of the DSM-IV that preceded it.

There is some controversy about including neurological disorders like Tourette's syndrome in the *DSM*. The practice derives from a time when anything that affected behavior was thought to be psychological, based on life events, poor self-control, or moral failings. Even medical problems like epilepsy and senile dementia were put on Freud's couch by many doctors during this era.

As explained in Chapter 1, *Introduction to Tourette's Syndrome,* TS has since been identified as a completely neurological condition. Some would argue that it should now be taken out of the *DSM*. However, *most* of the disorders once thought to be psychological are now known to have medical causes. As knowledge increases and medical tests are developed for TS and other conditions that affect the mind, either these tests will make their way into the *DSM* criteria for diagnosis, or disorders for which there are medical tests will migrate out of the *DSM*.

For now, however, TS is still diagnosed based on a checklist of symptoms. According to the *DSM-IV*, the following must be present to make a diagnosis of Tourette's syndrome:[1]

1. Both multiple motor and one or more vocal tics have been present at some time during the illness, although not necessarily concurrently. (A tic is a sudden, rapid, recurrent, non-rhythmic, stereotyped motor movement or vocalization.)

2. The tics occur many times a day (usually in bouts) nearly every day or intermittently throughout a period of more than one year, and during this period there was never a tic-free period of more than three consecutive months.

3. The disturbance causes marked distress or significant impairment in social, occupational, or other important areas of functioning.

4. The onset is before age 18 years.

5. The disturbance is not due to the direct physiological effects of a substance (e.g., stimulants) or a general medical condition (e.g., Huntington's disease or post-viral encephalitis).

Plenty of experts would like to pick a bone or two with this description. For example, some people with TS do have tics that could be described as rhythmic, or even downright syncopated, such as compulsions to tap out a drumbeat. And as noted in Chapter 1, the separation of vocal and motor tics may not make much sense.

Some people who definitely have TS report having tic-free periods that last longer than three months, especially once they reach adulthood.

The "marked distress" criteria may not apply to young children, or to particularly well-adjusted older patients, for that matter. In fact, the revised version of the *DSM* released in 2000 eliminated this criterion. Although it's rare, there are occasional reports of

TS that starts after age 18 (often it turns out that these patients had undiagnosed, long-forgotten tics in childhood—but if this isn't remembered by the patient himself, TS may not be diagnosed). Finally, the last criterion doesn't jibe with what's now known about autoimmune disorders and tics in some persons.

Experienced diagnosticians know about these controversies and are able to work within the *DSM-IV* criteria when evaluating a person with tics. If you feel that the doctor you are seeing is being too rigid in his approach, you may wish to seek a second opinion.

The American Psychiatric Association also uses a special system to rate people in five areas of function, each of which it calls an "axis": a center line about which something (in this case, psychiatric and behavioral symptoms) revolves. Each axis is considered individually, and then graphed as a separate part of the diagnosis. The axes are:

- **Axis I.** Major psychiatric disorders, such as obsessive-compulsive disorder or schizophrenia

- **Axis II.** Personality disorders (ingrained personality traits that cause the patient difficulty in life), mental retardation, or developmental delay

- **Axis III.** Physical disorders that can affect thought or behavior, such as epilepsy

- **Axis IV.** Stresses in the patient's life, such as being the victim of child abuse

- **Axis V.** Level of function described on a scale of 0 (minimal function) to 100 (perfect function)

Usually, any disorders listed on Axes I, II, and III are defined in the *DSM-IV.*

Items listed on Axis IV come from interviews with the person, or from reports by his family members or other caretakers.

The "score" listed on Axis V is based on everything the doctor learns during the diagnostic process. It is a subjective measure of how well the person handles everyday life at home and at school, and how well the person handles stressful situations. You may see an axis chart on diagnostic reports, mental health evaluations, or treatment plans.

The *ICD-10*

In Europe, Africa, and Asia, the diagnostic guide used most frequently is Revision 10 of the World Health Organization's *International Classification of Diseases* (*ICD-10*). The *ICD-10* lists TS as F 95.2, combined vocal and multiple motor tic disorder (de la Tourette's syndrome), within the category F95, which covers tic disorders in general.[2]

The *ICD-10* criteria are almost identical to those in the *DSM-IV.*

Other diagnostic tools

Getting to diagnosis isn't as simple as just opening the *DSM-IV* or the *ICD-10* and finding a match, of course. The fact that tics wax and wane over time, and the fact that many tics go unrecognized or are camouflaged by persons with TS, can make diagnosis difficult.

Several standardized tests have also been developed to help doctors in their quest for accurate diagnosis. Most of these questionnaires and checklists are designed to lead a person through a conversation about behaviors that may be tics, including many "habits" she may never have considered as possible tics. Without the use of either a questionnaire or a detailed interview, doctors can only note symptoms present during the diagnostic interview—a method that has obvious drawbacks. Usually the end result of using these testing methods is a composite score, often a measure of tic severity or frequency. Appendix C contains an extensive list of tests used to diagnose Tourette's syndrome.

Subtypes of Tourette's syndrome

The only subtype of Tourette's syndrome that has been officially identified is TS associated with PANDAS: pediatric autoimmune disorders associated with strep. This name describes TS that seems to begin or become markedly worse as a result of infection with the bacteria known as group A beta-hemolytic streptococcus (GABHS, *S. pyogenes*). It is not caused by strep itself, but by the body's immune response to strep. In some susceptible persons, this response sets in motion an autoimmune process. There are still questions in the medical community about what PANDAS is, and about how to diagnose it.

The only foolproof test for PANDAS involves coupling a positive screen for the blood marker associated with PANDAS, known as D8/17, and a medical diagnosis of Tourette's syndrome (or OCD).[3] However, as of this writing, there is no commercial blood test available for D8/17. Most of the children who have had this type of blood testing are enrolled in research programs investigating PANDAS.

In early 2001, preliminary results from serum antibody studies of children with PANDAS were released. The researchers reported that elevated levels of antibodies to at least one of two other proteins, ts83 and ts60, were found in 100 percent of their

PANDAS subjects. They said the ts83 protein is a tissue-specific calpain, while the ts60 protein is a tissue-specific calpastatin.[4]

Calpain is a cysteine proteinase—a type of protease based on the amino acid cysteine that begins the process of breaking down proteins. It has a ribbon-like structure, and requires calcium to become active. Calpastatin is a protease inhibitor created by calpain. Researchers suspect that the calpain-calpastatin system is involved in other motor disorders, such as Alzheimer's disease.[5] It will be interesting to see where this line of inquiry leads in TS and PANDAS.

Outside of a research setting, doctors who are knowledgeable about the TS-PANDAS connection look instead for a correlation between increased frequency and severity of tics and/or obsessive-compulsive behavior, and more easily available measures of strep infection. These include:

- **Strep throat swab.** The physician uses a cotton swab to take a sample from the person's throat. That sample is then cultured to see what sort of infection is affecting the throat, if any. If strep bacteria grow, the result is positive for strep infection. However, it's possible that no strep infection will be found, because the antibodies that actually cause symptom exacerbation in people with PANDAS may have already wiped it out. For that reason, a negative result from a strep throat swab does not rule out PANDAS, although a positive result coupled with increased TS and/or OCD symptoms can support a diagnosis of PANDAS.

- **Antistreptolysin O (ASO) titre.** The ASO titre is a blood test that measures the amount of antibodies to strep in a person's blood. Normal results are 200 International Units per milliliter of blood (IU/ml) or below for adults and for children under age 5; for children ages 5 through 12, 333 IU/ml is considered normal. ASO titre results may also be expressed in Todd units/milliliter, in which case the adult/preschool-child level should be 85 TL/ml or below, and the normal level for ages 5 through 12 should be 170 TL/ml or below. A significantly higher titre coupled with increased TS or OCD symptoms is considered strong evidence for PANDAS. However, only 75 to 85 percent of active strep infections can be detected with an ASO titre, and you have to take at least two titres to show that there has been an increase.

- **Anti-DNAse B (ADB) titre.** This antibody blood test is better than the ASO at uncovering signs of past strep infection. A titre that is two or three times the normal level coupled with increased TS or OCD symptoms is considered strong evidence for PANDAS. Normal ADB levels are 85 Todd units per milliliter of blood or less for adults, 170 TU/ml for children ages 5 through 12, and 60 TL/ml or less for children under 5 years of age. Up to 240 International Units per milliliter (IU/ml) is considered normal in adults.

The antineuronal antibody (ANA) is a blood test that searches for antibodies to brain (neuronal) matter. Early in the course of PANDAS research, some clinicians tried using this test to corroborate PANDAS. Although it has proved to be a useful research tool, it hasn't seemed to be very helpful for actual diagnosis.

As its full name implies, PANDAS focuses solely on autoimmune reactions to strep. TS symptom onset and exacerbations have also been reported in connection with other types of bacterial or viral infections, particularly viruses in the herpes family (see "Postencephalitic syndromes," later in this chapter). Whether these are at all related to co-occurring infection, and if so, whether they are directly caused by actual infection of the brain (encephalitis) by a bacteria or virus, or caused by autoimmune reactions similar to PANDAS, is as yet unknown. However, researchers believe that once the first autoimmune process has occurred, perhaps in response to strep, the body may develop autoimmune reactions to other infections.

Judy, mother of 21-year-old Gabe, strongly suspects that this is the case with her son:

> Gabe had frequent ear infections before the age of 18 months. He was in the first of Dr. Swedo's PANDAS studies at NIH at age 14. Before that time, we did not know to watch for an association between viral illness and exacerbation of TS symptoms.
>
> He did not experience increased tics during the period of the study, but his titers for rheumatoid arthritis (which he does not have any symptoms of) were very high. The blood tests also indicated that he had just gotten over mononucleosis, although he had no symptoms of the disease. We are dealing with a strange autoimmune system here for sure!

A large number of families affected by TS also report that autoimmune disorders like rheumatoid arthritis are also present in family members, which has led some researchers to suspect a general tendency toward autoimmune conditions in this population.[6] A higher than normal prevalence of allergies in people with TS has been reported.[7]

As PANDAS research moves forward, researchers are experimenting with other ways to measure immune system differences in people with TS and related disorders. In time, these tests may become standard for anyone who appears to have tics. For now, they are rarely used except in cases where there is a clear link between strep infection and increased symptoms.[8]

Several studies have been done, or are in progress, of families in which two or more people have TS. Based on the results seen so far, researchers believe that it takes a combination of several genes for TS to occur, and that in some cases an environmental insult—such as repeated or early strep infection—must also occur to set off the disorder.[9]

In other cases, there may be specific combinations of genes that always or almost always lead to TS. If these genes are ever identified, the purely genetic variant may eventually be defined as a subtype that can be diagnosed by genetic testing alone.

Chapter 6, *Medical Care,* includes a section on potential treatments for the PANDAS subtype of Tourette's syndrome.

Another subtype you may hear or read about is "TS+." This isn't really a special kind of TS, as the name seems to imply, but rather Tourette's syndrome plus one or more additional neurological conditions.

Rage behaviors, the most challenging symptoms seen in some people with TS, are strongly associated with having TS and an additional condition, usually OCD or bipolar disorder.

Differential diagnosis

There's a saying among neurologists who specialize in movement disorders: "Not everything that tics is Tourette's." Although Tourette's syndrome is more common than the conditions that are sometimes confused with it, it's often wise to consider other possibilities. This process is known as differential diagnosis—using deductive reasoning and observation to tell seemingly similar disorders apart. A frequent mistake is confusing TS with deliberate misbehavior. Another common error is blaming TS behaviors on ADHD, which often occurs with TS and may begin earlier. ADHD is discussed at length in Chapter 3, *Related Conditions.*

However, tourettism—tic-like movements that are not caused by TS or another tic disorder—is sometimes associated with other medical problems. Following are conditions (listed in alphabetical order) that physicians sometimes need to consider to arrive at a diagnosis. Generally speaking, most of these could only be confused with severe cases, not the mild symptoms that are more typical of Tourette's syndrome. Several of the conditions listed are quite rare, and all have significant differences from TS despite occasional confusion.

With the exception of substance abuse and drug side effects, discerning any of the following from TS would be a job for a neurologist, not a psychiatrist or psychologist.

The TSA and medical educators have produced a number of helpful guides, including papers and videos that compare one or more of these conditions with TS. These are geared toward doctors, although patients and families can sometimes benefit from going over such materials with a neurologist. Appendix A also includes sources of information about some of these conditions.

Cerebral palsy

Cerebral palsy is a catchall term for neurological conditions that begin in early childhood and that include spasticity (mild to severe effects on the child's ability to move arms, legs, and sometimes other body parts), ataxia (weakness, unsteady gait), and/or athetosis (slow, writhing movements of the arms and legs). Athetoid cerebral palsy is caused by damage to the basal ganglia, the same area of the brain where tics originate, so sometimes the movements can look like tics or chorea (see the next section, "Chorea") to the untrained eye.

Cerebral palsy has multiple causes. Unlike TS, however, the symptoms of cerebral palsy do not wax and wane.

Treatment options for cerebral palsy include physical therapy, occupational therapy, and medications that can help relax and/or tone the muscles.

Chorea

Chorea is a medical term for uncontrolled, rapid movements that are performed without purpose. If you think that sounds identical to tics, you're correct.

The official description of choreaform movements requires that there is no premonitory urge before the movement, that they do not occur in groups, and that the movements are more difficult to suppress than tics.[10] However, people with Sydenham's chorea do sometimes report that they feel compelled to perform certain movements, so that description may be called into question.

Sydenham's chorea is a movement disorder that occurs after as many as 10 percent of rheumatic fever cases.[11] It is caused by inflammation that occurs when antibodies to strep bind to nerve tissue in the basal ganglia. PANDAS research (see "Subtypes of Tourette's syndrome," earlier in this chapter), indicates that Sydenham's chorea and strep-linked TS may well be the same basic condition. However, Sydenham's chorea is more common in females than males, unlike TS in general, and it usually disappears within three to twelve months after infection.[12]

Huntington's chorea is a hereditary, degenerative disease caused by a mutation on chromosome 4. Symptoms include tic-like chorea, unusual gait, and often rage behaviors and mood problems. It can be diagnosed using genetic testing, and there are also characteristic findings on a CAT scan. Although half the children of adults with Huntington's inherit the gene, the disorder normally does not appear until adulthood. TS, on the other hand, always appears before age 18, and rarely worsens with age. TS never causes the severe degeneration seen in Huntington's chorea.[13]

Occasionally, the early stages of Huntington's chorea appear during the teen years. Since the onset of TS is unusual at that late age, doctors looking at late onset of tics sometimes order genetic testing—especially if there is a family history of Huntington's chorea or similar degenerative conditions.

There is no treatment at this time for Huntington's chorea, although medication and physical therapy can help minimize its symptoms for a time. Promising medications are under development, however.

Dystonia musculorum deformans

Dystonia musculorum deformans is a rare condition characterized by unusual movements that are sustained rather than rapid. Usually, these are whole-body movements—odd, frozen postures in which the person is "stuck" for quite some time. It is believed to be hereditary in many cases. Not only do the movements look different from typical tics, but they get worse with time, and they do not wax and wane.[14]

Treatment options include physical therapy and medications that can relax the muscles in the affected area.

Head injury

Head injuries can result in swollen or damaged brain tissue. If this affects the basal ganglia, tics may emerge. As the injury heals, the tics may or may not disappear, depending on whether the basal ganglia return to normal, or suffer permanent effects from the injury. Because the basal ganglia are deep in the brain, permanent injury is unlikely unless the injury penetrates the brain (like a gunshot wound) or causes blood to collect within the brain. In these cases, tics are likely to be the least of the patient's worries.

Naturally, a doctor would only consider this as a differential diagnosis if tics beg soon after a head injury occurs, or if a head injury was penetrative. An EEG would also be ordered to insure that the tic-like movements are not due to seizures, which are a more likely explanation, and which can also be caused by head injury.

Cathie, mother of 8-year-old Jason, says that for two years his TS symptoms were attributed to brain injury:

> Jason has hydrocephalus. When tics appeared, including face grimaces, eye blinks, shoulder shrugs, clothes-picking, skin-licking, grunting, repetition of words and phrases, toe-walking, and arm-flapping, at first everyone thought his issues were attributable to the brain compression he suffered when he had too much fluid pressure. Everyone, including the medical professionals, thought it would all go away with time.

Hyperekplexia

Hyperekplexia, also known as startle disease, is a term for exaggerated startle response. A person with hyperekplexia has unusual movements in response to outside stimuli only, not internal feelings. The movements may look a bit like complex tics, but the pattern of when and why they occur is different.

Hyperekplexia is believed to be a genetic disorder. So far, it does not seem to be caused by the genes associated with Tourette's syndrome. However, patients are sometimes helped with the same medications that are useful for reducing tics.

Lesch-Neyhan syndrome

Lesch-Neyhan syndrome is a hereditary disorder caused by a genetic mutation that disrupts purine metabolism. Purines are nitrogen compounds found in certain foods or medicines. The body itself can also make purines.

Symptoms include tics, coprolalia (involuntary blurting of obscene or derogatory words), self-mutilation, and severe developmental delay. These symptoms are almost always obvious before age 3, so Lesch-Neyhan syndrome is unlikely to be confused with TS. Doctors might consider this diagnosis if TS-like symptoms occur with mental retardation.

Special diets can be used to prevent worsening of symptoms.

Medication side effects

Amphetamine ("speed," "crank") abuse can produce tics, or make them worse. This is also true for cocaine and the street drug Ecstasy, although that may be because it is often "cut" with less-expensive street amphetamines to increase its psychoactive effects.

Prescription drugs can also cause movement problems, including tics. The effect of prescription stimulants on persons with underlying tic disorders is discussed at greater length in Chapter 6.

Neuroleptics, also known as antipsychotics, are drugs used to treat not only tic disorders, but also major mental illnesses, including schizophrenia. They are related to, but much stronger than, antihistamines. Various members of the neuroleptic family affect serotonin, dopamine, and other neurotransmitters in various ways. Neuroleptics include Haldol, Risperdal, and many others, which are discussed further in Chapter 6.

Prescribed correctly, these medications save lives. Prescribed incorrectly, they can cause several difficult side effects that include tic-like movements. Akisthesia is an uncomfortable condition in which the person is constantly in motion, as if "driven by a motor." Dystonia is a condition in which muscle tone and control is diminished, often affecting the head and neck, causing the person to frequently stick out his tongue. Parkinsonian symptoms involve tremor and unusual movements. Tardive dyskinesia is characterized by repetitive movements of the feet, legs, arms, body, and/ or face.

Akisthesia, dystonia, and parkinsonianism can usually be addressed by discontinuing the medication. Tardive dyskinesia, however, can be permanent. Possible methods for preventing and treating tardive dyskinesia are listed in Chapter 6.

Occasionally tics are reported as a side effect of antiepileptic drugs, including carbamazepine (Tegretol).

Generally speaking, tics caused by medication are an unacceptable side effect, and indicate that the dose taken may be too high, or that one medication is strengthening the effect of another. Anyone who currently takes prescription medications or who uses illegal drugs, even occasionally, should report new tics to his or her doctor. This can prevent misdiagnosis or dangerous drug interactions, even if Tourette's syndrome is confirmed.

Myoclonic seizures and partial complex seizures

Myoclonic seizures are a type of partial complex seizure, a form of epilepsy that affects only one part of the brain. Partial complex seizures don't cause convulsions, but they can include purposeless movements that can look very much like tics, including straightening of clothing, repetitive gestures, and even coprolalia (compulsive swearing) or copropraxia (compulsive use of obscene gestures).[15]

People with seizure disorders have abnormal EEG findings that are consistent with seizures. They also experience an altered mental state during their episodes, and generally have no memory of them. In contrast, people with TS are fully aware of their behavior while ticcing.

Seizure disorders can be treated with medication.

Myoclonic twitches

Myoclonic twitches (also called myoclonus or fasciculations) are uncontrolled movements of small muscles, frequently the muscle next to the eye's outside corner. These rhythmic movements tend to worsen under stress. They usually go away on their own once the stressful period ends—often never to return. Typical hiccups are a type of myoclonic twitch. Unlike tics, myoclonic twitches can't be predicted or suppressed.

Normally, myoclonic twitches are not treated.

Neuroacanthocytosis

Neuroacanthocytosis is a rare neurological disorder that affects the basal ganglia. It is sometimes genetic (as in McLeod's syndrome) and sometimes not. Patients have uncontrolled movements in several areas, loss of control over their reflexes, and sensory loss and weakness (peripheral neuropathy). Neuroacanthocytosis can be diagnosed through blood testing for abnormal red blood cells (acanthocytes).

The movements seen in neuroacanthocytosis are rarely tic-like, and the other symptoms do not match TS. In addition, neuroacanthocytosis appears during the teen or adult years, while TS is normally diagnosed much earlier.[16]

This disorder would only be considered as a differential diagnosis if tic-like movements begin in the late teens or beyond, or if they are accompanied by weakness and anemia.

Postencephalitic syndromes

Encephalitis is a blanket term for infection of the brain. There are at least 50 bacteria and viruses that can cause encephalitis, which can have effects ranging from unusual behavior to brain damage or even death.

Encephalitis lethargica, the "sleeping sickness" portrayed in neurologist Oliver Sacks' book *Awakenings* and the film of the same name, is now quite rare in North America. This form of encephalitis, which was epidemic from 1918 to 1926, was associated with tic-like movements, coprolalia, and uninhibited behavior. Doctors believe these effects were caused by irritation of or damage to the basal ganglia by influenza or a similar infectious disease. Other forms of encephalitis can also cause tics.

While encephalitis lethargica is now rare, other forms of encephalitis are actually becoming more common, as demonstrated by a spate of West Nile virus cases in New York in 2000. Doctors are likely to consider postencephalitic symptoms only if tics have occurred "out of the blue" following a severe illness. Treatment options depend on the virus or bacteria involved.

Sydenham's chorea is one type of postencephalitic syndrome (see "Chorea," earlier in this chapter). Tics have been reported following infection with the bacteria that causes Lyme disease[17], the human herpes virus[18], and other agents.

Torticollis

Spasmodic torticollis is an unusual movement disorder that affects the neck muscles, causing muscle spasms, neck-twisting, and abnormal postures. Its cause is unknown, although in some cases it may have to do with abnormal muscle fibers. If a person's only tics involve the neck, this condition might be considered.

Treatment includes antispasmodics and other medications. Physical therapy and bracing may also be helpful.

Wilson's disease

Wilson's disease is an inherited disorder that results in abnormal accumulation of copper in the liver and, eventually, other parts of the body. It is caused by a mutation on chromosome 13.

Along with tic-like movements, tremors, and rigid muscles, symptoms of Wilson's disease also include deteriorating mental abilities, eventually leading to dementia; personality changes; speech problems; and unstable behavior. Early stages of all these signs should be visible by age 10.[19]

Doctors diagnose Wilson's disease using chromosome testing. They may also order blood tests for hemolytic anemia and copper levels in the red blood cells. Another physical clue is the presence of a ring, the color of which can range from grayish green to reddish gold, around the edge of the cornea in the eye. This sign is called a Kayser-Fleisher ring.

Hair tests for copper are not a diagnostic tool for Wilson's disease, as they can only measure very recent exposure to copper.

If not recognized and treated early in life, the mental changes associated with Wilson's disease are irreversible, although the tic-like movements may disappear. Liver and kidney damage are likely, as are health problems due to hemolytic anemia.

Treatment involves removing excess copper and restricting copper intake.

What to do with a diagnosis

When you finally have a diagnosis of TS, where do you go from there? There are no therapies currently available that cure its underlying genetic or neurological causes, although medical treatments may address the PANDAS variant. Instead, TS can be treated in two complementary ways: with medication that reduces the number and severity of tics, and with lifestyle adjustments, including special education and parenting techniques. These treatments can help people with TS reach their full potential despite the disorder.

Many people with TS choose to avoid medical treatment, relying instead on controlling those manifestations of the disorder that they can, and learning to live with the rest. Others, including some people whose tics are almost unnoticeable, choose aggressive medical treatment.

Joyce chooses not to take medication for her tics:

> For me, getting a life that goes beyond TS has helped me ignore the tics, which are much milder now, anyway. I did community volunteer work for a couple of years after we moved here, so that people know me as the

school library lady, not as the weirdo who tics. I also find satisfaction in encouraging others with TS. These things don't make the tics disappear, but they do mean I have a life that is more than just tics. I see myself as a useful, capable member of the community.

Only you and your doctor can decide what course of action makes the most sense for you or your child, based on your individual circumstances, needs, and preferences.

CHAPTER 3

Related Conditions

MANY PEOPLE WITH TOURETTE'S syndrome have no other major health challenges. Some, however, have one or more additional conditions that can complicate diagnosis and treatment of TS. Doctors call these comorbid or secondary disorders.

This chapter discusses a wide variety of neurological and other conditions that are seen more often in people with TS than in the general population. It tells a little about what each one is, and how it is diagnosed and treated. Learning disabilities, which also sometimes accompany TS, are covered in Chapter 8, *School Issues*.

Obsessive-compulsive disorder

According to data from major TS clinics, about 40 percent of people diagnosed with Tourette's syndrome who seek treatment also have obsessive-compulsive disorder. The rate among people with mild cases, who are less likely to seek treatment, is probably lower.[1]

Like TS, OCD has genetic underpinnings and appears to be caused by differences in or damage to the basal ganglia.

Unlike tics, the thoughts and behaviors experienced by people with OCD are not "purposeless," but instead are linked with severe fears and anxieties. For example, a person with obsessional worries about germs might spend many hours each day carrying out elaborate sterilization procedures in order to eat and use the bathroom. The compulsive behaviors are responses to obsessional fear and anxiety: either they make the feelings go away, or they are designed specifically (although not necessarily reasonably) to prevent some bad thing from happening.

Grace, mother of 17-year-old Keith, says his obsessive-compulsive symptoms have been far more difficult to cope with than his tics:

> *For Keith, the worst is undoubtedly the obsessive-compulsive*
> *component, which drives him mad with frustration. He cannot at present*
> *watch a video without continually stopping and re-winding it, and he is*

literally shouting at his "voice" (his name for the compulsive urges) to leave him alone. His behaviors have included touching objects around him in sequence, going up or down stairs sideways or backward, having to miss every other stair or jump over certain ones, turning faucets on and off repeatedly and screwing them up impossibly tight, and having to check and re-check that his car door is locked after leaving it, among others.

OCD tends to present a bit differently in people with TS than in people with OCD alone. Some people with TS refer to their obsessions and compulsions as "brain tics"—obsessive thoughts or topic obsessions. Others feel a need to perform activities in a certain order, or to repeat actions (including tics) a certain number of times. Tic-like compulsions, such as compulsively organizing items on a shelf or lining up body parts symmetrically, are especially common.[2]

Some people with TS have classic OCD symptoms. The majority of people with OCD can be described as counters, cleaners, checkers, or hoarders—people whose obsessions and compulsions center on numbering and ordering items or activities; constantly cleaning to deter dirt, germs, or other contaminants; obsessively checking things to prevent harm; or uncontrollably collecting objects. Many people with OCD also have obsessions related to religion or morality ("scrupulosity").

According to people who have experienced both, obsessive-compulsive symptoms are usually more difficult to cope with than tics. The anxiety and fear associated with OCD can be absolutely overwhelming, and the rituals that evolve to ward it off can take over your life.

Mary, mother of 14-year-old Ryan, is currently searching for a new therapist. She says:

> *Ryan has ADD and OCD as well as facial, shoulder, and body tics. His symptoms include washing, avoidance, and hoarding.*
>
> *It has been very hard to find someone who knows how to treat OCD. The last therapist said my son's anxiety level was too high to do exposure and response prevention therapy.*
>
> *It has been devastating. Our son has become a prisoner to OCD, and to our house. It is very hard for him to have a teacher come to our home for instruction. He feels that the teacher brings in germs and contaminates the house.*
>
> *Ryan is now soon to be 15. His OCD and tics are worse than ever, and we are still struggling to find an experienced behavioral therapist.*

Luckily, there are now two well-tested treatments for obsessive-compulsive disorder: medication and cognitive behavioral therapy. The most effective medications for OCD are the selective serotonin reuptake inhibitors (SSRIs), a group that includes Prozac and Luvox. Some people have a better response to tricyclic antidepressants, particularly Anafranil, although those medications carry a greater risk of side effects. Drugs from either of these groups can be taken with medications used to control tics, but potency and effect of one or both drugs may be affected. If both types of medication are needed, it's especially important to work with a physician who is cautious and knowledgeable about current psychiatric medications. See Chapter 6, *Medical Care*, for more information about medications.

Cognitive behavioral therapy (CBT) is a type of psychotherapy. One version of CBT is known as exposure and response therapy. Through exposure to the anxiety-producing item or experience (dirt, animals, or the impulse to save every single newspaper "just in case," for instance) and therapeutic exercises designed to slowly reduce your sensation of fear and anxiety, you can slowly regain control over obsessions and compulsions. It's not all about willpower, either—"before and after" brain scans of people who have successfully used cognitive behavioral therapy show that changes in brain chemistry can occur through this process.[3]

Chris, mother of 7-year-old Kelsey, says:

> When we were in the grips of OCD before cognitive behavioral therapy, we all felt trapped. We were very fortunate to find a good therapist right away. We have not used any medications, but we just completed ten weeks of CBT and she is nearly symptom-free. I'm hopeful these days.

Along with in-person interviews, family histories, and the *DSM-IV* or *ICD-10* criteria, OCD symptom checklists are available for both adults and children. For adults, the list includes the Florida Obsessive-Compulsive Inventory (FOCI), the University of Hamburg Obsession-Compulsion Inventory Screening Form, and the Yale-Brown Obsessive Compulsive Scale (Y-BOCS). The Y-BOCS is considered the gold standard of OCD checklists. It doesn't diagnose OCD, but it does provide an easy way to rate the severity of a patient's obsessive-compulsive symptoms, and its detailed questions are helpful to professionals as they try to get the patient to describe symptoms that they may be reluctant to talk about.

Teenagers may find that the regular Y-BOCS meets their needs, but a special version called the CY-BOCS has been developed for use with children.

The Y-BOCS and CY-BOCS also give doctors a way to measure the efficiency of treatment: if a patient retakes the test and gets a lower score, that means symptoms are becoming less severe. These and other diagnostic tests for OCD are listed in Appendix C, *Diagnostic Tests for TS and Related Disorders*.

Attention deficit disorders

Attention deficit hyperactivity disorder (ADHD) is, basically, a neurologically based difficulty in paying attention. People with these disorders have a hard time focusing on one thing to the exclusion of everything else, are easily distracted, and may lack patience with activities that are frustrating or time-consuming. If a person is extremely active, to the point of having a hard time staying on task, the ADHD label might be used. If the person's symptoms do not include hyperactivity—the variant popularly known as ADD—the *DSM* calls it "ADHD, Predominantly Inattentive Type."

Lee, mother of 13-year-old Joseph, said his ADHD symptoms have had more impact on his school performance than his relatively mild tics:

> *Joseph needs flexibility within structure. If things are too flexible, they don't work; if they are too structured, they don't work. He needs choices. He needs work that engages him.*
>
> *He needs incentives to encourage him to work. I used to feel bad about that, until a friend asked me how many people I know who would go to work every day if they didn't get a salary.... Since he isn't motivated by adult approval, incentives help.*
>
> *Too much stimulation in the classroom does not work for him. He needs to be able to move around sometimes.*

ADHD is fairly common in the general population, but it is even more common among people with TS.[4] The following criteria for ADHD are from the *DSM-IV* criteria for ADHD.[5]

- Some hyperactive, inattentive, or impulsive symptoms must appear before the age of seven; symptoms must be present in two or more settings (such as at school and at home)

- The symptoms must cause real difficulty for the child

- The symptoms must not be due to another mental disorder, including TS

The "either/or" position in this last point is controversial with some clinicians. The symptoms of ADHD overlap with many other neurological disorders. The definition also doesn't address specific physical causes for attention deficit, such as sensory integration problems. To meet the criteria for ADHD, item 1 or 2 must be true:

1. Six or more of the following symptoms, persisting for at least six months, occurring frequently, and occurring to a degree inconsistent with the child's developmental level:

    a. Fails to pay attention to details, makes careless mistakes in schoolwork or other activities

    b. Difficulty sustaining attention in schoolwork, chores, or play activities

    c. Does not seem to listen when spoken to directly

    d. Failure to follow instructions, does not finish schoolwork or chores (not due to deliberate oppositional behavior or failure to understand instructions)

    e. Difficulty organizing tasks and activities

    f. Avoids, dislikes, or is reluctant to try tasks that require sustained mental effort, such as homework

    g. Loses things needed for tasks or activities, such as toys, homework assignments, or books

    h. Easily distracted by noise or other external stimuli

    i. Forgetful in daily activities

2. Six or more of the following symptoms of hyperactivity/impulsivity must be present, persisting for at least six months, and to a degree that is inconsistent with developmental level:

    a. Fidgets with hands or feet, squirms in seat

    b. Can't seem to remain seated in the classroom or other places where it is expected

    c. Runs and climbs excessively in inappropriate situations and places (in adolescents, this can be subjective feelings of restlessness)

    d. Has difficulty playing quietly

    e. Is physically very active—acts as if "driven by a motor"

    f. Talks excessively

    g. Displays impulsivity

h. Blurts out answers before questions have been completed, or out of turn

i. Can't seem to wait for turn in play or at school

j. Interrupts or intrudes on others by butting into conversations or games, invading others' personal space, etc.

Based on these criteria, the *DSM-IV* separates ADHD into four categories:

- ADHD, Predominantly Inattentive Type (314.00, ADHD-I, "ADD"). Child meets the criteria in section 1, but not in section 2. This is what's commonly called ADD: attention deficit without marked hyperactivity.

- ADHD, Predominantly Hyperactive-Impulsive Type (314.01, ADHD-I). Child meets the criteria in section 2, but not in section 1.

- ADHD, Combined Type (314.01, ADHD-C). Child meets the criteria in both section 1 and section 2.

- ADHD NOS (314.9). Child has prominent symptoms of hyperactivity/impulsivity and/or attention deficit, but doesn't meet all of the required criteria for any of the other three types. This diagnosis is sometimes used when the child has another primary condition, such as Tourette's syndrome, but also has symptoms of ADHD that are not fully explained by that disorder.

Children with TS have bodies that are almost constantly in motion simply because of their tics. Being diagnosed first with ADHD and later with TS is so common as to be a stereotype among people with Tourette's. Sometimes enough symptoms of ADHD are present that the person continues to carry both diagnoses; sometimes the TS label alone is kept and the ADHD diagnosis is discarded.

One problem with a combination of Tourette's and ADHD is that the stimulant medications often prescribed to treat ADHD can sometimes make tics worse. This and related treatment issues are discussed more fully in Chapter 6.

Anxiety and panic disorders

OCD is just one of several anxiety disorders. Anxiety disorders are common enough that almost everyone knows someone who suffers from them, but are somewhat more common in people with TS.[6] They include panic disorders, generalized anxiety disorder, post-traumatic stress syndrome, and extreme phobias of all sorts, from claustrophobia (fear of being in small, enclosed places) to arachnophobia (fear of spiders). Basically put, anxiety disorders all involve an extreme reaction to certain situations or stimuli, as the body puts its "fight or flight" system in motion for no good reason.

Like OCD, anxiety disorders can be treated with cognitive behavior therapy and/or medication.

Allergies

One very interesting study has found that allergies, including allergic rhinitis and asthma, are significantly more common in children with TS than in the general population.[7] This finding mirrors reports from parents of children with TS, and from adults with TS.

This is significant for several reasons. First, allergies are autoimmune disorders, so this finding seems to buttress the concept of immune-system involvement in TS. Second, many tics resemble the effects of allergies, including nose-twitching and repetitive sniffing, which means that children with TS frequently see an allergist before TS is diagnosed. Finally, some allergy medications contain stimulants that can worsen tic severity, and others may affect medications used to treat TS. This and related treatment issues are covered in Chapter 6.

Joyce, mother of 18-year-old John, says that he definitely has allergies but they don't seem to be closely linked with his TS:

> When we took John to have him tested for allergies, a number of food sensitivities were found. We placed him on a special diet. After six months I had him tested again, and found that he was now sensitive to foods that hadn't bothered him before, and that the foods he was sensitive to at first, he could now eat. I saw no difference in his behavior on the diet, nor did his teachers. I then chucked the whole idea and fed him like everyone else in the family. He was greatly relieved!

Autistic spectrum disorders

The autistic spectrum ranges from autistic disorder to Asperger's syndrome, with atypical and unspecified pervasive developmental disorders in the middle: in the *DSM-IV*, this family of conditions is classified as Pervasive Developmental Disorders, or PDDs.

Although the common perception is that people with autism cannot talk or relate to others, many people with an autistic spectrum disorder can do both—although their ability to maintain social relationships and communicate fluently with others tends to be limited. These conditions may occur with or without mental retardation. When mental retardation is present, the severity of autistic symptoms tends to be worse.

People with autism and other PDDs have a disordered sensory system. Their perceptions are scrambled, heightened, or diminished, making the world a confusing and even painful place. Like TS, autism appears to involve damage or differences in the basal ganglia, and has genetic underpinnings. Evidence is also emerging for immune-system differences in people with autism, including links to infections and PANDAS-like autoimmune problems.[8,9]

Linda, mother of 10-year-old William, says that PDD is her son's main challenge, with TS a secondary issue:

> William had only fifteen words or word approximations at age 2-and-a-half, his speech was very hard to understand, he was clumsy, and he didn't relate to other children much at all. Although his first neurological diagnosis was Tourette's because his tics were easily recognized, it was followed not long after by a diagnosis of PDD-NOS: Pervasive developmental disorder, not otherwise specified.
>
> We think of PDD as being his main diagnosis because it explains so many things about him, and we think of TS as being sort of a secondary thing that causes his tics. He fits the criteria for ADHD and OCD as well, and has the reaction to strep that fits with PANDAS. Sometimes we feel like it's all too much alphabet soup for such a little guy!

Among young people with TS, the autistic spectrum disorder known as Asperger's syndrome is being diagnosed with increasing frequency. People with Asperger's are often quite intelligent. However, social skills just don't come naturally to them at all, and they do not read social cues well. They don't have noticeable language delays; in fact, many are very early talkers and early readers (a symptom known as *hyperlexia*.) Most do have speech differences, most noticeably a tendency to lecture endlessly on topics of special interest like a pedantic "Little Professor."

Narrow areas of interest and a self-centered way of looking at the world characterize Asperger's syndrome. These interests may become full-fledged obsessions. Many people with Asperger's are highly successful in technology careers, such as computer programming and engineering, which both minimize contact with other people and make use of their special interests. Others find their progress hampered by social difficulties, or by comorbid conditions like TS or depression, which are fairly common in this group. Parents note that middle school and high school tend to be especially difficult times for these children, because their social difficulties are thrown into bold relief.

Another autistic spectrum disorder, Rett syndrome, deserves special mention because it is characterized by a specific type of movement. Rett syndrome has recently been linked to a gene known as MeCP2, which is located on the X chromosome. Almost all people with Rett syndrome are female, as the mutation is usually deadly to males before birth. People with Rett syndrome have tremor-like movements, wring their hands repetitively, and frequently have obsessions and compulsions.

Both obsessive-compulsive behavior and tic-like movements are fairly common in people with all autistic spectrum disorders. Obsessiveness is considered to be part of the diagnostic criteria for PDDs. The tic-like movements seen in autism are usually called stereotypic movements or stims (short for "self-stimulatory movements").

Some clinicians feel that there is no appreciable difference between tics and at least some stereotypic behaviors. However, some repetitive movements seen in persons with autistic spectrum disorders are significantly different from tics. These movements, such as hand-flapping and waving fingers rapidly in front of one's face for hours, appear to be performed either for pleasure or to block out unpleasant and overwhelming sensory phenomena. They are rhythmic rather than sudden and singular. It's entirely possible that the same movement—hand-flapping, for example—could be a tic under some circumstances and a stim in others. This makes diagnosing TS in people who also have a PDD more difficult.

One recent study found that at least 4.3 percent of children and teens with autism also have Tourette's syndrome, and that based on symptom reports, an additional 2.2 percent probably do as well.[10]

Another study placed the rate at 8.1 percent.[11] Because this is much higher than the rate of TS seen in the general population, it's considered very strong evidence for a genetic relationship between these two conditions.

There is currently no proven medical treatment for PDDs, although many of the medications used to treat TS, OCD, and ADHD benefit some people with autism. Medications aimed at treating underlying infection or autoimmune problems are also showing promise for some people with PDDs, and others respond well to special diets or supplements. The primary intervention used is intensive, one-to-one interaction and education, particularly the method known as Applied Behavior Analysis, often combined with speech therapy and occupational therapy.

Body dysmorphic disorder

Body dysmorphic disorder (BDD) is an obsession with imagined ugliness or deformity. The late-stage anorexic's insistence that he or she is still "fat" represents a similar kind of thinking.

People with BDD are frequently obsessed with individual physical features, or with the whole package. They may feel compelled to conduct elaborate grooming and dressing rituals to get their appearance "just right," and still avoid mirrors. Some adults with BDD pursue unnecessary cosmetic surgery; others hide away from society for fear that their appearance will offend others. Some are fixated on imagined body odor rather than appearance.

Recent research indicates that BDD is equally common in men and in women; co-occurs frequently with eating disorders, impulse disorders, and OCD; and responds to the same medications and therapeutic techniques as OCD. One study has found that about 37 percent of adults with OCD also meet the criteria for BDD.[12] Others have noted that it also occurs more often in persons with Tourette's syndrome than in the general population, and have suggested that it falls within a spectrum of "obsessive compulsive spectrum disorders" that includes both OCD and TS.[13]

Depression and manic depression

Unipolar, or "simple," depression is just that: depressed mood that lasts longer than two weeks, and is not due to another medical condition, the side effects of medication, or normal reaction to a major life event (such as grieving after a parent's death). It is the most common form of depression. Most people with unipolar depression have periods of feeling normal, including feeling happy.

Some people with Tourette's syndrome develop situational depression as a reaction to difficult symptoms like coprolalia, or to their actual or perceived social status. Others have clinical depression, which may or may not have roots in some of the same chemical differences that are involved in TS.[14] Whether or not depression and bipolar disorders are related medically to TS, they can certainly complicate diagnosis and treatment of TS, and should be taken into account by care professionals.

Bipolar I disorder used to be known as manic depression. People with Bipolar I swing into depression cyclically, and have had at least one manic episode. Some have also had hypomanic episodes. Hypomania is an abnormally elevated, expansive mood with such signs as hyperactivity, irritability, fast speech, and rapid-fire thinking. Mania takes these symptoms to the next level, in which the patient's thoughts and actions are out of control altogether.

Bipolar II disorder is defined as recurrent depression with hypomania, but not mania or mixed states. People with Bipolar II also tend to be more emotionally labile (moody) in between actual mood swings.

Cyclothymic disorder is also a bipolar disorder. It is defined as a chronic mood disturbance for at least a year. Both depressed and hypomanic moods are present, but there are no major depressive, manic, or mixed episodes. The patient must have gone without a period of normal mood for more than two months during the year. The cycles and moods are not as severe as those seen in Bipolar II. Seasonal Affective Disorder ("winter blues") is a form of cyclothymic disorder.

Marlene, mother of 8-year-old Billy, explains:

> Billy's TS, OCD, and ADHD were diagnosed first, and he was then diagnosed with cyclothymia this year. Billy specifically complained about the loss of feeling tired. It really disturbed him. He would go look in the mirror and say, "I look tired, so my body must be tired. But I don't feel tired." He could not fall asleep. He asked me to make an appointment with his psychiatrist.
>
> My concern about incipient bipolar disorder (which is rampant in our family) as a reason to avoid medicating the ADHD with stimulants was dismissed by the pediatrician, but not by the child psychiatrist.
>
> I hope that he does not have to suffer the severe psychic pain of full-blown bipolar disorder.

The cycles seen in bipolar disorders can be slow swings between mood states, or transient extremes of mood ("rapid cycling"). The rapid cycling variant, which is sometimes mistaken for ADHD in children, is more common in children and in adult women.

All of the bipolar disorders are slightly more common in adults with TS.[15] Bipolar disorders are often missed in children, but can begin in childhood or the teen years as well as in adulthood.

All forms of depression can be treated, usually with medication and sometimes with talk therapy as well, although not all patients find complete relief with current treatments. People who have TS and depression or a bipolar disorder will need to work with a physician who knows how to carefully adjust the doses of antidepressants and medications used for tic relief to get the best results and avoid side effects. In the case of bipolar disorders, it's essential to stabilize the person's mood medically before treating TS or any other comorbid disorder.

Developmental disorders

Tic-like behaviors are frequently seen in people with developmental disorders other than autism, including persons with mental retardation or Down syndrome.[16] As in autistic spectrum disorders, these stereotyped behaviors tend to be more rhythmic than typical tics. However, differentiating them from tics may be more a matter of semantics than an appreciable medical difference.

This correlation was at the root of the old concept of TS as a "degenerative" disorder: early researchers noticed that many mentally retarded patients in state institutions had tics, and presumed that tics were therefore a sign of intellectual degeneration. Recent genetic studies have instead found that reason for tics occurring in developmental disorders may lie in chromosomal differences that both have in common.[17]

Impulse disorders

Impulse disorders are problems that occur when one's impulses are not overridden, allowing a harmful or unwanted act to be committed. The category includes pyromania (compulsive fire-setting), kleptomania (compulsive stealing), pathological gambling, compulsive shopping, and more.

Trichotillomania (compulsive hair-pulling) is also classified as an impulse disorder in the *DSM-IV*. It is discussed separately in the section "Trichotillomania," later in this chapter.

Defining impulse disorders is complicated, and linking impulse disorders with TS is highly controversial. Dr. David Comings, author of several books on TS and related problems, is probably the most prominent advocate for this idea. Comings' research found a correlation between impulse disorders and TS.[18] Other studies have not substantiated all of his findings.

Impulsive behaviors, unlike tics, can be somewhat rewarding in their own right—for example, compulsive drinking produces intoxication, which might seem pleasant at first. But the definitions of impulse disorders in the *DSM* make it clear that behavior is in response to a vague urge, or to a sense of tension or anxiety, not a desire to get an item or harm others.

People with TS who have impulse disorders usually experience these cravings and impulses as unwanted feelings, and are guilt-ridden after acting upon them.

Pyromania deserves special mention because having a compulsion to set fires is serious business, and one that is likely to have strong personal and legal consequences. Fire-setting compulsions are seen more often in people under the age of 21, and are much more common in boys than in girls.[19] However, the vast majority of juvenile fire-setters do not have TS, and very few people with TS have problems with fire-setting. Treatment of impulse disorders is usually with cognitive behavioral therapy, particularly exposure and response techniques. Medication also helps some people, while others find group therapy useful.

Substance abuse and other addictions

Many people do not feel comfortable thinking of substance abuse as an illness, although the idea of alcoholism as a disease is gaining wider acceptance. Certainly, not everyone who uses or abuses alcohol or drugs is responding to a genetic compulsion—but it's equally possible that some are. Substance abuse is also not an uncommon strategy for dealing with the unpleasant symptoms of physical or mental illness, stress, or personal problems.

The combination of both a psychiatric diagnosis and substance abuse is called dual diagnosis, and there are some special programs available to treat both problems simultaneously. This can be a very important strategy, because there is strong evidence that even if a person gets great results from treatment, their mental illness is likely to return if the substance abuse disorder is not also treated. Likewise, reducing symptoms can contribute to more successful substance abuse treatment in dual-diagnosis patients.[20,21] Although TS is not a "mental illness" per se, it's still important to address it during treatment for substance abuse or addiction, and vice versa.

Alcohol and drugs are now known to have complex effects on the neurotransmitter system, effects that can feel even stronger and seemingly more desirable to people whose neurotransmitter system is out of balance.

The lifetime prevalence of alcohol abuse and dependence in people with OCD is estimated at 24.6 percent; the rate in persons with TS is said to be even higher.[22,23] An increased risk of substance abuse is expected if the picture is complicated by other neurological disorders, particularly ADHD or bipolar disorders. Current statistics do not seem to be available on the prevalence of drug abuse among people with TS, but studies indicate that for some people, the onset of anxiety disorders is associated with the use of drugs, particularly cocaine.[24] Some people with TS report that marijuana use reduces tic severity and frequency, which may cause some to become frequent users.[25] Medical researchers are following up on whether compounds found in marijuana are actually useful; see Chapter 6 for more information.

One researcher who believes there is a strong genetic link between Tourette's syndrome and substance abuse is Dr. David Comings, who has covered the topic at great length in several published studies and two books. His findings remain controversial, but they are certainly intriguing.[26,27]

Resources for help with substance abuse problems can be found in Appendix A.

Oppositional defiant disorder/conduct disorder

In the film "Rebel Without a Cause," the juvenile delinquent played by James Dean is asked what he's rebelling against, and replies, "Whaddaya got?" That's a good illustration of what psychiatrists mean by oppositional defiant disorder (ODD). Simply put, a person who's diagnosed with ODD typically defies authority, breaks the rules, and refuses to follow orders. Whether this is truly a psychiatric problem or instead an attempt to put a medical-sounding label on badly behaved delinquents is still a matter for debate. What's certain is that the impulsiveness that comes with TS can often be mistaken for ODD, and that ODD can be a very damaging label to carry.

When the same behaviors and attitudes are seen in an adult, the label applied by psychiatrists is conduct disorder (CD). A person who for no apparent reason constantly tests the limits of both patience and the law might be given this diagnosis. Like ODD, it's a controversial label that can carry stigma along with it.

Joyce has seen both ODD and now CD used to describe her son, John, who has TS, ADHD, and difficulties with anxiety:

> He has, on occasion, got into a lot of trouble both at school and at home for actions that, in retrospect, I realize were probably tics or compulsions. For example, his swearing, whether in context or not, has a compulsive quality about it. He himself says that he can't help it, and we have noticed that medication greatly helps with the problem.
>
> He has had problems with extreme agitation and anger since about fourth grade, and it gradually got worse as he grew into his teen years. His anxiety when in groups, as at school, seemed to be intense. All it took was a minor trigger to set off an explosion.

By eighth grade, he was extremely difficult, oppositional and defiant, skipping school, into drinking, smoking and drug use. About this time he got into trouble with the law and ended up getting assessed at a hospital. His psychiatrist agreed to a trial of Risperdal. Well, within a week we had our boy back. His surliness was gone, he was much more pleasant, he was much less oppositional, and behavioral programs began to have some effect on him. With the Risperdal, we do not see major rages and meltdowns. The anger is still there, but is usually much more controlled than before.

Quite a few people with a TS diagnosis are also given an ODD or CD diagnosis.[28] If Tourette's syndrome turns out to be the underlying reason for their impulsive, odd, or aggressive behaviors, these labels should definitely be removed. Judges, social workers, and others who might get a peek at someone's medical records understand these terms as medical euphemisms for "juvenile delinquent" or "habitual criminal," and may not be able to look past that snap judgment. Preconceived notions based on these labels can have serious repercussions when decisions about custody, treatment, or incarceration are made. As John's story illustrates, when oppositional behaviors are caused by neuropsychiatric problems, appropriate treatment can help.

Self-injurious behavior and dissociation

Sometimes a person with TS will have tics that cause injury, such as pressing hard on the eyes over and over, or repetitive arm motions that cause strained muscles. This isn't deliberate behavior, however, and is as hard to control as any other type of tic. While you can choose to ignore other types of tics, self-injurious tics demand treatment with medication, as a few people with TS have caused themselves actual harm. Self-injurious tics and ways to cope with them are discussed in Chapter 6.

Some people with TS have self-injurious behaviors that seem too deliberate to be "pure" tics, although it can be hard to tell one from the other. The most common forms of self-injurious behavior (SIB) in people with TS are skin-picking and scab-picking. People who pick at their skin or at areas of injured skin that are healing usually say they are responding to a premonitory sensation: an itch, a tingle, a feeling of tightness or "wrongness" very much like the sensations that often precede tics.

Skin- and scab-picking can cause scarring, especially in people who are prone to keloids, and it can also make the person more susceptible to infection through the broken skin. Parents whose young children are prone to this behavior may be able to use bandages to discourage it, although medication and cognitive-behavioral therapy are the most effective treatments.

There are more serious forms of SIB, including cutting, burning, the use of caustic chemicals, head-banging, deliberate breaking of bones, and even self-strangulation. This type of self-injurious behavior is usually done in private and kept hidden. It's not done for attention, and it's not an attempt at suicide, although serious injury or death can occur. It is also uncommon in persons with TS—but must be addressed immediately if it does occur.

Patients describe self-injury as more "addictive" than other compulsive behaviors. While SIB creates intense sensations, many who self-injure say their acts are not especially painful. SIB can result in dissociation, a sort of temporary high that's even stronger than the heightened emotions experienced by those who compulsively shoplift, gamble, eat, or have sex. Others with SIB report a heightened sense of awareness or "reality," and a numbing effect that also deadens psychic pain. Research is preliminary, but both of these paradoxical responses to pain and the addictive quality of SIB may be caused by the release of endorphins, the body's natural opiates. One clue to this is the effectiveness of the opiate-blocker drug naltrexone (ReVia) in at least some patients with SIB.[29]

In some cases, childhood abuse may set off self-injurious behavior, dissociation, or both. This does not mean that everyone who has self-injurious behavior or dissociative episodes has been abused.

Whether the mental link between pain and "escape" begins because of abuse or mere chance, that link can be hard to break once it has been established. Doctors who understand SIB and dissociation as biological disorders feel that it can be just another type of tic or compulsion. People with TS report both symptoms slightly more often than people in the general population do—and both have more serious repercussions than adjusting clothing or counting fence slats. Immediate and intensive treatment, usually including medication and cognitive behavioral therapy, is essential.[30]

Trichotillomania

Trichotillomania, compulsively pulling out one's own hair, is a common disorder that many clinicians believe is linked to OCD, and it is often reported by people with TS.[31] People with trichotillomania usually pull hair from their heads, but may also pull from any other area of the body. Some also tie knots in, roll, or save the hair that they pull.

Most people with trichotillomania say they pull hair in response to an anticipatory "tingle," itch, or sensory cue—the urge-response picture is so similar to ticcing that some researchers feel trichotillomania ought to be considered a tic rather than an OCD compulsion or an impulse disorder.

The behavior is not threatening to the person's health, but it can cause bald patches or even complete hair removal, leading to embarrassment and discomfort. Repeated pulling also commonly causes skin irritation.

Trichotillomania responds well to the same medications and therapeutic techniques used for OCD. While they are in treatment, people with trichotillomania may want to consider wigs, hats, and hair extensions that can cover bald areas on the scalp.

Another way of looking at TS

Recently, a few researchers have put forth the idea that separating out the many neurological disorders that seem to arise from damage to or difference in the structure of the basal ganglia according to special symptoms may obscure the larger picture. These researchers, led by Dr. Roger Kurlan, argue that patients and their physicians might be better served by thinking of all these conditions as variations on the same theme.

Dr. Kurlan and others have proposed looking at an entire spectrum of conditions, including not only Tourette's syndrome and obsessive-compulsive disorder but also ADHD, autistic spectrum disorders, and certain communication disorders, through the lens of basal ganglia dysfunction.[32,33]

This is an interesting view, and it may eventually encourage researchers whose topics are now separated by arbitrary labels to work more closely together. However, it's unlikely to have an impact on people seeking medical help. Most physicians prefer to be as specific as possible when making a diagnosis, and these separate classifications are unlikely to disappear from the *DSM-IV* and other diagnostic handbooks.

CHAPTER 4

Growing Up with Tourette's Syndrome

TOURETTE'S SYNDROME sometimes poses challenges to child development, and can create difficulties in family and community life for young people. Most kids with TS face at least some teasing. While most kids with TS do not have unmanageable behavior problems, they do tend to have trouble with temper tantrums and uninhibited behavior long past the usual age. A significant minority has developmental delays, and will need additional help.

This chapter discusses the non-medical effects of TS on children, adolescents, and their family members. Topics covered include common problems encountered by children with TS, effective parenting techniques for handling the behavioral issues of children with TS, and community support systems that provide the best possible environment for a child or adolescent with TS.

Because many children with TS have one or more learning disabilities or need some accommodations in school, school and special education services are covered in Chapter 8, *School Issues*. Subjects pertaining primarily to adults are covered in Chapter 5, *Living with Tourette's Syndrome*.

Kids and TS

Growing up with Tourette's syndrome can range from easy to terribly difficult, depending on the severity of your symptoms and how much social acceptance you encounter. Young people are not as well equipped as adults when it comes to handling misunderstandings and rejection, and that makes it challenging to have a disability that's both visible to others and poorly understood.

Except in the most severe cases, TS itself is not the issue—it's how other people react to or perceive TS, and how those reactions and perceptions are internalized by people with TS.

In years past, young people with TS had to deal with some extremely harmful notions about the condition, such as the persistent belief that tics were caused by "moral weakness." Today's children are less likely to encounter such attitudes, although it's always possible. Honest discussions can help prepare your child for encounters with adults who seem extremely punitive or disgusted by ticcing. Understanding prejudice and discussing ways to respond may help to protect your child from these hurtful views.

Most people who hassle kids about ticcing simply don't know that it's a neurological problem. They may have heard the term "nervous tics," and think that feeling nervous causes the tics. Or they may see a deliberately annoying behavior instead of a tic. The result of these misunderstandings is often comments that hurt, even though they may not be intended to do so.

Kids who tic have to deal with nosy comments on a regular basis. The remarks are often direct, even rude. Imagine dealing with a daily diet of comments like these:

- Stop fidgeting!
- What's wrong with you?
- Quit making that ugly face.
- You're driving me crazy with that tapping (fidgeting, twitching, humming…)
- You are the most nervous, twitchy kid I've ever seen.
- Is there something in your eye?
- You are so weird.
- Stop making that annoying noise.
- Keep your hands to yourself.
- Sit still.
- You're not even trying to control yourself.
- Just stop it!

These are the words that children with TS hear over and over every day. They're hissed by annoyed parents, yelled on the playground by other children, and said in front of classmates by angry teachers. They even come from strangers in supermarket lines, on the bus, or at soccer practice.

It's hard to measure exactly what living with constant disapproval does to a person's self-esteem, but the net effect is certainly not good. It seems likely that the longer a child with TS is blamed or even punished for ticcing, the more frequently he is made to feel ashamed or excluded, the more likely he is to develop a poor image of himself as a person. He may grow up feeling like a freak of nature, a socially unacceptable outsider.

Judy, mother of 21-year-old Gabe, looks back on the treatment he received from his peers with sadness:

> Some of Gabe's tics have caused physical pain, but all of them have caused terrible embarrassment to him, especially between sixth and ninth grades. He has become somewhat cautious with people he does not know well, and also of new situations. His demeanor does not speak of confidence, although he has a lot of positive things in his life. He seems unsure of the strong qualities he possesses. However, maturity and success are helping him overcome the self-doubt brought on by the teasing in former years.

Gaining self-acceptance and learning how to advocate for yourself is a basic survival skill for someone with TS. Without these basic achievements, young people like Gabe are very likely to approach life and relationships with caution rather than confidence.

The more extreme a child's tics are, and the less she knows about why they happen, the worse she is likely to feel about them.

Jennifer, mother of 12-year-old Ty, says his tics have affected his self-esteem and his ability to form strong relationships with other children:

> The verbal tics are harder for Ty to deal with, just because they draw attention to himself and he is very shy. Scouts became difficult and discouraging as he got older and had increased anxiety. Baseball was a passion, but he found with the ticcing that it was hard to concentrate on catching and throwing accurately. Ty recently joined a youth group, but has felt withdrawn since he is afraid of being misunderstood or ridiculed.
>
> He has few friends. He is very sensitive to the fact that not many kids socialize with him, and it has caused him to withdraw even further from others. He has wished for one good friend, but it hasn't happened yet.

Tools for self-protection

Kids with TS can persevere to soar above the challenges this disorder poses when armed with a diagnosis, solid information about TS, adult support, and tools for handling cutting comments with aplomb.

Kids with TS need and want to know as much about the disorder as they can. Many have come up with ideas about TS on their own that cause them excessive worry. They may fear that their tics will get worse as they get older, have negative feelings about having to take medication, or worry about how they look to the opposite sex. Frank and frequent conversations with parents, doctors, and counselors can keep these fears to a minimum.

Kids with TS need to hear that family and friends accept them, tics and all. It's true that sometimes their behaviors are annoying, but every kid does a few things that drive his parents nuts.

If you've never had a tic, it's hard to show your child that you really understand and sympathize. Meeting other children with TS through a support group, or reading about them in books, lets kids know they're not alone with their challenges. Handling rude comments is never easy, and what works for one child may not work for another. The standard advice is to not let nasty remarks bother you, but let's face it—they do bother most people. Coming up with a repertoire of witty comebacks can be helpful for some kids. Here are a few responses that have worked for others:

Katy, mother of 15-year-old Steve, says:

> Steve spent his first year of middle school in a school outside of our regular district, because the school he should have attended was still under construction. Being concerned about the transition of my TS/ADHD child to middle school in general, and to a school where he would be around a lot of kids he didn't know, I decided to provide each teacher with a brief, one-page handout about Steve's condition. The handout included a picture.
>
> The day in question Steve was in his homeroom and apparently made some little squeaky noise. The teacher stopped and said: "WHO is making that NOISE?" to which Steve replied, "It's me, it's my Tourette's."
>
> As you might imagine, dead silence followed from said teacher.

Lee's son Joseph has used both a factual approach and humor when questions make him uncomfortable:

> When Joseph was younger, 9 or so, he could stop adults and children from teasing him by telling them he "had a neurological condition."
>
> He also wears a clonidine patch on his back. When asked what it was for, he would tell the inquirer it was "for a snake bite." I'm not sure where that came from, but people never asked twice....

Many people with TS have a real gift for humor, and a little self-deprecating or even in-your-face humor can defuse problems much of the time, especially with peers.

Tools for changing the culture

Kids also need to know when to seek adult help with situations. A witty comeback is fine for the occasional rude comment, but extreme forms of teasing take too much of a toll for children to bear alone. Likewise, no child should be told to deal with physical attacks on his own. Look at what your standards would be for your peers—you could ignore or reply to rudeness, but you wouldn't accept someone at work punching you in the face.

Too often, adults put all the responsibility for handling the social implications of tic-cing on the shoulders of children. Adults tend to forget that most of the environments children must negotiate are set up and supervised by adults, or should be. When the adults in charge of homes, schools, sports leagues, and parks abdicate their responsibility to guide the actions of children, vulnerable kids—"different" kids—tend to bear the consequences.

If you parent a child with TS, or if you are a teacher, counselor, or other professional who wants to help, taking on the responsibility of building a culture that supports people with disabilities and differences really can make a difference.

Cathie, mother of 8-year-old Jason, says having caring adults involved in her son's community activities has been a plus:

> Trying to find ways of relating to him that are productive, as far as discipline and daily living go, makes a difference. Cub Scouts and Challenger baseball have been great. His special ed preschool teacher from years past is now his Sunday School teacher, so he does well there as she has the skills to work with him. This also makes me more comfortable about leaving him.

Adults have come a long way toward creating safer, more inclusive workplaces. It's hard to imagine, but 100 years ago pushing and shoving, slapped faces, and even fist-fights were not uncommon in some rough-and-tumble workplaces. Today, this is considered assault whether the perpetrator is a coworker or a supervisor. It's no longer socially or legally acceptable for bosses or coworkers to belittle others with comments about race, sex, or disability. Recent court cases have made the term "hostile environment" well known as a description for a workplace where some employees feel belittled, harassed, or even endangered. It's not that racism, sexism, homophobia, or negative feelings about people with disabilities have disappeared. Most adults have simply learned that while they may hold any views they please, imposing them on others in public is socially unacceptable—and could get you sued, or make you lose your job. Some people have changed their views, others have simply learned to get along better despite them. Only a very few need to be reminded with workplace discipline or a civil rights lawsuit.

Strides have also been made in most schools. Only three decades ago, teachers routinely used spanking and slapping to keep students in line, and "hazing" was a common and accepted rite of passage among high school and college boys. Now, most states have outlawed corporal punishment in schools, and incidents of hazing cause college fraternities to lose their charters. However, most of the changes have been in what adults do to children, not in changing how children deal with each other.

Sadly, teasing, harassment, bullying, and even physical attacks, when they occur in schools and affect children, are still dismissed with words like: "boys will be boys," or "kids can be cruel" far too often. In many neighborhoods, children with disabilities or other differences are shunned or even set upon, and their parents feel helpless to change the situation.

While it's true that children can easily fall into bad behavior, adults do have power over the choices children make. Many are simply afraid to exercise this power. When people do, it is possible to create schools, neighborhoods, and communities where people with disabilities or differences are accepted and valued, and where teasing and bullying is as unacceptable as it is at work.

The job begins at home, with educating young children about disabilities. A parent's tasks include stepping in to say that using hurtful words like "retard" and "spaz" is not acceptable, but it also includes making sure that children notice the presence and accomplishments of persons with disabilities. Beethoven's hearing impairment, Steven Hawking's wheelchair, and baseball player Jim Eisenreich's Tourette's syndrome can be reference points for discussions about what people with disabilities offer our community. These chats are not just helpful for kids who have a disability and their siblings, but for all children.

There are several books available about children with TS (see Appendix A, *Resources,* for a list). Sharing these with a child who has TS helps with self-understanding.

Sharing them with a group of that child's peers can help them understand and accept as well.

Schools and other community settings can outlaw teasing and bullying. Deliberate adoption of policies on diversity that include disability is a start, but adult supervision and guidance is really the key. Often young bullies will readily admit that being able to get away with it is a primary reason for their actions. If not allowed the opportunity to prey on other kids, they might take out their frustrations in some other way.

Sometimes kids get out of line verbally or physically, but incidents should not escalate or be repeated if adults are on the lookout for problems. Just as there are school rules about using foul language in class, we need school rules about harassing children with disabilities. When adults hear kids taunted for riding the "short bus" or being in special ed, they have a duty to step in.

Many people don't say anything because they are at a loss about what to say. A simple "I'm sorry, but it's not okay to make fun of other people for having a disability," or "At this school, we don't use those words because they hurt people's feelings," can help. Talking about disabilities in general and encouraging sensitivity to others with differences, including discussing what words like "retarded" actually mean, can help eliminate misconceptions that some children may have and make this kind of teasing socially unacceptable.

A consistent and wise response to physical incidents is also important. Some schools are now adopting "zero tolerance" policies about violence and threats of violence. This is certainly one way to approach the problem, and in some situations it may be a proper one. But "zero tolerance" policies punish without addressing the root of the problem—indeed, under these policies the child who was the victim of a bully may be suspended along with the perpetrator!

Once a fight begins, it's hard for adults to see who was at fault, and "fault" is hard to assign when taunts and punches have been thrown on both sides. Finding out what the core issues are takes more time and effort than blanket suspensions do, but it can make a real difference in violence prevention.

It shouldn't be assumed that a kid with TS is always the victim when it comes to teasing and fighting. Recent research indicates that children who bully others tend to be kids who have experienced teasing and bullying themselves, and this is a category that many young kids with tics fall into. Research also shows that bullies pick victims who are more anxious than other children, and therefore more likely to react to bullying with satisfying emotional outbursts.[1] The same child can be both a bully and a victim, depending on the circumstances. In either case, compassion and help are needed more than punishment if the cycle is to be broken.

Some kids with TS do have a tendency toward aggression, even blind rages, and this can get them into serious trouble if unchecked. A thin-skinned kid with a hair-trigger temper will find it much more difficult to handle a rude comment than one who is confident and in control. Social scientists who study bullying in schools call these children "provocative victims": students whose social deficits are like a permanent "kick me" sign in the eyes of bullies.[2] When a child with TS does appear to be part of the problem rather than strictly a victim, the best strategy is probably working on anger management skills, social skills, and improved self-esteem, not doling out stiff punishment.

Teasing and bullying in schools is beginning to have legal consequences as well. Several recent court cases have demanded—and won—financial damages against schools and school districts that allowed hostile environments to harm children. Disability harassment is considered discrimination under Title II of the Americans with Disabilities Act, and under Section 504 of the Rehabilitation Act,[3] Successful Supreme Court claims regarding harassment at school have also been brought on constitutional grounds under Title IX of the Equal Access Act of 1984, indicating that a civil rights/ Constitutional defense can also succeed.[4]

In 2000, US Secretary of Education Richard Riley issued a policy letter to school principals, superintendents, and college and university presidents about this issue. Along with spelling out the legal consequences of permitting harassment of students with disabilities, Riley's letter reminded them that:

> Disability harassment can have a profound impact on students, raise safety concerns, and erode efforts to ensure that students with disabilities have equal access to the myriad benefits that an education offers. Indeed, harassment can seriously interfere with the ability of students with disabilities to receive an education critical to their advancement.

As defined by Riley, "disability harassment" may include verbal acts, such as name-calling, graphic or written statements, and physical conduct that threatens, harms, or humiliates a disabled child. Here are some examples of the kind of conduct covered by Riley's directive, taken from an article by the Learning Disabilities Association of America:[5]

- Several students continually remark out loud to other students during class that a student with dyslexia is "retarded" or "deaf and dumb" and does not belong in the class. As a result, the harassed student has difficulty doing work in class and her grades decline.

- A teacher subjects a student to inappropriate physical restraint because of conduct related to the disability, with the result that the student tries to avoid school through increased absences.

- A school administrator repeatedly denies a student with a disability access to lunch, field trips, assemblies, and extracurricular activities as punishment for taking time off school for required services related to the disability.

- A professor repeatedly belittles and criticizes a student with a disability for using accommodations in the class, with the result that the student is so discouraged that she has great difficulty performing in class and learning.

- Students continually taunt or belittle a student with mental retardation by mocking and intimidating him so he does not participate in class.

As Riley's letter makes clear, legally actionable conduct is either extreme (physical assault) or repeated, and it must prevent a child from accessing educational opportunities or benefits. Similar standards apply in community settings, most of which are also covered by the Americans with Disabilities Act (ADA), a civil rights law.

Parents and helping professionals who feel that a child is being subjected to disability harassment have many options, ranging from direct intervention to going to court. The advocacy groups listed in Appendix A can help, as can school officials committed to preventing problems.

There are now prepared curricula on bullying prevention. Schools can adopt programs like the Committee for Children's "Steps to Respect" (see *http://www.cfchildren. org/str.html* for more information), which uses lesson plans based on popular children's books to talk about teasing, bullying, and violence in elementary schools. It specifically addresses issues of disability and "difference," and includes skill-building lessons to help students develop empathy, friendship, and self-esteem skills. The Committee for Children notes that success of its program and similar efforts depends greatly on gaining the commitment of the entire school staff, which also receives training in prevention and problem-solving techniques.[6]

An excellent web site, *http://www.bullying.org,* addresses related issues.

TS and child development

Tourette's syndrome usually appears in school-age children. Some kids with TS had no previous neurological symptoms worth noting—their tics seemed to appear out of the blue. For many others, the emergence of tics is simply the most noticeable sign that something about these children is different.

Many parents of children with TS note that they saw differences in their child's behavior from a fairly early age, long before tics were noticed. High activity level and extreme impulsivity, often leading to an early diagnosis of ADHD, is a common tale. For others, developmental delays and social anxiety were the earliest symptoms seen.

Joyce, mother of 18-year-old John, tells her story:

> When John was 4, before we noticed his eye-blinking, I was concerned about his poor language development. He was barely speaking in sentences by then. I had him in for hearing tests. No problems were found, but he was described as extremely withdrawn. When he began kindergarten, he began to show signs of separation anxiety and school phobia. The tics began when he was about 4 years old. We noticed rapid eye-blinking, but thought that perhaps he was just anxious about starting school.

Except in the case of children who have autism or mental retardation in addition to TS, the developmental delays seen are usually mild. They generally don't affect intellectual or academic ability, although there are a few specific learning disabilities that are more common in people with TS (see Chapter 8 for more information). Parents of kids in this category report that their child acts as though he is a few years younger than his peers, and prefers the company of younger children.

The term a lot of parents use is "the 2/3 rule," meaning that they expect their child with TS to be about 2/3 as advanced developmentally as other kids his age, at least in some areas. While his academic achievement may be on-target or even high, his behavior and social skills lag behind those of his peers.

Debbie, mother of 18-year-old David and 10-year-old Nate, says:

> David is susceptible to friends' suggestions, which could include bad influences, but so far we have been lucky. There are many times that he appears to be looking at the world through the eyes of a 12-year-old, rather than a mature 18-year-old—it's the old 2/3 rule.

Adults out there see him as a talented, hard-working young adult, but there are times when we get a completely different picture at home.

The good news is that social development does catch up in time. You may be able to hurry the process along a little by accessing formal social skills training, which should be available at school or through a counselor or therapist.

In social skills training, kids discuss appropriate and inappropriate behavior, and work on improving their skills. It's often done in groups rather than individually, allowing participants to practice on each other before they try out their newfound skills on typically developing peers. Skills practiced include things like learning how to read "body language" and facial expressions, so as not to miss social cues; turn-taking; and conversational skills.

Effective parenting

Most kids with TS pose no special challenges when it comes to childrearing. Although having tics can add to natural feelings of self-consciousness, especially during the awkward years of puberty, that stage usually passes quickly if a child has grown up with a strong self-image.

Parents find extra skills invaluable, however, when a child or teen has severe tics, an especially high level of impulsivity, or additional neurological problems. Some kids with TS challenge all the traditional rules of parenting. With help, you can develop the sensitivity and skill you need to cope well with these unique children and their symptoms.

The first thing to do is to recognize tics for what they are: almost impossible to control. Yes, children can often learn to delay or camouflage tics, but it's not possible to stop ticcing for long. Even deliberately stopping for a short while takes a great deal of concentration, and may make it impossible for the child to pay attention or do anything else other than concentrating on not ticcing.

Many people with TS note that the more reaction a tic gets, the more anxiety the person ticcing feels about it. The result is usually more of the unwanted tic, not less. So learn to accept and ignore tics as much as possible. Less anxiety usually means less ticcing.

If a tic harms no one, it can be ignored completely. If it harms no one but is annoying—for example, a vocal tic that always seems to erupt when you're at the movies—work together on strategies for handling it discreetly. Brainstorm solutions for substituting a less obtrusive movement, sound, or word for the one that annoys, offends, or distracts.

Come up with guidelines for where and when your child can relax and "let out" her tics, such as before the movie, after the movie, or during a quick trip to the bathroom. Let her know that you understand this isn't something she wants to do, and that you want her to be relaxed and have fun when she's out in the community, at home, and at school.

Basic techniques

Most children with TS respond well to fairly traditional parenting techniques, the sort of ideas you could pick up in any good parenting class. Basic suggestions for improving behavior include:

- Catch kids doing the right thing, not just the wrong thing. Studies have shown consistently that for most children, praise is far more motivating than punishment.

- Employ rewards for positive behavior—but do so judiciously. "Star charts" and point systems are often effective ways to turn behavior around, but if used too often they can actually make good behavior dependent on rewards, or simply lose effectiveness.

- Let the punishment fit the "crime" by employing natural and logical consequences whenever possible. For example, if your child throws a fit because he doesn't want to wear a coat to school, let him leave without his coat. If he gets cold, that's a natural consequence of refusing to wear his coat.

- Involve kids themselves in making rules and deciding on consequences for breaking them.

- Avoid corporal punishment, which can encourage the use of violence as a way to solve problems—exactly the outcome you're trying to avoid.

Appendix A includes a list of books, web sites, and other materials on helpful parenting techniques for kids with neurological differences.

Parents whose children with TS occasionally have difficult behaviors stress that developing a flexible approach, prioritizing, and understanding are key to coping. Sometimes basic parenting techniques work, but sometimes they don't. Extreme rigidity is not the same thing as consistency.

Brenda, grandmother of ten-year-old Charisse, says putting consistency and kindness together works for her family, although it's not always an easy combination:

> I've found that schedules, routines, and providing an environment
> where she knows what to expect relieves her stress and seems to comfort
> her. She very much likes "tradition": Regular mealtimes, bathing times,
> bedtime routines, and morning activities where she knows what to expect
> all result in a happier child.
>
> It's sometimes difficult to choose which behavior to address and which
> to ignore. Balancing our expectations with her ability to control behaviors
> is difficult.
>
> I tend to ignore or try to redirect her when she is being difficult. I find
> this quite easy to do, but my daughter, on the other hand, is concerned
> that Charisse will come to expect this from people in her life, and will not
> accept that most of the world won't accommodate her in this way. We've
> agreed to balance this, but continue my way for now so she can enjoy her
> childhood more, without every little issue being dealt with.
>
> It's a tough balancing act for the whole family.

Techniques for handling extreme behaviors

Some children with TS have difficult behaviors every day. Some fly into rages easily, often without regard for logic—and without logic, tactics like natural and logical consequences just don't make a dent. There is good reason to believe that these behaviors, like tics, are something that some people with TS cannot easily control.[7] Of course, the world is going to demand that children learn to control them, and that's when new parenting techniques can help.

If you're coping with rages, self-injurious behaviors, or other extreme situations, begin by examining what circumstances seem to bring on the most difficult behaviors. If you can pinpoint at least some of your child's triggers, you've made the first step toward preventing blow-ups.

Maria, mother of 4-year-old Jesse, has identified triggers and learned to head off trouble by avoiding them whenever possible:

> We do see extreme agitation and rages, usually when he is striving to
> do something perfectly, yet rushing because of his ADHD. Add his poor

fine-motor skills, and he is set for the highest frustration. For example, trying to put on his socks and his shoes. When he can't get his fingers to work as fast as he wants them to, he blows up.

If he ever says he is frustrated, even once, that's a sign that he must be removed from the situation. If he says, "I'm frustrated" three times, he will blow up, and this will be followed by twenty minutes of continuous ticcing.

We also can't mention good things to him in advance. If I say, "We will go to grandmother's tomorrow," he will immediately want to go now, and if that is not possible, he will rage. I can't mention a toy if I don't know where it is, because once he hears the name he will want it—and if I cannot find it, he will rage.

A number of parents interviewed for this book strongly recommended the parenting ideas presented Dr. Ross Greene's book *The Explosive Child* (see listing in Appendix A). Greene relies on the latest research in neuropsychiatry, which has documented what parents of kids with TS and related disorders knew all along—sometimes their kids really are different. Their difficult behaviors are not deliberate attempts to manipulate adults, but reactions to out-of-control emotions, difficulty in processing some types of information effectively, and poor self-control.

Greene points toward built-in inflexibility as the basic problem, suggests many strategies for defusing conflicts, and provides several different strategies for helping children who are "chronically inflexible" and "explosive" learn better approaches to difficult situations. If a child's developmental skills for dealing with frustration appropriately are delayed, he argues, natural and logical consequences, chart and reward systems, and other typical interventions are unlikely to work. Instead, parents should examine what triggers rages, eliminate triggers where possible, and teach skills that help the child build flexibility and tolerance for frustration.

One of his best-known ideas, the "basket system," is especially helpful for families who need a new approach to handling discipline creatively. Parents must assert their authority where issues of safety are concerned—these are what Greene would call "Basket A" issues, areas where there is no flexibility at all. Beyond these areas, issues might fit into several other "baskets," depending on how much flexibility parents feel comfortable with. So while protecting siblings from hitting is a Basket A issue, picking up your socks right now might be a Basket B or C issue.[8]

Experienced parents have come up with many ways to handle rage behaviors. Lucy, mother of 12-year-old Richard, tells some of her strategies:

> The best approach, in my experience, is to try to avoid the rage starting in the first place. Start making some notes about the times when his behaviors escalate, and look for commonalties. Are certain times of the day harder for him? Then try to avoid changes in routine during those times of day. Is he better after he eats? Then feed him before attempting a change in routine. Are there any little "signs" in the hour or so preceding the rage/bad behavior to clue you in that it is coming? If so, try to steer him to whatever is calming for him—and teach him to notice these signs also.

> If the rage is already present, then the most important step is to get him somewhere where he cannot harm himself, others, or property. Prepare for this stage BEFORE it happens.

> Set up a "safe place" in your home, a place where he can go and not be at risk to himself or to others. We all say we don't have such a place in our homes, but as a wise therapist once pointed out to me, you can't afford NOT to have such a place! It may be a bed, or a walk-in closet, or a bathroom, or a corner of the garage. Agree with your child in advance where his safe place will be and what will be in there. Then, when he starts to lose control, tell him to go there until he is in control again. If he refuses, bodily take him there. Teach him to go there on his own, and praise him when he does go there on his own.

> Be sure there is nothing in this one place that he could use to harm himself. Do put comforting items there—a blanket, a pillow, some small soft objects that it would be okay for him to hit or throw, etc.

> Richard has two "safe places": the top bunk above his own bed, and his walk-in closet. The top bunk has a pillow, blanket, and lots of stuffed animals. He can go snuggle up there by himself, or he can throw the stuffed animals on the floor of his room (he will later have to pick them up). In the closet is a light switch so he can choose to be in the dark or in the light, a punching bag, a pillow, a blanket, a basket of small toys, etc.

> Stay calm during the rage—it's not easy, but you must try to step back and not take personally what he says or does during the rage. Your job during the rage is to keep everyone safe; you can mother him again after

things have calmed down. Don't try to reason with him or argue with him during the rage; he can't respond with logic at that time. If Richard starts to do something dangerous or make threats, I tell him in a very controlled, even voice, "I will not allow you to harm yourself or to harm anyone else. If you harm any property, you will be responsible for repairing the damage or paying to replace it." Sometimes I say this two or three times in a row, in a very controlled fashion.

Some people can use a "safe place" for self-calming, others choose meditation, strenuous exercise, or substituting an acceptable aggressive act, such as bopping a punching bag, for unacceptable outbursts.

Lee, mother of 13-year-old Joseph, tells about some of her strategies:

Joseph has had trouble with extreme agitation and rages. These are more likely to occur if he is in an unfamiliar situation or with people he doesn't know well, or is hungry, rushed, or tired. Also, this is much more common when his OCD is waxing.

When he is starting to rage I will ask him how I can help. Usually he wants me to stay with him, but not too close because he doesn't want to hurt me.

We keep old phone books around that can always be torn up. A box of tissues is good in a pinch. Sometimes I line up old, plastic flowerpots on the railing of the deck for him to knock off. We fly by the seat of our pants a lot!

The more helpful options you can come up with, the more likely you are to have the right intervention available when it's most needed.

The Southern California chapter of the Tourette Syndrome Association (TSA) worked with McDonald Productions to produce a video, "Bending the Rules," that does an excellent job of presenting fresh ideas on effective discipline for kids with TS. This video is now available through the Tourette Syndrome Spectrum Disorder Association (TSDA), which is listed in Appendix A.

The national TSA has produced a groundbreaking pamphlet on neurologically based rage behaviors, which families can use as a starting point for talking with schools, doctors, and therapists. These and other materials on behavior management for kids who do have challenges beyond the ordinary are listed in Appendix A.

Getting expert help

You know your child best, and are more likely than even the best "behavior expert" to recognize what triggers rage and other difficult behaviors, and what works to help your child regain control. However, when your best efforts aren't doing the trick, it may be helpful to call on expert services.

TSA, TSDA, and other organizations hold conferences and workshops that often feature speakers who present ideas about managing difficult behaviors. Help may also be available through your school district, county mental health department, or a therapist, psychologist, or psychiatrist. In some cases, your health insurance may pay for this assistance, including parent training as well as direct work with your child.

If you find that immobilizing your child is sometimes necessary (physical restraint, or "holds") for safety reasons, be sure to seek out training in appropriate physical restraint methods. Improperly applied holds can cause injury or even death. Non-violent crisis intervention training should be available through a nursing education program, or possibly at a local hospital, as nurses and other health-care personnel need this type of instruction to protect themselves from dangerous patients. Crisis Prevention Institute Inc., listed in Appendix A, also sponsors this type of training around the country.

Resorting to physical restraint should not be a common occurrence, however. Using holds frequently is a good indicator that you need to add some new ideas to your bag of tricks, or that it's time to call for additional expert help.

When rages and other extreme behavior problems are chronic and self-calming strategies are not working, medication or medication changes may be recommended. If your child's safety or the safety of others is at risk, taking this strategy under consideration may be wise, even if your child does not have severe tics. Medication choices are discussed in Chapter 6, *Medical Care*.

Public dilemmas

When rages occur at home, you have the advantage of knowing the environment and having the privacy needed to deal with the situation as you see fit. When meltdowns occur in a public place, such as a supermarket or public park, it's not so easy.

Your first concern must be safety. If that means physically restraining your child, that's okay. However, you may attract unwanted attention from people who want to berate your child, or even you. Having a pre-printed card available to hand off to these people while you try to get the situation under control can help.

Medical identification cards are available from the national TSA, or you can print up your own at a copy center. These cards can also be helpful if your child has socially unacceptable tics, such as coprolalia, that could attract unwanted attention.

A card's text might read:

> My child has a neurological disorder, Tourette's syndrome, that causes uncontrolled movements and sounds, and that sometimes causes behavior problems. If you would like to know more about Tourette's syndrome, please call the Tourette's Syndrome Association at (718) 224-2999.

Occasionally a bystander will misunderstand what's going on and call the police. At times like these, having a card on hand can really help.

In some areas, the police department maintains a registry of persons with disabilities whose behavior could be misconstrued as threatening or so odd as to require police attention. Signing up with a registry gives the police solid information to work with before officers respond to potentially confusing situations, whether they occur in your home or in public.

Parents who are aware of the early signs of an impending meltdown can often remove the child from the situation, which is usually the best strategy. It's not very convenient if you're in the middle of grocery shopping, but dealing with a public tantrum is even less convenient. Retreating to your car, a nearby park, or another quiet place can give your child a chance to regain control before he loses it entirely.

Once a rage has actually occurred, it's essential to give the person time to recover. It's also important for the person to make reparations for his or her behavior, if possible.

If you find that certain situations often or almost always set the stage for rage, see if you can find ways to identify the root problem. Older children may be able to tell you exactly what it is that sets them off, but with younger children your powers of observation will have to suffice.

Once you've identified the root problem, you can choose to either address it or to help your child avoid the situation. For example, if you notice that long shopping trips are frequently the setting for difficult episodes, solutions could range from taking short trips to just one store per day rather than a mall or large department store, both environments that are overwhelming for some kids; avoiding stores that use flickering fluorescents or loud music, if those are a problem for your child; bringing along snacks and an activity bag if the triggers seem to be hunger or boredom; or doing your shopping without the kids.

Sibling issues

Parents of children with TS often find that they spend a great deal of time working with the affected child or children, sometimes to the detriment of brothers and sisters. That can lead to all sorts of acting-out behavior by other children in the family.

Resentment is a natural reaction. Siblings may ask themselves why the kid with TS seems to get the most attention, and try a few attention-getting things themselves. Another common reaction is just withdrawing from the situation, hiding in their bedrooms, throwing themselves into after-school activities, or hanging out at friend's houses where the drama level is lower.

When a child with TS has difficult behaviors in addition to tics, the need of siblings for adequate attention can easily be overlooked. This can set up some very difficult family dynamics.

Debbie, mother of 18-year-old David, 10-year-old Nate, and five other children, says:

> Nate is the least popular child in the family. Deep down, I think everybody loves him, but nobody wants to be his roommate. His rages naturally upset his siblings. He is very "bothered" by his siblings, but cannot recognize when he is "bothering" one of them.

Although your child with TS may have neurological reasons for his increased impulsivity or aggression, that doesn't mean it's all right for his siblings to bear the brunt of it. You must set ground rules that protect siblings and their personal property to avoid fanning the flames.

Some siblings become ultra-protective of their brother or sister with TS, others try to pretend they aren't even related to avoid embarrassment. The healthiest response is probably somewhere between these two extremes.

Joyce struggles to cope with sibling rivalry that's compounded by her 18-year-old son's TS, which includes rage behaviors:

> John's behaviors have significantly affected every member of the immediate family, somewhat affected our extended family, and impacted every facet of our lives. His actual tics have not been terribly problematic, although it took a long time for some of the family to accept them as non-threatening. The vocal ones have been more difficult, especially some of the coprolalia-like tics—having him suddenly insert "bumslimer" into conversations was a little disconcerting, to say the least.

But the aggression and anger directed at his dad and sister, the defiance, the oppositionality…these have been the hardest. It is very hard to deal with behaviors that are neurologically based but look deliberate, and not feel that some personal vendetta is being fought.

John's TS has skewed family dynamics immensely. I have been pushed into the referee position, keeping the snarling animals apart. John's sister alternately feels pity for him or wants to kill him, and all the kids feel bound to protect Dad from John.

All siblings need to know that their individual accomplishments and needs are important to you. You may not be able to give each kid equal time, but with careful scheduling you can make sure that each one gets some special, individual time with you. If necessary, arrange for respite care to make time for nurturing siblings. Be sure that your children have opportunities to discuss their feelings about their sibling's behavior, and about how it impacts them at school and in the neighborhood, with you in private.

If siblings are experiencing personal problems as a result of the child with TS's behavior—for example, if they have frequently been the target of tantrums, or are being teased at school because of their sibling—they can benefit from individual counseling.

Try to explain TS to your other children in terms they can understand. Younger children may need reassurance that it's not a disease they can catch.

Building a support system

Every kid needs to find a place where his talents shine, and a way to create a positive life in the community beyond school and home. Children with challenges need a community support system that includes extended family whenever possible, same-age peers, and adults whose relationship to the child is personal, not merely professional.

Your allies in creating this kind of support system include grandparents, aunts and uncles, scout leaders, athletic coaches, members of your religious congregation, even shopkeepers who see your child on a regular basis. You don't need to tell these folks everything there is to know about TS, just enough to encourage them to accept and care about your child as a person. Always stress the positive aspects, the things your child can do well, as well as discussing any difficulties he may exhibit.

Maria, mother of 4-year-old Jesse, says:

> Through careful researching, I have found lessons or day camps where
> his issues are accepted and his interests encouraged. You have to make a
> lot of phone calls and make visits to determine this.
>
> My sister refuses to deal with the issue, but the rest of my family is
> great.

Parents of kids with TS also need support, and sometimes it isn't forthcoming. Many parents report that old friendships end because of their child's behavior, and that even neighbors and relatives sometimes shun them.

Judy, mother of 21-year-old Gabe, feels like she has coped on her own for most of her son's life with TS:

> I had very little extended family support, as they live a distance away
> and also chose to tell me, when they did see him, that Gabe didn't have
> much of a problem, that they had never heard of TS, and that no one in
> either family has ever had it. They didn't understand the concept of tic
> suppression, nor did they know the extent to which he was subject to
> rejection by former friends and others. They never knew the depth of
> sadness I have experienced because my son, at age nine, suddenly
> developed this disorder.
>
> My friends supported me, but there was little known about TS back
> then and little if any support in the community.

Some old friends, neighbors, and relatives want to know more, and may draw closer to you. Others will drift away, unable to cope with this change in your family's situation. Some people are simply uncomfortable with disability, others may not understand why you have less time to spend with them, or feel that you have become too serious because of your child's challenges.

You may find that parents you meet through a local TSA chamber are the first people who really understand. Many fast friendships are made through formal and online support groups.

Brenda says an activity group especially for girls with TS has been a good fit for her granddaughter:

> Only just recently, we found a group in Toronto that works with young
> girls with Tourette's and comorbid disorders by providing weekend camps
> and day trips. The cost is high, and for families without resources this

would be difficult, but it was wonderful to find some services that focused on girls and their challenges with Tourette's. There are some private donations available to assist with the cost for those eligible.

Support groups

In the US, the Tourette Syndrome Association is the main sponsor of TS-specific support groups for families and for people with TS, although there are also independent support groups and, in California, the TSDA. To find a group in your area, contact a national organization and/or check with a local hospital or newspaper.

Support groups may meet monthly or more often. Some meetings feature speakers invited to talk about topics of interest, while others are simply informal get-togethers. Small groups tend to meet in members' homes, while larger groups might rent a church hall or a room in the public library.

Rindy, mother of 14-year-old Shawn, has found support in many different quarters:

> *I look for support from other TS parents, including (probably most instrumentally) those on online support lists and medical professionals.*
>
> *I also rely on parents of children at church who have different disabilities, but who understand how to circumvent systems problems such as those in school. People at church who can provide names of former coworkers in the school system who can help us have been especially helpful at interpreting tests, getting appropriate placements and services within the school.*
>
> *It would have been helpful through the years to have respite care. Leaving the kids with sitters, grandparents who live far away and don't understand, or friends inexperienced with neurological issues has not been adequate or reliable at giving us the rest we need as parents. On the other hand, a few close friends who have experience with similar neurological issues, who have a lot of patience and love, and who have been able to take the kids for short periods of time have been irreplaceable.*

You don't have to be a member to attend a TSA meeting, although joining the organization or putting a few dollars in for refreshments is welcomed. Many TSA groups sponsor occasional social events, such as summer picnics or holiday parties, as well as meetings. Some hold local, regional, or state conferences. There is also a national TSA conference each year, and both members and non-members are always welcome.

If you are too far away from the closest TSA group to attend regularly, see if you can attend occasionally and continue your contact via letters, phone calls, or email. Just knowing there's someone you can reach when you're in need goes a long way.

If there's no local TSA support group and there doesn't seem to be enough families coping with TS to form one, you may want to seek out a group for parents of children with disabilities in general. Organizations like Easter Seals sponsor groups like these, as do some mental health clinics and school districts. The National Alliance for the Mentally Ill (NAMI), the largest US organization for persons and families affected by mental illness, also welcomes people coping with Tourette's syndrome. NAMI sponsors many local groups, and is listed in Appendix A along with other groups that may be helpful, such as CHADD.

Online support

Internet support groups (also called listervs) are free email discussions on specific topics of interest. Each subscriber receives a copy of an email sent by any member of the group. Some active groups generate dozens of messages a day. If you subscribe to the "digest" mode, you will receive one email containing all of the messages posted that day. Email discussion groups are an excellent way to connect with people in similar circumstances. Several Internet support groups discuss Tourette's syndrome and related issues.

Most online support groups work like a round-robin letter: each question, story, or piece of advice is broadcast to all list members, who can then comment or reply to the individual or the whole group. Some operate through the World Wide Web, allowing you to read and send messages through a web site.

Linda, mother of 10-year-old William, relies on an online support group:

> I'll never forget how wonderful it was to find other people were out there dealing with very complicated kids like my boy. I had tried local TSA meetings, but they were in a suburban area (I'm in the city) and it seemed that not many of the families were dealing with comorbid disorders in addition to TS.
>
> I got online and found POV-Twitch—now known as Sunrise Tourette—about four years ago. At first I was all questions. Four years later, I probably answer more questions than I ask. The help and support are worth it, and it's great to be able to call on the list members any time, day or night.

It's not a cyberspace-only thing, either. It turned out that one member lived not too far away, and we have met or spoken on the phone a few times. I visited another when I was in her area for a conference. Some members make a point of meeting during the annual national TSA conference also.

Many email groups have a moderator who sets rules about who can join the group and what topics are off-limits (divisive issues like politics and religion, for example). Sometimes the moderator also steers the course of conversations. Other groups are more of a free-for-all, which works well as long as no one gets offended or uses the group as a forum for sales-oriented posts or personal diatribes. Several computer-based discussion and support groups are listed in Appendix A.

Online groups are especially good support options for people who live in rural areas, where an in-person support group may not be available. You don't even have to own a computer to take advantage of these—you can probably log on via an Internet-equipped computer at your public library. Any email software, including free programs and software you get through commercial services like America Online, can be used to subscribe to and participate in these groups.

Family counseling

A counselor who is knowledgeable about the impact of TS on families can make a huge difference.

The hallmarks of good family therapy are a strong knowledge base about your family's issues, finding a counselor who is a good listener, and being willing to try some new techniques as a family. Issues you might want to discuss are Tourette's syndrome, parenting styles, family dynamics, and special difficulties that complicate the situation, such as stepfamily blending.

Joyce says that family therapy with a good counselor can augment your own efforts:

As a family, we have had a number of people working with us to help us cope with the situation we are in. John's school counselor referred us to a member of a private team that worked for the school district to deal with children who have severe behavioral problems. We saw this therapist for a while as a family.

When we moved, I immediately got in touch with mental health services in the new area and arranged for John to see the child and youth coordinator for counseling. He saw her, and we got support from her, for several years. We also managed to get a childcare worker to work with John on behavioral issues, anxiety, fears, socialization, etc.

The focus of all these counselors has been on family dynamics, and somewhat on behavioral plans and interventions. As parents, we have benefited mostly from knowing that others were sharing the load.

Often family therapists do both group and individual work in different sessions. This gives each family member a chance to talk in confidence about personal feelings, and then provides the entire family with a forum for improving how the unit works together.

Brenda, grandmother of 10-year-old Charisse, has not found as much help in family therapy as she had hoped for:

We did have some family therapy early after Charisse was diagnosed. I don't believe any of the strategies to cope with problems suggested were of any help to Charisse or our family. We have learned more from books such as The Explosive Child, *and in particular from an online discussion list that I belong to. In fact, I'm convinced that the list and the knowledge I've gained there has been the single most helpful thing for all of us…. it's been amazing. This has helped us cope better and understand TS related symptoms.*

Hopes and fears

Whenever a child has a disability, parents and other caretakers spend a great deal of time wondering what the future will bring. In the case of TS, the answer is likely to be a positive outcome. Children with tics have grown up to be everything from truck drivers and cooks to sculptors and surgeons. Very few adults with TS find that it has a negative impact on their job prospects, dating success, or personal achievements. Here are some of the worries and hopes expressed by parents of young people with Tourette's syndrome:

I hope that he finishes high school. I hope that someone will marry him, "warts" and all. I hope that he will find something that he enjoys doing and be successful at that. He has a winning personality, and older children, teens, and adults really take to him.

• • • • •

I fear that potential employers won't allow for his needs, and won't really see past some of his irritating behavior to see his skills and talents.

• • • • •

We worry. She is so bright and has such potential. We worry particularly about the teenage years—we pray she'll continue with her education and not get off track. We feel if she completes her education and finds something she loves in terms of career, her potential is limitless. But, we accept that if she isn't interested in something, then she is very careless and restless. It will be important for her to choose a career where she has great interest and dedication.

• • • • •

I just want my kids to finish school, find gainful employment, and eventually get married. The employment I see as being the most difficult. I know I will worry about their academic success when they get older.

• • • • •

I think once my son is grown up he will do fine. I think he will find a niche and do well as an adult. I don't think it will always be easy for him, but he already has to try so hard to do things that other kids can do without trying that he has tremendous strength.

• • • • •

I worry that others will judge him for his tics, and not give him a chance.

• • • • •

I have a strong sense that his sense of humor, intelligence, and curiosity will help him get through any difficulties posed by Tourette's syndrome. I hope that I'm right.

CHAPTER 5

Living with Tourette's Syndrome

MANY ADULTS with Tourette's syndrome cope well, but for others, the disorder can cause ongoing difficulties. TS can create problems in adult social situations, community life, and employment. These challenges are usually far more difficult to surmount than the condition's medical ramifications. This chapter discusses some non-medical effects of TS on adults.

Topics covered include common problems encountered by adults with TS, including coping with self-esteem issues, other people's perceptions, discrimination, relationships, and parenting. It also covers some severe problems, such as rage and self-injurious behaviors. Finally, it addresses legal problems related to TS symptoms and building a support system. Similar issues that are specific to children are covered in Chapter 4, *Growing Up with Tourette's Syndrome*.

Common problems

Low self-esteem is probably the most common challenge faced by adults with TS who experience ongoing difficulties, and it's no minor matter. Many of today's adults with TS have lived a lifetime of denigration, self-reproach, and missed opportunities because they grew up in a time when the disorder was rarely recognized, hard to treat, and frequently misunderstood.

Keith, who was not correctly diagnosed until age 43, has often been made to feel ashamed about his tics:

> *Biting my nails has been a blow to my self-esteem since I can first remember. I was made to feel ashamed of it by my parents. I have spent half my life hiding my fingernails, even while working as a computer programmer/analyst/VP of MIS and constantly at a keyboard in view of others. Many other tics (picking my nose and scabs comes to mind first)*

had a similar, but less pronounced, effect, but this one stands out in my mind more than any other.

My parents basically tried to beat my tics, hyperactivity, and depression out of me. They have spent the time since I left their house ridiculing just about every aspect of my personality. I didn't begin to develop any self-esteem until I was diagnosed.

Counseling is often very helpful for adults who want to move forward with their lives despite past teasing and mistreatment. Adults with TS also cite setting and meeting ambitious goals as one of the best ways to silence those nagging voices of doubt.

Another common problem is bumping up against a lack of knowledge about TS. Even though tics are fairly common, many people have never noticed someone with obvious tics or multiple tics, and may not have heard of Tourette's syndrome. While no one should have to put up with blatantly rude remarks, consider taking the opportunity to politely educate those who ask about your tics. Of course, not everyone with TS is comfortable talking about his personal situation. You may want to keep a couple of brochures on hand, or carry a card that includes the TSA's phone number.

Stereotypes and the media

Although erroneous beliefs about TS have largely faded, adults with TS still face stereotypes about people who tic. Unfortunately, these tired ideas are sometimes reinforced by media portrayals. Actors commonly use tics as a comic device, or to give a screen villain a twitchy, sinister demeanor. Conversely, tics are seldom seen in a sympathetic character.

When Tourette's syndrome is actually used as a plot device, usually either the most severe, melodramatic symptoms of TS are shown as the disorder's common face, or TS is played for laughs, as in the insulting depiction of a woman with TS who must hire a prostitute to obtain male companionship in the movie "Deuce Bigalow, Male Gigolo." Comedians and radio show hosts have often been known to use TS as a topic of ridicule, probably without realizing that their attempts at humor can have an impact on the quality of life of people who have the disorder.

True, no one should look to the popular media for medical information or affirmation, but like other minorities, people with disabilities prefer honest portrayals. The TSA sends official letters of protest when TV and film studios commit particularly egregious sins. If you are offended by something you see or hear in the media, don't hesitate to let the show's producer or sponsors know. Likewise, when you see a sensitive, accurate portrayal of someone with TS, let them know you appreciate it. It helps to keep your sense of perspective and humor when you see an inaccurate or negative presentation of TS in the media, of course.

Waxing, waning, and medicating

People with just a little knowledge about TS, a class that includes many employers, tend to believe that tics can be wiped out with medication. But as people with TS know, medication doesn't work all the time, and neither do self-control or tic-stopping tricks. There is no magic pill for TS.

Another tough issue is getting other people to comprehend the waxing and waning nature of TS. Let's say you complete a job interview or meet a potential date during one of your tic-free periods. What will your new employer or date think when you start to have tics again?

Judy, mother of 21-year-old Gabe, says Gabe worries less about his TS even though he has experienced several waxing and waning periods in recent years:

> *His tics had essentially disappeared by age 15. At age 19, while away at college, Gabe had an exacerbation of ticcing and also had OCD added to his diagnosis. At age 21 he is on medication, the ticcing is mild, and the OCD is gone. Go figure!*
>
> *Maturation has helped a lot in his adjustment to TS. He is a handsome, athletic young man, and those attributes have greatly helped his acceptance by his peers throughout high school and college. Also, relaxation techniques have helped through tough times.*

There are also valid reasons to reduce or discontinue taking medication at times, even when it is effective. If you develop another medical condition that requires treatment, such as high blood pressure or diabetes, your new medication may interfere with your TS medication. Some medications used for tic control are not absolutely safe during pregnancy, and others may become more or less effective as your body chemistry changes with age (see Chapter 6, *Medical Care*, for more information about specific medications). You may also feel that certain kinds of side effects, such as sexual dysfunction, are okay for a while but not forever. Deciding what is an acceptable trade-off is up to you, not the social acceptability standards of others. After all, you're the one who has to deal with side effects and health risks, as well as increased ticcing.

Jen, mother of 6-year-old Paul, decided from the start that he should be able to make decisions about medication:

> When we told him there was medicine he could take to stop his painful tics, he literally jumped up and down, and said he would use his Christmas money to buy it. That is when I realized that he needs to be in control of his body and the meds he takes.
>
> However, clonidine knocked him out cold. No way he could take it any other time than at bedtime—we tried for months. Finally, we asked him if he wanted to stop taking the meds and he said yes, because it makes him so sleepy.

Higher education and careers

The same US laws that protect students under 18 from discrimination in schools, Title III of the Americans with Disabilities Act and Section 504 of the Rehabilitation Act of 1973, also cover adult students.

Students in special education programs who are between the ages of 18 and either 21 or 22, depending on the state, are entitled to continue receiving educational services until they have achieved a high school diploma or an equivalent qualification. In some cases, transition services can be written into an IEP to continue certain public school services past graduation.

The ADA prohibits discrimination against disabled persons in public facilities. This has been defined in multiple court decisions as encompassing both private and public colleges, including graduate schools and technical schools. It also applies to licensing boards, such as those that confer credentials or certify professionals in medicine, law, and other fields.

One case specific to Tourette's syndrome is Cohen v. Boston University. Joanne Cohen, a graduate student pursuing a Masters of Social Work degree at Boston University, was refused readmission to the MSW program after leaving temporarily. In court, the University claimed it was because Cohen could not do academic work at a graduate level and because she had problems forming relationships, despite the fact that she had good undergraduate grades and excellent evaluations from her supervisors in a community counseling program for persons with disabilities. It emerged that the real reason was Cohen's TS, which included coprolalia: for example, as stated in a US Department of Justice brief submitted in Cohen's defense, one of her former professors sent the admission committee a memo saying: "If she is still uttering in this manner, I do not see a place for her in clinical social work."[1]

The Department of Justice argued that Cohen's disability was not sufficient grounds to prevent her from attending the school or having a career in social work, and noted that the issues cited other than her TS were not substantiated by evidence, leading it to believe they were a pretext for disability discrimination. Unfortunately, Cohen did not win her case, so a positive precedent has not yet been set.

Some people with TS need accommodations to do well in trade school or college, such as taking a lighter course load to reduce stress level, taping lectures or having lecture notes provided, or taking breaks during long classes. The same types of accommodations are commonly made for students with learning disabilities, which are also an issue for some people with TS. Others find that they thrive in the self-directed, self-paced environment of college.

Joyce, age 53, is one of those who liked much of school:

> *I do very well with innovative, interesting teachers and courses. I think I do better with visual learning techniques, as I tend to zone out in lectures—I have found a tape recorder quite helpful.*
>
> *As a student, I do well in a traditional classroom, with peace, quiet, firmness, and structure. I also do well with home-study courses, where there is no pressure except what I put on myself. Although I have some attention difficulties, they did not interfere with my learning enough to be a problem: I graduated with a Bachelor of Science degree in Physics, and then attended a one-year teacher-training course.*

Many colleges and trade schools now have employees who work to ensure that students with disabilities do well. They can help you if problems do occur. Check in with your student support office or student union for more information. Unless a student is taking part in a formal transition program through the school district, vocational rehabilitation, or another agency, he or she must identify himself to the campus office in charge of disability issues.

Work issues

Adults with TS struggle to decide when to reveal that they have the condition, and just how much need be explained to bosses and coworkers. Most Western and Asian countries offer employees at least some protection from disability discrimination on the job. In the US, the Americans with Disabilities Act (ADA) makes it illegal to refuse to hire a person simply because she has, or appears to have, a disability—as long as that disability will not prevent her from doing the job. Thus, it's better to not mention TS during a job interview, if possible.

Careful preparation for job applications and interviews can help you avoid job discrimination. Make an honest assessment of your skills and job history when deciding what job to apply for. Working with a job counselor can help you prepare your résumé and practice interviewing skills. Apply only for jobs that you are able to do, as employers have the right to reject you if you are not qualified for the job. If you have a choice, choose to work for a company with a large workforce, as it is less likely to discriminate and more likely to offer group life and health insurance.

Interviewers are only allowed to discuss a job applicant's disabilities if they are visible or if the applicant brings up the topic. Accordingly, you don't need to volunteer information about your TS during a job interview, but you should address your tics if they are noticed. Be as matter-of-fact as possible, and offer to provide additional information on TS if your potential employer feels it could affect your fitness for the position. If you do choose to volunteer information about your TS, or if the interviewer asks you to, you may want to let your prospective employer know if you don't have coprolalia (compulsive swearing). Some people have heard of only this part of TS, and it could make a prospective employer nervous.

If you do in fact have coprolalia and wish to address it in the interview, concentrate on whether it would affect your ability to do the job. For example, a position as a front-office receptionist or public relations specialist might be compromised by coprolalia, while a position as a carpenter, computer programmer, or product designer might not.

Unless you have specific mental or physical limitations that affect the type of work for which you are applying, the fact that you have TS should have no bearing on your qualifications for the job. An employer cannot refuse to hire you simply because you have a neurological condition. Knowing your rights, and preparing strategies for your job interview can make the difference between being hired and being rejected. The following suggestions on how to conduct yourself during a job interview may help:[2]

- Do not volunteer information about your medical history. Employers have the right only to determine if you are capable of performing the job, not the right to ask about personal or confidential information during an interview.

- Under the Americans with Disabilities Act, employers cannot ask about medical history, require you to take a medical exam, or ask for medical records unless they have made a job offer.

- Do not lie on a job application or during an interview. You can be fired later if your dishonesty is discovered. Instead, answer only the specific questions asked. Try to steer the conversation towards your current ability to do the job, rather than explaining your past.

- Do not ask about health insurance until you have been offered a job. Before accepting the job, get the benefits information and review it thoroughly.

- If your medical history becomes an issue after the job offer, get a letter from your physician that briefly outlines your treatment and stresses your current good health and ability to do the job. Ask the doctor to let you review the letter prior to giving it to your potential employer. If your doctor is willing, you might even prepare this kind of letter yourself and give it to your doctor for a signature.

See the web site of the US Equal Employment Opportunity Commission (EEOC) at *http://www.eeoc.gov* for technical assistance documents on Pre-Employment Disability-Related Questions and Medical Examinations. The EEOC also has a document on the definition of disability used in federal civil rights (anti-discrimination) laws.

Both federal contractors and federal aid recipients (hospitals, universities, etc.) are required to engage in affirmative employment action for people with disabilities. If you are seeking a job with one of these employers, inquire about its affirmative action program.

Americans with Disabilities Act

The Americans with Disabilities Act of 1990 (ADA) prohibits many types of job discrimination based on actual disability, perceived disability, or history of a disability by employers, employment agencies, state and local governments, and labor unions. Any employer with fifteen or more workers must comply with the ADA.

In addition, most states and some cities have laws that prohibit discrimination based on disabilities, although what these laws cover varies widely. If your state or city has laws that provide more protections than the ADA, those laws prevail. If the ADA provides more protection than local or state laws, it prevails.

The ADA requires that the employer may not make medical inquiries of an applicant, unless one of the below is true:

- Applicant has a visible disability
- Applicant has voluntarily disclosed his medical history

Such questions must be limited to asking the applicant to describe or demonstrate how she would perform essential job functions. Medical inquiries are allowed after a job offer has been made, or during a pre-employment medical exam. Employers must provide "reasonable accommodations" unless it causes undue hardship. An accommodation is a change in duties or work hours to help employees during or after treatment, when symptoms are worse, or when new health issues arise. An employer does not have to make these changes if they would be very costly, disruptive, or unsafe. If it seems likely that an increase in tics due to waxing symptoms or necessary medication changes could jeopardize your job, work proactively with your employer to make needed accommodations.

Employers may not discriminate because of family illness. For instance, if an employee has a child who has Tourette's syndrome, the employer cannot treat the employee differently because she thinks the employee will miss work or file expensive health insurance claims.

Employers are not required to provide health insurance, but if an employer does offer health insurance, it must do so fairly to all employees.

The Equal Employment Opportunity Commission enforces Title 1 of the ADA, the section that covers employment. Call (800) 669-4000 for EEOC enforcement information and (800) 669-3362 for enforcement publications. Other sections of the ADA are enforced by, or have their enforcement coordinated by, the US Department of Justice (Civil Rights Division, Public Access Section). The Justice Department's ADA web site is *http://www.usdoj.gov/crt/ada/html*.

Canadian Human Rights Act

In Canada, the Canadian Human Rights Act provides essentially the same rights as the ADA. The Canadian Human Rights Commission administers the act. You can get further information by calling the national office at (613) 995-1151.

If you feel that you have been discriminated against due to your disability or a relative's disability, contact the EEOC, the Canadian Human Rights Commission, or the appropriate agency in your country promptly. In the US, a charge of discrimination generally must be filed within 180 days of when you learned of the discriminatory act. Although you do not need an attorney to file a complaint, an attorney experienced in job discrimination law can help you draft the complaint, making it more likely to be successful.

The Federal Rehabilitation Act

The Federal Rehabilitation Act bans public employers and private employers that receive public funds from discriminating on the basis of disability. The following employees are not covered by the ADA, but are by the Rehabilitation Act:

- Employees of the executive branch of the federal government. (Section 501 of the Rehabilitation Act)

- Employees of employers that receive federal contracts and have fewer than fifteen workers. (Section 503 of the Rehabilitation Act)

- Employees of employers that receive federal financial assistance and have fewer than fifteen workers. (Section 504 of the Rehabilitation Act)

If you are a federal employee (section 501), you must file a claim within thirty days of the job action against you. If you are an employee whose employer has a federal contract (section 503), you must file a complaint within 180 days with your local Office of the US Department of Labor, Office of Federal Contract Compliance Programs. If your employer receives federal funds (Section 504), you have up to 180 days to file a complaint with the federal agency that provided funds to your employer, or you can file a lawsuit in a federal court. The Federal Rehabilitation Act is enforced by the Civil Rights Division of the Department of Justice, (202) 514-4609.

Section 504 of the Rehabilitation Act of 1973 includes protections for adults attending school or working for employers who get at least some public funds. That list includes colleges, government bodies, and many non-profits, and may sometimes cover private firms that accept government contracts.

If you live outside the US, talk to your national Tourette's syndrome organization or a disability rights group about the laws that affect you on the job. If you live in one of the nations of the European Union, you can cite European Union civil rights regulations as well as applicable local or national disability rights laws.

Unfortunately, employment law for people with disabilities is still evolving, in the US and elsewhere. As recently as 2000, the Michigan Court of Appeals upheld the firing of a supermarket employee with Tourette's syndrome who had coprolalia, despite recognizing that the symptom was involuntary. The employee in question, a 21-year-old bagger, had requested a position with less public contact when his coprolalia offended customers, but was refused.[3,4]

On the other hand, some employees with TS have used the ADA and similar laws to protect their right to work. In 1996, one employee with upper-body tics overturned his firing and won both back pay and punitive damages. Many others have cited the ADA's protection to retain their jobs or get needed accommodations without going to court.[5]

There is one catch to the ADA, however: it applies only if your TS presents a significant disability or if your employer believes that it does—even if that belief is based on misconceptions about TS. This has led to a Catch-22 situation for many people with neurological conditions or mental illness: yes, there are drugs available that can treat the symptoms of these conditions, but those drugs don't work consistently for everyone, and may not work at all for some. They also carry with them side effects and dangers. Recent Supreme Court cases uphold the idea that if a disability can be corrected with medication, eyeglasses, or other temporary measures, it does not qualify for ADA protection, despite many lower-court cases that say otherwise. Future challenges can be expected in this area of law; indeed, California recently passed a bill that removes the "significant impairment" criteria for persons in that state.

One way around this roadblock is showing that the medication itself creates a disability. Haldol, for example, effectively suppresses tics for many people who take it, but it also tends to cause drowsiness and "brain fog." Slow thinking and falling asleep on the job may actually be quite a bit more disabling to you than your tics ever were, and may qualify you for ADA protection even though the tics you are taking it to treat do not.

An attorney can explain where you stand legally and may be able to help you fix the problem without going to court. Mediation is an increasingly popular and less costly option.

Getting and keeping a job are concerns for most adults with TS, but being treated properly on the job also matters. The ADA and other civil rights laws do protect you against workplace harassment based on your disability. As with other types of harassment cases, it's important to let harassers know exactly how you feel about their actions, to keep detailed records of incidents, and to go through any formal grievance procedure your company or labor union has before filing a lawsuit.

Most large firms have a staff member who handles internal complaints of sexual or racial harassment. This is probably the right person to see first if you find that your tics have become the topic of rude remarks, practical jokes, or other cruel actions by fellow employees or supervisors.

If you're not sure how to handle a workplace problem related to your TS symptoms, call your state's protection and advocacy system for free advice (see Appendix A,

Resources). Some TSA chapters can also refer you to legal counsel, and occasionally the National TSA gets involved in prominent or groundbreaking cases.

Chantal says that TS has generally been a non-issue on the job:

> *I've not had to really "handle" TS in the workplace, except for an occasional question from the kids I teach. Usually they're quite satisfied with my tongue-in-cheek response.*
>
> *I've always been able to camouflage my TS, though now I'm more comfortable with it and I don't mind so much people noticing. However, my friends tell me that I move around so much that it's hard to tell I tic with all the other movements going on. One could say in my case that I have ADHD with TS as a comorbid disorder. I've always had what was called back then "nervous habits." However, most people did not notice. If they did, I would get the odd question about why I do what I do, and that would be it.*

Medical leave

If you need to be away from work temporarily due to worsening symptoms or treatment needs, you may have legal job protection available to you. Since August 1993, the Family and Medical Leave Act (FMLA) has protected US workers in large companies who need a leave of absence. Only employees who work 25 hours per week or more for one year are covered, and only if they work for a company with 50 or more employees within a 75-mile radius. The Family and Medical Leave Act:

- Provides twelve weeks of unpaid leave during any twelve-month period for one's own medical needs or to care for a seriously ill spouse, child, or parent. Sometimes employees can take intermittent leave, which means shortening your normal work schedule.

- Provides twelve weeks of unpaid leave for the birth, adoption, or fostering of a child.

- Requires employers to continue benefits, including health insurance, during the leave period.

- Requires employees to attempt to schedule leaves so as not to disrupt the workplace, and to give 30 days' notice if possible.

- Requires employers to put returning employees in the same position or in an equivalent position.

Employers should have procedures in place for medical leaves covered by the FMLA. Usually you will need to present your employer with documentation from your doctor stating why the leave is necessary, and how long it is expected to last.

The FMLA is enforced by the Employment Standards Administration, Wage and Hour Division, US Department of Labor, and the courts. You can find the nearest Wage and Hour Division office in the US Government pages of your telephone directory. You have up to two years to file a FMLA complaint or a lawsuit if your employer does not abide by the law.

Relationships

The workplace isn't the only environment in which talking about TS can be problematic. Relationships can also be a minefield for people with unusual behaviors. Adults with TS often find that the top issue, as with job interviews, is disclosure: Do you work it into conversation on a first date? Do you wait until your date notices a tic or two? Do you brush it off as something minor or launch into a complete explanation?

There's no one-size-fits-all answer—it all depends on the severity of your symptoms, how much they affect you, and your comfort level in talking about your TS.

Starting close and intimate relationships is hard for people at times, whether they have Tourette's syndrome or not. Some people with TS have a more difficult time starting relationships than do others, particularly those who have experienced rejection in the past because of their symptoms. No one else can decide the right time or the right way for you to disclose your TS. You might want to find out right away whether someone you are interested in has very negative feelings about TS. On the other hand, you may wish to establish a relationship first so that the person cares for you and will be less likely to respond negatively.

Some people with TS feel strongly that quick honesty is the best policy, while others feel equally strongly that it's better to wait a while. Some people find any imperfection in a potential mate impossible to live with—and these are people that you're probably better off without. Others are completely nonjudgmental. But most people fall somewhere in the middle. Remember, if the person you're dealing with likes you as a person, your tics may make them curious or even a little scared, but hopefully they'll remain secondary to your personal charms.

Joyce, age 53, began ticcing again after years with "invisible" TS:

> *As an adult, I had many tic-free years to develop my relationships with others. When the tics came along, most just accepted them as part of me,*

and things continued on as usual. However, inside myself I didn't feel the same, so I withdrew a lot from those around me. It has taken me the last seven years to stop feeling that way and regain some of what I lost by my own withdrawal. It has helped that the tics have waned again to very mild, and I don't feel like such a weirdo anymore. If I still had severe tics, I don't know where I would be.

As Joyce's story illustrates, the problem is sometimes less in how other people react to you than in how you handle their reactions. A strong sense of self can influence how others see you. Their curiosity won't be interpreted as insulting or make you feel strange, but will instead allow you to open up and "be yourself" in their company.

Adults, especially adult men, do sometimes struggle with teasing from friends. Jibes can start as a bit of good-natured fun, but if your new nickname or jokes about your tics hurt your feelings, you have a right to ask for a moratorium on Tourette humor.

Family planning and heredity

One of the more difficult questions that adults with TS ask themselves is whether or not they will pass the disorder on to their children. The short answer is that there's no way to tell.

A number of family studies have been done, and transmission rates have ranged from around 2 percent to 36 percent. In a few families, the transmission rate appears to be even higher. Male children who have first-degree relatives (parents or siblings) with TS have five times greater risk of also having TS than those who do not have first-degree relatives with TS; female children who have first-degree relatives with TS are two times as likely as their counterparts to have TS (but have a higher risk than the boys of having OCD).[6] In other words, an adult with TS may have a one in 1,250 chance of having a daughter with TS, while his chance of having a son with TS might be one in 500 or higher.

There is no genetic testing or prenatal testing available for TS at this time. As a result, there's no way to calculate your personal risk of transmitting the TS gene or genes to your children. There's also no way to know whether even with the genes your children would develop TS in the absence of additional "triggers," such as strep infection.

Deciding whether to have children is a highly individual decision. If you are concerned about having a child with TS, talk it over with your doctor and a genetic counselor to get a clear view of the risks involved.

To find a qualified genetic counselor, check with the staff of a good local hospital or, in the US, contact the National Society of Genetic Counselors at (610) 872-7608 or on the Web at *http://www.nsgc.org*.

If you have concerns about whether you should take a specific TS medication during pregnancy or while breastfeeding, see Chapter 6, and discuss your medications with your doctor before planning a pregnancy.

Special issues

You may never have to deal with the issues discussed in this section, but it's best to be prepared. Everyone with TS should be well informed about these concerns in case other people's misconceptions interfere with their lives in the future. If someone says that "all" people with TS have uncontrollable cursing, rage behaviors, or some other symptom, you will have the information you need to knowledgably contradict their assertion.

Rage behaviors

The issue of "rage attacks" in persons with Tourette's syndrome is controversial. There's really no argument that some experience this symptom, but people with TS and the research community have been reluctant to talk publicly about it until quite recently. There is a legitimate fear that this information could be used to stereotype people with TS—most of whom do not have rage attacks—as violent, disturbed, and dangerous.

Indeed, lawyers have already attempted in at least one case to use this symptom as an excuse for murder, portraying TS-linked rage as sudden and uncontrollable. The defense was unsuccessful, but the unwelcome attention that it brought to people with TS worried advocates.[7]

The truth is that people with TS who do have episodes of rage find them embarrassing and frightening. They are usually guilt-ridden about what they've said or done during an episode and wish there was some way—any way—to prevent rages from occurring.[8]

No one is quite sure what causes these episodes, although information is starting to emerge. Angry feelings are certainly not unique to people with TS. Some researchers theorize that the impulse-control system, already weaker in people with TS, loses its grip because of a decrease of particular chemicals during stressful episodes.[9]

Early study results indicate that almost all persons with TS-linked rage episodes have one or more additional conditions.[10]

Joyce tells about what sets off rage episodes for her, and how she copes:

> *I find that when I am in a situation where I feel any kind of pressure or danger, like case conferences, meetings with social workers, confrontational situations with bureaucrats, or snotty store clerks, I am much more likely to get extremely agitated, and get into a rage. I have blown up in stores, in offices, in case conferences, and occasionally at home. The trigger may be extremely minor, but the situation sets the stage. Often it can be set off by my sense of injustice, powerlessness, or unfairness. I have literally "seen red" and can feel the rage rising within me. I also feel powerless to stop it.*
>
> *Taking a break, even for a few minutes, can help defuse the rage. But I may not be able to initiate the break myself; having another person along as an advocate helps a lot.*

Although the impulse to blow your stack can feel overwhelming, as Joyce notes, prevention is almost always possible. Options include recognizing your personal "rage triggers" and avoiding situations that involve them, recognizing symptoms of impending rage and excusing yourself from the company of others, learning stress and behavior control techniques that work for you, and considering new medication or medication changes that can give you increased control.

Specialized anger management counseling programs are available. Although they are usually not geared specifically to TS, the techniques they impart are universally helpful.

If rage episodes are a concern for you, it's a good idea to come up with multiple setting-based strategies. For example, if you're at home when an episode begins, it may be practical to hop on your bicycle and ride until you're exhausted. If you're at work, that may not be possible, but running up and down several flights of stairs, stepping out for coffee, or arranging to leave early may be.

Some people who have recurring difficulties have found that breaking up their work-day with strenuous exercise sessions, either at a gym or at a nearby park or track, seems to redirect some of their angry energy.

The advice often given to parents of children who have rage episodes is to help them find and use a "safe place" when they start to feel out of control. Adults can also employ this strategy. Some people find a small, dark space comforting, while others find that overwhelming feelings fade fastest when they're outdoors. Retreating to your car may suffice in a pinch. Try different possibilities until you find an instant retreat that works for you.

Rage episodes can be hard to control, but they're even harder to explain. People with TS must be careful to present this difficult symptom as an explanation for behavior, but never an excuse. Focus on the medical nature of the problem rather than the issues that happen to set you off, and concentrate on how you can best maintain control, regain control, and avoid offending or harming anyone due to rage. Even though you can't prevent these feelings, you do have a responsibility to limit how they impact others.

Self-injurious behaviors

Self-injurious behavior (SIB) is defined as any self-inflicted, deliberate action that causes physical harm. Examples of SIB include skin-picking, biting, tearing off cuticles or nails, burning, cutting, or hitting. SIB is somewhat more common in people with TS, especially if OCD is added to the mix, but it is distinct from self-injurious tics because it is deliberate behavior.

SIB is a medical problem, and you should not be ashamed or embarrassed about it. Some medical professionals, especially those who work in emergency rooms, do not have a good understanding of SIB. They may express resentment or even anger when you seek treatment. Look for a professional who can work with you on a regular, ongoing basis to reduce this painful and dangerous symptom.

Some counselors have been trained to believe that SIB is always a response to past (or even "repressed") trauma, but this is often not the case. Don't allow yourself to be pressured by a therapist who puts forward theories that don't make sense based on what you know about yourself. Many therapists are available who look at SIB as a complex neurological problem, and can help you find harm-reduction strategies that work.

Treatment is available for SIB. Options include medication, including anti-anxiety agents, antidepressants, and sometimes opiate-blockers like naltrexone; cognitive behavioral therapy; and support groups. You would be surprised at how many people, with or without TS, battle with SIB.

Trichotillomania (compulsive hair-pulling) is sometimes described as a form of SIB, although people who have it report that it is more tic-like. It does respond to the same treatments as do tics or OCD.

Two other forms of self-injury seen somewhat more frequently in people with TS are body dysmorphic disorder (BDD) and eating disorders. The harm experienced due to body dysmorphic disorder can be entirely psychological, but that does not make it less painful. Persons with BDD imagine that they are imperfect, fat, misshapen, or ugly, and may hide themselves, harm themselves, or even seek cosmetic surgery to fix their imagined flaws.

One could think of eating disorders like anorexia and bulimia as a form of BDD, since they are often based on a false body image, but they can also stand on their own. Persons with eating disorders can manifest many different types of symptoms, from self-starvation in the most extreme and deadly forms of anorexia, to binge eating or dangerously controlled diets.

Any form of eating disorder requires immediate, expert medical treatment. Disordered eating habits, as well as compulsive vomiting or laxative use, can create electrolyte imbalances that may lead to seizures and damage the teeth, throat, heart, stomach, and kidneys. Eating disorders are especially dangerous in elderly people and those who have medical conditions that could be aggravated by even slight deviations from good eating habits, but they also can and do cause injury and death to otherwise healthy young adults.

As in the case of SIB, some therapists have been trained to believe that body dysmorphic disorder and eating disorders result from mental, physical, or sexual trauma. If you don't feel this applies to you but the counselor continues to insist on pursuing this theory, seek another medical professional who is experienced at treating BDD and eating disorders in persons with TS and/or OCD.

Coprolalia and copropraxia

Coprolalia and its cousin copropraxia (compulsive use of obscene gestures) are the two symptoms no one with TS wants to have. They are the most notorious and embarrassing of all behaviors associated with TS. Estimates of the number of people with TS who have coprolalia at some time in their life range from 10 to 15 percent.[11]

There are also degrees of severity with both coprolalia and copropraxia. Many people with TS have experienced what could be called "mental coprolalia": obsessive repetition of obscene, derogatory, or blasphemous words within your mind, but not out loud. It may take great energy to make this annoying inner voice shut up. Often the words are offensive to the person thinking them, who may devise OCD-like rituals to prevent them from popping up and perhaps do penance when they do.

Some people with mental coprolalia feel the urge to shout out these words but are able to repress it. This takes a great amount of willpower. The urge may be more likely in certain situations, such as when the person is under stress or in the worst possible place to use this type of language—church, for example. The effort to not utter these unwanted terms can be so strenuous that people who experience the urge often start avoiding places they would otherwise like to be.

Joyce says she was tormented by mental coprolalia, a symptom that has since gone away:

> Shouting was a major problem for a while, and required a great amount of effort to suppress. This has been especially problematic at religious gatherings, and I have a horror of blasting out a shout during a prayer or other solemn time, yet the urge is strongest when I know that expressing a tic would be the most embarrassing.
>
> Because of my religious beliefs, I have an intense fear of coprolalia, so that when I had the mental coprolalia a couple years ago, this inhibited my participation in religious services to a degree. I was so fearful that what I had so far kept inside my mind might suddenly burst out aloud.

The next level of severity involves those who cannot always prevent unwanted words from slipping out, but who are usually able to disguise or camouflage their utterances. For example, a person might successfully strive to shout "freak," "fork," or "duck" when she feels compelled to yell out a similar-sounding obscenity, or might incorporate a throat-clearing sound into the word so that it's not easily recognized. Others are able to whisper the word, or hold back the symptom until they are alone.

Substitutes can also be found for rude gestures, although your substitute or cover-up will probably attract plenty of attention on its own.

As with repressing mental coprolalia, all of these strategies take a great deal of mental effort, making it hard to pay attention to anything else. The stronger and more frequent the urge becomes, the more difficult it becomes to resist.

Finally, some people with TS do experience coprolalia or copropraxia that is almost impossible to control, even for a short time. Medication may or may not reduce its severity, but because this symptom is so difficult to live with, it's worth trying several different medication possibilities.

If you gain no relief from medication, the best strategy is probably to be forthright about your condition when the situation arises. Most people with coprolalia already go out of their way to avoid offending others, but it's not necessary to lock yourself away from humanity—after all, they're only words. However, since others may consider certain terms to be "fighting words" (especially racial epithets and blasphemous words), caution is certainly warranted.

As of yet, no one has found a special therapy that can cure coprolalia or copropraxia. Anything that reduces your anxiety level, including your anxiety about saying inappropriate words, may be helpful. Giving yourself scheduled breaks during which you are free to use any language you wish may also help.

Carrying brochures or cards that explain about TS and/or coprolalia and copropraxia can help others understand you better. Speaking frankly about this symptom with coworkers, employees at stores you frequent, and others in the community can help to clear the air. Once people know you as a person and understand that these utterances are out of character and unintentional, they are more likely to forgive and forget your outbursts.

A sample card for an adult might read:

> *Hi! My name is _____.*
>
> *You may receive this card as a friend, employer, or fellow student. As I have a visible and sometimes vivid neurological disorder, Tourette's syndrome, it helps me introduce myself and explain a bit about what you may see or hear.*
>
> *TS symptoms include involuntary movements and vocalizations, sometimes including obscenities. Symptoms can also appear alone or as outbursts.*
>
> *All I ask is for you to look beyond Tourette's syndrome to see someone who in all other ways is normal, and who in many ways excels.*
>
> *If you would like to know more about TS, please ask me, or call the Tourette Syndrome Association at (718) 224-2999.*

There is one bit of good news about coprolalia and copropraxia: like all other tics, these symptoms tend to wax and wane over time. Most people with TS will never experience coprolalia (other than perhaps the mental variant), and of those who do, most will eventually be free of it for at least a while.

Many persons with TS also find themselves mirroring behaviors that they see, a behavior known as echopraxia. Normally this isn't too much of a problem, but in certain kinds of workplaces it could be.

Legal problems

Coprolalia, copropraxia, rage behaviors, and sometimes even tics can occasionally lead to unwanted attention from law enforcement. This happens often enough that a short video, "Not the Usual Suspects," is available for educating police officers about TS. If you would like to use this video, contact the Tourette Syndrome Foundation of Canada (TSF), listed in Appendix A. The TSF has copies available to loan, and is also producing a new video that will be applicable to a wider variety of persons in authority, such as security guards. You may want to carry literature about TS or a medical identification card with you if your symptoms cause you worry when in the community.

A few US states have laws on the books about the use of four-letter words or racial epithets. Generally speaking, these laws are rarely enforced except in extreme cases, where speech is deliberately used to offend or demean. There has been at least one instance in which a "hate speech" law has been applied to a person with TS, but it was found not to apply because the speech was not voluntary.[12]

One high-profile case about TS in a community was settled in August 2000, and offers hope to people whose symptoms may disturb others. Jeffrey Marthon, a Chicago man with TS, lived in a condominium community for many years. In 1998 the acting president of the condominium association moved into the unit above Marthon's and immediately began to complain about his neighbor's vocal tics. He actually convinced the condominium association board to threaten Marthon and his wife with fines and eviction if Marthon could not stop making noise. According to court documents, the threatening language was extreme: one board member said Marthon should "go around with pillows on his feet and a gag in his mouth," and all persons with TS should be "put in an institution."[13]

With help from a local civil rights law group, Marthon was able to invoke the Fair Housing Act, which was written to protect people with disabilities from unfair treatment. He decided that he would prefer to move rather than remaining near the neighbor who had treated him badly, and was awarded a $385,000 settlement.[14]

The Marthon case is believed to be the first TS-related suit brought under the Fair Housing Act, but it probably will not be the last. Many people with vocal tics and rage behaviors have run afoul of landlords, condominium associations, co-op boards, and neighbors over the years. Of course, if you can take steps to minimize the impact of your symptoms on your neighbors, you should—but you certainly shouldn't be forced from your home because of your symptoms.

TS can sometimes contribute to other kinds of legal problems. As mentioned earlier in this chapter, it's never an excuse, but it may be part of the explanation. For example, drug and alcohol abuse are somewhat more common in people with TS, although it hasn't yet been determined if this is because of impulsivity, genetic predisposition, or "self-medication."[15]

A few researchers, notably Dr. David Comings, have linked TS with a propensity toward other types of crimes, such as fire-setting.[16] This linkage is tenuous and controversial. If you feel that TS or a comorbid disorder, such as OCD, is steering you toward legal trouble, seek specialized counseling to deal with the symptom. People who have had this experience—for example, people who have had a compulsion to shoplift—often are helped by cognitive behavioral therapy and/or medication.

Building a support system

Everyone needs a support system to fall back on, whether it's made up of family members, old friends, or a Tourette's syndrome support group.

Amy Wilensky's memoir, *Passing for Normal* (see Appendix A), includes a touching anecdote about how hard it can be to attend your first TS support group meeting— and what a relief it can be to meet other adults coping with the condition. Once you've made it through the door, your reaction is likely to be "Finally, other people like me!"

Some TSA chapters have more than one group, often with one structured around issues concerning children and parenting, and another just for adults with TS. In larger cities there may be further divisions, such as people with TS who are in recovery (Alcoholics Anonymous or Narcotics Anonymous members), young adults with TS, or people whose TS symptoms are especially severe.

These divisions provide evidence that not every TS support group is a good fit for everyone. As with any other group of people, there's always a chance that you won't feel comfortable with some of the personalities involved. If that's the case, see if another group is available, found your own, or look online for support.

Online support groups are discussed in Chapter 4, but they also deserve a mention here. Since most people with active, major TS symptoms are children and teens, most online groups center on parenting issues. However, adults with TS are more than welcome in almost all such groups (after all, quite a few of the parents have TS themselves).

You may feel more comfortable discussing issues like sexuality and marital problems in a group strictly for adults. And if you can't find one you like, it's easy enough to start your own—talk to your Internet Service Provider about list-management options.

Keith, age 43, found a unique way to blow off steam and meet accepting people:

> I skydive. It is the perfect sport for a hyperactive adrenaline junkie with a three-minute attention span! It also has a very accepting community; many skydivers are "weird," and things like tics that the corporate world, or golfers or tennis players, would look down on, are generally accepted without mention at the Drop Zone.
>
> For support, I rely on others with the disorder, including the Sunrise Tourette list, my fiancée (who also has TS), and Alcoholics Anonymous (where many undiagnosed TSers reside!)

It's your life

In the end, Tourette's syndrome should not limit your life choices, although there may be times when you'll need to be assertive about your rights. Set your goals as if TS didn't matter—because in the end, it really doesn't. People with TS have found success in family life, community organizations, and every sort of profession. The only thing that can hold you back is attitude: your own as well as other people's.

Judy, Gabe's mother, boasts that thanks to his basic good nature and perseverance, he has achieved far more than doctors could have predicted when we was a child:

> Gabe is faring well in the adult world. He graduated from college in May. He has an exceptional job, and is planning to apply to medical school next year or the year after.
>
> When a child fails through a lack of acceptance, we all suffer as a society. When a child succeeds, and becomes a contributing member of society, we all benefit.
>
> I am very proud of my son.

CHAPTER 6

Medical Care

PEOPLE WITH TS have more choices than ever before when it comes to medical care. This chapter covers all of the current medical treatment options.

There are now several medications available for treating the symptoms of Tourette's syndrome, each of which may have different levels of effectiveness for each individual. Many people with TS decide to forgo medical treatment for their symptoms some or all of the time. The more you know about the medication choices available to you, the better equipped you are to make wise decisions.

This chapter also includes a section on emerging treatment possibilities that show promise for people with TS. Although these options are not available from your doctor as of this writing in Spring 2001, you may be able to access them through clinical trials or, once they have gained interim or official approval, through your physician.

One special section discusses treatment possibilities for PANDAS (pediatric autoimmune disorders associated with strep), a variant of TS that is related to bacterial infection. The next section lists medications used to treat the three conditions commonly seen in people with TS: OCD, ADHD, and anxiety disorders. These medications sometimes interact with those used for TS, so it's important to understand how they work and what kinds of problems can develop.

You'll find important information about side effects and medication interactions in this chapter. It also includes a section on hospital-based care, which is occasionally needed by people with TS.

Chapter 7, *Other Interventions,* explains non-medication treatment options, including talk therapy, occupational therapy, alternative medicine, and more.

History of TS treatment

Until the late 1940s, a wide variety of herbal concoctions were tried in various areas of the world to treat Tourette's syndrome. Psychotherapy, hypnosis, breathing exercises, inhalation of carbon dioxide, and even restraints were used. Doctors and patients tried drugs for fever, bromides, medications for infection, and phenobarbital (an anti-epilepsy drug), as well as surgical procedures ranging from tonsillectomy to lobotomy. Occasionally, patients seemed to get better, but modern observers looking back on these cases suspect that any benefits seen were probably due to the natural waxing and waning course of TS. Since most doctors did not follow up with their patients after treatment, long-term outcomes were rarely known.[1]

The first real breakthrough came in the mid 1950s, when a few doctors began trying a new medication: chlorpromazine, better known by the brand name Thorazine. Thorazine was originally developed as an antihistamine. During the course of testing, its makers found that it also helped with psychosis—the first drug to do so reliably, and a true breakthrough in the medical treatment of mental illness. Thorazine was the original member of a family of medications that has since grown to include dozens, perhaps hundreds, of pharmaceuticals now known as antipsychotics or neuroleptics.

Thorazine reduces the transmission of the neurotransmitter dopamine throughout the central nervous system. Unfortunately, that's a bit like using a sledgehammer to tap in a tiny nail. Too much Thorazine causes tremors, stiff movements, and cognitive problems that resemble the symptoms of Parkinson's disease, a degenerative movement disorder caused by a lack of dopamine. Thorazine was also found to carry a high risk of causing tardive dyskinesia, another serious and permanent movement disorder, after a long period of use. So although a few doctors did use Thorazine to treat TS and reported success, others were reluctant to risk it.

A related drug, haloperidol, is sold under the brand name Haldol. Unlike Thorazine, Haldol seems to restrict its antidopamine activity to the basal ganglia, the part of the brain where tics originate, and nearby areas. The first report of success in treating TS with Haldol appeared in 1961, and was followed by the launch of multiple studies to test the drug's effectiveness in both adults and children.[2]

It worked—and disproved the psychoanalytic theories about TS that were still in vogue. Unfortunately, Haldol also has drawbacks. Although it is safer than Thorazine, it still creates a fairly high risk for tardive dyskinesia and other serious side effects. Many doctors felt reasonably comfortable prescribing it to fully informed adults, but were less sure about suggesting it for children, who are the majority of TS patients in need of treatment.

Haldol is still widely used to treat TS, but safer alternatives have been developed over the past several decades. Continued research has produced neuroleptics with fewer risks and side effects, and new variants whose action is even more carefully targeted arrive every few years (see "Neuroleptics," later in this chapter). These "atypical" neuro-leptics, particularly Risperdal, are highly effective.

Two more drugs, clonidine (Catapres) and guanfacine (Tenex), also work well to reduce tics. These drugs have even fewer side effects than either the old or atypical neuroleptics, although they aren't appropriate for people with low blood pressure or certain kinds of health problems (see "Clonidine and guanfacine," later in this chapter).

Other drugs under investigation as treatments for TS have already gained approval and popularity outside the US (see "Other medications for TS," later in this chapter).

Medication basics

The words "psychiatric medication" strike fear into the hearts of many, much more so than the words "diabetes medication" or "allergy medication," even though those drugs can also be dangerous if improperly used. Part of that fear is based on fact: some drugs used to treat brain disorders can have serious side effects, particularly the older, stronger, less specific drugs. Unfortunately, another part of that fear is based on scare stories in the popular press and online, particularly when it comes to giving medication to children.

The truth is that almost all drugs used to treat medical problems have risks. You can minimize those risks by making thoughtful choices about when medication is and isn't necessary, by choosing a physician whose medication decisions are well-informed and cautious, and by monitoring your own health carefully to recognize and avoid unusual reactions or side effects.

Making smart choices

If your healthcare provider is considering prescribing medication for your TS symp-toms, he should start by assessing those symptoms. He should ask you which symptoms you can live with, and which ones you can't. This gives you a range of choices beyond simply medicating or not medicating. For example, a person who has both OCD and TS may feel that her OCD symptoms have the greatest impact on her enjoyment of life, and are well worth taking medication for, while the side effects of medications she has tried for TS seem worse than having tics. Another person may feel that the minor side effects he experiences from his TS medication are no problem when compared to the muscle strain and embarrassment he has experienced from constant ticcing.

Your choice to take or not take medication should be based on personal criteria, including quality of life, physical comfort, and your or your child's emotional comfort level about having tics. Most people choose to take medication only when their symptoms interfere with everyday activities.

Jen, mother of 6-year-old Paul, did not want her son to take medication at first:

> He was hiding his tics for a long time. He thought they were bad because he could not stop them. His head began to jerk to one side and he would tuck his chin into his neck. It scared me greatly because it distorted his face so much. The jerking to the side tic was so painful that it pushed me off of the medication fence. My husband and I did not want to try medication, but when our child was in pain, we changed our minds.
>
> Clonidine made him so tired. I hated when he was on the meds, but the painful tics stopped. We stopped the meds after school was out, and have not needed them since, even after school started again.

Your doctor should always explain medication choices and changes to you and, if you are the parent of a child with TS who is old enough to understand, to your child. Better informed healthcare consumers are more likely to take their medication faithfully, and less likely to ignore problems that may emerge.

Take the time to research different medications so you can have an informed discussion with your doctor. This chapter's capsule descriptions are a good start, but much more information about prescription drugs can be found in books about medications or online, including on pharmaceutical company web sites (see Appendix A, *Resources,* for some pointers).

You may also want to talk to people who have tried a particular medication that you're considering. This can be helpful, but remember that your or your child's personal body chemistry has a great deal to do with how well a medication will work. One person's disaster drug may be another person's miracle drug.

Research is especially important for people who have more than one health condition that requires medication. Doctors are not always aware of every possible interaction between drugs, so checking to make sure that your new TS medication won't affect the activity of drugs you already take is an excellent idea.

Roadblocks to choices

Your choices may be limited by insurance or HMO rules, regulatory approval, and occasionally, medical misinformation.

In some cases, doctors are bound by HMO regulations that limit them to prescribing approved drugs from a list called a formulary. You can get around these restrictions, but your physician will need to document her reason for using an off-formulary drug to gain approval. You may have to pay more if you or your child is prescribed an off-formulary medication.

The use of medications to treat conditions for which they have not been FDA-approved is rarely an issue. Known as "off-label" use, this is a common practice. In fact, the majority of prescriptions written in the US are for "off-label" uses. For example, drugs approved for adults are frequently prescribed at weight-specific doses for children, and drugs approved for one condition are often prescribed for others if doctors know they will be useful.

Sometimes doctors have personal preferences based on their treatment experience. If you are unsure why your doctor chose one drug instead of another that you may have heard good things about, ask him about his reasons.

A few doctors still believe, probably based on reading older medical literature, that Haldol is the drug of choice for treating TS. If you can't choose a better-informed doctor, you can provide your doctor with the latest advice from TS advocacy groups or other current sources to help guide her towards a more informed decision. Of course, Haldol is still the medication that works best for some people with TS—it's just not the first, or even the second, that should be tried.

Dose selection

Selecting the correct dose for a patient is more of an art than a science, despite the availability of manufacturers' guidelines. Doctors usually start with these recommendations, which are based on the patient's weight and/or age. Your doctor should also take into account your medical history, particularly your response to other medications, when choosing an initial dose. Differences in individual metabolism, and the use of other medications (including vitamins and herbal supplements) affect optimal doses for individuals.

When it comes to children, there is one dosage rule that should almost always be followed: start low, and go slow. This rule is probably best for adults as well. If a person is given too high of a starting dose, or if medications are increased to the full therapeutic dose over just a few days, difficult side effects are far more likely to occur. Gradual *titration* (increase in dosage) over a period of weeks can make all the difference, although it may take longer to see positive effects. However, when TS symptoms are severely disabling—for example, self-injurious tics—you may want to start with a higher dose despite the increased risk.

Although occasionally people report dramatic results in just a week or so, the medications used to treat TS normally take a few weeks to have a noticeable therapeutic effect. The changes can be so gradual that patients sometimes think that a drug is not working, only to realize after a few more weeks of use that they are ticcing much less frequently. It's rare for there to be a moment where you say, "My gosh, it's working!" Instead, there's a gradual decrease in symptoms.

Often you will notice drug side effects long before you notice drug benefits. Minor side effects, such as dry mouth or sleepiness, occur as your body struggles to get used to the new medication. These should pass within a few days or weeks. Ask your doctor about any serious or persistent side effects (see "Medication side effects," later in this chapter).

Start, add, or increase only one drug at a time to ensure that you see a medication's true effects, if possible. You shouldn't make major dietary changes or start taking an herbal remedy, vitamin, or supplement at the same time as starting a new medication. Otherwise, it's hard to find the cause of a benefit or side effect.

Here are some points to keep in mind:

- Do not start or stop taking any prescription medication on your own. This includes taking medication prescribed for someone else.

- Follow dose size, dosage time, and other instructions ("take with food," etc.) to the letter.

- Tell both your physician and pharmacist about all other prescription medications you or your child takes.

- Inform your physician and pharmacist about over-the-counter (OTC) drugs you or your child takes. Aspirin, ibuprofen, decongestants, non-prescription asthma inhalers, Alka-Seltzer and similar medications, and cough syrup are just some of the common substances that sometimes cause dangerous side effects when mixed with prescription drugs.

- Inform your doctor about your use, or your child's use or suspected use, of alcohol, tobacco, and any illegal drugs.

- Tell your doctor about any supplements, herbs, vitamins other than a regular daily multivitamin, and special diets that you or your child is trying. If your doctor is unsure about how a medication might interact with an herbal remedy or supplement, you may need to help him find more information. Most doctors are not well informed about the chemical action of nutritional supplements, herbal medicines, and dietary changes, but many are willing to work with you on these matters.

- Call your pharmacist right away if you suspect that you or your child has been given the wrong medication or the wrong dosage. Such errors do occur, and your pharmacist should be able to either reassure you or fix the problem.

- Ask your physician or pharmacist about any side effects specifically related to female reproduction and nursing if you are pregnant, breastfeeding, or could become pregnant.

- Ask about the risks of male reproductive side effects if you are actively trying to father a child.

Prior to giving your child any drug or taking one yourself, you should be given basic information, including answers to the following questions:

- What is the dosage?

- How many times a day should it be given?

- What are the common, and the rare, side effects?

- What should I do if side effects occur?

- Will the drug interact with any over-the-counter drugs, such as Alka-Seltzer or Tylenol? Will it interact with any herbal medicines or vitamins?

- Will I be counseled on the details of how to avoid risks such as drinking alcohol, smoking cigarettes or marijuana, and pregnancy?

- What should I do if I forget a dose?

- What are both the trade and generic names of the drug?

- Should I buy the generic version?

- Will this drug affect my vision, dental health, energy level, or sexual function? If so, are there remedies for these problems?

Special drug formulas

Drugs often come in a limited number of sizes. Even the least powerful pill may be too much for some patients to start with, especially for younger children. Following are some options that can help: A number of psychiatric medications, including Prozac, Risperdal, and Haldol, are available in liquid form. Liquids can be measured out in tiny doses and increased very gradually. Incidentally, liquid medications can be easily administered to children who refuse pills. You may even be able to mix them with food or drinks. (Check with your pharmacist first, as some cannot, and some may not be taken with certain juices, soft drinks, or milk.)

Some pills can be broken into fractions. Pill splitters are available at most pharmacies for just this purpose. Make sure it's okay to split a medication before you go this route, however: time-release medications and some pills with special coatings will not work properly when broken. Generally speaking, if the pill is scored down the middle, you can split it. If it isn't, ask your pharmacist, or call the manufacturer's customer hotline.

Some pills that are too small to split can be crushed and divided into equal parts. Again, ask your pharmacist before doing this, as it's difficult to get precise doses with crushed pills. Tiny mortar and pestle sets can be found at health food or cookware shops. You can buy empty gel caps to put the powder in, or you may be able to mix it into food or drink.

Some medications come in patch or cream form. Don't cut patches to get a smaller dose or to move up to a larger dose gradually. Doing so will keep the medication from being absorbed properly.

Patches should be placed on a padded, non-bony part of the body that doesn't flex too much. Many teens and adults prefer the upper arm area; children are more likely to leave them alone if you place them on an inaccessible area of the back.

Many patches need to be securely covered to deliver the full dose. If the patch comes with overlays that don't work well, try using the transparent, waterproof dressing Tegaderm. Younger children may enjoy the large, decorated Nexcare "Tattoos" bandages.

Medication patches cause rashes in some people with sensitive skin. Changing the patch location each time (or even daily) can minimize this problem. Ask your doctor about anti-inflammatory creams to try if the problem persists. Some people report that coating the skin with a small amount of Maalox helps.

Compounding pharmacies make medications to order in their own labs. For example, these facilities can make a liquid version of a prescription drug that's normally available in tablet form only. Compounding pharmacies are especially helpful to individuals with allergy problems, as many typical pills and syrups contain common allergens, including eggs, soy, corn, and dyes.

If a hypoallergenic version isn't available from the manufacturer, seek out a compounding pharmacy. If there isn't one where you live, several allow patients with valid prescriptions to order over the phone, by mail, or via the Internet. Just use a search engine like AltaVista (*http://www.altavista.com*) or Google (*http://www.google.com*) to search for the term "compounding pharmacy." As always with Internet-based or mail-order businesses, check references before you pay for goods or services. Several mail-order pharmacies, some of which compound medications, are listed in Appendix A.

Maria, mother of 4-year-old Jesse, found that switching medication formulas made a difference:

> *Risperdal took care of the vocal tics, and at a very high dose helped the nighttime ticcing. There has been no weight gain, but it stimulates his appetite and immediately after his nighttime dose, he "hangs out" in the refrigerator.*
>
> *However, the Risperdal tablet includes lactose. He is lactose-intolerant, so it gave him diarrhea. The solution that doesn't have lactose in it is fine.*

Prescription notes

You may see some odd initials on your prescriptions or pill bottles. Most of them stand for Latin words, so they are hard to figure out on your own. Here are some of the most common abbreviations used by doctors and pharmacists:

Abbreviation	Latin Term	Meaning
ac	ante cibum	Take before meals
bid	bis in die	Take twice a day
gtt	guttae	Drops
pc	post cibum	Take after meals
po	per os	Take by mouth
prn	pro re nata	Take as needed
qd	quaque die	Take once a day
qh	quaque hora	Take every hour
qid	quater in die	Take four times a day

Abbreviation	Latin Term	Meaning
q(number)h	quaque (number) hora	Take every (number) of hours
q hs	quaque hora somni	Take at bedtime
q day	quaque day	Take once per day
tid	ter in die	Take three times a day
ut dict.	ut dictum	Take as directed

In the US, most pharmacies also use colored stickers and letter codes to let you know about medication side effects and risks. If the picture or wording doesn't make sense to you, ask your pharmacist to explain its meaning.

Blood tests

Taking blood levels is part of a regular routine for some people who take medications for Tourette's syndrome. For example, liver or heart function may need to be tested before a particular drug is tried, and perhaps at regular intervals during its use. Liver function is assessed with a blood test that checks the level of certain enzymes.

The insert that comes with your medication includes recommendations about how often you need blood tests, if at all. Experienced doctors have found that repeated blood tests are rarely needed on otherwise healthy patients whose medication is effective. If you have health problems that place you at special risk, such as heart or liver problems, regular blood tests become more important. Talk to your doctor about what kind of tests he recommends when using your medication, how often you need the tests, and why they are necessary.

Other blood tests measure how much of the medication is found in the blood. Your doctor can compare this level to a chart of therapeutic blood levels: amounts of the medication that have been found to be effective in patients of various sizes and ages. The timing of blood draws can be important. Doctors usually aim for a "trough" level, meaning taking blood toward the end of a dose's presumed effectiveness. For example, if you normally take your medication at 8 A.M. and 5 P.M., late afternoon would be your best choice for having blood drawn for a trough level.

Lucy, mother of 13-year-old Richard, shares her tips for better blood draws:

> *Tip #1: Butterfly needles. They are much tinier and take longer to draw the blood, but there is far less pain involved.*

> *Tip #2: Listen to the kid. This seems obvious, but you'd be surprised how often the technicians don't bother with it. If the kid says he has the*

best veins in his left arm, start looking for a vein in his left arm. If he says
he can keep the blood flowing sitting up better than lying down...let him
sit up. One of my sons has unusually deep veins; every technician seems
to have to learn this the hard way. We are grateful for the occasional tech
who believes him and doesn't assume the previous techs just didn't have
his or her "magic touch."

Tip #3: Have some small reward available for afterwards. Even a small
container of fruit juice is much appreciated after a blood draw.

Always ask where your therapeutic blood level and current blood level are when you are tested. Observant people can catch potentially dangerous mistakes. Typical problems include blood assessed with the wrong blood test, misinterpreted levels, and getting someone else's paperwork.

Once a therapeutic level has been reached, your main job is to try to keep that level steady. Sometimes this requires raising the dose of medication over time. It's as if the body gets used to the drug, and requires more to get the same effect. This isn't the same as becoming addicted. It may just reflect how your metabolism adjusts to your medication.

Good phlebotomists (blood-draw specialists) do not cause bruising or more than a twinge of pain when they do their job, unless you bruise very easily or have a low pain threshold. If this is the case, let the phlebotomist know—she may have a better way to obtain the sample. Numbing ointments (like EMLA cream) can help, although in some cases they cause the veins to constrict. You may have to experiment to find what works best for you.

People who do not have regular access to quality lab facilities, such as those living in remote areas, may have a very difficult time keeping up with a testing schedule. Talk to your healthcare provider about alternative ways to handle the need for monthly testing, such as having a visiting home-health nurse do the blood draw in your home and then mailing the vial to a lab for testing.

Understanding blood test results

Blood test results can be difficult to understand, unless you're a doctor. Here's some basic information about the three most common tests requested for patients taking medications for Tourette's:

- **Liver function tests.** The liver is the body's center for eliminating toxins. Since many medications include or produce toxins, they can put stress on the liver.

Blood tests can check the levels of liver (hepatic) enzymes. These enzymes result from the death of liver cells. Since the liver is constantly regenerating itself, some of these enzymes should always be present. When you take a medication that's metabolized by the liver, they will be a bit higher than usual. What your doctor looks out for is an enzyme level that's much too high. The three liver enzymes most commonly checked are:

- AST (aspartate amino transferase). AST is also known as SGOT (serum glutamic-oxaloacetic transaminase) or aspartate transaminase.

- ALT (alanine amino transferase). ALT is also known as SGPT (serum glutamate pyruvate transaminase) or alanine transaminase.

- GGT (gamma glutamyl transpeptidase).

For people in good health, the levels of all three liver enzymes are usually below 25. Simply taking certain medications can double the level of liver enzymes. If the level goes over 70, that's generally considered cause for concern. If you have known liver problems or are experiencing health problems that could be caused by liver problems, your doctor might also be concerned about levels between 35 and 70. High liver enzyme levels can also indicate heart problems.

- WBC count. WBC stands for white blood cells, which are also known as lymphocytes. A healthy number of white blood cells in your blood indicate a properly functioning immune system, a very elevated number can indicate the presence of infection, and a very low number can indicate either a suppressed immune system or an infection that has overwhelmed your body's defenses. The WBC count is included in a CBC count (see below).

- CBC count. CBC stands for complete blood cell, and as the name indicates, this test measures the numbers of various types of cells that should be present in your blood. It returns levels for both red and white blood cells, blood platelets, and subgroups of these cells. Typical, normal values returned from a CBC count are listed in the following table.

CBC Test Component	Expected Result
WBC (white blood cells)	5,000–10,000 WBCs per cubic millimeter of blood
HGB (hemoglobin)	12–15 grams per 100 cubic centimeters of blood
Hct (hematocrit)	31–43 percent of whole blood
RBC (red blood cells)	4–5.2 million RBCs per cubic millimeter of blood
Platelets	130,000–500,000 platelets per cubic millimeter of blood
MCV (mean corpuscular volume)	74–85, an expression of the average size of red blood cells

Normal CBC values for a specific person depend on that person's age, size, state of general health, and medications used. If one of your results on this or any other blood test seems to be outside the normal range, ask your doctor whether it should be a concern or not. Individual variations can occur, and may not indicate a problem.

Electrocardiogram (EKG)

In addition to blood tests, your heart function may need to be monitored by regular blood-pressure tests, physical exams, and sometimes an electrocardiogram (EKG). The EKG can be done in the doctor's office, and since it uses wires that stick on the chest with an adhesive patch or gooey substance, it doesn't hurt at all. You just have to lie still (not always an easy task for kids). The wires are attached to a mechanical device or to a computer, much like an EEG machine, resulting in a graph of the electrical activity of the heart rate. Your doctor can "read" this graph to discern problems with or changes in heart function.

Learning more about medications

The information in the following sections about specific drugs is taken from the *Physician's Desk Reference,* pharmaceutical company literature, and other reputable sources. This information is accurate as of this writing, but new findings may emerge. Check out medications using a detailed drug reference book, such as those listed in Appendix A, to make sure you are aware of all possible side effects and interactions.

The Tourette Syndrome Association reports on the latest treatment information through its newsletter, web site, and annual convention. It is probably the most up-to-date lay source for medication data that's specific to TS. The TSA provides a full medication reference online at *http://www.tourettesyndrome.org.*

The National Alliance for the Mentally Ill is also a good resource for information on new drugs for neurological disorders in general. Its web site (*http://www.nami.org*) often features "consumer reviews" of new drugs and previews of medications now undergoing clinical trials.

The Child Psychopharmacology Information Service maintains online medication guides at *http://www.psychiatry.wisc.edu/cpis.htm,* and can be reached by phone at (608) 827-2470.

Neuroleptics

Neuroleptics are the class of drugs most frequently prescribed for Tourette's syndrome. This section begins with a list of the most recent neuroleptics. Known to doctors as *atypical neuroleptics,* these drugs are considered much safer and easier to take than their predecessors. Risperdal is the atypical neuroleptic tested most extensively for use in TS.[3]

Brenda, grandmother of 10-year-old Charisse, says a low dose of Risperdal has had noticeable benefits:

> Charisse has had rages since she was about 3 years old. They escalated and continued until she was put on Risperdal. On Risperdal she sometimes begins to rage, but appears to have increased control to pull back and change direction.
>
> Charisse has always been on fairly low doses. Currently she is off the Risperdal for the summer so we can evaluate how and what it is doing for her.
>
> She has experienced significant weight gain while on Risperdal. We feel this would be such a wonderful medication except for that complication.

The minor side effects seen most often with the neuroleptics are sedation (sleepiness) and weight gain. Sometimes stimulants are prescribed to counteract these problems (see "Medications for ADHD," later in this chapter). Other people choose complementary therapies, such as diet and exercise programs, vitamins, or herbal remedies, to offset these effects (see Chapter 7 for more information). Be sure to tell your doctor about any complementary therapies that you try, as some can actually interfere or interact with neuroleptics.

Onset or increase of bedwetting and daytime wetting (enuresis) is also sometimes seen in children taking these medications. Reducing the dose or changing its timing can help with this uncomfortable problem. Different toileting schedules can also help, and occasionally a second medication is added. Talk to your doctor if this occurs.

Certain major side effects are sometimes associated with neuroleptics, including neuroleptic malignant syndrome (NMS), extrapyramidal side effects, and tardive dyskinesia. See the section "Major side effects," later in this chapter, for definitions of and more information about these dangers.

Tourette's syndrome experts recommend that people who need a neuroleptic rather than a milder medication like clonidine or guanfacine should try one of the atypical neuroleptics first. The following drugs are atypical neuroleptics. Of these, only Risperdal and Zyprexa are routinely used to treat TS.

Clozaril

Generic name: Clozapine

Use: Schizophrenia

Action, if known: Atypical neuroleptic—this medication works against the hormone acetylcholine.

Side effects: You may experience sedation, fever (temporary), changes in blood pressure or heartbeat, overproduction of saliva, or tremor. Major dangers include agranulocytosis (a serious blood condition), seizures, neuroleptic malignant syndrome (NMS), and tardive dyskinesia.

Known interaction hazards: Avoid alcohol, CNS system depressants, drugs for high blood pressure, tricyclic antidepressants, and similar drugs, or use with caution. The danger of NMS increases when Clozaril is used with lithium.

Tips: Weekly blood tests are required. Women, people with low white blood cell counts, and some people of Ashkenazi Jewish descent have a higher risk of agranulocytosis (severe, potentially fatal loss of white blood cells) when taking this drug. People with heart disease, glaucoma, prostate trouble, or liver or kidney disease need careful monitoring. Smoking cigarettes can affect how quickly your body uses Clozaril. You may want to supplement with vitamin E, which may protect against tardive dyskinesia.

Risperdal

Generic name: Risperidone

Use: Psychosis, schizophrenia, rage/aggression

Action, if known: Atypical neuroleptic—this medication affects serotonin and dopamine, and raises the level of the hormone prolactin.

Side effects: You may experience sedation, headache, runny nose, anxiety, or insomnia. Weight gain, especially in children, may occur. Risks include neuroleptic malignant syndrome (NMS) and tardive dyskinesia.

Known interaction hazards: Risperdal decreases the action of L-Dopa. It also interacts with carbamazepine and clozapine, and may make SSRI antidepressants stronger or weaker.

Tips: You should have an EKG before starting Risperdal and regular heart monitoring while taking it. In some patients, Risperdal (and possibly other atypical neuroleptics) may increase obsessive-compulsive symptoms. You may want to supplement with vitamin E, which may protect against tardive dyskinesia.

Seroquel

Generic name: Quetiapine

Use: Psychosis, rage/aggression

Action, if known: Atypical neuroleptic—this drug is believed to increase the availability of serotonin and dopamine at specific receptors in the brain.

Side effects: Drowsiness, dizziness, sedation, agitation, nausea, changes in appetite, weight gain or loss, or sexual dysfunction may occur. Seroquel lowers the seizure threshold. It also carries a danger of neuroleptic malignant syndrome (NMS), extrapyramidal side effects, and tardive dyskinesia.

Known interaction hazards: The effects of this drug can be made dangerously strong by alcohol and all central nervous system (CNS) depressants, including tranquilizers, sedatives, OTC sleep aids, and narcotics, as well as the anti-epilepsy drug phenytoin. It may interfere with the effects of drugs for high blood pressure. Seroquel's action may be increased by other drugs, including ketoconazole, erythromycin, clarithromycin, diltiazam, verapamil, and nefazodone.

Tips: This drug can cause extra sensitivity to heat. People with liver or kidney problems, heart disease, thyroid problems, or low blood pressure should be monitored while taking Seroquel. You may want to supplement with vitamin E, which may protect against tardive dyskinesia.

Zeldox, Geodon

Generic name: Ziprasidone

Use: Schizophrenia, psychosis, rage/aggression

Action, if known: Atypical neuroleptic affects production and use of dopamine, serotonin, and norepinephrine. It also has some antihistamine effects, and is an alpha-adrenergic blocker.

Side effects: You may experience drowsiness, dizziness, agitation, tremor, nausea, reduced appetite, lightheadedness, rash, increased light sensitivity, increased blood pressure, or cold-like symptoms. It carries a risk of neuroleptic malignant syndrome (NMS) and tardive dyskinesia. Zeldox can lower the seizure threshold.

Known interaction hazards: Avoid alcohol and all CNS depressants, including tranquilizers, sedatives, OTC sleep aids, and narcotics. Zeldox may strengthen the action of drugs that lower your blood pressure, including clonidine and guanfacine. It may counteract L-Dopa and similar drugs. Its action may be strengthened by carbamazepine and ketoconazole. According to its manufacturer, Pfizer, Zeldox is less likely to interact with other medications than other atypical neuroleptics, including lithium and oral contraceptives.

Tips: You should have an EKG before starting Zeldox, as well as regular heart monitoring while taking this drug, which can lengthen the QT/QTc interval. It should not be used with other drugs that also have this effect, including quinidine, dofetilide, pimozide, thioridazine, moxifloxacin, and sparfloxicin. It is not recommended for people with existing heart or liver problems, or for people with disturbed electrolyte balance (such as persons with anorexia.) This is a very new drug, and just got FDA approval for US use in February 2001. According to research carried out by its manufacturer, it is much less likely to cause rapid weight gain than other atypical antipsychotics, and may be safer for people who have diabetes or high cholesterol because it has less effect on insulin and cholesterol rates. Zeldox capsules contain lactose, so if you are lactose intolerant you may want to see if a lactose-free version can be compounded for you. This drug may increase the risk of birth defects. Talk to your doctor if you could become pregnant.

Zyprexa

Generic name: Olanzapine

Use: Psychosis, rage/aggression, tics; also used in cases of hard-to-treat OCD, depression (usually with an antidepressant), or bipolar disorders (usually with a mood stabilizer.)

Action, if known: Atypical neuroleptic—this medication blocks uptake of dopamine and serotonin at certain receptors, and may have other actions.

Side effects: Headache, agitation, dry mouth, hostility, disinhibition, insomnia, slurred speech, neuroleptic malignant syndrome (NMS), tardive dyskinesia, dizziness, and seizures could occur.

Known interaction hazards: Alcohol and carbamazepine add to the sedating action of this drug. Zyprexa strengthens the effect of medications for high blood pressure, including clonidine and guanfacine.

Tips: Zyprexa can increase your sensitivity to heat. If you smoke, you may need to take Zyprexa more frequently. You may want to supplement with vitamin E, which may protect against tardive dyskinesia.

If the atypical neuroleptics do not work and your tics remain very difficult to cope with, your doctor may recommend trying one of the older neuroleptics, despite their high potential for side effects. Haldol is the most frequent choice among drugs in this class. Orap was the second most common choice until recently, when it was found to react badly with a number of common prescription drugs. If Haldol is not effective for you, either alone or in combination with other medications, your doctor may suggest one of the other old-line neuroleptics from the following list.

Catapres

Generic name: Clonidine

Use: High blood pressure, ADHD, tics/Tourette's syndrome, extreme impulsivity, migraine, drug and alcohol withdrawal aid, ulcerative colitis, childhood growth delay.

Action, if known: Clonidine stimulates alpha-adrenergic receptors in the brain and spinal cord to widen blood vessels, and stimulates similar receptors throughout the body. This reduces the heart rate, relaxes blood vessels, and may have other effects.

Side effects: This drug can cause dry mouth, dizziness, constipation, sedation, unusually vivid or disturbing dreams, and weight gain.

Known interaction hazards: Clonidine can interact with other medications for blood pressure, and its activity is blocked by tricyclic antidepressants, such as Anafranil. It can have an additive effect with certain antihistamines that also lower blood pressure.

Tips: Do not use clonidine if you have slow heart rate or AV node conduction problems, disease of the blood vessels in the brain, or chronic kidney failure. Clonidine is not recommended for persons with depression. You can become tolerant of clonidine, requiring a higher dose. You should have regular eye exams, as clonidine can affect the retina. You can diminish oral clonidine's sedating effect by taking all or the largest part of your dose at bedtime. This can help people who have sleep problems in addition to TS. The time-release Catapres patch is far less sedating than oral clonidine for most patients. Do not stop using clonidine suddenly. Your doctor can supervise a slow withdrawal program to avoid risking a sudden, dangerous rise in blood pressure. Symptoms of this problem include rapid heartbeat, sweating, nervousness, and headache. A cream version of clonidine is also available.

Clonidine and guanfacine

Clonidine (Catapres) and guanfacine (Tenex) were originally developed to treat high blood pressure, but were found to reduce the level of tics in people with TS who also happened to need treatment for hypertension. This accidental discovery has allowed many people to switch over from the neuroleptic medications traditionally used to treat tic disorders.

Andrea, mother of 17-year-old Robbie, says he found clonidine and then guanfacine quite helpful:

> *From age 9 to age 15, Robbie was on clonidine for the tics and Ritalin for ADHD. His doctor felt that Desoxyn and Tenex would be better, since he wouldn't have to take them during the school day. He has been taking them for the past two years.*

Robbie had a skin rash when he used the Catapres patch. Other
than that, he has had good experiences with medication. It helps with
concentration and tic reduction.

Clonidine and guanfacine have also shown promise specifically for treating TS-linked rages, and are gaining popularity as non-stimulant medications for ADHD. They are particularly valuable when a person has sleep disturbance in addition to TS.

Etrafon, Trilafon, Triavil

Generic name: Amitriptyline/perphenazine (Trilafon includes only perphenazine)

Use: Depression, panic disorder, chronic pain, eating disorders, severe PMS

Action, if known: Perphenazine is a neuroleptic with qualities similar to those of a tricyclic antidepressant—it blocks norepinephrine and serotonin use, and works against the hormone acetylcholine. In Etrafon and Triavil, perphenazine is combined with amitriptyline (Elavil), a tricyclic antidepressant.

Side effects: Side effects may include sedation, tremor, seizures, dry mouth, and light sensitivity. It can cause mood swings in people with bipolar disorders. This drug carries a risk of tardive dyskinesia, extrapyramidal side effects, and neuroleptic malignant syndrome.

Known interaction hazards: This drug can interact dangerously with alcohol, MAOI antidepressants, blood pressure medications (including clonidine and guanfacine), and thyroid medications. Its action is strengthened by bicarbonate of soda (found in Alka-Seltzer and other digestive remedies), acetazolamide, procainamide, and quinidine. Cimetidine, methylphenidate, Thorazine and similar drugs, oral contraceptives, nicotine (including cigarettes), charcoal tablets, and estrogen may interfere with Etrafon's action in the body.

Tips: Avoid extreme heat when taking this drug. Etrafon is not recommended for use by people with severe depression, lung disease, severe asthma, or liver disease. Take this medication with food if stomach upset occurs. You may want to supplement with vitamin E, which may protect against tardive dyskinesia.

Haldol, Haldol Decanoate

Generic name: Haloperidol

Use: Psychosis, tics/Tourette's syndrome, schizophrenia

Action, if known: This drug affects the hypothalamus gland in the brain, which in turn affects metabolism, body temperature, alertness, muscle tone, and hormone production.

Side effects: Haldol can lower the seizure threshold. Sedation, jaundice (temporary), anemia, changes in blood pressure or heartbeat, or dizziness may occur.

Known interaction hazards: Alcohol and other CNS depressants, narcotics, and tranquilizers (including OTC sleep aids) add to the sedating action of Haldol. Its action is strengthened by lithium, causing a greater risk of encephalopathic syndrome. Haldol strengthens the effects of tricyclic antidepressants. Anticholinergic medications may make Haldol less effective. This drug carries a risk of tardive dyskinesia, extrapyramidal side effects, and neuroleptic malignant syndrome.

Tips: Haldol is not recommended for people who have low blood pressure, Parkinson's disease, or diseases of the blood, kidneys, or liver. You may want to supplement with vitamin E, which may protect against tardive dyskinesia.

Loxipax, Loxitane

Generic name: Loxapine

Use: Psychosis

Action, if known: Loxipax blocks or changes the use of dopamine in several areas of the brain.

Side effects: Loxipax may suppress the gag or cough reflex. Other side effects may include sedation, depression, light sensitivity, jaundice (temporary), anemia, changes in blood pressure or heartbeat, or dry mouth. This drug lowers the seizure threshold.

It also carries a risk of tardive dyskinesia, extrapyramidal side effects, and neuroleptic malignant syndrome.

Known interaction hazards: Alcohol, any tranquilizer or CNS depressant (including OTC sleep aids), antacids, lithium, and tricyclic antidepressants may interact with Loxipax.

Tips: The drugs Motipress and Motival contain both loxapine and the anti-anxiety medication nortriptyline. You may want to supplement with vitamin E, which may protect against tardive dyskinesia.

Mellaril

Generic name: Thioridazine hydrochloride

Use: Psychosis, depression with anxiety, aggression

Action, if known: Phenothiazine neuroleptic—this drug affects the hypothalamus gland in the brain, which in turn affects metabolism, body temperature, alertness, muscle tone, and hormone production.

Side effects: Mellaril may suppress the gag or cough reflex. Other side effects may include sedation, depression, light sensitivity, jaundice (temporary), anemia, changes in blood pressure or heartbeat, or dry mouth. This drug lowers the seizure threshold. It also carries a risk of tardive dyskinesia, extrapyramidal side effects, and neuroleptic malignant syndrome. Mellaril can lengthen the QT interval, a measure of heart activity that can be picked up on an EKG. In susceptible persons, this could cause potentially fatal heart arrhythmias.

Known interaction hazards: Mellaril interacts with alcohol, any tranquilizer or CNS depressant (including OTC sleep aids), antacids, lithium, and tricyclic antidepressants. It loses effectiveness when you eat or drink items containing caffeine.

Tips: Mellaril can increase your sensitivity to heat. This medication is usually not recommended for people with blood, liver, kidney, or heart disease; low blood pressure; or Parkinson's disease. Take it with food if stomach upset occurs. You may want to supplement with vitamin E, which may protect against tardive dyskinesia.

Moban, Lidone

Generic name: Molindone

Use: Psychosis

Action, if known: Dihydroindolone neuroleptic

Side effects: Moban may cause drowsiness, sedation, depression, nausea, or dry mouth. This drug carries a risk of tardive dyskinesia, extrapyramidal side effects, and neuroleptic malignant syndrome.

Known interaction hazards: Moban can interact with alcohol and all other CNS depressants, tranquilizers (including OTC sleep aids), barbiturates, anesthetics, tricyclic antidepressants, and lithium. It may have negative interactions with many other medications, including other neuroleptics, Asendin, phenytoin, and Cylert. Smoking can interfere with the action of this drug.

Tips: People with liver disease or Parkinson's disease should not take Moban. Take with food if stomach upset occurs. You may want to supplement with vitamin E, which may protect against tardive dyskinesia. Moban is available in a liquid formulation (Moban Concentrate). This medication is not available in Canada.

Navane

Generic name: Thiothixene

Use: Psychosis

Action, if known: Thiothixene neuroleptic—this drug affects the hypothalamus gland in the brain, which in turn affects metabolism, body temperature, alertness, muscle tone, and hormone production.

Side effects: Sedation, depression, light sensitivity, jaundice (temporary), anemia, changes in blood pressure or heartbeat. Danger of tardive dyskinesia, extrapyramidal side effects, neuroleptic malignant syndrome.

Known interaction hazards: Alcohol, any other tranquilizer or CNS depressant (including OTC sleep aids), antacids, lithium, and tricyclic antidepressants interact with Navane. Do not combine this drug with propranolol. Its effect may be reduced by the use of anticholinergic medications like L-Dopa.

Tips: Avoid extreme heat when taking Navane. This medication is usually not recommended for people with blood, liver, kidney, or heart disease; low blood pressure; or Parkinson's disease. Take it with food if stomach upset occurs. You may want to supplement with vitamin E, which may protect against tardive dyskinesia.

Orap

Generic name: Pimozide

Use: Psychosis, severe tics/Tourette's syndrome, schizophrenia

Action, if known: Neuroleptic—affects the amount and action of dopamine in the brain.

Side effects: Extrapyramidal side effects, such as restlessness and unusual movements, can occur when using Orap, which also carries a risk of tardive dyskinesia and neuroleptic malignant syndrome (NMS).

Known interaction hazards: Talk to your doctor before taking any other drug with Orap. Antihistamines (including OTC cold and allergy remedies), anticholinergic drugs, certain kinds of antibiotics, antifungal drugs, protease inhibitors used to treat AIDS, and several other drugs can interact dangerously with Orap. Alcohol, other CNS depressants, tranquilizers (including OTC sleep aids) can also combine with Orap to cause dangerous levels of sedation. Taking other neuroleptics with Orap increases your risk for tardive dyskinesia, neuroleptic malignant syndrome, and extrapyramidal side effects. Taking tricyclic antidepressants and many other medications with heart effects can increase your risk for heart problems with Orap. Your doctor may need to adjust dosages of other medications you take, especially anti-seizure drugs. Do not take Orap with grapefruit juice.

Tips: You should have an EKG before starting Orap, and regular heart monitoring while taking it. Orap is considered more risky than some other old-line neuroleptics, as well as the atypical neuroleptics. Make sure you have exhausted your other options first. You may want to supplement with vitamin E, which may protect against tardive dyskinesia.

Prolixin, Prolixin Decanoate

Generic name: Fluphenazine

Use: Psychosis

Action, if known: Phenothiazine neuroleptic—this drug affects the hypothalamus gland in the brain, which in turn affects metabolism, body temperature, alertness, muscle tone, and hormone production.

Side effects: Prolixin may suppress the gag or cough reflex. Side effects may include sedation, depression, light sensitivity, jaundice (temporary), anemia, and changes in blood pressure or heartbeat. This drug carries a risk of tardive dyskinesia, extrapyramidal side effects, and neuroleptic malignant syndrome.

Known interaction hazards: Prolixin combined with alcohol, any tranquilizer or CNS depressant (including OTC sleep aids), antacids, lithium, or tricyclic antidepressants can lead to dangerous levels of sedation. It loses effectiveness when you eat or drink items containing caffeine. Charcoal can block the action of this drug.

Tips: Prolixin can increase your sensitivity to heat. This medication is usually not recommended for people with blood, liver, kidney, or heart disease; low blood pressure; or Parkinson's disease. Take it with food if stomach upset occurs. You may want to supplement with vitamin E, which may protect against tardive dyskinesia.

Serentil

Generic name: Mesoridazine

Use: Psychosis

Action, if known: Phenothiazine neuroleptic—this drug affects the hypothalamus gland in the brain, which in turn affects metabolism, body temperature, alertness, muscle tone, and hormone production. It blocks dopamine receptors in the mesolimbic system, increasing turnover of dopamine.

Side effects: Drowsiness, dizziness, sedation, agitation, nausea, changes in appetite, weight gain or loss, and sexual dysfunction are sometimes associated with Serentil. It also lowers the seizure threshold. This drug carries a risk of tardive dyskinesia, neuroleptic malignant syndrome, and extrapyramidal side effects. Serentil can lengthen the QT interval, a measure of heart activity that can be picked up on an EKG. In susceptible persons, this could cause potentially fatal heart arrhythmias.

Known interaction hazards: When Serentil is taken with alcohol or other CNS depressants, including tranquilizers, sedatives, OTC sleep aids, and narcotics, dangerous levels of sedation can occur. It interacts with atropine, phosphorus insecticides, and quinidine as well. Charcoal can block the action of this drug.

Tips: This drug can increase your sensitivity to heat. You will need regular blood tests and eye exams while taking Serentil. This drug is not recommended for people with severe depression, bone marrow depression, liver or heart disease. If you have high blood pressure, you will need careful monitoring while taking Serentil. You may want to supplement with vitamin E, which may protect against tardive dyskinesia.

Stelazine, Vesprin

Generic name: Trifluoperazine

Use: Psychosis

Action, if known: Phenothiazine neuroleptic—this drug affects the hypothalamus gland in the brain, which in turn affects metabolism, body temperature, alertness, muscle tone, and hormone production. It blocks dopamine receptors in the mesolimbic system, increasing turnover of dopamine.

Side effects: Stelazine may suppress the gag or cough reflex. Other side effects can include sedation, depression, light sensitivity, jaundice (temporary), anemia, or changes in blood pressure or heartbeat. This drug carries a risk of tardive dyskinesia, extrapyramidal side effects, and neuroleptic malignant syndrome.

Known interaction hazards: Combining Stelazine with alcohol, any tranquilizer or CNS depressant (including OTC sleep aids), antacids, lithium, or tricyclic antidepressants can lead to dangerous levels of sedation. This drug loses effectiveness when you eat or drink items containing caffeine. Charcoal can block the action of this drug.

Tips: Stelazine can increase your sensitivity to heat. You may want to supplement with vitamin E, which may protect against tardive dyskinesia. This medication is usually not recommended for people with blood, liver, kidney, or heart disease; low blood pressure; or Parkinson's disease. If you have thyroid problems, use extreme caution. Take it with food if stomach upset occurs.

Thorazine

Generic name: Chlorpromazine

Use: Psychosis, schizophrenia

Action, if known: Phenothiazine neuroleptic—this drug affects the hypothalamus gland in the brain, which in turn affects metabolism, body temperature, alertness, muscle tone, and hormone production. It interferes with the action of dopamine in the basal ganglia, mesolimbic area, and medulla, and has anticholinergic effects.

Side effects: Thorazine may suppress the gag or cough reflex. Other side effects may include sedation, depression, light sensitivity, jaundice (temporary), anemia, changes in blood pressure or heartbeat, or dry mouth. Thorazine lowers the seizure threshold. This drug carries a risk of tardive dyskinesia, extrapyramidal side effects, and neuroleptic malignant syndrome.

Known interaction hazards: Combining Thorazine with alcohol, any tranquilizer or CNS depressant (including OTC sleep aids), antacids, lithium, or tricyclic antidepressants can lead to dangerous levels of sedation. It loses effectiveness when you eat or drink items containing caffeine. Charcoal can block the action of this drug.

Tips: Thorazine can increase your sensitivity to heat. This medication is usually not recommended for people with blood, liver, kidney, or heart disease; low blood pressure; Reye's disease; or Parkinson's disease. Take with food if stomach upset occurs. You may want to supplement with vitamin E, which may protect against tardive dyskinesia.

Tenex

Generic name: Guanfacine

Use: Tic disorders/Tourette's syndrome and high blood pressure, migraines, extreme nausea, heroin withdrawal aid, ADHD.

Action, if known: Guanfacine stimulates the central nervous system to relax and widen blood vessels, increasing blood flow and reducing blood pressure. It may also have other effects.

Side effects: Sleepiness, changes in blood pressure or heart rate, or nausea may occur.

Known interaction hazards: Alcohol and other CNS depressants plus guanfacine can cause extreme sedation. Its effects may be counteracted by stimulants such as Ritalin, many non-prescription drugs, estrogen and oral contraceptives, indomethacin, ibuprofen, and non-steroidal anti-inflammatory drugs. It could also have an additive effect with certain antihistamines that also lower blood pressure.

Tips: If you take another medication that lowers blood pressure, your doctor will need to adjust your Tenex dose accordingly to prevent problems. Taking all or the largest part of your dose at bedtime can diminish guanfacine's sedating effect. This can help people who have sleep problems in addition to TS.

Other medications for TS

Quite a few other medications for Tourette's syndrome have been considered over the years. Some of these are similar to drugs in current use, while others have a different pharmacological action that reduces tics. Researchers are currently studying the following options, but they are just some of the possibilities that have been considered over the years. Some are already in use outside the US.

Botox

A combination of botulinum toxin type A (Botox) and the muscle relaxant baclofen (Lioresol) has been investigated in one large trial as a treatment for TS. Botox alone has been the subject of a few smaller investigations. Botox has been used for many years to treat spasticity due to cerebral palsy, and other conditions as well. Early results have been promising, particularly for vocal tics.[5,6,7] It is also being used more widely for eye and other facial tics.

Cannabinoids

Receptors for cannabinoids, active compounds found in *Cannabis sativa* (marijuana) and *Cannabis indica* (hemp), are found in large numbers in the basal ganglia of the brain. Researchers suspect that they are involved in some way with controlling motor activity, and that they may affect the activity of neurotransmitters within this area of the brain. Cannabinoids may affect the uptake of dopamine, among other actions. Based on this information and on anecdotal reports of tic reduction from smoking marijuana, researchers have recently begun looking into the use of marijuana or derivatives to treat TS. Early results have been promising, and have placed TS on the "approved list" of conditions for medical marijuana use in some areas where it is legal.[8,9] Cannabinoids may also be useful for persons with tardive dyskinesia, a movement disorder caused by some medications used to treat TS. However, marijuana smoke, like cigarette smoke, is dangerous to the lungs and may be carcinogenic.

Inversine

Inversine (mecamylamine HCI) is an older drug for high blood pressure. It blocks nicotine uptake in the brain and relaxes blood vessels. This might seem an unlikely treatment for TS, considering that nicotine itself has shown some promise as a medication for tics. Researchers believe that mecamylamine actually binds to nicotine receptors, and may therefore set off similar neurotransmitter activity.[10]

Side effects of Inversine can include dizziness, blurred vision, nausea, dry mouth, and constipation. One of the reasons it fell out of favor for hypertension treatment is that it interacts with many other medications, including sulfa drugs and antibiotics, and its action is strengthened by antacids, bicarbonate of soda, acetazolamide, potassium or sodium citrate, and citric acid. It also decreases the effects of ambenonium, neostigmine, and pyridostigmine. Those with bladder, kidney, prostate, or bowel problems require regular monitoring while taking Inversine. It may make glaucoma and heart problems worse.

Inversine is currently being studied as a specific treatment for TS-linked rage and aggression. The TSA is sponsoring clinical trials at the University of Florida.

Ketanserin

Ketanserin is an interesting drug that seems to have multiple actions. When taken internally, it blocks the 5-HT2A receptor of serotonin. It not only lowers blood pressure, but also seems to decrease the secretion of testosterone, cause platelets to clump together more easily, and affect anxiety levels. It appears to have hormonal effects as well. One recent study found it useful for treating TS in children.[11]

Nicotine

Sold under the brand names Habitrol, Nicoderm, Nicotrol, and ProStep, the main medical use for nicotine is as an aid to stopping smoking. However, some doctors prescribe nicotine and related compounds to increase the activity of neuroleptics without increasing the dose. Researchers are currently investigating nicotine for tic reduction.[12,13]

Nicotine affects many central nervous system functions, and not all of its actions are known. People with insulin-dependent diabetes, heart problems, liver or kidney disease, high blood pressure, or pheochromocytoma require careful monitoring when using nicotine in any form (including cigarettes).

The use of nicotine as a primary or secondary treatment for TS is still under investigation, and doctors do not recommend trying this on your own. Of course, smoking is not recommended as a TS treatment—tobacco smoke is hazardous to the lungs and can cause lung cancer, emphysema, and other serious health problems. Smokeless tobacco (snuff, chewing tobacco) can also cause cancer.

Ondansetron

Sold under the brand name Zofran, ondansetron is normally used as an anti-nausea drug. It is also a selective serotonin blocker, working at 5-HT3 serotonin receptors. The most common side effects reported are headache, constipation, and dry mouth; some patients also report abdominal pain and nausea. One recent trial showed that this medication was associated with a significant decrease in tics for most patients.[14]

Interestingly, ondansetron has also been found useful in the treatment of bulimia, an eating disorder that is seen much more often in persons with OCD, and somewhat more often in persons with TS.[15]

Tetrabenazine

Tetrabenazine (TBZ, also marketed under the names Regulin and Nitoman) depletes dopamine in nerve endings, and so it may interact with other drugs that affect dopamine production or use. Tetrabenazine is not FDA-approved for sale in the US, but is widely available elsewhere. US patients may obtain it through compassionate use programs or through mail-order arrangements. It is sometimes used in Canada, Europe, and Japan as a treatment for TS, and is also the only drug currently known to ease the effects of tardive dyskinesia. Tetrabenazine sometimes causes depression as a side effect.

Surgical options

As in OCD, surgical treatment of Tourette's syndrome is seen as strictly a last resort, when ticcing is extremely severe or self-injurious, and no medications are effective. Many types of surgical treatments were tried unsuccessfully before medication became available.

Recently a more precise type of surgical treatment was tried on one patient with some success. Rather than removing, cutting, or deliberately damaging (lesioning) a part of the brain, the surgeons used an implanted electrode to deliver high-frequency stimulation to the thalamus, a brain structure tightly connected with the basal ganglia. The procedure is similar to electrode stimulation methods currently being tested for patients with untreatable epilepsy. The doctors reported that their patient, who had severe TS and had not found relief with any medication, had much-improved symptoms.[16] Much research is necessary to determine if this is a viable treatment option for severe symptoms of TS.

Treatment for PANDAS

Pediatric autoimmune neurological disorders associated with strep—PANDAS—is the name given to TS or OCD symptoms that begin or worsen after a strep infection. See Chapter 2, *Diagnosis,* for more information about how PANDAS is identified.

The simplest treatment that has been suggested for PANDAS is prophylactic antibiotics, usually amoxicillin or Augmentin (amoxicillin/clavulanate). The antibiotics are given to prevent reinfection with strep, not to treat PANDAS itself. If strep infection does not recur, the theory goes, neither will PANDAS symptoms. This treatment is standard for cases of rheumatic fever, and is often effective in preventing Sydenham's chorea (see Chapter 2 for more information on this strep-linked movement disorder).

Of course, taking antibiotics on a long-term basis is not without risk. It can make life-threatening infections harder to treat due to the development of antibiotic resistance, and gastrointestinal problems tend to occur as antibiotics kill off the gut bacteria that aid digestion. Yogurt with live cultures and other "probiotics" can preserve and replenish gut bacteria.

The PANDAS research team at the National Institute of Mental Health (NIMH) currently recommends giving antibiotics only to treat verified strep infection, not for prevention.[17]

One substance that attacks existing strep antibodies is intravenous gammaglobulin (IVIG). This substance is given through an intravenous drip. Studies at NIMH have shown that IVIG is highly effective for treating PANDAS. It does not cure the disorder permanently, but it usually ends the current outbreak.

However, IVIG is a blood product derived from multiple donors, which means there is a remote possibility that those who receive it could also receive an unknown virus. It is screened for known bacteria and viruses, of course. IVIG is used to treat many medical conditions, and it is in short supply. That can make it hard to get and expensive. NIMH has issued a warning that IVIG for PANDAS should not be used outside of a research setting at this time.[18]

Plasmapheresis is a method that removes strep antibodies from the blood. Plasmapheresis is similar to dialysis, in that blood is removed, treated, and then returned to the patient. Like IVIG, plasmapheresis carries some dangers, and is expensive and invasive. As with IVIG, NIMH researchers warn against using this treatment outside of a research setting.[19]

Some physicians have also induced immunosuppression with steroids, such as Prednisone, to treat PANDAS. This has not been tested in clinical trials. Prednisone and similar drugs can have serious side effects, and deliberately suppressing the immune system can make a person's system vulnerable to infection. This treatment is not recommended. Steroids have also been implicated in worsening tics.[20]

In sum, there are currently no proven, accepted treatments for PANDAS-linked TS outside of clinical trials. This situation may change soon. In the meantime, persons who fit the criteria for PANDAS should contact a TS specialty clinic or NIMH for information about clinical trials and the latest treatment recommendations.

Medications for related conditions

OCD, ADHD, and anxiety disorders are common companions of Tourette's syndrome. If you choose to take medication for one of these conditions in addition to TS medication, make sure you and your doctor are aware of the potential for interactions and increased side effects.

If you have epilepsy or bipolar disorder in addition to TS, it's best to work closely with an expert in psychopharmacology, the management of psychiatric medications. There is a high possibility of interactions between TS medications and anti-epileptic drugs or mood stabilizers, and these conditions add complexity to the course of Tourette's syndrome.[21]

Medications for OCD

The drugs prescribed for OCD are all slightly different from each other, although all of them are also used to treat clinical depression. They include Anafranil, which is in a family of medications called the tricyclic antidepressants; as well as the entire drug family known as the selective serotonin reuptake inhibitors (SSRIs). The SSRIs include Celexa, Luvox, Paxil, Prozac, and Zoloft.

Some people find that their OCD symptoms remit when they take the medication Effexor (see the section "Medications for anxiety," later in this chapter), which doctors usually prescribe for anxiety. Effexor actually has a very similar chemical profile to Anafranil, but no hard data is available about its usefulness for OCD.

Anafranil was the first medication approved specifically to treat OCD. It reduces obsessions and compulsions by blocking the reuptake of the neurotransmitters norepinephrine and serotonin, and works against the hormone acetylcholine. Today Anafranil is rarely the first choice for treating OCD, particularly for children, because it carries a higher risk of side effects than the SSRIs. However, it is highly effective for many patients, and still in wide use. None of the other tricyclic antidepressants are FDA-approved for use against OCD, but they are occasionally effective for patients who have not responded well to other choices.

While the SSRIs all inhibit the reuptake (absorption) of serotonin at certain nerve terminals, each member of the SSRI family has unique qualities and actions. For example, Celexa, Paxil, and Luvox tend to be sedating, while Prozac and Zoloft tend to be energizing. For this reason, doctors may want to try Celexa, Paxil, or Luvox for a person who has OCD and anxiety or hyperactivity, while indicating Prozac or Zoloft for a person with OCD and depression or fatigue. These qualities can be particularly important to remember when the SSRIs are combined with other medications. For instance, combining a sedating SSRI with a neuroleptic can sometimes produce an exponential increase in sedation.

Medications frequently used to treat OCD include the following.

Anafranil

Generic name: Clomipramine hydrochloride

Use: OCD and obsessive-compulsive behavior, depression, panic disorder, chronic pain, eating disorders, severe PMS. Anafranil is sometimes prescribed to treat herpes lesions or arthritis, indicating that it may also have antiviral or anti-inflammatory qualities. It is FDA-approved for use in children with OCD age 10 and older.

Action, if known: Tricyclic antidepressant—Anafranil blocks the reuptake of norepinephrine and serotonin, and works against the hormone acetylcholine. It has weak antihistamine properties.

Side effects: Anafranil can cause sedation, tremor, seizures, dry mouth, light sensitivity, mood swings in people with bipolar disorders, and weight gain. It lowers the seizure threshold, and can cause sexual side effects.

Known interaction hazards: Combining Anafranil with alcohol, MAOI antidepressants, blood pressure medications (including clonidine and guanfacine), or thyroid medication can be dangerous. Estrogen, bicarbonate of soda (as in Alka-Seltzer and other OTC remedies), acetazolamide, procainamide, and quinidine all increase the activity of this drug. Cimetidine, methylphenidate, Thorazine and similar drugs (neuroleptics), oral contraceptives, nicotine (including cigarettes), charcoal tablets, and estrogen may interfere with Anafranil's action in the body.

Tips: Take Anafranil with food if stomach upset occurs. Take the bulk of your dose at bedtime to reduce sedation, if so directed.

Celexa

Generic name: Citalopram

Use: Depression. Some doctors are, however, experimenting with this relatively new (to the US) SSRI as an OCD medication. It is not yet FDA-approved for treating OCD in children, although clinical experience indicates it is effective for some patients.

Action, if known: SSRI—Celexa increases the amount of active serotonin in the brain. It usually has a calming and/or sedating effect.

Side effects: Celexa can cause dry mouth, insomnia or restless sleep, increased sweating, or nausea. It is reportedly less likely to cause sexual dysfunction than other SSRIs. Celexa lowers the seizure threshold, and can cause mood swings in people with bi-polar disorders.

Known interaction hazards: Celexa and alcohol can be a dangerous combo. Celexa should never be taken with an MAOI antidepressant, or soon after stopping an MAOI. Use Celexa with caution if you take a drug that affects the liver, such as ketoconazole, or the macrolides.

Tips: People with liver or kidney disease need regular monitoring while taking Celexa.

Luvox

Generic name: Fluvoxamine maleate

Use: OCD, social phobia, depression. Luvox is FDA-approved for use by children with OCD age 8 and older.

Action, if known: SSRI—Luvox increases the amount of active serotonin in the brain. It usually has a calming and/or sedating effect.

Side effects: Luvox can cause headache, insomnia, sleepiness, nervousness, nausea, dry mouth, diarrhea or constipation, or sexual dysfunction. It lowers the seizure threshold, and can cause mood swings in people with bipolar disorders.

Known interaction hazards: Never take Luvox with an MAOI antidepressant, or soon after stopping a MAOI. Luvox's action is strengthened by tricyclic antidepressants and lithium. It can strengthen the action of many medications, including clozapine, diltiazem, methadone, some beta-blockers and antihistamines, Haldol and other neuroleptics.

Tips: Avoid taking this drug if you have liver disease. Smoking cigarettes may make it less effective. Luvox does not bind to protein in the body, unlike the other SSRIs, and may have a very different effect in some people.

Paxil, Seroxat

Generic name: Paroxetine hydrochloride

Use: OCD, panic disorder, social phobia, depression. Paxil is not yet FDA-approved for use by children with OCD, although clinical experience indicates it is effective for adult patients.

Action, if known: SSRI—Paxil increases the amount of active serotonin in the brain. It usually has a calming and/or sedating effect.

Side effects: Paxil can cause headache, insomnia or restless sleep, dizziness, tremor, nausea, weakness, sexual dysfunction, or dry mouth. It lowers the seizure threshold, and can cause mood swings in people with bipolar disorders.

Known interaction hazards: Paxil should not be taken with alcohol. Never take it with an MAOI antidepressant, or soon after stopping an MAOI. Paxil strengthens the action of warfarin, theophylline, and procyclidine. It also changes how digoxin and phenytoin act in the body.

Tips: People with liver or kidney disease should be monitored regularly while taking Paxil. This medication has a short life in the body, so missed doses may be more likely to cause side effects.

Prozac

Generic name: Fluoxetine hydrochloride

Use: OCD, depression. Prozac is also sometimes used to treat eating disorders, ADHD, narcolepsy, migraine/chronic headache, Tourette's syndrome, and social phobia. Prozac is not yet FDA-approved for use by children with OCD, although studies indicate that it is effective.

Action, if known: SSRI—Prozac increases the amount of active serotonin in the brain. It may have an energizing effect.

Side effects: Prozac can cause headache, insomnia or restless sleep, dizziness, tremor, nausea, weakness, sexual dysfunction, dry mouth, itchy skin and/or rash. It may cause changes in appetite and weight. Prozac lowers the seizure threshold, and can cause mood swings, especially manic episodes, in people with bipolar disorders.

Known interaction hazards: Prozac should not be taken with alcohol or other central nervous system depressants. Never take this drug with an MAOI antidepressant, or soon after stopping an MAOI. Do not take OTC or prescription cold or allergy remedies containing cyproheptadine or dextromethorphan with Prozac. This drug's action is increased by tricyclic antidepressants. It strengthens the action of lithium, phenytoin, neuroleptic drugs, carbamazepine, and cyclosporine. It reduces the effectiveness of BuSpar.

Tips: Prozac has a long life in your body. People with liver or kidney disease should be monitored while taking Prozac.

Zoloft

Generic name: Sertraline hydrochloride

Use: OCD, panic disorder, depression. Zoloft is FDA-approved for use by children with OCD.

Action, if known: SSRI—Zoloft increases the amount of active serotonin in the brain. It has an energizing quality.

Side effects: Zoloft can cause dry mouth, headache, tremor, diarrhea, nausea, or sexual dysfunction. It may cause mood swings, especially manic episodes, in people with bipolar disorders. It lowers the seizure threshold.

Known interaction hazards: Zoloft should not be taken with alcohol or any other central nervous system depressant. Never take this drug with an MAOI antidepressant, or soon after stopping an MAOI. Zoloft strengthens the action of benzodiazepine drugs and warfarin. Its action is strengthened by cimetidine. It may affect the therapeutic level of lithium.

Tips: People with liver or kidney disease need careful monitoring while taking Zoloft.

If none of these medications works, either alone or in combination with others, doctors may look for an alternative reason for the person's obsessive-compulsive symptoms: an autistic spectrum disorder, a genetic disorder, head trauma, or an infectious cause, such as PANDAS. The presence of one of these conditions could suggest a different course of treatment.

If none of these approaches works, there may be other alternatives. A very few patients with severe OCD have found relief by undergoing brain surgery. One technique that has shown some promise recently involves microsurgery to destroy tissue in the orbitofrontal cortex of the brain. For obvious reasons, brain surgery is reserved for extreme cases that do not respond to any other type of medical or therapeutic treatment.[22]

A new treatment, transcranial magnetic stimulation (TMS), is currently being tested. Although it is not yet commercially available, patients might be able to access this treatment by signing up for a research study.

Electroconvulsive therapy (also known as ECT or electroshock therapy) is not recommended for treatment-resistant OCD, although it is sometimes very effective for treatment-resistant depression.

Medications for ADHD

Many people feel that stimulant medications for ADHD are overused in the US, while doctors say that some patients who could benefit from ADHD medication don't receive it.[23] Some people also worry about the long-term effects of drugs like Ritalin, and about dangers associated with their use, including the possibility that stimulants can cause tics.

For almost 80 years, doctors have used stimulant medications to treat ADHD-like symptoms in both children and adults. They are safe and effective for many people who have serious attention problems.[24] However, medication is not a cure for ADHD, and it is not safe and effective for all people.

Medication should be only part of a treatment plan for ADHD—unfortunately, for many children it is the entire treatment plan. It's no substitute for special education services and one-on-one work on skill development. The best outcomes for kids with ADHD are seen when both medication and adjustments to the child's environment are made.[25] Useful adjustments include setting up and using organization systems for schoolwork, adjusting homework assignments and work periods to better fit the child's attention span, and identifying and using the child's most effective learning skills.

Sandi says 14-year-old Brian responds well to organizational and motivational strategies:

> You need to attack these things both behaviorally and medically. One of the problems I've identified with Brian is that he can't break down tasks into different steps. So if I tell him to clean his room, it is overwhelming and he can't get it done. But, if I tell him to make his bed; then tell him to put his dirty clothes in the hamper; and then tell him to put his Nintendo games away, his room eventually will get clean.
>
> If I tell him to do his homework, I experience the same thing. But if I tell him to open his science book then, he will do his science homework. Then I need to tell him to open his math book. These things seem elementary, but they aren't to our kids.
>
> I've taught him to put all of the things he needs to bring home in a special folder. If I ask him if he has anything for me, the answer is usually "no." But if I ask for the folder, then invariably there is something in there. So, now when he gets home, I tell him to take everything out of his backpack and put the books in a pile. Start with the top book and put it

back into the backpack. Eventually, he comes to the folder of stuff for mom, and then actually gives it to me.

One other issue is the stuff he doesn't tell me or waits to the last minute for—for this, he suffers the consequences. I am not going out at 11 P.M. to buy poster board or a belt or anything else.

Stimulants affect the level of dopamine available at synapses. Ritalin and Dexedrine block dopamine reuptake, as well as affecting some enzymes in the synapse that work against dopamine. Other stimulants simply cause neurons to release dopamine directly. Stimulants are also believed to increase how much norepinephrine is released from the sympathetic nervous system, and to inhibit this neurotransmitter's reuptake by the caudate nucleus. In addition, these drugs increase the flow of blood to all parts of the brain.

Stimulants all work similarly, but for different lengths of time, and with varying danger of the dreaded "rebound effect." This phenomenon's symptoms range from mania-like euphoria to depression or aggression. You can address the rebound effect by careful dosing. Ritalin is the shortest-acting stimulant, and therefore the one with which the greatest amount of rebound trouble occurs. Doctors often prescribe Ritalin doses at two-and-a-half to three-hour intervals, with half of a regular dose at bedtime to permit better sleep. A sustained-release version of Ritalin (Ritalin SR) is available, but gets low marks from patients when used alone. A new longer-acting version of Ritalin, Concerta, was developed specifically to avoid both rebound and daytime dosing. Dexedrine has a longer life (four to six hours), and the Dexedrine Spansule formulation can maintain its beneficial effects for up to eight hours. Adderall combines several different stimulants, which tends to create a smoother effect.

Stimulants and tics

If you've followed the controversy around the use of Ritalin as a treatment for ADHD, you may have heard that stimulants "cause" Tourette's syndrome in children. Repeated studies have shown that this is not the case, although stimulants can sometimes make tics worse or more frequent, and may therefore make an underlying tic disorder more obvious.[26] However, there are people who find that taking stimulants actually reduces their tics. For most people, it has no effect.

Some people with TS report that taking Ritalin increases their level of aggression and can cause mania-like behavior. Researchers have recently noted that stimulant medications can have this effect for some persons with bipolar disorders, which can either coexist with or be mistaken for ADHD in children.[27] You may want to avoid these if you or your child experiences this kind of reaction to stimulants, or if you have a strong family history of bipolar disorders.

Brenda, grandmother of Charisse, tells about their unpleasant experience with Ritalin:

> Charisse was far less stable on Ritalin than off. We were actually frightened by her reaction to this medication. Even her teachers noticed her anger, irritability and loss of appetite. She was moody, and had increased sleep problems. It was definitely not helping her in any way.

Jennifer, mother of 12-year-old Ty, reports that Ritalin has been helpful despite side effects:

> Ritalin has been the most useful medication to date. Although it seems to increase his ticcing, it helps him concentrate. It is the one that we have gone back to every time after trying a new medication. He had no noticeable difference with Cylert, Adderall, Catapres, or Cylexa. Provigil caused hallucinations and goofy behavior, but no noticeable improvements whatsoever in actions or academics.

Stimulants do not increase ticcing for some people with TS, but they do for others. Work closely with your doctor when first trying a stimulant to ensure safety and achieve the best results.

Stimulant medications used to treat ADHD follow.

Adderall

Generic name: Dextroamphetamine/amphetamine

Use: ADHD.

Action, if known: Central nervous system (CNS) stimulant

Side effects: Adderall can cause loss of appetite, weight loss, headache, insomnia, dizziness, increased heart rate, and agitation. It may increase tic severity in people with an underlying tic disorder.

Known interaction hazards: Vitamin C supplements, citrus juices, citric acid, more than four cans per day of soda pop, or taking this medication with food can reduce its effectiveness.

Tips: Make sure you drink plenty of water while taking Adderall, even if you're not thirsty. Adderall is not as well known as Ritalin, but it may be a better choice for many patients. It time-releases different amphetamine compounds smoothly over several hours, resulting in a lower chance of rebound.

Concerta

Generic name: Methylphenidate

Use: ADHD

Action, if known: CNS stimulant

Side effects: See listing for Ritalin.

Known interaction hazards: See listing for Ritalin.

Tips: Concerta is a time-release version of Ritalin. It provides smooth delivery of medication throughout the day with a single morning dose, eliminating the need for taking medication at school or work, and potentially eliminating rebound effects.

Cylert

Generic name: Pemoline

Use: ADHD, narcolepsy

Action, if known: CNS stimulant

Side effects: Cylert can cause irritability, insomnia, appetite changes, or depression. It lowers the seizure threshold.

Known interaction hazards: Cylert strengthens the action of other CNS stimulants. It may increase tic severity in people with an underlying tic disorder. Vitamin C supplements, citrus juices, citric acid, drinking more than four cans per day of soda pop, or taking this medication with food can reduce its effectiveness.

Tips: You will need to have liver enzyme tests frequently while taking Cylert—those with known liver problems may need to avoid this medication. It is not recommended for people with psychosis. You can take Cylert with food if stomach upset occurs, but the dose may need to be adjusted. Make sure you drink plenty of water, even if you're not thirsty. Cylert has a long action period, but because of the potential for liver problems and other complications it is rarely used unless all of the other ADHD medications have failed to have positive effects and behavioral strategies are ineffective.

Dexedrine, Dexedrine Spansules, Das, Dexampex, Dextrostat, Ferndex, Oxydess

Generic name: Dextroamphetamine sulfate

Use: ADHD

Action, if known: CNS stimulant

Side effects: Dexedrine can cause agitation, restlessness, aggressive behavior, dizziness, insomnia, headache, tremor, dry mouth, change in appetite, or weight loss. It may raise blood pressure. It may increase tic severity in people with an underlying tic disorder.

Known interaction hazards: Do not use Dexedrine with MAOI antidepressants. It interacts with tricyclic antidepressants, meperidine, phenobarbital, phenytoin, propoxyphene, acetazolamide, thiazides, and some medications for stomach distress. Vitamin C supplements, citrus juices, citric acid, drinking more than four cans per day of soda pop, or taking this medication with food can reduce its effectiveness.

Tips: If you are diabetic, discuss your use of insulin and oral anti-diabetes drugs with your doctor, as Dexedrine may force a change in dosage. It is not recommended for people with psychosis. Make sure you drink plenty of water, even if you're not thirsty, while taking this medication.

Desoxyn

Generic name: Methamphetamine, MTH

Use: ADHD, narcolepsy

Action, if known: CNS stimulant

Side effects: Desoxyn can cause agitation, restlessness, aggressive behavior, dizziness, insomnia, headache, or tremor. It may raise your blood pressure. It may increase tic severity in people with an underlying tic disorder.

Known interaction hazards: Never use Desoxyn with an MAOI antidepressant. Its effects may be counteracted by barbiturates, tranquilizers (including OTC sleep aids), and tricyclic antidepressants. Desoxyn may strengthen the action of other CNS stimulants, including caffeine and OTC cold and allergy medications. Its action is strengthened by cetazolamide and sodium bicarbonate (found in Alka-Seltzer and similar over-the-counter remedies), and it may interact with some medications for gastrointestinal problems. Vitamin C supplements, citrus juices, citric acid, drinking more than four cans per day of soda pop, or taking this medication with food can reduce its effectiveness.

Tips: This is the most powerful and potentially addictive of the stimulants, and is well known as a drug of abuse. For these reasons, Desoxyn is rarely prescribed for ADHD in the US. If you are diabetic, discuss your use of insulin and oral anti-diabetes drugs with your doctor, as Desoxyn may force a change in dosage. It is not recommended for people with psychosis. Make sure you drink plenty of water, even if you're not thirsty, while taking this medication.

Provigil

Generic name: Modafinil

Use: ADHD, narcolepsy. Approved for narcolepsy only in the US.

Action, if known: CNS stimulant

Side effects: Provigil can cause agitation, restlessness, aggressive behavior, dizziness, nausea, or insomnia. It may raise your blood pressure. Some people experience more infectious illnesses when taking this drug.

Known interaction hazards: Never use Provigil with an MAOI antidepressant. Its effects may be counteracted by barbiturates, tranquilizers (including OTC sleep aids), and tricyclic antidepressants. Provigil may strengthen the action of other CNS stimulants, including caffeine and OTC cold and allergy medications.

Tips: This medication is not recommended for people with psychosis.

Ritalin

Generic name: Methylphenidate hydrochloride

Use: ADHD, narcolepsy, social phobia

Action, if known: CNS stimulant

Side effects: Ritalin can cause agitation, restlessness, aggressive behavior, dizziness, insomnia, headache, tremor, or loss of appetite and/or weight. It may raise your blood pressure. It may increase tic severity in people with an underlying tic disorder.

Known interaction hazards: Ritalin should not be taken with alcohol. Its action is strengthened by MAOI antidepressants to a high degree. It strengthens the action of tricyclic antidepressants, and reduces the action of guanethidine. Vitamin C supplements, citrus juices, citric acid, drinking more than four cans per day of soda pop, or taking this medication with food can reduce its effectiveness.

Tips: The rebound effect can be bad with Ritalin, which has the shortest life of the stimulants commonly used for ADHD. Some doctors combine Ritalin SR with regular Ritalin for the smoothest effect (SR's action is said to be erratic). Make sure you drink plenty of water, even if you're not thirsty. Some people, including quite a few doctors, swear that the brand name Ritalin is superior to its generic counterpart. It may be worth trying the brand-name version if the generic didn't work well. See also listing for Concerta, above.

Non-stimulant medications for ADHD

Clonidine (Catapres) and guanfacine (Tenex) are medications originally developed to reduce blood pressure in persons with hypertension, but they also appear to reduce both hyperactivity and tics in some persons. They have become an important alternative to stimulants for people who have both TS and ADHD, or who have ADHD and a family history of tic disorders. See the section "Clonidine and guanfacine," earlier in this chapter, for more detailed information about these medications.

A new non-stimulant medication, tomoxetine, is currently being clinically tested for ADHD. Early reports indicate that it is effective and does not cause sleeplessness or other side effects associated with stimulants.[28] At least two other non-stimulant treatments for ADHD were also under development as of spring 2001, and are expected to gain FDA approval by 2002, if clinical trials are successful.[29]

Wellbutrin (buproprion, also sold under the brand name Zyban), normally used to treat depression, is also effective as an ADHD medication for some persons. However, it can lower the seizure threshold, and one study has found that it increased tics in children with both ADHD and TS.[30]

Medications for anxiety

Anxiety is an important component of OCD, and many people with OCD also suffer from other anxiety disorders, such as panic attacks. An SSRI can often relieve these symptoms, but in more severe cases you may be prescribed an anti-anxiety medication (tranquilizer). Some people with TS but not OCD also have one of these anxiety disorders.

Depending on your needs and your doctor's advice, these medications may be taken daily or on an "as-needed" basis. Often, they are prescribed as a temporary measure only. These medications may be prescribed to you for non-psychiatric conditions as well, including irritable bowel syndrome, seizure disorders, restless leg syndrome, and muscle spasms.

Most of them do have a potential for addiction and abuse, so be careful about their use and storage. Some are not FDA-approved for use by children, and speaking generally, their use should be avoided unless other strategies for reducing your anxiety level are ineffective.

Anti-anxiety medications include:

Ativan	lorazepam	Serax	oxazepam
BuSpar	buspirone	Tranxene	clorazepate
Centrax	prazepam	Valium	diazepam
Klonopin	clonazepam	Xanax	alprazolam
Librium	chlordiazepoxide		

Most of the medications on this list do much more than reducing anxiety. They tend to be sedating, and can cause a myriad of unpleasant side effects, including a disoriented feeling, blurred vision, confusion, and tremor. When added to other medications that also cause sedation, dangerous levels of physical and mental slowing can be experienced if dosages of both drugs are not carefully adjusted.

Treatment for self-injurious tics and behaviors

The use of medication as a primary treatment for self-injurious tics or behavior is problematic. Most of the time, the medication chosen is a neuroleptic, often at high doses that can cause serious side effects.[31] If the action is a tic, a short course of medication may be helpful, but if the action is carried out on purpose or as a physical compulsion, it may not. In fact, neuroleptics sometimes increase compulsive behavior.

Opiate blockers, notably naltrexone (ReVia) can successfully blunt self-injurious behaviors in some people. Most of the research has been done on persons with autism and/or mental retardation.[32] Autism may include disruptions to the body's own opiate system, so this intervention might make sense in that specific population. It seems less likely to be effective for persons with TS only.

OCD medications are also effective for many persons with compulsive self-injury.[33] Interpersonal therapy, anxiety reduction, functional behavior analysis followed by behavior modification techniques, increased supervision, and possibly hospitalization for the patient's own safety are also used.

Although rarely used in the developed world anymore, binding techniques have historically been tried to temporarily prevent self-injury from, for example, a tic that involves flailing arms or punching oneself. An adult might choose to use this method under medical supervision, but ethical considerations could prevent using it for a child.

You can also use protective equipment to prevent injury from self-injurious tics or behavior. Special helmets are available that prevent injury from head-banging, for example, and gloves may be worn to circumvent skin-picking or scratching.

One of the most common compulsive behaviors is fingernail-biting and picking at the skin surrounding the fingernails or toenails, which is seen in many people who don't have TS or OCD. Nasty-tasting solutions that can be painted onto the nails are available over-the-counter at drugstores, but are not always effective in stopping this compulsive behavior. Some people with compulsive nail-biting have opted to have artificial nails applied. Biting these doesn't seem to produce the same effect as chewing on your natural nails, which may help you eventually end the habit. Artificial nails can be shaped in short styles for men as well as in various styles for women.

Tooth-grinding (bruxism) can be either a compulsive behavior or a side effect of some medications used to treat OCD or TS. It can cause serious damage to the teeth, as well as jaw pain. If it's a problem for you or your child, talk to your dentist: it's actually a fairly common issue, for a variety of reasons. He can fit you with a custom-made bite guard to wear at night, which is when this most commonly occurs. Over-the-counter bite guards are also available, and some people find them satisfactory even though the fit will not be as exact. These can usually be found in tooth-whitening kits.

If self-injurious behavior involves the use of objects, such as knives, obviously these items should be kept out of reach. Some parents have chosen to install a lock on a drawer where necessary sharp objects like kitchen knives can be stored, and to remove burn hazards.

Medication interactions

The practice of taking more than one medication to treat the same health condition is known as polypharmacy. Done with careful supervision and adequate professional knowledge, it can help people with even the most complex medical problems. Done haphazardly, it can be dangerous.

There are additional concerns when a person needs to take multiple drugs for different conditions. It doesn't really matter whether the additional medications you take are for a secondary psychiatric condition like OCD, or for another health problem like diabetes, rheumatoid arthritis, or HIV infection. Mixing medications requires careful attention to detail, and this is difficult when medications for TS are prescribed and managed by a psychiatrist while medications for another problem are prescribed and managed by your regular doctor or a second specialist.

Lee, mother of 13-year-old Joseph, has long-term experience with managing multiple prescriptions for multiple conditions. Joseph has OCD, ADHD, and Asperger's syndrome (a mild form of autism) in addition to TS, and also has PANDAS-like immune-system problems that exacerbate his difficulties:

> Paxil, clonidine, Adderall, and Neurontin seem to work well for him at this point. Ritalin made his heart skip beats, and Dexedrine gave him full-body tics. Depakote seemed to totally disinhibit him, and he sure seemed manic on it to me. Risperdal gave him the "rages from nowhere," and seemed to exacerbate his OCD. He also hated Risperdal and Depakote because they made his thinking cloudy. He had a reaction to lithium where he looked palsied.

Be sure to tell your doctor about any non-prescription drugs you take. Over-the-counter remedies are among the top reasons for medication failure and medication problems, and are often overlooked. Most people think of items like cough syrup, aspirin, ibuprofen, and Alka-Seltzer as benign, but as a glance at the drug listings earlier in this chapter shows, many of them can counteract or strengthen prescription drugs. Some interactions are potentially very dangerous: for example, taking cold remedies that contain non-prescription stimulants with your prescription stimulants could cause a racing heartbeat, or even a heart attack.

Anyone who needs to take a regular, maintenance medication for a chronic condition like Tourette's syndrome should ask their doctor and pharmacist for a list of over-the-counter remedies that are safe to take with that medication.

Interactions between drugs and herbal or vitamin supplements are also an increasingly common problem. St. John's Wort, a popular herbal remedy for mild depression, was recently found to interact with protease inhibitors prescribed to treat AIDS, and is believed to affect the potency of many other drugs, including anticancer agents and birth control pills.[34] St. John's Wort and the supplement SAM-e definitely affect the serotonin system, and therefore should not be taken with other drugs that do, including most medications for OCD and some for TS.

Even items in your refrigerator can interact with your medicine. Grapefruit juice, for example, prevents the breakdown of certain medications, while some can't be taken with any citrus juice or with soda pop. Taking other drugs with food can help or hinder their absorption.

Two types of interactions deserve special mention, because they involve drugs more likely to be taken by people with TS. Serotonin syndrome, described in the section "Major side effects" later in this chapter, is potentially deadly. The other hazard involves mixing any medication with one of the monoamineoxidase inhibitors (MAOIs), such as Aurorex, Parnate, or Nardil. These older antidepressants, which inhibit the body from metabolizing the neurotransmitters serotonin, norepinephrine, and dopamine, are not prescribed very often anymore. They have unpleasant and even life-threatening interactions with many other drugs, including common over-the-counter medications. People taking MAOIs must also follow a special diet, because these medications interact with natural compounds found in many foods. The list of proscribed foods includes chocolate, aged cheeses, beer, and more. If you or your child must take a MAOI, check for warning labels on all medications and foods, and familiarize yourself thoroughly with the dietary restrictions.

Medication side effects

The same dose of a medication can cause terrible side effects in one person, and none at all in another. The difference isn't in the drug itself, but in subtle differences in body chemistry.

Most of these are probably genetically based, but there are only tests for a very few of the differences that have been identified. For example, one study found that between 5 and 8 percent of Caucasians produce abnormally low levels of an enzyme that's needed to flush common anti-depressant and blood-pressure medications out of the body safely.[35] These people either can't take these drugs safely, or can take only tiny doses. On the other hand, fully one-third of persons of Somali descent were found to have a genetic difference that prevents them from benefiting from all but the highest doses of these same drugs.[36]

The emerging science of figuring out who can and can't take certain medications is known as pharmacogenomics, and it's still in its infancy. Until reliable tests have been developed—and until some of the issues surrounding confidentiality of genetic information have been addressed—most people will continue to find out about drug side effects the hard way.

Certain side effects are associated with psychiatric drugs, including those used to treat TS. You may experience none, one or two minor problems, or even one or more serious side effects. The best way to avoid side effects is to work with a physician who believes in careful, gradual titration of medications, and who watches out for interactions with other drugs.

When taking a new medication, pay extra attention to how you feel, and report anything unusual to your doctor.

Minor side effects

Although some people call these side effects "minor" because they usually don't endanger health, you may consider them quite major. If these or other side effects really bother you or your child, talk to your doctor to find a solution:

- **Unwanted behavior changes.** Sometimes called behavioral side effects (BSEs), these can include increased hyperactivity and abnormally elevated mood, provocative and uninhibited behavior, and in a few cases aggression. These changes are usually mild, and may fade in time or respond to lowering the dose slightly. They are more common with the SSRIs used to treat OCD than with medications for TS. If behavior changes are more severe or long-lasting, they may signal an underlying tendency toward bipolar disorders (manic depression and related conditions). If so, you may need to stop taking the medication, or your doctor may prescribe a mood stabilizer, such as lithium or Depakote, and add the other medication again later.

- **Dry mouth.** This side effect, caused by decreased saliva production, comes from the secondary action of certain drugs on the neurotransmitter acetylcholine. Usually it's a minor annoyance, but it can contribute to tooth decay, especially in children who wear braces; and it can also exacerbate tooth-grinding. Drinking plenty of water to relieve the dryness, brushing your teeth frequently, and perhaps using a fluoride mouthwash should also help. Sugarless mints or gum sometimes improve comfort by increasing saliva production. In extreme cases, you may want to use nighttime mouth guards to prevent tooth damage from grinding, or a doctor may recommend a special moistening spray, mouthwash, or medication.

- **Nausea.** This side effect results from the action of medications on serotonin receptors in the gastrointestinal tract. It usually goes away after a few weeks. In the meantime, changes in diet and eating small, frequent meals can relieve symptoms. Check with your doctor before using any over-the-counter stomach remedy.

- **Weight gain or loss.** Serotonin is the target of many psychiatric drugs. This neurotransmitter controls the inner feeling of having eaten enough food. People taking drugs that affect serotonin may report increased or decreased appetite, and ensuing weight gain or loss. Weight gain is a frequent problem for people who take neuroleptics, and can also occur with SSRIs. These symptoms are best addressed by dietary changes and, for weight gain, regular exercise. Some clinicians think these drugs may also reset the metabolism, because some patients on controlled diets still gain weight. In these cases, adjustments to dose or adding another medication to treat this side effect may be tried. Stimulants are the most commonly used medications to offset weight gain, although some clinicians report success from using low doses (25 to 50 micrograms per day), of the thyroid hormone Cytomel. Patients with eating disorders need to be especially careful about medications that cause appetite changes, including the SSRIs.

- **Sexual side effects.** Many psychiatric medications tend to dampen sexual impulses and lower responsiveness to sexual stimulation, including the ability to achieve erection or orgasm. Obviously, this is more of a problem for adults, but it's one that parents should consider and discuss with teenagers. Strategies including lowering the medication dose; adding a second medication, such as

Effexor, Wellbutrin, BuSpar, or Edronax, that raises sexual response in some patients; using Viagra; trying herbal remedies that may affect sexual response; or working on sensitization techniques with a professional sex therapist. Ritalin (and presumably other stimulants) may actually increase sexual response for some people.

Major side effects

You should call your physician immediately if you or your child ever experiences seizures, heart palpitations, blood in the urine or stool, or other serious symptoms. If your doctor is not available on short notice, report to an emergency room. These symptoms may be related to medication, or they may signify another health condition that needs attention.

The side effects listed below are signs of serious trouble, and they always warrant immediate medical help:

- **Agranulocytosis.** Agranulocytosis is a severe, potentially fatal loss of white blood cells.

- **Akasthisia.** This is an intense, continual, internal sensation of physical restlessness, "itchiness," and jumpiness—a need to move constantly. A person with akasthisia will look and feel uncomfortable if she tries to be still.

- **Bradyphrenia.** This term denotes slowed thought processes.

- **Dystonia.** Muscle rigidity and uncontrollable muscle spasms are called dystonia. They are associated primarily with the neuroleptics.

- **Encephalopathic syndrome.** The symptoms of encephalopathic syndrome are similar to those of neuroleptic malignant syndrome (see below), of which it may be a variant. It is usually associated with lithium toxicity.

- **Extrapyramidal side effects (EPS).** The physical symptoms of EPS include tremor, slurred speech, akathisia (motor restlessness), dystonia (muscle rigidity), anxiety, distress, paranoia, and bradyphrenia (slowed thought processes). It is associated primarily with the neuroleptics.

- **Hyperkinesia.** This term means excessive motor activity, the physical expression of akisthesia. In children this can mimic common hyperactivity, but the movements may seem both driven and purposeless.

- **Neuroleptic malignant syndrome (NMS).** This potentially fatal condition is characterized by rigid muscle movements, fever, irregular pulse and heartbeat, rapid heartbeat, irregular blood pressure, heavy sweating, and strange states of mind. Discontinue the medication immediately and call your doctor if these symptoms occur. In extreme cases, you may need emergency care at a hospital. Physicians should report episodes of NMS to the Neuroleptic Malignant Syndrome Information Service (*http://www.nmsis.org*), which has set up a registry to help researchers reduce the incidence of this problem. NMS is associated primarily with neuroleptics, although it can also occur with tricyclic antidepressants or other medications.

- **Oculogyric crisis.** A person in the throes of oculogyric crisis has a frozen upward gaze, often a very strange-looking facial expression and eye movements, and has contorted facial and neck muscles.

- **Orthostatic hypotension.** This is dangerously low blood pressure caused by alpha-adrenergic blockade. It is associated primarily with the neuroleptics. Some people who take SSRIs experience dizziness when they stand up suddenly, which is also caused by a drop in blood pressure but is not considered harmful.

- **Parkinsonian symptoms.** These symptoms mimic the neurological disorder Parkinson's disease, hence the name. They include cognitive slowing, muscle and joint stiffness, tremor, and unusually stiff and unstable gait. Associated primarily with the neuroleptics, these symptoms are caused by too little dopamine activity.

- **Seizures.** Some of the medications used to treat TS and associated conditions can lower your susceptibility to seizures. This effect is rarely a problem, but it is something patients and parents should be aware of, especially if there is a family history of seizure disorders. Other than convulsions, which are easy to recognize, mild seizures can mimic fainting spells, dizziness, short-term memory loss, strange sensations, such as feeling as if your mind is detached from your body or feelings of déjà vu, and hearing or seeing things that aren't there.

- **Serotonin syndrome.** When the brain is bombarded with too much serotonin (for example, from combining two antidepressants), a person may experience shivers, headaches, diarrhea, profuse sweating, confusion, and akisthesia. If this happens, stop taking the antidepressant(s) or any other medication that you know affects serotonin immediately, and see your doctor without delay. In extreme cases, serotonin syndrome can be fatal. That's why patients taking prescription antidepressants should not also take "natural" antidepressants, such as St. John's Wort.

- **Tardive dyskinesia (TD).** TD is a drug-induced movement disorder characterized by twisting motions of the hands and feet, and smacking or chewing movements of the mouth. Rippling movements of the tongue muscles are considered an early warning sign. Discontinue the medication immediately and call your doctor if these symptoms occur. Between 10 and 20 percent of long-term users of the older neuroleptic drugs, such as Haldol and Thorazine, eventually develop this disorder.[37] The atypical neuroleptics seem far less likely to cause TD, and those patients who do get TD have usually taken very large doses over many years. A very few cases of TD have been associated with tricyclic antidepressants and some mood stabilizers.

- Some physicians recommend that people who take drugs that carry a risk for tardive dyskinesia also take vitamin E supplements, which appear to stave off the disorder in some people. If TD is caught early, it may reverse itself once the medication is stopped.

- Some people experience TD-like symptoms while discontinuing a neuroleptic drug. These should pass in time.

- For those who are already affected by TD, only one medication is currently known to help: tetrabenazine (see the section "Other medications for TS," earlier in this chapter.)

These are serious and painful side effects, the kind that understandably make people want to stop taking their medicine. Careful medication choices and dosage adjustment should reduce them, and complimentary adjustments to diet, vitamins, supplements, and relaxation techniques may also help.

Joyce, age 53, has had one of the more serious side effects associated with TS medication:

> I had lots of problems with sedation right from the start of taking tetrabenazine, becoming very tired and drowsy. Eventually I developed akasthisia, which really bothered me in late afternoon and evening, to the point where I would be pounding my legs with my fists, trying to make the squirmy, twitchy, nasty feelings stop. I discontinued this drug.

Discontinuing medication

Sometimes a doctor will ask that all medication be withdrawn for a while to give him a baseline look at which symptoms are caused by the disorder and which are caused by medication. If it is not managed well, this process is exceptionally trying. You can stop taking very few medications immediately without causing distress—with some, such as clonidine, stopping cold can even be life-threatening.

Gradually tapering off to a lower dose and then to none is almost always the best approach. Patients should be carefully monitored for signs of trouble. In some cases (such as for discontinuing benzodiazepine tranquilizer use after several years), you may need a hospital setting or extra-careful home supervision during medication withdrawal.

Ask your doctor about symptoms to expect during the withdrawal period. He might be able to recommend over-the-counter or dietary remedies for likely problems, such as diarrhea or nausea. Decide on non-medication strategies for dealing with problems that could occur as drugs are tapered off.

Although the medications used for TS are not addictive in the usual sense, some people do report withdrawal-like symptoms when they stop taking one of these medications. Doctors find that these symptoms may be prevented by increasing the dose of a new medication while tapering off the old one. If your physician approves, you can try over-the-counter remedies for countering symptoms such as nausea or fatigue during medication changes. Unfortunately, sometimes medications do not work again when they are reintroduced.

Hospitals and treatment centers

Tourette's syndrome itself is rarely treated in a hospital, but there are several situations that may cause an adult or child with TS to need hospitalization. Here are some of the possibilities:

- When a person is a danger to himself, either through suicide threats or attempts, or through self-injurious behavior.

- When a person is a danger to others because of aggressive, assaultive behavior or serious threats.

- When a person's medical symptoms and/or behavior cannot be safely managed at home, even with the addition of medication and support services.

- When a person is suffering from severe medication reactions or unusual symptoms that are too difficult medically to handle at home, including status tics (the rare condition of having constant, uncontrollable ticcing).

- When a person with TS complicated by substance abuse needs intense medical supervision during the detox process.

- When a person with TS has another medical problem that requires hospital treatment.

If you or your child has a problem that requires hospitalization, confer with your primary care physician, any specialists involved, and the hospital staff. These experts can ensure that your diagnosis and current medical treatments are thoroughly understood. They can also make sure that any additional needs, such as TS medication management, therapy, and special education services, are met in the hospital.

Lucy's son has needed inpatient care on several occasions. Educating the staff has been the key to a successful experience:

> When Richard was 8, the hospital's doctor didn't believe he had TS. He said neither he nor the staff had seen him tic. However, he pointed out, Richard did have this funny habit of jumping up every few minutes and running to his room. I asked him if anyone had ever followed my son, or had asked him why he did this. No, he replied. So I asked Richard. He was going to his room to tic in private, because he didn't want all those people to see him tic!
>
> I got him out of that hospital, got him to a doctor who specialized in TS within a matter of days, and got the diagnosis in writing.
>
> Even today, at age 13, when all the medical personnel KNOW he has TS, they still don't necessarily know a tic when they see (or hear) one. Just yesterday he lost a point on his contract at the hospital for "making noises" during the school session. Needless to say, the noises were a long-standing tic that the staff thought he was doing on purpose.

Make sure that your TS medications are listed on your chart if you are entering the hospital for surgery. Neuroleptics affect what kind of anesthesia should be chosen, and you may have to discontinue clonidine or guanfacine a few hours before your surgery because of their effect on blood pressure.

If you or your child is injured due to a suicide attempt, self-injurious behavior, self-injurious ticcing, or a drug overdose, go directly to the nearest emergency room. Call your primary care physician and/or psychiatrist to let him know what's going on. ER workers are sometimes not familiar with TS symptoms, and may need help to understand about tics. The presence of a physician, friend, or parent who can advocate for proper care should help.

You may have to wait a long time to see someone in the ER, especially if it's a busy weekend night or most personnel are attending to life-or-death emergencies. Probably the first person you'll see is an intake worker, who will get your health insurance information and other basic details.

After admission to the ER, you should next see a triage nurse, who's specially trained to assess your situation. Let this person know what your greatest concerns are, especially if you feel you or your child could be in danger or a danger to others. When you go to the ER, bring any medications, supplements, and herbal remedies that you or your child uses. If you have used or suspect that your child has recently used, any illegal drugs or alcohol, let the emergency room personnel know right away. These things affect what medical intervention they can safely use. You may also want to bring a book that you or your child enjoys, a Walkman with tapes of soothing music, toys, and a change of clothes in case of overnight admission. If there's no time to collect these items, don't worry—you can have someone else deliver them to you later at the hospital when the situation stabilizes.

Once you or your child has been admitted to the ER, you'll see a doctor and/or nurses. They may check blood pressure and heartbeat; take blood or urine samples to test for drugs, alcohol, infection, or medication blood levels; and give emergency medical treatment, including drugs. Make sure you understand the effects of any medications you are given, especially if you or your child will be released immediately after treatment rather than being held for observation. There may be some delay in getting needed medications for your child. If you have brought emergency medications for your child, ask if they may be used while you wait for help.

For mental health crises that do not involve an immediate risk to life, it helps to have a plan worked out in advance. The best place to start is, of course, the doctor who provides your TS-related healthcare. If you haven't already set up a plan, call your doctor and ask for an emergency evaluation. If it is after hours or your doctor is unavailable, call your primary care provider, general practitioner, or HMO and ask for an immediate referral. In some cases you may need to go to the ER for safety's sake until a doctor can arrive.

If you reach your doctor, he should ask you to come in immediately if the situation warrants it. If you think you'll need help getting to his office, say so—he may be able to send a mental health aide or other staff member to your assistance. If this kind of help is not available through his office, ask your spouse, other relatives, friends, neighbors, or even the police for help. In some areas, your county or provincial mental health department may be able to send someone out. If your child is physically difficult to control or at risk for self-harm, the momentary embarrassment you may feel from asking for help will rapidly be overshadowed by the need to ensure her safety.

Some larger cities have a separate "ER alternative" for mental health emergencies, known as a mental health triage center. In these centers, trained personnel are on staff 24 hours a day to deal with crisis situations. Psychiatrists, appropriate medications, and security measures are on hand to meet your needs. Whenever possible, the environment is carefully constructed to be as peaceful, quiet and non-threatening as possible. There may be a play area for younger children.

Usually a triage specialist will meet with you within just a few minutes. As in the ER, the triage nurse will assess you or your child's condition and start the process of obtaining treatment. Vital signs checks, blood and urine samples, and interviews with patients are often performed quickly. She may also interview you and/or your child.

Whether you go to your psychiatrist's office, the ER, or a mental health triage center, the criteria for hospital admission will be largely the same. If you or your child can be stabilized right there, you may be sent home with medications and care instructions. Alternatively, you or your child may be held for overnight observation, or admitted for short- or long-term treatment.

People with HMOs or managed care plans may be required to jump through some hoops before admission is approved. Many people have reported that it's extremely hard to get a family member admitted even when he is a suicide risk or when the family is in danger from his violent actions. Others note that some facilities release patients far too early, often due less to positive treatment outcomes than to negative news from the person's insurance company. Your doctor is your most important ally when you need admission or a longer stay.

Psychiatric facilities

There are many different types of hospital settings for psychiatric care. Most are a special psychiatric wing within a local hospital. Mental health units are usually locked wards, to both protect the patients themselves and to prevent escape. They are designed mostly for short-term care, holding persons for observation for a few days or weeks.

People in need of long-term hospitalization are usually sent to a standalone mental facility. Choices include private facilities, therapeutic residential care facilities that specialize in treating mentally ill or emotionally disturbed youth or adults, and public mental hospitals. Generally speaking, public mental hospitals in the US get only the most difficult-to-treat cases, along with uninsured patients. This is not necessarily the case elsewhere in the world, where publicly funded mental health care may be available to all citizens.

The type of facility matters far less than the appropriateness of its program. Facilities for children and teens need to have a strong education program to prevent patients from slipping too far behind in school. All staff members should be medically savvy, knowledgeable about the latest advances in treatment, and have therapy options that are appropriate for each person's age and needs. For example, facilities that accept very young children should have play therapists on staff, and programs for teens and adults should have considerable resources for treating drug and alcohol addiction when it occurs along with psychiatric problems. They should be ready and willing to work closely with family members and other outside helpers. Cleanliness and basic safety are important issues too, as are human decency and kindness.

A lot of the time you have to go with your gut instinct. If the staff members you meet appear to be well trained, competent, and gentle with the people in their care, that's a good sign, as is the presence of a sense of humor.

If you have time, talk to your local TSA chapter, another TS advocacy group, or a nearby NAMI chapter to get other people's opinions about facilities you are considering. If you or your child is difficult to treat with the usual medications and therapies, you may want to consider a research-oriented hospital, up to and including the special facilities available at the National Institutes of Health in Bethesda, Maryland.

When you or your child are in a high-quality hospital or residential care facility, you should feel reasonably comfortable with the care and the environment.

Children's psychiatric facilities

Tourette's syndrome rarely requires hospital treatment, but sometimes a child with TS will need inpatient care due to severe symptoms or other psychiatric conditions. Many children's psychiatric units have very strict regulations about appearance, smoking, language, and activities. Teens are very likely to resent being told that they can't wear their favorite heavy metal T-shirt, or that they must hand over jewelry upon admittance. Let them know that these appearance issues are the hospital's rules, not yours, and that they're usually there to protect more sensitive patients from being offended or harmed.

Ask about consequences for breaking the rules. Punitive enforcement is not a good thing. Many hospitals use a token economy or level system to reinforce positive behavior on the ward. As noted in Chapter 4, *Growing Up with Tourette's Syndrome,* this form of behavior modification is often ineffective with kids who have TS, as are behavior contracts.

When your child is first admitted to a hospital or residential program, you may not be able to see her for a period of time, possibly based on her behavior on the ward. You should be able to meet with the staff during this period, however, and start planning her treatment and after-care program. Once you do get to visit, be prepared for some ugly words, especially if she was admitted against her will. Anxiety and fear may cause oppositional behavior. This seems to be a part of the adjustment process, and it should pass.

Alternatively, you may be shocked to see your child looking "drugged up." Be sure that you discuss your concerns with the staff, and that any medications given are to treat the condition, not to simply control your child's behavior. If your child still seems to be in a haze after the first few days, overmedication is a possibility, and should be addressed. Ask what medications are being used and at what doses. You can talk to your child's regular psychiatrist about the medications and about what you have seen at the hospital.

If your child is in the hospital for a long time or has been admitted before, she will probably adjust to the routine quite well. You may even find that your visits are less of a special treat than they were at first, as your child eagerly waits to go back to playing or chatting with the other kids on the ward. This can be disconcerting for parents, but be assured that regular visits from you are essential to your child's well being, even if she doesn't act like it.

One thing that usually isn't a great idea is visits from your child's friends. Most mental-health facilities do not allow these for underage patients, but if your child's does, make sure they are supervised and that you have control over which friends are allowed in. Supportive friends are wonderful, but friends who encourage your child to blame you for his problems, leave the facility, or refuse medication are not. "Friends" who try to sneak in drugs or alcohol for your child are even worse. If you suspect this may be happening, contact the staff immediately.

Your child may be disturbed or frightened by the behavior of some other patients. Most children's psychiatric facilities care for people with a wide variety of conditions, ranging from eating disorders to schizophrenia to neurological problems, such as Tourette's syndrome. He will see some children who are very, very ill, and others who are well on their way to recovery. When you visit, talk to your child about anything he may have seen or heard that bothers him. He may feel uncomfortable bringing up these concerns in group or individual therapy sessions. Information about other mental illnesses or neurological disorders should be able to help him better understand what his fellow patients may be experiencing.

Be sure to share information about echopraxia with the unit's staff if you get reports about your child copying the behaviors of other patients.

A good hospital is probably the safest possible place for you or your child to be while in a mental or medical health crisis. Medication reactions can be carefully observed, therapy can be delivered on a daily basis, and professionals can help families rally around a treatment and recovery plan.

Hospital problems

Many of us get our ideas about mental hospitals from old movies like "The Snake Pit," depictions of past years' horrors in films like "Frances" (the story of actress Frances Farmer), or books by people who suffered in horrid institutions. Today, there are many good hospital programs, and there are still some that verge on the criminal. Danger signs include frequent use of physical restraints and isolation rooms to control "dangerous" patients, a reliance on psychoanalysis as the primary cure for neurological conditions, lack of knowledge about the most current medications, and poor relationships with family members, schools, and outside care providers.

It appears that staff members at some facilities still blame parents, spouses, and patients themselves for their symptoms. This attitude undermines self-confidence, can prevent people from getting proper treatment, and drives people away from those they need most—the family members charged with the responsibility to care for them when they leave the hospital.

There's no reason for patients or family members to tolerate hostility from administrators or staff. Of course, no one is perfect. But suggestions for change within the family can only be listened to in an atmosphere of mutual assistance, in which family members are seen as an essential source of information, and as the greatest resource for helping a person continue his or her recovery outside of residential care.

If you or your family member lands in a facility that can't seem to change its attitude, do what you can to find a better location.

Certain treatments used in mental hospitals have gained notoriety. These include electroshock therapy, insulin shock therapy, wet sheet packs, aversives, restraints, and isolation. None of these treatments is recommended for use with patients who have TS. Any treatment program that relies on these is substandard.

Bruce's severe OCD and TS put him in the hospital several times during his teen years. He looks back on many of these experiences with bitterness:

> In my stay at the general hospital, I was very badly mistreated. My doctor refused to believe I have a severe case of Tourette's syndrome with obsessive-compulsive disorder when it was relatively obvious. He very rudely implied that I was a disturbed, trouble-making teenager who was trying get out of school because I did not like work, and who was manipulating and upsetting my family. At this point in time I was overwhelmed and tortured horribly by my disorder. He told me if I wasn't in school that I should be out looking for a job.
>
> Another doctor also looked after me at the hospital for a little while, and instructed the nursing staff to make me walk down to the TV room every mealtime to get my tray. At this point in time my disorder was making me go through many processes to get from place to place, it was taking me about an hour to simply walk through a doorway. The doctor was aware of all this and the awful torture it put me through, but even after me and my sister had a talk with her she still made me walk an hour or so to get each meal. By then my meals were cold. Sometimes I didn't even eat.
>
> I don't know what the nurses on floor three were instructed to do by the first doctor, but they were threatening to restrain me if I didn't walk fast enough to my room, and some of them were refusing to help me out with problems.
>
> This wasn't the worst of my problems. The next time we came to the general hospital I was having psychological breakdowns, and the same doctor made us wait at least three hours before he would see us. By the time he did see us, he was refusing to admit me to the hospital. He was angry with my parents because they had taken me to Toronto to see a Tourette's syndrome specialist. He implied I was making up my symptoms.
>
> The last time at the hospital was the worst. When my parents left the hospital, I began to do my rituals. I was certain if I didn't do certain rituals that something terrible was going to happen to my sisters and my mom and dad. I was panic-stricken and asked to use the phone so that I could make sure they were okay. They refused to let me use the phone and they put me in restraints. Each day when I did my rituals they tied

*me to the bed and told me I didn't have obsessive compulsive disorder,
when I was already diagnosed by a specialist who assured me I have
OCD, not a conduct disorder. They left me tied up in that bed so long
I wet my bed. They didn't even let me go to the bathroom. They made me
lay in it for an hour. I was also so overdosed on the medication the doctor
had me on that I wasn't allowed visitors because they didn't want my
friends to see what they were doing to me. Soon I passed out from all the
medication and it took my parents and the nurses five hours to wake me
up. Is that something to do to a 15-year-old boy? It still disturbs me.*

Growing and changing

No matter what kind of medical care you choose for yourself or your child, your
needs will change over time. A medication that works at age 12 may not be the best
choice for an 18-year-old. A medication that was highly effective for a young adult
may become less so after menopause, or when combined with medication needed for
aging-related problems.

Your tics are likely to decrease as you grow older. You may find that you no longer
need to take medication because your tics are much milder than they once were.
Obsessive-compulsive symptoms, on the other hand, may grow stronger and require
treatment. You may discover that seeing a counselor, a massage therapist, or another
alternative health practitioner who helps improve your quality of life becomes more
important to you than some forms of traditional medical treatment.

Always work closely with your doctor when you are considering discontinuing any
medication or other form of medical treatment.

CHAPTER 7

Other Interventions

THIS CHAPTER DESCRIBES various non-medication treatment approaches. It covers a wide variety of complementary treatments that may be helpful for easing your TS symptoms or battling the side effects of medications. It also discusses talk therapy (particularly cognitive behavioral therapy) and stress reduction techniques.

Complementary therapies

In recent years there has been increasing research on mind-body medicine and its effect on coping with the symptoms of illness. Complementary therapies (also called adjunctive therapies) are those that can be expected to add something beneficial to an ongoing medical treatment program. Helpful adjunctive therapies include relaxation, biofeedback, massage, visualization, acupuncture, meditation, aromatherapy, and prayer.

Alternative treatments

Alternative treatments are often defined as those that are used in place of conventional medical treatment or, if used in addition to treatment, that may have effects like those of medication, including unknown or adverse effects.

Alternative treatments are usually based on word-of-mouth endorsements, also known as anecdotal evidence. Medical therapy is based on scientific studies using large groups of patients.

It is extremely important that you discuss with your doctor any therapy that involves ingestion or injection of a substance (including herbs, vitamins, special diets, or enemas). A physician's involvement is necessary to prevent harm and to maintain the effectiveness of conventional medication.

Evaluating complementary/alternative interventions

No matter what kind of complementary practitioner or therapy you choose, it's just as important to be a smart consumer in this area as it is with traditional medicine. Unfortunately, it can be more difficult. Medications approved by the FDA undergo rigorous testing. Study results and detailed information about these compounds are available in books, journal articles, online, or directly from the manufacturers.

With "natural" remedies, that's not always the case. It seems like every week another paperback book appears making wild claims for a "new" antioxidant compound, herbal medication, or holistic therapy. The online bookstore Amazon.com lists nearly thirty titles about St. John's Wort alone! These books—not to mention magazine articles, web sites, and semi-informed friends—sometimes wrap conjecture up in a thin veneer of science. They may reference studies that are misinterpreted, that appeared in disreputable journals, or that were so poorly designed or biased that no journal would publish them.

Some supplement salespeople, particularly those who take part in multilevel marketing schemes, seem to have taken lessons from their predecessors from the days of the traveling medicine show. They have little to lose by making outrageous claims for their products, and much to gain financially. Here are just a few of the unsupported claims found in a single five-minute sweep of supplement-sales sites on the Internet:

- "Glutathione slows the aging clock, prevents disease and increases life."
- "Pycogenol…dramatically relieves ADD/ADHD, improves skin smoothness and elasticity, reduces prostate inflammation and other inflammatory conditions, reduces diabetic retinopathy and neuropathy, improves circulation and enhances cell vitality…" [And, according to this site, cures almost anything else that might ail you!]
- "Sage and Bee Pollen nourish the brain."
- "Soybean lecithin has been found to clean out veins and arteries—dissolve the gooey sludge cholesterol—and thus increase circulation, relieve heart, vein and artery problems. It has cured many diabetics—cured brain clots, strokes, paralyzed legs, hands and arms!"

Take the time to browse your local health food or vitamin store's shelves, and you'll probably spot a number of products that are deceptively advertised. Some companies try to deceive you with sound-alike names, packaging that mimics other products, or suggestive names that hint at cures.

Other colorful bottles of pills contain substances that can't actually be absorbed by the body in oral form—for example, "DNA" (deoxyribonucleic acid, the building block of human genetic material) graces the shelves of some shops. One site for a manufacturer of this useless supplement claims, "it is the key element in the reprogramming and stimulation of lazy cells to avoid, improve, or correct problems in the respiratory, digestive, nervous, or glandular systems." Some brands of "DNA" are apparently nothing but capsules of brewer's yeast. Brewer's yeast is high in nucleic acids, the compounds the body uses to build DNA, but there's no evidence that your body can use nucleic acids taken orally to build better DNA. Brewer's yeast is a good, inexpensive source of vitamin B and the mineral chromium, but these "DNA" pills cost 40 times as much as an equivalent amount of brewer's yeast.

Some other supplements contain the end products of internal processes, such as glutathione, instead of the precursors needed for the body to carry out these processes and make a sufficient supply on its own, such as vitamin E. This approach also may not work. When in doubt, consult with your doctor or a competent nutritionist.

How can you assess supplement claims? Start by relying primarily on reputable reference books for your basic information, rather than on advertisements or the popular press. Watch out for any product whose salespeople claim it will "cure" anything. Supplements and vitamins may enhance health and promote wellness, but they rarely affect cures.

Jennifer, mother of 12-year-old Ty, says she tried one such product with unpleasant results:

> We tried a kava-kava, garlic, gingko biloba, ginseng, maté, rauvolfia, rosemary, and white willow combination touted by a company as a "cure" for ADHD symptoms. All it did was cause my son to not sleep for several days in a row and make his heart pound.

Watch out for advertising claims that a supplement is universally useful. The worst offenders in supplement advertising tout their wares as cure-alls for a multitude of unrelated conditions in an effort to make the most sales.

If a company claims to be the only one to know the secret powers of a natural substance, beware.

Be especially cautious when sales pitches are written in pseudoscientific language that doesn't hold up under close examination with a dictionary. This is a popular ploy. For example, one product that has occasionally been peddled to parents of kids with TS claims to "support cellular communication through a dietary supplement of monosaccharides needed for glycoconjugate synthesis." Translated into plain English, that means: it's a sugar pill.

You can check with the National Center for Complementary and Alternative Medicine (listed in Appendix A, *Resources*) to see if any scientific evidence backs up the treatment that interests you.

Even when you have examined the science behind a vitamin or supplement treatment, there's still the problem of quality and purity. It's almost impossible for consumers to know for sure that a tablet or powder contains the substances advertised at the strength and purity promised. Whenever possible, do business with reputable manufacturers, companies that back up their products with potency guarantees or standards. In most European countries, potency is governed by government standards; in the US, it's a matter of corporate choice.

Check the credentials of alternative healthcare providers, just as you would with any other specialist. The section "Adjunctive/complementary treatment systems," later in this chapter, includes information on how to check these credentials. Beware of any practitioner who will provide complementary therapy only if you stop conventional treatments.

Talk with other people who have gone through the treatment. Be sure to find out how much the therapy costs, as your insurance company may not pay for complementary treatments.

Take all the information you have gathered to your doctor to discuss any positive or negative impact that it may have on current medical treatment.

Whatever you do, don't operate behind your doctor's back. If you're philosophically incompatible, you should simply part ways—but you need a medical expert on your team.

Adjunctive/complementary treatment systems

In the US, at least one out of three patients relies on complementary or adjunctive therapies for some ailments. While there is no secret natural cure for Tourette's syndrome, the holistic approach to patient care used by good complementary medicine practitioners often helps people maintain optimal general health through adequate diet, stress reduction, and vitamin, mineral, or herbal supplements if needed.

Following are brief descriptions of the most common adjunctive and complementary medicine systems.

Acupuncture

Developed in China, acupuncture is based on the concept of *ch'i,* an energy force that is believed to course through the human body. If your *ch'i* is blocked, acupuncture theory states, illness results. Acupuncturists use tiny needles inserted into the skin at specific points to undo these blockages.

Modern acupuncturists use disposable needles to ensure sterility. Some also employ heat (moxibustion), noninvasive lasers, magnetic devices, essential oils, or electrical stimulation. Many have expertise in other Chinese or Western complementary therapies, such as herbal medicine.

If you do try acupuncture, you may encounter terms and practices that are unfamiliar to you. Acupuncture, and Chinese medicine in general, works from a different set of explanations than Western medicine. Ask your practitioner about anything you don't understand.

Studies funded by the National Institutes of Health have found that acupuncture does help some conditions, including chronic pain, and works well as an adjunct to other methods in the treatment of drug addiction. Western doctors think that the needles somehow influence the body's production of natural opioid chemicals and neurotransmitters.[1]

Reputable research indicates that properly applied acupuncture treatments may help regulate gastrointestinal functions, which could be good news for people with GI distress due to TS medications.[2] Other studies have indicated (but not proven) that acupuncture may heal nerve damage.[3]

Acupuncture is commonly used in China to help people with TS. One journal article on acupuncture for TS has been published in English. In it, the acupuncture specialists worked with over 100 patients with TS, and discerned two different patterns of the disorder using diagnostic methods based on traditional Chinese medicine. They claimed a 73 percent cure rate, with an additional 19 percent improvement rate, from their intensive and carefully designed acupuncture treatment plan.[4] If this had been a TS medication study, those results would be considered astounding. However, not enough information is available about how tic severity and remission were judged after the study, or about how long patients were followed after the study's end. Until more is known, perhaps the most that can be said is that a good acupuncturist might be a worthwhile addition to your healthcare team.

Acupuncture licensing rules vary from state to state. A complete guide can be found on the Web at *http://www.acupuncture.com/StateLaws/StateLaws.htm*. Most states require, at minimum, that acupuncturists meet the criteria set by the National Certification Commission for Acupuncture and Oriental Medicine. You can reach NCCAOM at (703) 548-9004 or on the Web at *http://www.nccaom.org*.

Acupressure and reflexology are other complementary treatments that borrow much from acupuncture's basic concepts. These therapies use physical pressure or movement rather than needles to stimulate the same points targeted in acupuncture.

Chiropractic

Chiropractors make adjustments to the spine and related body structures. Some people with back pain find relief through chiropractics.

People with major tics often experience muscle and joint pain due to their repetitive movements. Chiropractors are experienced at helping people work through these kinds of injuries, and may help you feel better quicker. Some chiropractors also offer advice on diet, vitamins, and supplements that may be useful.

One study of an adult TS patient found that his symptoms became less severe over a three-month course of chiropractic adjustments, although they did not disappear, and the chiropractor noted that a natural waning of symptoms was a possibility. Perhaps more important to the patient's well being, his stress level also decreased markedly.[5]

In the US, state boards license chiropractors. To find out about licensing in your state, contact the Federation of Chiropractic Licensing Boards at (970) 356-3500 or on the Web at *http://www.fclb.org*.

Homeopathy

Homeopathy is based on the principle that remedies containing infinitesimal amounts of substances that could cause the medical condition being treated can instead prod the immune system into action against the condition. Homeopathy is a fairly mainstream medical practice in the UK, although repeated studies have not verified that it works.[6]

In the US and Canada, homeopathic physicians are not licensed to practice medicine. However, some MDs and NDs do recommend homeopathic treatments, and a few homeopaths are fully licensed physicians. For information about homeopathic medicine and licensing for homeopaths in North America, contact the National Center for Homeopathy at (703) 548-7790 or on the Web at *http://www.homeopathic.org*.

Although homeopathic remedies can often be purchased at health-food stores, responsible practitioners recommend seeing a homeopathic doctor before choosing remedies. The remedies are generally used only as part of an overall treatment plan that may include diet changes and stress reduction. Even if the remedies themselves are of no value, as many skeptics believe, you might benefit from this part of the program.

Naturopathy

Naturopaths are licensed to practice medicine in some US states, some Canadian provinces, and some other countries. They are trained and licensed as naturopathic doctors (ND). Naturopaths tend to see themselves as "wellness promoters," not just people who treat the disease. Their practice stresses prevention of disease through diet, exercise, and vitamins. They may prescribe herbal remedies or Western pharmaceuticals (in states where they are licensed to do so) to those with illness, and may also suggest and/or administer complementary therapies like hydrotherapy (special baths or wet packs) or massage.

Naturopaths vary in their personal philosophy about Western medicine. Some will refer patients elsewhere for ailments they feel are out of their league; others prefer to rely solely on nutritional and natural medicine.

People who want to try herbal remedies and nutritional interventions like the ones mentioned in this chapter can choose a naturopath as their primary care provider. Take care when making a choice, however: In the US, some people calling themselves naturopaths have not completed an accredited program. Properly licensed naturopaths receive medical training roughly comparable to traditional ("allopathic") medical school, though with a different emphasis.

For information about finding a licensed naturopath in the US or Canada, contact the American Association of Naturopathic Physicians (*http://www.naturopathic.org*) or the Canadian Naturopathic Association (*http://www.naturopathic.org/canada/Canada.Assoc. List.html*).

Orthomolecular medicine

Orthomolecular medicine relies mostly on using vitamins and nutrition to prevent or cure illness. The most famous proponent of orthomolecular medicine was its late founder, Dr. Linus Pauling. Better known for receiving the 1954 Nobel Prize for Chemistry and the 1962 Nobel Prize for Peace, Pauling spent most of his later life studying and publicizing the effects of megadoses of vitamins, particularly Vitamin C. Many of Dr. Pauling's more extravagant claims have not been substantiated, but his reputation as a scientist forced the medical establishment to take his ideas seriously.

Some MDs are firm believers in orthomolecular medicine, and Pauling's principles underlie many of the megadose vitamin concoctions in health-food stores. Since large doses of vitamins can have side effects as well as potential benefits, discuss what you should expect with your doctor if he wants to try an orthomolecular approach. You shouldn't do megadose vitamin therapy without consulting a physician or a competent nutritionist. See the section "Supplements and herbal remedies," later in this chapter, for more information about vitamins that appear to be useful for some persons with TS.

If a practitioner says she is an orthomolecular physician or doctor, that should mean that she is a licensed MD or DO. You can check on the status of a physician's license with your state Medical Licensing Board. If a practitioner says he is board-certified, you can confirm it with the American Board of Medical Specialties at (847) 491-9091 or online at *http://www.certifieddoctors.com*. An appropriate board certification for an orthomolecular psychiatrist would be Psychiatry or Neurology.

Unfortunately, some persons presenting themselves as orthomolecular physicians or psychiatrists are not licensed MDs.

Osteopathy

Osteopathic physicians are trained as primary care providers first, although they may then specialize as pediatricians, surgeons, allergists, etc. They stress preventative care, and look closely at the role of body structure in the disease process. In the UK, licensed osteopaths participate in the National Health program. They are licensed to practice medicine in all US states, and use the initials DO (Doctor of Osteopathy) instead of MD.

Osteopaths may operate somewhat like chiropractors, adjusting the musculoskelatal system to effect improvement. You can find out if an osteopath is licensed to practice medicine in your state by calling your State Medical Board or State Osteopathic Board. You can find out more about DO certification and find a practitioner through the American Osteopathy Association at (800) 621-1773 or online at *http://www.aoa-net.org*.

One area of osteopathy-related treatment, craniosacral therapy, is often recommended for children with neurological challenges. Although osteopath John Upledger developed it, trained members of other professions, including some occupational therapists and physical therapists, also practice craniosacral therapy.

Although anecdotal reports indicate that some people with TS find craniosacral therapy useful, there have not been any peer-reviewed studies published on the topic. Some practitioners make claims of being able to "cure" TS, which has certainly not been proven.

Ayurvedic and Chinese traditional medicine

Indigenous peoples everywhere have medical systems based on the use of herbal remedies. Two of these, India's Ayurveda and traditional Chinese medicine, have been systematized and studied to a great extent. The Ayurvedic medicine concept revolves around a life force called *prana,* while Chinese traditionalists talk about *ch'i,* as mentioned in the previous section on acupuncture.

Ayurvedic practitioners will give you a thorough exam and then tell you what "type" you are according to their diagnostic system. Then they'll suggest an appropriate diet, lifestyle adjustments, and probably therapeutic meditation. They may also have various suggestions about cleaning out your digestive tract.

Chinese traditional practitioners take a very similar approach, although their dietary recommendations are usually less strict than a typical Ayurvedic plan.

There is a vast array of Ayurvedic and Chinese herbal remedies. Some of these concoctions are probably quite effective, while others could be dangerous to your health. If possible, try to find out exactly which herbs are in a potion, and check out their effects. For example, the popular Chinese herb Ma Huang (ephedra) is a common ingredient in traditional "nerve tonics." It is also a powerful central nervous system stimulant, and should be taken with caution.

It is far safer to work closely with a practitioner who knows your state of health and can monitor you during treatment than it is to purchase Chinese or Ayurvedic remedies over the counter. A review of the literature in English does not reveal any surveys or studies of Chinese, Ayurvedic, or other traditional herbal remedies for TS, although some people do use them. See the section, "Supplements and herbal remedies," later in this chapter for more information.

In the US, the primary certification agency for practitioners of Chinese medicine is the National Certification Commission for Acupuncture and Oriental Medicine. You can reach NCCAOM at (703) 548-9004 or on the Web at *http://www.nccaom.org*.

There is no US certification commission for Ayurvedic practitioners. The most active group promoting Ayurveda in the US is the National Institute of Ayurvedic Medicine, which can be reached at (914) 278-8700 or online at *http://niam.com/corp-web/index.htm*.

Sensory integration

The theories behind sensory integration (SI) were first developed by an occupational therapist and researcher, Jean Ayres. In the US and Canada, many occupational therapists are at least familiar with the principles of SI, although most of the best practitioners are certified through Sensory Integration International. SII, which is listed in Appendix A along with related resources, will provide parents with a list of trained therapists and evaluators.

In the UK, the treatment methods recommended by educational psychologist Madeleine Portwood (*http://web.ukonline.co.uk/members/madeleine.portwood/index.htm*) for children with developmental dyspraxia are very similar to SI.

Sensory integration work is based on the idea that people with motor or sensory problems have difficulty processing the information their body receives through the various senses. SI exercises are intended to reduce sensory disturbances related to touch, movement, and gravity. These disturbances can occur in any or all of the following areas:

- **Processing.** This ability involves how quickly (or if) the sensation reaches the central nervous system to be interpreted.

- **Analysis.** This ability governs how the person interprets the sensation.

- **Organization.** This ability decides how the person responds to their analysis of the sensation.

- **Memory.** This ability controls how (or if) the person remembers similar sensations and proper responses from the past.

Disturbances can occur in either the traditional five senses (sight, hearing, smell, taste, and touch) or in less well-known senses—senses that actually have a greater effect on gross-motor development. SI exercises generally work on the latter. These "whole body" senses are:

- **Tactile.** The tactile sense is based in the system created by the entire skin surface and the nerves that serve it; this sense processes information taken in via all types of touch.

- **Proprioceptive.** This sense is based in the muscles, ligaments, joints, and the nerves that serve them, this sense processes information about where the body and its various parts are in space.

- **Vestibular.** The vestibular sense is based mostly in the inner ear, which acts as a sort of internal carpenter's level; this sense processes information about how the body interacts with gravity as it moves and attempts to retain its balance.

Most of us never think about these senses, unless they are suddenly disordered in some way, such as from an inner-ear infection, a dizziness-producing carnival ride, or a leg that "falls asleep" and causes stumbling. Infants and young children learn to interpret the world around them through these senses, however. If the information comes in all wrong or cannot be processed properly, the world is a confusing place. Imagine trying to play with a toy when your clothing was causing intense discomfort, for example. The tactile, proprioceptive, and vestibular senses are our most elemental ways to relate to the environment—they're with us from the earliest nervous-system development in the womb. Problems in this area are fundamental, because they interfere with the ability to learn the basic skills that are the building blocks for all others.

Luckily, sensory integration work can help most people who experience difficulties in this area get better control of the information they take in. SI activities are usually quite simple. Special equipment is not a must, although some parents have used swings, hammocks, and small items that can be obtained from catalogs. The following list offers a few examples of typical SI activities that may be done at home:

- For tactile-sensitivity problems (under- or over-sensitivity):
  - The so-called *Wilbarger brushing* technique is based on the use of firm strokes with a soft surgical brush (available inexpensively from medical-supply stores) on the back, arms, and legs. Brushing is interspersed with joint compression, in which the elbows, arm sockets, knees, and hip joints are pushed

together firmly several times in succession. It's hard to explain this practice in print—it's really something you should be taught in person.

- Handling materials with a variety of textures, such as wet or dry sand, shaving cream, dry beans, and water. Children can be encouraged to play with the materials, even put them on their arms, legs, or face if appropriate.

- Deep-pressure massage or hugs.

- Making a "kid burrito" by rolling the child up tightly in a blanket, or a "kid sandwich" by (carefully) squishing the child between two gymnastic mats or sofa cushions.

- Taking care to also avoid introducing people with tactile oversensitivity to unnecessary unpleasant sensations. Clothing problems are very common in this group, with tags and scratchy materials being frequent offenders. Incidentally, tactile issues are a common cause of hyperactive behavior.

- For proprioceptive problems:

  - Swinging (clinics often use a big therapy swing that lets the person swing in a prone position).

  - Jumping on a small trampoline.

  - The joint-compression technique mentioned above.

- For vestibular problems:

  - Walking on a balance beam.

  - Balancing on a large "therapy ball" as it moves.

  - OT work aimed at strengthening and developing gross-motor skills (people with vestibular problems tend to have low muscle tone).

  - Exercises that encourage "crossing the midline": using the left hand and arm on the right side of the body, and vice versa. Examples include some kinds of dancing, and rocking from side to side.

  - Stair climbing.

Most of these exercises actually work on more than one sense at once. Activities can be combined and varied to keep SI work fun—and most children *do* think it's fun! Adults with long-term sensory issues may have a hard time getting started with an SI program, especially since some of the activities may seem childish or silly.

In addition to exercises that reduce sensory defensiveness, or that help the undersensitive patient integrate and process sensations, clinicians recommend making a *sensory diet* part of daily activities at home and at school. This means integrating soothing sensory experiences into daily activities at a regular interval. These activities could include:

- Slow repetitive rhythmic movements, such as Tai Chi, water aerobics, or using a rocking chair.

- Firm pressure on the skin, from hugs, compression devices, or another source.

- "Heavy work," such as moving furniture, carrying heavy bags, or lifting weights.

- Activities done upside down, such as headstands or tumbling.

Supplements and herbal remedies

It seems like everyone is trying supplements these days, whether it's gingko biloba for failing memory, or chondroitin and glucosamine for creaky joints. They've become a big business, and fill entire sections in supermarkets. Many people with TS are interested in what supplements can do for them.

Sandi says 14-year-old Brian has had excellent results from an antioxidant, grapeseed extract, although the lack of clinical studies to back its use is a concern for his doctor:

> *I heard several people make positive comments about grapeseed extract and how it has helped their children control their tics. I did a little research about it, and everything I read about it was positive in terms of its health benefits. It is a very potent antioxidant and has been implicated in protecting people against heart disease and cancer. However, I read nothing about it helping neurological problems. More importantly, I read nothing that would imply there were any health risks in using it. So, I broached the subject with my son's psychiatrist. His response was that it couldn't hurt, but he was skeptical that it would provide any benefits.*
>
> *Initially, we started with a small dose and found no results. However, upon more research, I found out the recommended dosages were 1 to 2 milligrams per pound of body weight when using grapeseed extract for medicinal purposes, instead of just as a preventive measure. We upped the dosage, and the results have been incredible. We have been able to reduce my son's clonidine from .25 mg per day to .05 mg per day.*
>
> *The best result is that my son stopped having rage attacks. In fact, when occasionally, he appears to have some anger management problems, the first thing I'll ask him is if he took his grapeseed extract. Invariably,*

the answer is that he forgot. Within fifteen minutes of taking it, he is back to being himself.

My son's psychiatrist is absolutely amazed at our results. Unfortunately, he says that he cannot recommend it to other patients because it has not passed clinical trials. Yet he freely admits the results in my son have been staggering, and if his own child were to be similarly afflicted, then he would absolutely try it.

While some people have reported benefits from various supplements, others have not, and there have not yet been any scientific studies on the use of vitamins or herbs for TS.

There has, however, been a great deal of research on the effects of vitamins and other supplements on persons with autism. Since as many as 20 percent of persons with autism also have TS, it is possible that there are at least some biochemical similarities between the two.[7] Numerous clinical trials, including double-blind, placebo-controlled studies, have shown that supplementing with fairly high doses of vitamin B6 and magnesium helps to reduce the symptoms of autism for at least some patients.[8]

A number of parents have found that these vitamins and related substances are also helpful for their kids with TS, and some adults with TS take them regularly as well. One parent, Bonnie Grimaldi, has made B vitamins a part of her extensive supplement/ diet plan, which you can find online at *http://hometown.aol.com/bonniegr/BONNIE_1. HTM.*

The B vitamin family includes thiamin (B1), riboflavin (B2), niacin (B3), pantothenic acid (B4), pyrixodine (B6), cobalamin (B12), and folic acid. B vitamins in general are depleted by stress and anxiety. B2 is specifically affected by certain medications, including Anafranil and some other antidepressants.

The B vitamin most frequently recommended for both autism and TS is B6, which should be taken with magnesium and folic acid to ensure proper absorption. Folic acid itself is also important for proper immune system and nervous system function. B6 is essential for metabolism of amino acids, proteins, fatty acids, and starches, and for the production and proper use of neurotransmitters. B6 binds to the same receptors as natural corticosteroids, and may regulate steroid production by this mechanism.

An old-time remedy, cod-liver oil, has recently gained prominence in the autism community, and also appears on some lists of suggested supplements for people with TS. Cod liver oil contains high doses of vitamin A, and is also rich in Omega-3 fatty acids. See the section "Essential fatty acids," later in this chapter, for more information.

Skullcap (*Scutellaria lateriflora*) is an herb with a long history of use for treating tic disorders in several parts of the world. It is also a medium-strength sedative. No studies have been done on this traditional remedy in regards to TS, although research on a Chinese herb in the same family (*Scutellaria baicalensis*) found that it had anti-bacterial and antihistamine properties, and seemed to affect the lipid system.[9] Skull-cap should not be taken with prescription sedatives or neuroleptics.

Clinical studies have indicated that a carbohydrate called inositol, one of the active ingredients in lecithin, may be helpful for some people with obsessive-compulsive disorder.[10] Other studies have found evidence of benefits for people with depression, panic disorder, and autism.[11] It has not been tested specifically for TS.

Inositol plays a part in the chemical process that carries messages for certain neuro-transmitters, including serotonin and acetylcholine. It also seems to help boost the activity of serotonin receptors. It may help repair damaged areas of the myelin sheath that surrounds and protects nerves.

Inositol can be found in lecithin (phosphatidyl choline) a phospholipid found mostly in high-fat foods. Lecithin also contains choline, a substance needed by the brain for processes related to memory, learning, and mental alertness, as well as to the manu-facture of cell membranes and the neurotransmitter acetylcholine.

Lecithin is oil-based, so it gets rancid easily. It should be refrigerated. Lecithin cap-sules are available, but many people prefer the soft lecithin granules. These are a nice addition to fruit-juice smoothies, adding a thicker texture.

See also the section "Fixing sleep problems," later in this chapter, which lists herbal remedies and supplements that may help with insomnia.

Supplement cautions

It's very important to let your doctor know about any supplement your child takes, whether it is vitamin, mineral, or herb. There are many possible interactions between these substances and prescription drugs. Here are just a few that are known at this time:[12]

- Echinacea adds to the toxic effects some medications have on the liver, including anabolic steroids, amiodarone, methotrexate, and ketoconazole, increasing the risk of liver failure.

- The antimigraine effects of feverfew may be negated by nonsteroidal anti-inflammatory drugs (NSAIDs), including aspirin.

- Feverfew, garlic, Gingko biloba, ginger, and ginseng alter bleeding time, and so should not be used with anticoagulant drugs like warfarin. You should also report use of these supplements to your doctor if you are going to have surgery.

- When taken with phenelzine sulfate, ginseng can cause headache, tremor, and mania.

- Ginseng (and other herbs that may affect the hormonal system) may add to or work against the effects of estrogens, corticosteroids, or oral contraceptives.

- St. John's Wort (and any other "natural" antidepressant, such as SAM-e) may add to the effects of prescription antidepressants, increasing the risk of serotonin syndrome. It also appears to impact the effectiveness of a wide variety of other prescription drugs.

- Valerian (and any other herbal sedative) should not be used with barbiturates or other prescription sedatives, because of an increased risk of over-sedation—and even coma or death.

- Kyushin, licorice, plantain, uzara root, hawthorn, and ginseng may interfere with the medical action of digoxin, as well as with digoxin monitoring.

- Evening primrose oil and borage oil may lower the seizure threshold, and so should not be used by people with seizure disorders, or with prescription anticonvulsants.

- The Ayurvedic remedy Shankapulshpi may decrease phenytoin levels as well as diminish drug efficacy.

- Kava-kava can cause coma when combined with alprazolam. It can also damage the liver if used for more than thirty days in a row. It could worsen the effects of other drugs that can harm the liver, including many psychiatric medications.

- Immunostimulants like echinacea and antioxidants should not be given with drugs that suppress the immune system, such as corticosteroids or cyclosporine.

- St. John's Wort, saw palmetto, and some other herbs have high levels of tannic acids, which may inhibit iron absorption.

- Karela, ginseng, and some other herbs may affect blood glucose levels, and so should not be used by diabetic patients.

- Folic acid blocks the action of the seizure medication Dilantin.

There are surely many more unknown reactions that could occur between natural and pharmaceutical remedies.

Desperate to find something that works to reduce difficult symptoms, parents and adult patients tend to pile on the interventions. That makes it hard to tell when something really is working—or if it would work without interference from some other remedy. To get the clearest picture possible of any complementary interventions, you must introduce them independent of each other, and independent of new pharmaceuticals or therapeutic interventions.

Keep careful, daily records of supplements and dietary changes you introduce, when they are given and in what amounts, what brands you used, and any visible effects that you observe. If after four to six weeks you have not seen improvements with a supplement, benefits are unlikely. Dietary changes, bodywork, and other interventions may take much longer to show beneficial effects.

The Herbal PDR, listed in Appendix A, provides the results of medical research on herbal remedies.

One of the best online resources for information on medicinal herbs is MedHerb.com (*http://www.medherb.com*), which is sponsored by the professional journal *Medical Herbalism.* It includes information about herbs used in Western, Asian, Ayurvedic, and other traditional medicine systems, with links to scientific studies, and information on adverse reactions.

Vitamin cautions

Vitamins are generally safe to take, but you need to take age, size, and metabolism into account. Purchase a basic guide to vitamins and minerals that includes information about toxicity symptoms before starting any vitamin-based program. Each individual metabolizes vitamins and minerals differently, and some people may be more or less susceptible to potential toxic effects. Along with your doctor's guidance, a good reference book can help you avoid problems.

Also, take vitamin-company sales pitches and dosage recommendations with a grain of salt. Consult a physician or a professional nutritionist who does not sell supplements for unbiased, individualized advice.

Vitamin and mineral formulas are often recommended for people with disordered eating habits, including those who have been diagnosed with anorexia or bulimia. Because the mineral deficiencies associated with eating disorders can be life threatening, these patients should take only supplements recommended by a physician.

Vitamins A and D are fat-soluble, so they are stored in the body's fat cells for later use. Having a little socked away for a rainy day is probably okay, but if you take too much, hypervitaminosis may develop. Symptoms of hypervitaminosis A include orangeish, itchy skin; loss of appetite; increased fatigue; and hard, painful swellings on the arms, legs, or back of the head. Symptoms of hypervitaminosis D include hypercalcemia, osteoporosis, and kidney problems.

Don't overdo it with any fat-soluble vitamin, and take care with fish-oil supplements, including cod liver oil, which is very high in both vitamins A and D.

If you or your child experiences behavioral side effects or tingling of the hands and feet while taking B6, cut back on the dosage temporarily, and make sure it is accompanied by the correct amount of magnesium.

If you experience flushing when taking niacin, look for a "no-flush" brand that is buffered. As niacin can lower your blood pressure, be cautious about using it with drugs like clonidine or guanfacine.

Immune system support

For those who have the PANDAS variant of TS or whose symptoms seem to be made worse by other infections or illnesses, a healthy diet and certain supplements might help. On the other hand, remedies that put your immune system into overdrive, such as echinacea, could make symptoms worse.

The immune system needs an adequate supply of nutrients, and sometimes a little help from antioxidants. Antioxidant compounds scavenge the bloodstream for particles called free radicals. Free radicals damage healthy cells and cause inflammation of tissues, causing the immune system to jump into action over and over again.

Antioxidants

Antioxidants are often recommended as general health and immune-system boosters, although those eating a healthy, balanced diet normally do not need to take them in supplement form. There is no research showing that they can play a role in treating TS, although some people do report benefits. Antioxidant substances include the following.

- **Vitamin A (retinol)**. This vitamin has antioxidant properties, and also helps maintain the mucous lining of the intestines. It is essential for growth, vision, reproduction, and immune function. It may help fight viral infections and improve night vision. Pregnant women should avoid vitamin A supplements unless advised to take them by their physician, as too much can contribute to miscarriage.

- Vitamin C (ascorbic acid). Vitamin C is a very powerful antioxidant. It may shorten the length of colds, and improve the basic health of people with many medical conditions. Actual Vitamin C deficiency, known as scurvy, is now rare. One population in which it does occur, however, is people who start using mega-doses of C and then suddenly stop. The acidic nature of ascorbic acid can also contribute to kidney stones. (The buffered form, calcium ascorbate, is more easily tolerated.) As the cautions mentioned here indicate, megadoses of C shouldn't be taken without consulting your physician first. If you do choose to take large doses of vitamin C, accompany it with vitamin E. Be sure to tell your doctor if you take vitamin C supplements, as it can alter some lab results.

- Vitamin E (alpha tocopherol). Vitamin E is believed to be important for proper immune-system functioning. It protects cells from free radical damage, and helps the body build tissues, muscles, and red blood cells. People who take neuroleptics, tricyclic antidepressants, or other medications that carry a known risk for tardive dyskinesia should take vitamin E supplements. This vitamin appears to protect against and reduce the symptoms of this drug-induced movement disorder.

- Beta carotene. This nutrient is related to vitamin A, and is found in dark green leafy vegetables and yellow-orange vegetables. It's best to get it through the diet rather than from a supplement.

- Coenzyme Q10 (CoQ10, ubiquinone). This is a vitamin-like antioxidant, one of the strongest available. It's part of the cellular process that uses fats, sugars, and amino acids to produce the energy molecule ATP. It is said to boost immune-system function and help GI tract problems.

- Gingko biloba. This extract of the gingko tree is advertised as an herb to improve memory. There is some clinical evidence for this claim. It is an antioxidant, and is prescribed in Germany for treatment of dementia. It is believed to increase blood flow to the brain and body. It may help revive sexual response in people taking SSRIs, by increasing blood flow to the genitals.

- Glutathione peroxidase. This substance is an antioxidant peptide manufactured by the body. You need to have enough selenium, vitamin C, and vitamin E to make it. There's no need to supplement directly with glutathione itself.

- Selenium. The mineral selenium works with vitamin E to produce the antioxidant peptide glutathione peroxidase. Selenium deficiency occurs in some people with celiac disease and other autoimmune disorders, so if you or your child experiences GI tract problems, you may want to use a supplement of this mineral, preferably in its easily absorbed chelated form (L-selenomethionane).

- **Zinc.** Zinc is an antioxidant mineral. If you or your child experiences GI tract problems, you may want to use a supplement of this mineral in its easiest to-absorb chelated form (zinc aspartate or zinc picolinate).

- **Proanthocyanidins (OPCs, Pycogenol, grapeseed oil).** These are the active ingredients in several naturally occurring antioxidant compounds. Grape seed oil is just what its name indicates, while Pycogenol is a brand-name formulation derived from maritime pine bark. Some people with TS who have tried grape seed oil report beneficial effects for reduced aggression, tic reduction, and improved immune-system function.

- **Cat's claw (una de gato, maca, *Untaria tomentosa*).** Cat's claw is an herbal anti-oxidant from the Peruvian rainforest. It also has antiviral and anti-inflammatory qualities, and has become a mainstay of Mexican folk medicine. It contains plant sterols (compounds related to steroids), among other active ingredients.

Lee says that grapeseed oil seems to be helpful for her son, while other natural alternatives were not:

> We have tried vitamin B, but this seemed to make his OCD worse. Melatonin for sleep seemed to make OCD worse. But when we tried grapeseed oil, all of the sudden, after eleven years of telling him to use words to express frustration, he was able to. Grapeseed oil also seems to perhaps reduce tics. We tried several brands that seemed to not work for him until we found one that did. Now we stick with that brand.

Minerals

There is no current medical research linking mineral deficiency to TS, but an adequate supply of minerals is essential for optimal health. Some are also necessary for utilizing certain vitamins. Three minerals—selenium, calcium, and magnesium—are particularly important for nervous system function.

The mineral selenium is listed earlier in this chapter, in the section "Antioxidants."

Calcium is important for the regulation of impulses in the nervous system and for neurotransmitter production. However, excessive levels of calcium (hypocalcinuria) can result in stupor.

Magnesium is important for the regulation of impulses in the nervous system and neurotransmitter production. If you are supplementing with vitamin B6, you will need to add magnesium as well. Magnesium also lowers blood pressure by blocking calcium channels and dilates blood vessels, so watch out for interactions with medications that have similar or opposite actions.

Essential fatty acids (EFAs)

Essential fatty acids (EFAs) are substances needed to build cells, and also to support the body's anti-inflammatory response. They are the "good" polyunsaturated fats that improve cardiovascular health when substituted for the "bad" saturated fats. There are two major types of EFAs, Omega-3 and Omega-6.

Two Omega-3 fatty acids are found in oily, cold-water fish: eicosapentaenoic acid (EPA) and docosahexanoic acid (DHA). Another Omega-3 fatty acid, alpha-linoleic acid, is found in flaxseed and perilla oils, among other sources.

The Omega-6 fatty acid family includes linoleic acid and its derivatives, including gammalinolenic acid (GLA), dihomogamma-linolenic acid (DGLA), and arachidonic acid (AA). These substances also come from animal fats and some plants, such as evening primrose oil (EPO), which is a good source of GLA; flaxseed oil; black-currant seed oil; hemp-seed oil; and borage oil, which contains both GLA and very long chain fatty acids (VLCFAs).

Researchers believe that achieving a dietary balance between Omega-3 and Omega-6 fatty acids provides the most benefits. The ratios usually recommended are 3:1 or 4:1 Omega-6 to Omega-3.[13]

VLCFAs can be irritating to the liver and central nervous system, so large amounts are not recommended for children, people with nervous-system disorders (such as TS), or people taking medications that put a heavy load on the liver. Oils with a high VLCFA content include borage oil, canola oil, peanut oil (including the oil in peanut butter), and mustard-seed oil.

When oils are heated, most will convert at least part of their fatty acids into trans fatty acids, which are substances to be avoided. Hemp oil is one of the few that can resist this heat-driven conversion progress, and has recently become available for cooking and medicinal use in the US.

The heart and blood vessels aren't the only beneficiaries of EFAs, however. Some people with autoimmune diseases that involve the nervous system say EFAs are very helpful in reducing symptoms. Recent research in psychiatry has found that Omega-3 fatty acids can act as a mood stabilizer for some people with bipolar disorders.[14] Studies have recently been announced that will look at EFAs as a treatment for autism and other mental conditions.[15] How fatty acids help is still unknown, but they are essential for building and maintaining the myelin sheath that surrounds nerve fibers and ensures the proper conduction of messages along the nerves.

No proven benefits from EFAs have yet been found that apply specifically to people with Tourette's syndrome.

Some EFA sources you may hear about follow.

- **Cod liver oil.** High in Omega-3 fatty acids, cod liver oil is also loaded with vitamins A and D. Look for a high-quality, toxicology tested source of cod liver oil, because mercury and other toxins could be deposited in the fish's liver if it was exposed to these substances. In the US, Kirkman Labs can provide carefully tested cod liver oil. You can reach Kirkman at (503) 682-5678 or online at *http://www.kirkmansales.com*.

- **Fish body oil.** Like cod liver oil, fish body oil is made from oily, cold-water fish that are high in valuable Omega-3 fatty acids. However, there is less risk of mercury and other toxins in these oils, as they are not made from fish liver.

- **OmegaBrite.** This is a new EFA supplement designed by the researcher who headed NIMH's clinical trials on EFAs in bipolar disorder, Dr. Andrew Stoll. Based on fish body oil, it is toxicology tested, and comes in gel cap form. For more information, contact the manufacturer at (800) 383-2030 or online at *http://www.omegabrite.com*.

- **Evening primrose oil (EPO).** Evening primrose oil is one of the best EFA sources around, and has become a very popular supplement as a result. It contains high amounts of Omega-6 fatty acids, as do borage oil, flax-seed oil, and blackcurrant seed oil. Evening primrose oil has been reported to lower the threshold for frontal-lobe seizures, however, so people who have these types of seizures should exercise caution. EPO and other plant-source oils are available in liquid form or as gel caps from several different companies.

- **Efalex and Efamol.** These brand name EFA supplements are made by Efamol Neutriceuticals Inc. Efalex was specifically created to treat developmental dyspraxia in the UK, and is widely touted as a supplement for people with ADD or ADHD as well. Efalex contains a mix of Omega-3 fish oil, Omega-6 EPO and thyme oil, and Vitamin E. Efamol, marketed as a treatment for PMS, combines EPO; vitamins B6, C, and E; niacin, zinc, and magnesium. Both of these commercial EFA supplements are now available in the US and Canada as well, and can be purchased by mail order. Unlike some supplement manufacturers, Efamol adheres to strict manufacturing standards, and also sponsors reputable research. You can reach Efamol at (877) 458-6400 or on the Web at *http://www.efamol.com.*

- **Monolaurin.** This substance is made by the body from lauric acid, another medium-chain fatty acid that is found in abundance in coconuts and some other foods, including human breast milk. It is known to have anti-bacterial and anti-viral properties. Monolaurin may be the active ingredient in colostrum, the "pre-milk" all mammals produce to jump-start a newborn's immune system. Cow colostrum is actually available in supplement form in some areas.

It's great if you can get your EFAs in food. Low-fat diets are one reason some people, especially those who are trying to lose weight, may not get enough. Many cold-pressed salad oils, including safflower, sunflower, corn, and canola oils, do contain EFAs. When these oils are processed with heat, however, the fatty acids may be changed or destroyed. Oily fish are another great source for EFAs, although again, the oil's benefits may be lost with cooking.

Diabetics may experience adverse effects from an overload of EFAs, and should consult their physician before supplementing with EFA products.

DMG

Dimethylglycine (DMG, calcium pangamate, pangamic acid, "vitamin B15") is a naturally occurring amino acid that may help some people tolerate stress, reduce the frequency of seizures, and strengthen the immune system. DMG changes the way your body uses folic acid, so you may need to supplement with that vitamin. Increased hyperactivity may result from a lack of folic acid when taking DMG.

A related product, trimethylglycine (TMG) was recently introduced. It is available in liquid form.

Both DMG and TMG have roles in the chemical reactions that increase serotonin levels. Those who take medications that also affect serotonin should take care with these supplements.

Herbal antibiotics

Several herbs appear to have antiseptic, antiviral, antifungal, or antibiotic properties. They have not been researched as treatments for TS, although some people are trying them as a gentler preventative for PANDAS than antibiotics.

Obviously, if these substances are active, you should use them carefully and sparingly, despite the claims of certain manufacturers who encourage daily use for disease prevention. Those who prefer herbal remedies might want to try cat's claw or grapeseed oil, both mentioned in the section "Antioxidants," earlier in this chapter, or one of the following options:

- Bitter melon (*Momordica charantia*). An antiviral from the Chinese herbal pharmacopoeia, bitter melon is the plant from which the active ingredient in some protease inhibitors (the powerful drugs used to combat AIDS) is derived.

- Echinacea (*Echinacea purpurea*). An herbal antiseptic, echinacea also dilates blood vessels. It is said to have antispasmodic qualities as well.

- Goldenseal (*Hydrastis canadensis*). Goldenseal is an alkaloid isoquinoline derivative related to the minor opium alkaloids. Its active ingredient, hydrastine, elevates blood pressure. This is a very strong herb that has antiseptic properties when taken internally or applied to the skin in powder or salve form. It acts on the mucous membranes of the GI tract when taken internally.

- SPV-30. Derived from the European boxwood tree, SPV-30 is a fairly new item in this category. It apparently includes some antiviral and steroidal (anti-inflammatory) compounds, and has become very popular among people with AIDS as an alternative to pharmaceutical antivirals.

Probiotics

Probiotics counteract the harmful effects of antibiotics. As most people who have taken a course of penicillin know, these valuable medications can cause digestive distress even as they heal infection. Probiotics are substances that attempt to restore the friendly intestinal cultures that help you digest food. By replenishing the ranks of friendly bacteria, they keep a lid on unfriendly yeasts, such as Candida albicans, that can cause troublesome symptoms.

Commercial probiotic supplements usually combine a number of substances, sometimes including digestive enzymes, helpful bacteria, garlic, and other items. These can help you remain more comfortable when taking antibiotics.

- Biotin. A vitamin related to the B family, biotin is normally produced by friendly bacteria in the digestive tract. Replenishing this flora should ensure enough biotin, but some people do choose to take it directly.

- **Caprylic acid.** This fatty acid is said to be active against yeast in the digestive tract. Medium chain triglycerides (MCT oil, also called caprylic/capric triglycerides) is a liquid source of caprylic acid.

- **Garlic.** The active ingredients in garlic are said to be active against yeast in the digestive tract. You can swallow whole cloves raw, or take it in a supplement.

- *Lactobacillus acidophilus, Bifidobacterium bifidum, Lactobacillus bulgaricus.* These friendly bacteria are more familiar to most of us as the "active cultures" found in some yogurts. Yogurt itself is a good probiotic for those who eat dairy products.

- **Soil-based organisms (SBOs).** SBOs are microbes found in organic soils. They are believed to help the body produce important enzymes. Some people believe that modern food-processing techniques have left people deficient in these, so they take SBO supplements. These are increasingly added to probiotic supplements. No scientific information about their benefits is available at this time.

Talk therapy

There are many types of "talk therapy," but one thing ties them all together: forming a therapeutic relationship with another person. That relationship may be more important to success than anything else, especially with people who experience excessive guilt and pain as a result of their symptoms.

Sometimes psychiatrists provide therapy services, but most focus on medication issues. Psychologists specialize in talk therapy. Therapists, counselors, and some social workers also provide talk therapy.

Cognitive behavioral therapy

Cognitive-behavioral therapy concentrates on the here and now. It's an intensely practical kind of help that gives people tools they can use. It can't make ticcing stop, but it has been proven to help with obsessive-compulsive symptoms and anxiety, which many people with TS feel are far harder to deal with than tics, and which can make tics worse.

The basic concept of CBT is simple: by changing your behavior, you can eventually change how you think and feel. That's the reverse of what many people would expect. CBT usually works fairly quickly, and it relies mostly on action, not insight.

That makes it easier for very young children and people whose thought processes may be disordered due to mental illness.

One type of CBT is exposure and response prevention (often abbreviated as E&RP). It means exposing yourself to the very thing that causes fear and anxiety, and using all your strength to simply accept the experience instead of relying on compulsions to counteract it or having a panic attack. If you've ever seen a television documentary that showed anxious people taking elevators, walking onto airplanes, or touching something dirty with the help of a therapist, you've seen an example of E&RP in action.

Lee, mother of 13-year-old Joseph, says that cognitive behavioral therapy has been an important part of his treatment plan:

> *Finally last year we found a therapist that Joseph can stand. Before that it was like pulling teeth. This woman is wonderful with him. She uses some cognitive-behavioral stuff with him, but she also aligns herself with him against whatever he perceives as the problem, and works with him there. She uses a lot of logic in working with him to show him how his behavior causes different outcomes.*

The cognitive part of CBT helps you learn that your brain is sending out error messages, and teaches you how to recognize and respond to these errors in ways that are more functional. Although the focus is not on gaining insight into one's deepest psyche, you do gain insight into the nature of your symptoms. You learn to test the false realities that anxiety and obsessive-compulsive thinking present.

Therapists then work to help you challenge the rationality of your own thought patterns, introducing more realistic ways of seeing the world. More frequently, they simply encourage you to test out your own faulty hypotheses: If you don't wash your hands four times, will your father really become ill? If you take the escalator, will you really fall over the side? This side of CBT is also known as cognitive restructuring.

The behavioral part of CBT involves changing behaviors by learning specific techniques, such as exposure and response prevention, relaxation, and anxiety prevention. This is also known as self-instructional training, problem-solving therapy, or stress inoculation.

Rindy, mother of 14-year-old Shawn, says this approach has been helpful for him:

> *We have seen several psychologists in the past who were not helpful, because they didn't know about TS. The psychologist Shawn has most*

recently seen is well known in the area for his work with ADHD kids,
and he's been very helpful with guiding me through school issues and
has been a strong advocate for Shawn.

His focus with Shawn was to get him to see the physical changes within
himself so that he can recognize and abort rages before they happen.

He continues to see his psychiatrist who does his medication
management, but very little is done there except discussion around
medication/side effect issues. Both doctors have been invaluable resources
to me for ideas on how to handle Shawn at home; both think that Ross
Greene's book is right on.

Habit reversal

Although cognitive behavioral therapy techniques have proved effective for all kinds
of symptoms based on cognitive error messages, it's true that some are harder to handle than others. The most difficult to manage, according to experienced therapists,
are compulsions that have an automatic, tic-like quality, such as hair-pulling (trichotillomania) or tapping. A CBT variation known as habit reversal is usually used for
these, with varying degrees of success.

The basics of habit reversal for tic control are:

- **Awareness training.** Becoming aware of the sensations that precede a tic and any
  other factors, such as stress or anxiety, that make that tic more likely.

- **Competing response training.** Coming up with a repertoire of other responses to
  those same factors, such as using stress reduction techniques, breathing slowly, or
  performing a less-obtrusive movement.

- **Social support.** Involving family members in reminding the person to use competing responses, and praising him for doing so.

- **Motivational strategies.** Using self-chosen rewards as a motivating factor to
  encourage using competing responses.

Habit reversal starts with becoming aware of the behavior and when it occurs. With
young children, this may require observation and a verbal reminder by the parent;
older kids and adults can use a journal or checklist to track when and how the need
to do the behavior occurs.

As you become more attuned to when you do the targeted behavior, you will be
encouraged to look for triggers. In trichotillomania, hair-pulling may be a response

to noticeable stress, boredom, or a physical sensation. You may have one trigger or several.

Next, the therapist will ask you to look at the whole sequence that leads to the behavior. For instance, a person with trichotillomania may start pulling hair due to an odd physical sensation on the scalp, and the first movement may be an almost absentminded movement of the hand to the head. The person may then touch and stroke various hairs until she finds the one that "feels right" to pull. The behavior may end there, or may continue on to involve pulling out many hairs, perhaps from the eyebrows or other parts of the body as well. Once you know what all the steps in the process are, you can use cognitive behavioral therapy techniques, such as exposure and response prevention, to stop the process at any point along the line.

The eventual goal is to recognize the sensation on your scalp that usually leads to pulling out hair, and respond to it differently. You can experiment with different responses to the situation that compete with and therefore prevent hair pulling. For instance, you might respond to the sensation by brushing your hair, squeezing a rubber ball with the hand you usually use to pull, or pressing your hands together. You don't want to turn the response into yet another compulsive behavior, of course, just to short-circuit the hair-pulling compulsion. For that reason, you may want to come up with multiple responses to try. Probably some will be effective, while others are not.

As anxiety rises due to resisting the compulsion, you can use relaxation techniques to fight back. If you add social support and motivational strategies, carrying out the competing responses becomes that much easier.

It's important to note that while CBT can help people who have tic-like compulsions, it is not very effective for preventing actual tics. Tics are less voluntary in nature than compulsions. CBT techniques can often help people with tics cope better with the anxiety they cause, however, and can sometimes be used to temporarily suppress an impending tic in a situation where it would be especially unwelcome, without the usual build-up of severe anxiety and discomfort. Tics cannot be suppressed forever, though—this use of relaxation and anxiety prevention techniques is strictly a temporary coping mechanism.

It's also important for people to have a choice about using habit reversal and other forms of behavior modification. Research shows that strict behavior modification techniques can actually worsen tic frequency by increasing stress.[16]

Simple tic substitution is a creative strategy frequently employed by people with TS. Substituting a nonsense word or a word's equivalent in Latin when you feel the urge to blurt out a curse word, poking holes in a piece of scrap fabric rather than one's own clothes, or tensing rather than flailing out with your arm are just three examples of tic substitutions. Substitution is usually experienced as much less frustrating than actually suppressing a tic.

Social skill-building

The social world is fraught with problems for young people with TS. Their unusual behaviors can make them social pariahs or the targets of bullying. Some suffer from OCD or social phobia (another anxiety disorder) as well, compounding the problem. The feelings of fear and anxiety that accompany obsessive-compulsive symptoms have a particularly strong impact on the ability to socialize, but many people find that their embarrassment about ticcing is also a factor.

Many people with TS thrive in social situations, where their quick wit and verbal precocity may give them a distinct advantage. Some others, however, can benefit from explicit training in social skills. Usually delivered in a group setting, social skills instruction covers topics like how to have a conversation, playing well with others, etiquette and proper behavior, and sometimes personal grooming issues. The group may be made up of children or teens who all have TS or a related disorder, youth with a variety of disabilities, or a mix of children with and without special needs. These groups may be available through mental health clinics. Others are set up by psychiatrists, or are part of group therapy programs or formal mental-health support groups for kids.

Some people prefer to work on social skills in a one-on-one setting. Social skills work can also be incorporated into school programs, since school is often the primary social setting for young people with TS. The most successful approaches use direct modeling and role-playing, allowing the child to try on different responses to social situations without risk of failure. Sometimes a "buddy system" or "circle of friends" approach is used to incorporate the child with TS into the social life of the classroom and the school. If adults are careful to choose the right partners, this can be a very workable strategy.

A number of social skills curriculums have been developed that schools can purchase. Parents can also try the suggestions found in books like *Playground Politics,* listed in Appendix A.

Parents and teachers should act as "emotion coaches" with children who have social skills difficulties, helping them to recognize and manage their own emotions more effectively. You can help your child label the feelings and behaviors that cause him social distress, and think up strategies for dealing with these difficulties. There are posters, books, and entire curricula available for working on emotion awareness with young children or those with severe social deficits.

Debbie, mother of 10-year-old Nate, says:

> We had to teach him the correct facial expressions when being reprimanded. He once got recess taken away because he giggled when the principal reprimanded him. I informed the teachers and principal of the problem. On another occasion, a teacher was reprimanding his class and he began to giggle. Another teacher quietly reminded him that this was not the appropriate social response, and Nate "straightened" his face.

Perhaps the two greatest social skills you can help your child develop are a sense of humor and flexibility. These will help him weather life's setbacks even better than good manners or conversation skills.

Adults with TS sometimes wish that a "refresher course" in social skills was available, especially if their TS went untreated for many years. Working one-on-one with a therapist can help adults gain increased emotional and social skills.

You might also enjoy working with a "coach," a professional who helps people (usually those with ADD or ADHD) handle ongoing problems with organization, motivation and social skills. You can find out more about ADD coaching services and concepts on the Web at *http://add.miningco.com/health/add/library/weekly/aa011299. htm?pid=2750&cob=home.*

Neurobiofeedback

Neurobiofeedback, also known as EEG biofeedback, relies on an electroencephalograph (EEG) machine that has a computer-screen readout. While hooked up to this machine, you see patterns that correspond to your brainwaves on screen, and learn various mental strategies to modify them.

One study of people with simple and complex tics showed a good response to this technique.[17] Neurobiofeedback also helps people cope with anxiety.

Neurobiofeedback has become one of the most widely touted non-medication therapies for TS, even though the medical evidence is still rather slim. If you're interested in trying it, be sure to check out the firm you choose. Some are not reputable. Your best choice is a neurobiofeedback center that is associated with a hospital. While this therapy shows some promise, it requires constant practice and may come at a high cost.

You can reach the Association for Applied Psychophysiology and Biofeedback, a trade organization for centers offering this service, at (800) 477-8892.

Stress reduction

Methods to reduce stress are valuable supportive therapies for people with TS. What works for one person may not for another, but time-tested stress-busters include bodywork, prayer, meditation, dance, music, and exercise.

Even very young patients can benefit from simple stress-reduction techniques, especially basic relaxation exercises designed for their age level. Simply learning how to count to ten when faced with stress can go a long way. Having ways to deal with stress proactively can prevent many of the behavioral problems that are sometimes associated with TS.

Andrea, mother of 17-year-old Robbie, says stress has been a persistent problem for her son:

> When Robbie is under stress (usually self-imposed) he will rage either at others or at himself. He is a high IQ child and has high expectations for himself, as well as the ones others place on him. So he sometimes overloads himself and can't meet his expectations and then rages.
>
> He was so careful at school not to display the annoying tics that he became extremely stressed. One teacher said it seemed as if he was wound too tightly. When he would come home from school he would literally explode either in tears or extreme delightful exuberance.
>
> Simplification of everything is helpful. With Robbie, removing the usual pressure from school has helped a lot. I don't add to the pressure to get good grades, I allow him to miss school if he needs a day off, I haven't insisted that he get a job, etc. This may not be helpful with other kids, but Robbie is one of those self-motivated kids who put pressure on themselves to perform.

You can work with your therapist to identify tics or compulsive behaviors that you perform in response to stress, or that get worse when you're stressed out. Then you can gradually replace these uncomfortable behaviors with techniques that really work.

Aromatherapy

Some people swear by aromatherapy as a stress-buster. This practice involves using essential oils or other scents that have a calming effect. The nose does have a direct line to the brain, so it can't hurt to try. Adding oils with a calming scent to a warm bath might be especially relaxing.

Bodywork

Bodywork is a catchall term for any type of therapy that involves massaging or manipulating the body. If ticcing makes you sore and stressed out, bodywork can be a comforting solution. Massage in particular can soothe sore muscles and lower your stress level. There are many different types of massage, ranging from vigorous Swedish and Russian styles to shiatsu, which incorporates techniques similar to those used in acupressure.

Chiropractic and craniosacral therapy, mentioned earlier in this chapter, are two other forms of bodywork. There are many more. One of the nicer things about bodywork is that you can try different styles and practitioners at a relatively low cost per session until you find the right technique for you.

Exercise

Exercise is not only useful for reducing stress; it also strengthens your muscles, which reduces the likelihood of strain and pain from repetitive movements of those muscles.

In addition, many people with TS report that vigorous exercise is a great rage-stopper. Done regularly, it burns off excess energy; done when a rage seems imminent, it channels your energy and activity into something that benefits you and harms no one else.

If you have OCD in addition to TS, watch out for exercise becoming a compulsion. Set a sensible program and stick to it, but resist the impulse to "punish yourself" with exercise or to repeat exercises that weren't done just right.

Meditation

Specific forms of meditation are sometimes taught as part of therapy programs. They give patients a silent tool they can use when pressure is overwhelming, even at school or at work. Meditation programs differ in their approach, but most encourage you to become more aware of your physical and mental relaxation response. This allows you to relax more quickly when you wish.

Prayer

All religions encourage some form of prayer or prayerful meditation. Talk to your religious advisor about methods that may be especially well suited for handling stressful situations. "Centering prayer" is one name used for meditation-like techniques used in a specifically Christian context, but there are similar traditions within other faiths.

Fixing sleep problems

Sleep disorders are frequently seen in people with Tourette's syndrome. Nighttime movements, neurotransmitter differences, and factors as yet unknown can cause sleep disorders.[18] It is rare for doctors to recommend sleeping pills nowadays, as their continued use can lead to dependency. However, if disturbed sleep is a persistent problem, you may want to talk to your psychiatrist about changing your medications for TS or other conditions, or about rearranging when you take them. Medications are often a key factor in both sleeplessness and over-sleeping.

For example, some of the neuroleptics used to treat TS can be sedating during the day, leading to poor sleep at night. If you take a stimulant like Ritalin or Adderall, it could also be contributing to sleeplessness. Switching to a different medication, avoiding the use of stimulating medications like Prozac or Adderall in the evening, or taking sedating medications like Paxil or Risperdal in the evening can contribute to improved sleep patterns.

For 10-year-old Charisse, clonidine has shown benefit for both tic reduction and addressing insomnia:

> Charisse also takes clonidine in the evening to help TS symptoms and to help her sleep. Before being put on clonidine, she would be up until 2 A.M., still active and wide-awake. Her ADHD is quite severe, and the clonidine helps her get much-needed rest.

There are also non-medication strategies that can help. Setting a bedtime and a wake-up time and sticking to them is often essential, even if there's a big test tomorrow or a rock concert tonight, and even if it's Saturday morning and you want to sleep in. Obviously, this is not going to be a popular point with teenagers who delight in lazy weekend mornings, or young adults who want to share in the nightlife of their peers.

The following advice applies to anyone who occasionally experiences insomnia:

* Avoid unnecessary artificial stimulants and depressants, such as coffee, tea, and alcohol.

- Avoid over-the-counter medications with a stimulating or depressive effect, such as over-the-counter allergy preparations, aspirin with caffeine, No-Doz and other over-the-counter stimulants, and most commercial cough syrups.

- Avoid exciting television programs, music, or games right before bed. Parents can decide when their child's activity level should start to wind down slowly.

- Use your bed for sleeping only, not for reading, watching television, or playing. This helps associate the concepts of "bed" and "sleep" in your mind.

- If you can't get to sleep at the proper time, don't just lie there tossing and turning. Get out of bed, and do something really, really boring—like housework, or putting together an old jigsaw puzzle.

- Make a relaxing—but time-limited—ritual part of bedtime. For young children this could be a story with mom and some warm milk. Teens might prefer using a computer or reading for twenty minutes at a certain time, followed by brushing teeth, donning pajamas, laying out tomorrow's school clothes, or other end-of-the-day chores. A nice, long bath is another great way to end the day for adults.

- Some people find certain scents very soporific, and have added aromatherapy to their relaxation plan. These can be added to oil and massaged into the skin for a doubly relaxing effect.

- The use of relaxation audiotapes or background noise machines helps some people get to sleep or return to sleep.

- Special breathing and muscle relaxation techniques can help.

Melatonin

Melatonin (MLT), a hormone produced by the pineal gland, is responsible for helping you sleep and for maintaining other biochemical rhythms. Melatonin supplements given about half an hour before bed are sometimes useful for addressing sleep problems. Their effect may decrease over time.

Some studies have found that taking a melatonin supplement on a regular basis can make depression worse, so be careful when using this supplement. Supplementing directly with any kind of hormone can be problematic in the long run, as in some cases the person's body may respond by producing less of the natural substance.

If you do decide to try melatonin, talk about it with your doctor or psychiatrist, and set up a dosage plan and observation schedule first.

Other sleep supplements

Simply taking a good multivitamin may help regulate sleep. Vitamin deficiencies implicated in insomnia and/or hypersomnia (over-sleeping) include the B vitamins (especially B2 and niacin), potassium, and magnesium. Vitamin B2 helps the body convert the amino acid tryptophan into compounds that raise blood levels of the neurotransmitter serotonin. Serotonin levels rise before and during sleep.

You may be tempted to try "natural" sleep aids. Of the herbal options mentioned in this section, chamomile is probably the safest and mildest. Avoid using other central nervous system depressants, including alcohol, at the same time as these substances (using alcohol as a "sleep aid" can be very counterproductive, as it tends to lead to late-night wakening.) Other depressants may add to the sedative action of the active ingredients in some of these substances, with possibly dangerous effects.

These supplements also don't work for everyone. Brenda, grandmother of 10-year-old Charisse, says:

> We tried valerian to see if this could help with sleep. We had to mix it with juice, as it tasted horrid. There was no improvement that we could discern.

Indeed, although these herbal potions are not as dangerous as prescription sleeping pills, they are also not inconsequential. It's never a good thing to be dependent on a pill to sleep, and little is known about the long-term effects of herbal sleep aids, or of their over-the-counter counterparts (Ny-Tol, etc.)

Supplements believed to affect sleep patterns include the following.

- Valerian (*Valeriana officinalis*). Valerian is a strong herbal sedative (and one of the secret ingredients in the soporific liqueur Jagermeister). It should not be given to young children, but may help teens and adults fight occasional insomnia.

- Kava-kava (*Piper methysticum*). This mild sedative herb has been used for centuries in the South Pacific. It has a slight potential for abuse, although such misuse is rare.

- Chamomile (*Anthemis nobilis*). Chamomile is a mild but effective sedative traditionally used to treat sleep disorders or stomach upsets. It is a member of the daisy family, so avoid this herb if you are allergic to its cousin, ragweed.

- Passion flower (*Passiflora incarnata*). This botanical has sedative, antispasmodic, and anti-inflammatory effects.

- Skullcap (*Scutellaria lateriflora*). Skullcap is an herbal sedative that has traditionally been used to treat tic disorders and muscle spasms, as well as seizure disorders, insomnia, and anxiety. Other traditional uses include menstrual irregularity and breast pain, indicating that it may have hormonal effects.

- Hops (*Humulus lupulus*). This herb is used to flavor beer, and the reason beer makes many people sleepy. It's available in capsules or as a dried herb for use in tea, and works as a gentle sleep aid.

- Tryptophan. This amino acid that raises the levels of serotonin in the brain. It's not currently available in the US due to a badly contaminated batch several years ago, but it is sold over-the-counter in Europe and by prescription in Canada. It appears to help regulate sleep, and to have an antidepressant effect not unlike that of an SSRI. For that reason, do not use this substance if you take any pharmaceutical antidepressant. If you can purchase tryptophan, buy it from a trustworthy source. Take it at bedtime with sweetened milk or fruit juice, and add vitamin B6 for maximum effect.

- 5-HTP (5-hydroxytryptophan). The substance 5-HTP is synthesized from tryptophan, and is an even more direct precursor to serotonin than tryptophan. It is available in the US. It appears to help regulate sleep, and to have an antidepressant effect not unlike that of an SSRI. For that reason, do not use this substance if you take any pharmaceutical antidepressant.

- Taurine. This is another amino acid that can counteract insomnia. It works by slowing down nerve impulses.

- Black cohosh (Cimicifuga racemosa, squaw root). Black cohosh is a nervous system depressant and sedative, is often used by people with autoimmune conditions for its anti-inflammatory effects. Its active ingredient appears to bind to estrogen receptor sites, so it may cause hormonal activity.

- GABA (gaba-amino butyric acid). GABA is an amino-acid-like compound that inhibits the activity of certain neurotransmitters. You shouldn't take anti-epilepsy medications or mood stabilizers with GABA supplements, unless your physician recommends it and oversees the process. Supplementation with over-the-counter GABA is sometimes recommended for anxiety, nervous tension, and insomnia, especially insomnia associated with racing thoughts. If you experience shortness of breath, tingling, or numbness in your hands or feet when taking GABA, lower or discontinue this supplement.

Valerian, kava-kava, passionflower, and skullcap can help to ease extreme anxiety as well as insomnia, but their sedating qualities must be taken into account.

Dietary changes

If you suspect that you or your child has food allergies, pursue allergy testing and eliminate any allergens from your diet. A good allergist can help you try an elimination diet and other steps to discover and deal with food allergies.

Most people with TS who find that their symptoms improve with dietary changes don't have allergies per se. They simply have food intolerances, or need to avoid additives that interfere with certain processes in the body.

Sometimes the offending item makes itself obvious, according to Debbie, mother of 10-year-old Nate:

> We usually avoid milk. He drinks soy milk instead. If he has too many milk products, his behavior is "off the wall." He can occasionally have something, such as pizza or cheesecake, but never with a glass of milk, and never in large quantities.

When the problem is an additive, such as a food coloring or artificial flavor, it can be harder to uncover. Bonnie Grimaldi, parent of a son with TS who has become almost symptom-free while taking certain vitamins and changing his diet, recommends avoiding caffeine, aspartame (NutraSweet), MSG (monosodium glutamate), caramel color, vanillin and yellow #5 (tartrazine). She notes that some people are also sensitive to other food dyes, particularly red dye #40.[19]

Grace, mother of 17-year-old Keith, says:

> We haven't seen any changes in his TS symptoms, but when Keith was little we tried dietary changes to help with the hyperactivity, to no real effect. However, we know now to avoid tartrazine, excessive caffeine, and NutraSweet. These additives do make a difference, even though foods did not.

Quite a few physicians treating people with autism have noted that some of their patients benefit from removing dairy products and gluten (the protein found in wheat and some other grains) from the diet, an approach first discovered by parents who noticed that these foods seemed to affect their children's behavior.[20] This approach may be useful to some persons with TS as well, particularly those who also have an autistic spectrum disorder, or who have gastrointestinal problems.

Many popular diet books claim that a particular eating regimen will boost your immune system function. Immune-boosting claims have been made (and sometimes substantiated in limited clinical research) for a wide variety of foods, including red wine, tofu, miso (fermented soybean paste), kale, and yams. For the average person, a healthy, balanced diet is sufficient. If you have known or suspected immune-system dysfunction, however, you might want to research some of these options.

Exploring your alternatives

Complementary therapies are always a topic of interest when people with TS get together, simply because of the intolerable side effects many have experienced using accepted medical treatments.

If you would like to know more about complementary approaches to TS, the newsletter *Latitudes,* listed in Appendix A, covers this territory in depth. There are also a number of online resources that discuss various therapies, practitioners, and products. Just remember to maintain a skeptical view when you encounter claims that sound too good to be true, as they usually are just that.

CHAPTER 8

School Issues

TOURETTE'S SYNDROME CAN HAVE profound developmental and behavioral effects, which sometimes makes it an issue in the classroom. Several options are available for children who need extra help at school due to behaviors and developmental issues associated with TS.

This chapter helps you learn how to navigate the education system, including using the special education system to assist your child in achieving his best in school. It includes specific tips for handling TS behaviors in the classroom, with a special section on handling "difficult" TS behaviors that may distract other students or be seen as disciplinary issues, such as spitting, vocal tics, coprolalia, and full-body tics. It concludes with information on planning for a smooth transition to adulthood and independence.

It covers US education laws and practices, as well as education in other English-speaking countries.

Tourette's syndrome goes to school

Tourette's syndrome manifests itself in such varied ways that there's no way to predict what interventions students with TS require, if any. But when teachers, school administrators, and parents take the time to consider each child's individual needs, they can develop programs that give children with TS the best chance to learn.

For 10-year-old Nate, both the impact of TS on his school performance and modifications needed to deal with it have been minor:

> Nate was diagnosed with TS at age 6. He cannot pass tests with long columns of matching, such as matching questions 1 through 26 with answers A through Z—even if he knows the answers, he cannot find them. When the teacher keeps the questions and answers within sets of five (1–5 matched to A–E, and so on) and draws a line on Nate's paper after each set, my son can pass.

> *Teachers have also made him an "errand boy" so that he could get up and move around with permission.*

> *The teacher has been known to give him a grade "on his level." For instance, his report card may say "S–L," meaning satisfactory on his level.*

Accommodating disability is not always such an easy task for schools, however. In 1999, the US Department of Education released its most recent annual report on special education. This document trumpeted the excellent news that thanks to new laws, parental efforts, and better teaching methods, 31 percent more students with disabilities are now receiving high-school diplomas. Buried in this report was the sad news that this trend does not yet extend to children with "emotional disturbances," the special education category under which many children with TS are (usually erroneously) served. According to the DOE, an outrageous 55 percent of "emotionally disturbed" children leave school without earning a diploma. They also fail more courses, earn lower GPAs, miss more school, and are held back more often than students with other types of disabilities.[1]

That's a shameful record, and one that must be changed. Children with mental retardation, children whose physical disabilities confine them to wheelchairs, and those with other health problems are making great strides in accessing an education. This wasn't always the case. These changes have only come about through the efforts of dedicated parents and education researchers, working in concert with teachers, school administrators, and lawmakers to revamp school programs for the disabled. Students with mental or neurological problems deserve the same consideration.

For students with TS, most of the school problems that parents report center around a lack of current knowledge about TS, which sometimes creates misconceptions and even fear when teachers and schools encounter the disorder. Parents can do four things to dispel ignorance and fear of Tourette's syndrome in schools:

- Communicate with their child's school about the diagnosis. The potential stigma of labeling a child with Tourette's syndrome is far less serious than what will happen if the school labels the same child as a behavior problem, or as a lazy student who refuses to do his work.

- Use the special education laws to get classroom support for children with TS when needed.

- Educate the educators: provide reading material about TS, and make yourself available to teachers, counselors, and administrators who want to know more.

- Contact a TS advocacy group about holding an in-service presentation for your child's teacher and other school personnel.

Parents need to warn schools about adopting "generic" solutions, however. Each child's need for and response to interventions will differ. For that reason, no single school program is successful for all students who have TS.

Defining the problem

Children aren't always forthcoming about the symptoms that really bother them or get in the way of school success. They may say that everything's fine, even when their grades and behavior indicate otherwise. Sometimes the child is not aware of the root problem, is unable to put it into words, or is embarrassed about either the nature of the problem or about being singled out for special attention.

Teachers and parents should begin by observing the child's behavior during different types of school tasks, including during homework sessions. Certain subjects or situations may emerge as clear problem areas, while the child has no difficulties with others.

Make note of both problem areas and strengths—often you can call upon the child's strengths to deal with problems. For example, a child might have excellent visual and artistic skills, but find reading difficult. This child may shine at charts and geometry, but find "word problems" a chore. You may be able to use visual learning methods to address the reading difficulty, and thereby improve both reading and math competency.

Testing is an important step, both to figure out where the child is academically in various subjects, and to find out whether the child has specific learning disabilities. In the US, testing for learning disabilities is available at no cost to parents through the public schools. If your child's teacher is the first to notice that he is struggling, she can refer him for testing. Parents can also request a referral by talking with the teacher, school psychologist or child development specialist, or principal, or by calling the special education department directly.

You can also pursue testing through private programs, although the school system may not be willing to create a program for your child based on the results (see "Special education for students with TS," later in this chapter).

Sometimes the issue isn't as easy as identifying a learning disability or a different learning style. This is especially true when the problem is based on internal thought processes, such as obsessive thoughts that make concentrating difficult.

There are several symptoms linked to TS or its frequent companion, OCD, that school-age children find particularly distracting. These include:

- Physical or vocal tics that are hard to suppress in the classroom, and the anxiety that comes from trying to constantly suppress them

- Physical or vocal tics that disturb other students or the teacher, leading to ostracism, embarrassment, and sometimes punishment

- "Mental tics", such as counting words as they are being said or while reading, or counting other items in the classroom—for example, compulsions to repeat words, numbers, or phrases to oneself or out loud are sometimes the culprit when a child is slow to answer questions or process information

- Disruptive complex tics that include wanting to smell, touch, or look at other students

- Obsessions with "good" or "bad" numbers that cause students to avoid certain math problems, pages in books, or sentences with that number of words

- "Evening up" behavior, which can extend to wreaking havoc with mathematics, reading, and drawing

- Compulsions to read each word or number perfectly or follow steps with precision, causing students to start over again if they make even small errors

- Compulsion to re-read due to doubt that the first reading was done properly; compulsion to rewrite due to similar perfectionism or other obsessions

- OCD-linked contamination fears involving school bathrooms or classroom surfaces that other children have touched

- Overwhelming topic obsessions that make other subjects boring

- Specific OCD-linked rituals that are time-consuming, such as handwashing or checking rituals, or that cause severe anxiety if they are not carried out

- Anxiety that is disguised as vague illness, such as stomachaches

- Social phobia, sometimes caused by medications, that limits interaction with other students, making group projects, oral reports, and other types of school-work extremely stressful

- Attention deficits due to ADHD

Ten-year-old Ian tells how a topic obsession was disruptive in school:

> When I was 6, everything I did had to do with squids. I would look at
> a certain book that had pictures of squids in it in our class and count the
> legs. Some of the pictures were not right; they had fourteen or fifteen legs
> instead of ten. That made me mad and I wanted to talk about it a lot.
> People did not understand why I cared.

Special school problems

Certain school problems linked with TS are especially difficult. These include behaviors, such as spitting, touching, vocal tics, coprolalia, and full-body tics, that may distract other students; specific learning disabilities, particularly dyscalculia, dysgraphia and dyslexia; the use of medications at school; and "zero tolerance" disciplinary systems. Teasing and bullying are sometimes an issue as well. They are discussed in Chapter 4, *Growing Up with Tourette's Syndrome.*

When dealing with these problems, teachers, administrators and parents have to be careful not to stigmatize students with TS. When choosing solutions, always involve the student and classmates where appropriate, and look for solutions that don't set the student with TS apart from others. For example, putting the child with TS in a study carrel in the back of the classroom all of the time is likely to make him feel singled out, while simply making the study carrel available as needed gives him control. Providing a student with two work areas or occasionally having him run errands for the teacher (even fictitious errands, if need be) can give her a chance to move around without having to ask permission in public.

Often the issue is not the child's behavior so much as its effect on other students, or their reactions to it. If you and your child feel comfortable about it, educate classmates about TS at the beginning of the year, and make sure information is available when new symptoms appear.

Distraction

Perhaps the biggest problem for students with Tourette's syndrome is getting distracted from tasks by tics. Ticcing, trying to suppress tics, and dealing with other students' comments about tics all take time away from paying attention in class and completing schoolwork. If a teacher hasn't been informed about the child's diagnosis, she might think the child is willfully ignoring her lectures, when he is instead fighting hard to stay focused. Distractibility is increased when a child has OCD or ADD/ADHD as well as TS.

Medication can help, but until it takes effect (and for those students who do not respond to medication), classroom modifications are necessary. Eliminating unnecessary distractions is an important step, especially for students who are extremely sensitive to noise, smells, and visual clutter. These students may find that working in a resource room, quiet library, or individual study carrel is a good idea when they are having trouble concentrating.

Classrooms can be designed to minimize sensory overload. This change will benefit not only the student with TS, but will probably help many of his classmates as well.

Spitting tics

Spitting is a fairly common tic, and it can take many different forms. Kids with spitting tics need to be encouraged to find "workarounds" that prevent health risks to other students. Spitting into a handkerchief or wastebasket are two obvious ones. Moving the child closer to the door so this tic can be carried out in the bathroom or hall may also work. Fellow students also need to be told that the spitting is a tic, not an attempt to "gross them out."

Touching tics

Tics that involve touching other kids are an area where TS and the rights of others in the class can collide. Some kids may be bothered, while others are not. If the behavior is very minor (occasionally tapping another student's shoulder, for example) and you can help the other children accept it, that's great. If that's not possible, if the touching is frequent, or if it involves touching buttocks, crotch areas, or breasts, work with the student who has TS to come up with solutions. These might include changing the classroom layout to minimize physical contact between all students, or helping the student use "tic substitution" strategies.

One strategy that has worked for several classroom teachers is instituting the "three foot rule": declaring that when in line, at their desks, or walking around the classrooms, all students must maintain a three-foot distance from each other. You might use a three-foot ribbon or a tape measure to help the students visualize that distance. Obviously, this rule will not work for PE class and for certain classroom activities that require children to work in close proximity, but it's a start.

Vocal tics

When vocal tics erupt in the classroom, they tend to be distracting at first. However, they can't be helped, and must be accepted. Teachers should not discipline children with TS for having vocal tics—instead they should model tolerance, acceptance, and caring. If you studiously ignore them, a child's vocal tics tend to become just one more bit of background noise in the classroom, no more distracting than the click of the clock or rustling papers.

Sometimes special situations arise in which a student's vocal tics might be more distracting than usual. For example, if students are required to take a time-limited exam that will decide their college placement or graduation status, all of the students will want the test-taking environment to be as distraction-free as possible. Talk with the student who has TS about how he wants to handle the situation. Providing him (or all of the students) with a study carrel during the exam, or allowing the student with TS to take the test in an alternate location, are two possible solutions out of many.

Coprolalia

Coprolalia is not a common tic, but can present some very knotty problems when it occurs at school. All schools have rules about the use of profane or otherwise inappropriate language, but you can't prevent coprolalia with punishment.

It's best to address the issue head-on with other students, and to help them understand not only that the symptom is as involuntary as their classmate's other tics, but that it is very embarrassing for the child.

Parents and therapists may also be able to help the child use tic substitution techniques to blunt the impact of coprolalia in the classroom, while being careful to let the child know that he needn't expend all his energy on suppressing tics. Providing a special hall pass that the child can use when tics need to be expressed is also useful.

Full-body tics

Like vocal tics, these should simply be ignored. Providing a special hall pass that the child can use when tics need to be expressed can sometimes come in handy.

If a complex, full-body tic exposes the student with TS or classmates to harm (head-banging, for example, or leg movements that could result in someone getting kicked), look at practical solutions for preventing the harm, not the tic. Moving desks, adding a soft surface to a desk, or allowing a student to sit on the floor or in a chair without a desk as needed can minimize banging and flying furniture.

Specific learning disabilities

Some types of learning disabilities are seen considerably more often in students with TS.[2] When these are identified through appropriate testing, the outcome is decreased stress and improved academic performance.

Dyscalculia is a learning disability that affects mastery of mathematical concepts. Children with this challenge may find math easier if they use manipulatives and other visual aids to learn and practice new concepts. They may also have difficulty with learning to sight-read music, understanding musical concepts, and dancing— music and rhythm are all about mathematics.

Dysgraphia is a learning disability that specifically affects the child's ability to write. Many children with TS are delayed with learning how to write, and particularly with learning to write in cursive letters. Occupational therapy aimed at developing "pre-writing" skills, such as appropriate fine-motor control and hand-eye coordination, is important. Learning keyboarding skills is a great workaround for kids who never master the art of beautiful handwriting.[3]

Dyslexia is a learning disability that affects how a child reads. Not all children with dyslexia reverse letters, although many do. What all persons with dyslexia have in common is difficulties with tracking with their eyes while reading (a visual-spatial skill) and automatically recognizing the differences between letters (a visual-perceptual skill). There are many techniques that are helpful for students with dyslexia, including special curricula, devices that visually isolate the line being read to prevent confusion, using large-type materials, and sometimes even using colored overlays while reading.

Both dyslexia and dysgraphia can affect a child's performance on written assignments.

Rindy, mother of 14-year-old Shawn, says:

> Shawn's school problems have been in the area of written expression and with handwriting. The handwriting difficulty is related to his tics as well as to fine-motor problems and lack of hand strength, leading to an unorthodox grip.
>
> In addition, there are problems with getting his thoughts down on paper. He can speak entire paragraphs; ask him to write it down and you get a few words, usually not even a full sentence. The accommodation for this situation has been to provide him access to computers at school, resulting in much improvement.
>
> The special education department has also been working with him for three years in such areas as webbing, outlining, and organizational and

study skills, with much improvement. When originally assessed by the school in fifth grade, he was about two years behind, but now he is working pretty much at grade level.

Keeping the stress down by reducing the workload has been the biggest factor in keeping him from being overloaded. Modifications have been to shorten assignments and make them relevant—otherwise he resists doing them, because he doesn't see the point in doing something "boring and stupid"—and providing a study hall with the special ed teacher. She tracks his progress on a daily basis, and coordinates work loads with the regular ed teachers. We communicate frequently via e-mail. I let her know if he's stressed out at home so they can keep things stable at school, since stress in one environment overflows into others.

It's also been very important to place him with faculty who are flexible and watchful. Teachers who are into power struggles and/or are rigid and authoritarian have been disastrous.

Speech problems

One speech problem seen more often in children with TS is cluttering, also known as tachyphemia. A person who clutters repeats a word or phrase two or more times—it's a bit like stuttering, except that the person gets stuck on an entire word rather than a difficult sound. Some speech experts think cluttering may actually be a type of vocal tic.[4]

Like stuttering, cluttering responds well to speech therapy that focuses on speaking slowly, reducing your anxiety about speaking, and working on sounds that tend to trip your tongue. People with a tendency to clutter may never lose it, but instead develop a repertoire of tricks to minimize or cover up the problem.

Unusual speech rates, rhythms, and tones are also sometimes seen in kids with TS, along with temporary bouts of stuttering, and difficulties with mediating speech intensity and volume. These issues are similar to speech problems seen in verbal children with autistic spectrum disorders. They also respond well to specifically targeted speech therapy.

Transitions

Some students find that transitions during the school day are especially difficult. These kids do their best work when the number of classroom and personnel changes is limited, either by being in an inclusive special education classroom or by spending longer blocks of time in the same classroom.

Alternatively, they may need extra time to get from class to class. Teachers can release them a few minutes early, allowing them to make it to the next class without having to navigate crowded, noisy hallways.

Perfectionism

Perfectionism is a serious problem for some students who have both TS and OCD. In school, this might lead to excellent performance sometimes, and to problems at other times. For example, perfectionists often find handwriting and drawing intensely frustrating. They may try to get letters, numbers, and drawings absolutely perfect, to the point of writing, erasing, and rewriting figures over and over. Even simple math assignments can become torturous as they check and re-check their answers, or attempt to make their numbers perfectly shaped and lined up on the page.

Parents and teachers can work together on strategies like these:

- Be directive rather than offering choices.
- Spell out specific standards of quality so that students don't set their own bar too high.
- Allow students to prepare assignments on a typewriter or computer rather than by hand.
- Permit checking math homework answers once (and only once) with a calculator.
- Shorten assignments as needed to allow completion within the time allotted.

Many students are able to let go of perfectionist goals when working within time limits, especially if there are limits attached to each item rather than an entire set of items. Others find that time limits are the straw that breaks the camel's back, adding extra pressure to a task that's already hard.

Procrastination

Procrastination is sometimes the result of perfectionism. Students may start a school project over and over, throwing away half-finished versions or ruminating endlessly over what they should do. Alternatively, they may choose goals that are too ambitious to attain in the time given, leading to extreme frustration. As the deadline gets closer, anxiety increases, and may reach paralyzing intensity. The result is work left undone, despite the fact that thinking and worrying about the project has occupied far more hours of time than would have been needed to complete it.

Other students procrastinate because they have problems with executive function, the internal process of planning and executing a project. These kids respond well to explicit instructions and "road maps" on how to get started, how to stay on track, and how to complete their work on time.

Setting achievable goals and coming up with a system to meet them can prevent both types of procrastinators from sabotaging themselves. It's important to uncover the issues behind procrastination first, so the right strategy can be chosen.

Organization and study skills

Like students with ADHD, kids with TS can almost always benefit from general instruction in study and schoolwork skills, including systems for remembering, organizing, and completing classroom work, homework, and special projects. Successful strategies used by some students include:

- Breaking up large projects into small, manageable tasks, each with its own deadline

- Learning formulas that, if followed, will always turn out a serviceable essay or report

- Using an assignment or agenda book that teachers and parents check each day

- Using visual organizing systems, such as color-coded folders or sticky notes, to keep assignments organized and on time

- Setting a specific amount of time aside daily for schoolwork

- Keeping an extra set of books at home for days when they have been left at school

Of course, parents should provide a good environment for studying at home, and ensure that extracurricular activities, medical appointments, and family activities do not disrupt a child's regular study sessions.

Jennifer's 12-year-old son Ty began to have problems in junior high:

> This year is the first time that we have run into problems with the regular school setting. The move to middle school has been difficult, and we have run into many problems with getting homework done and assignments completed. So far no accommodations have been made, but

we've requested a special education assessment to evaluate if he qualifies for any type of assistance. Ty has had many emotional, crying episodes since this year started.

Kids with TS may benefit from working with a tutor on certain types of subjects or projects. The tutor could be an adult volunteer or resource room teacher, but many students have had equally good results from working with a peer or slightly older student whose study skills are particularly good. Tutors should pay special attention not just to helping with the problem topic or project, but to imparting general guidelines and ideas about studying and doing schoolwork.

Medications at school

Many children and teens with TS can take all their medication at home, and this is the best way to avoid school medication problems. Generally speaking, kids prefer not to take medicine at school. Some need to take daytime doses, though, and these have to be administered at school.

In any school there are many, many children who have daily medication needs, ranging from Ritalin to asthma inhalers. Your child will not be seen as unusual if he needs to take a pill every day. In fact, he'll probably have to wait in line.

On the other hand, schools these days are very concerned about student drug use. Drug policies usually include prescription medications and over-the-counter drugs, such as aspirin, as well as illicit drugs. Make sure you have a copy of your child's school's policy on using prescription and non-prescription medications at school to avoid problems. It is very rare for even a teenager to be allowed to self-administer medication at school. The usual exceptions to this rule are medications to treat life-threatening symptoms that could emerge suddenly, such as emergency asthma inhalers or an anaphylactic shock kit for students with severe allergies. Medications other than these must usually be kept and administered by a school employee.

Thirteen-year-old Richard now has an "as-needed" medication at his disposal at school, with help from a cooperative administration and his mother:

> *We had to give the school nurse a signed order by the doctor to give the medicine "PRN," and then I gave my own written instructions: they could give it once per day based on their judgment; if they thought he needed it a second time, they had to call me first for verbal permission.*

Emergency or "as-needed" psychiatric medications are problematic for schools. Unless they have a medical person on staff, they will naturally be unsure of when to allow their use. If your doctor prescribes this kind of medication for your child, the pill bottle should say "use as needed" or "PRN" (from the Latin *pro re nata,* meaning "as circumstances dictate"). Ask your physician to write a brief statement about when school personnel should give the medication out. Alternatively, you could write this statement yourself. Older children and teens should know the symptoms that these drugs can help with and be able to ask for them independently. The medications most commonly prescribed in this way to children with TS are tranquilizers and other anti-anxiety drugs. They are very helpful when used properly.

Medications should be properly stored. The pill bottle's label or pharmacy insert should tell you if a medication needs refrigeration or should simply be stored away from light or heat. For safety's sake, medications should be kept in a locked drawer or cabinet. This will prevent misuse, abuse, and theft. Ask to see where your child's medications will be kept.

If your school has an on-site health clinic or nurse's office, that's probably the best place for your child to get and take his medication. If it does not, someone who is neither licensed nor trained in how to handle medication-related problems will give out medications. This is a major problem for many families whose children need to take medication at school. School secretaries and teachers are frequently pressed into the role of pill-pushers, and it's rarely one that they relish. Incidentally, in hospitals and nursing homes, a Certified Medication Aide (CMA) license is the minimum qualification required for employees who give medication to patients.

If your child takes medication daily, make sure there is some sort of checklist used to monitor compliance. The person in charge should actually *see* the child take the medication, not hand it out and let the child walk away. Check the child's mouth to make sure the pills were swallowed, if necessary. Ask to see the medication compliance checklist at least once a semester, and talk to your child about whether he is getting his meds regularly. Know how many tablets you have sent to school, and when they should run out.

Sometimes a psychiatrist working at the school prescribes medication to students, with parental permission. Occasionally someone without a license to practice medicine, such as a psychologist or school counselor, may tell parents that their child should take a certain medication. In either case, parents have the right to refuse medication for their child, and to ask for a second opinion.

Zero tolerance policies

Due to recent episodes of violence, many US schools are taking a hard line on verbal threats, aggressive or assaultive behavior, and even on the presence of students with behavioral, emotional, or neurological disorders in schools. In some cases, this campaign has crossed over from prudent caution to violating the rights of special education students. For example, some districts have announced that all assaults (a category that includes hitting, biting, and even playground pushing) will result in police being called to actually arrest the student. Students have been suspended or threatened with expulsion for angrily saying things like "I wish this school would burn down" or for threatening the school bully with a stick hastily grabbed off the ground.

Joyce, mother of 18-year-old John, is dealing with how these new policies have impacted her son's education:

> John has had problems with extreme agitation and anger since about
> fourth grade, and it gradually got worse as he grew to his teen years. His
> anxiety when in groups, as at school, seemed to be intense—all it took
> was a minor trigger to set off an explosion. His junior high school staff
> was persuaded that perhaps I might know a bit about what I was talking
> about, and was quite cooperative. However, when John got to senior high
> (grade ten), there was a much more rigid stance, a "zero-tolerance"
> policy, and he rather quickly ended up being suspended indefinitely from
> school for kicking his aide, and thrust into my hands for home-schooling.

Some students with TS will break school rules, and not necessarily as a result of their illness. When they do so, they must pay the price. However, if a student covered by an IEP is suspended for more than ten days in one school year or is expelled, the district is responsible for finding an appropriate alternative educational setting immediately, and for continuing to implement the IEP. Suspension of a disabled student for more than ten days requires parental permission or a court order. The district is also required to do a functional behavior assessment and create a functional behavioral intervention plan if this has not already been done, or to take a new look at the existing plan in light of the incident.

Suspensions of longer than ten days constitute a change of placement, and that means that an IEP meeting must be called immediately. Special education law does not spell out exactly how this procedure should work, so districts may not have a plan in place to deal with emergency placements. Parents have reported that many school districts respond by putting the student on homebound instruction until a new placement can be found. This may or may not be acceptable. Delivery of therapeutic or related services may be a problem on homebound instruction. Parents will probably have to get involved to prevent the search process from dragging on too long.

These protections apply to students with a special education IEP or other formal agreement with the district, and also to students whose parents have requested a special education assessment or written a letter of concern about the child to school personnel (if the parent is illiterate or cannot write, a verbal inquiry will suffice) before the incident occurred, students whose behavior and performance should have indicated a disability to any objective observer, and students about whom district personnel have expressed concern before the incident.

Expulsion is an even more serious matter. Parents must be informed in writing about the district's intention to seek expulsion, and this document must include clear reasons for this action, evidence, and information about the child's procedural rights. There must be an assessment before expulsion can take place, and parents must also be informed about this in writing. A disabled student can be expelled only if all safeguards are provided and all procedures are followed.

Expulsion for a disabled student does not mean the same thing as it does for a garden-variety behavior problem. It's technically a forced change of placement. By expelling the student, the district has determined that the current placement is not working. It must then find an appropriate placement, which means revisiting the IEP.

Schools do have a duty to protect other students, faculty, and staff, even when the behavior is a manifestation of a child's disability. Case law has upheld the idea that if a student cannot be safely maintained in a less restrictive setting, the district has the right to place the student in a more restrictive setting. The devil is in the details, of course. Parents in these situations find they carry the burden of proving that the district did not do all it could to keep the student in his regular classroom.

If you or the school suspects that your child's misbehavior is the result of her disability, a functional behavior assessment (FBA) and a functional intervention plan (FIP) must be initiated once the child has been out of school for ten days. The FBA should include the following:

- A clear description of the problem behavior, including the pattern or sequence of behavior observed

- Time and place when the behavior occurs (setting and antecedents)

- The current consequences attached to the behavior

- A hypothesis about the cause and effect of the behavior

- Direct observation data

The FBA should determine whether the behavior was actually a manifestation of the disability, why it happened, and how it can be prevented in the future. If the child has already been identified as in need of special education services, this process is somewhat easier. If he has not, parents should be sure that a special education evaluation is started immediately to protect the child's educational rights (see "Special education for students with TS," later in this chapter).

The functional intervention plan should derive from the functional behavior assessment, and consist of guidelines for modifying the student's environment to improve behavior, and for teaching the student positive alternative behavior. Creating a workable plan may require testing several hypotheses about the behavior using different interventions. Administrators must follow this procedure whenever a special education student has a long-lasting behavior problem, or if he has any behavior problem that puts him at danger for suspension, expulsion, or arrest.

For a child who rages, the functional behavior assessment could be used to find out if there is an environmental trigger, and the functional intervention plan could provide ways to prevent the behavior. These might include removing the environmental trigger, designating a safe place for the child to go when he feels the warning signs of impending rage, training personnel in safe restraint techniques, or providing emergency medication.

Parents of a child who is sometimes aggressive or assaultive often secretly worry that he could turn his rage on others, with serious or even deadly results. Considering the rash of school killings in the late 1990s, this is a logical worry. After fifteen students and teachers were killed by a pair of gun-toting students at Columbine High School in Littleton, Colorado, both the press and legislative arenas were filled with calls to remove "problem students" from schools. One of the students involved, Eric Harris, had previously been prescribed Luvox, a medication frequently used to treat OCD, and some newspapers speculated that Harris suffered from the disorder. Suddenly the discussion about inclusion of students with mental illness took on an ugly tone, with some commentators and worried parents calling for students with emotional and behavioral problems to be kept away from public schools.

In fact, a look at the facts about teens guilty of school shootings who were supposedly under the care of a psychiatrist reveals that their care was generally cursory—perhaps a single visit and a quickly discarded prescription.

Responsible parents can do much to ensure that their child does not become the perpetrator of such crimes. Almost every teen involved in a school killing has had several traits in common. They have been very depressed, usually suicidal; and they have had easy access to weapons, little parental oversight, and no special program of supports at school. Most had been the victims of teasing and mistreatment at school, with no intervention from school administrators. All parents need to ensure that weapons are not easily available to children, that kids in need receive proper medical care, and that schools are part of the solution to emotional and behavioral problems.

If your child develops a fascination with weapons and violence, you must intervene immediately. Although intrusive violent thoughts are relatively common in TS, overpowering guilt normally accompanies them. On the off chance that your child might prove the exception to the rule, however, don't wait to get help if it is needed—call on all possible resources in his school and in the community.

As a result of school violence, several states and the federal government are considering laws that would mandate the arrest and incarceration (pending a hearing before a judge) of any child who brings a gun to school. If your child is ever in this situation, you should be able to use this opportunity to get him into a diversion program with psychiatric support. Unfortunately, some of the proposed laws go far beyond suspending special education services and rights for students with guns, and may represent a serious threat to special education services for a wider group who pose little if any risk to others.

The widespread adoption of zero tolerance policies has become a major issue for students coping with TS, and for school systems as well. One solution is putting a behavior plan in place at school that can be followed in case of an incident for any student who experiences behavioral difficulties, even if problems have so far occurred only at home. Parents can let teachers know about any triggers and warning signs that they have discovered, helping teachers intervene early and prevent problems when possible. A proactive approach provides protection not only for the student with a disability, but also for others who might be affected by his actions.

Designing a program

Once the problem or problems have been defined, it's time to look for solutions. You may have to try a few ideas out before you find a workable solution. Often the child or teen already knows some strategies that work, and simply needs your approval to put them into place.

Teachers and parents can find a treasure trove of specific ideas for accommodations and modifications in the book *Teaching the Tiger,* which is listed in Appendix A, *Resources.* This practical volume is highly recommended for anyone planning an education program for a child with Tourette's syndrome, OCD, and/or ADHD. It includes hundreds of invaluable classroom ideas, organizational hints, and ideas about IEP and 504 plan goals for students with TS. The Tourette Syndrome Association also has videos and pamphlets available for teachers, school psychologists, and even classmates, and has developed a well-received Education Curriculum package for schools.

Flexible programs are most likely to meet an individual student's needs. Due to the waxing and waning nature of tics and other symptoms, students with TS may have long periods during which their symptoms are minimal. Teachers can take advantage of these lulls to help them make up missed assignments or move ahead rapidly, leaving room to relax a bit when symptoms are more severe. Accommodations not needed at the moment can be suspended until symptoms flare up again.

Special education for students with TS

In the US, discriminating against the disabled is illegal in almost every setting, including schools. The Individuals with Disabilities Education Act (IDEA) specifically mandates that all children receive a free and appropriate education (referred to in special education circles as a "FAPE"), regardless of disability. That means providing, free of charge, special education programs, speech therapy, occupational therapy, physical therapy, psychiatric services, and other interventions that can help the child learn.

Several laws protect your child's access to an education. These include:

- Section 504 of the Rehabilitation Act of 1973
- The Individuals with Disabilities Education Act (IDEA)
- The Americans with Disabilities Act (ADA)
- Other state and Federal laws concerning disability rights and special education

504 plans

At the very least, any child with TS should have a 504 plan in place—an agreement between the child's family and the school about accommodations that can help him attend school successfully.

Section 504 of the Rehabilitation Act of 1973, one of the very first laws mandating educational help for students with disabilities, lays out the regulations for such plans. A 504 plan is usually written by a team made up of the parents and teachers or school administration, with minimal involvement by the school district's administrators. It is a simpler and less detailed process than writing an IEP (see "IDEA and special education," later in this chapter,) but it also doesn't cover as many contingencies.

Unlike special education eligibility, Section 504 eligibility is not based on having a certain type of disability. Instead, it is based on:

- Having a physical or mental impairment that substantially limits a major life activity, such as learning. Learning is not the only activity that applies: 504 plans can cover other major life activities, such as breathing, walking, controlling your own behavior, and socialization.

- Having a record of such an impairment, such as a medical diagnosis.

- Being regarded as having such an impairment.

A 504 plan is a good idea even if your child has never had an academic or behavior problem in school. The nature of TS dictates that new symptoms could emerge at any time, and have unexpected effects on school performance. Your child's 504 plan can put procedures into place regarding who will give out medication and where it will be stored, communication between home and school, the use of certain organization systems for homework and books, exemption from timed tests, or what to do if your child has a difficult behavior episode at school.

Judy, mother of 21-year-old Gabe, says a 504 plan was sufficient to help him get through school:

> Gabe was in a regular classroom with a 504 agreement in place. When he needed to, he got added time for tests and/or assignments, and he could take the tests alone. When his tics affected his work, he was allowed extensions. (This worked better with some teachers than others.)
>
> I always set up meetings with all of his teachers at the beginning of the school year, after the guidance counselor spoke to them. I left a packet with each teacher explaining the history of Gabe's TS—what he has and, despite the sensationalism of the media, what he does not have.

Children and teens with TS are prone to the occasional meltdown, and this is one area where a 504 plan shines. Episodes of anxiety, rage, or unusual behavior may occur in response to stress, fear, teasing, illness, missed medications, or simply out of the blue. You can develop a response in advance and put it in place via a 504 plan. It can include procedures for giving emergency medication, calling for outside help, and keeping the child and others safe until that help arrives. Without advance planning, it's easy for a bad day to turn into a crisis.

A letter from your child's doctor, psychiatrist, or therapist is helpful for getting a 504 plan approved. If the professional makes specific suggestions, that's even better.

If you apply for 504 status and are still denied services, appeal this decision to your school district's 504 compliance officer. If that doesn't produce results, contact your state's Office of Civil Rights. If your child has been diagnosed with Tourette's syndrome, the school should not deny him this limited protection under any circumstances—a 504 plan is the very least that any child with a health impairment qualifies for. Some special education advocates recommend that parents request a 504 evaluation at the same time they start the IEP process. This can mean asking the 504 compliance officer to attend your IEP meetings. It may confuse your district because it isn't a common practice, but it will save time by ensuring the delivery of some services and accommodations even if special education services are denied and you have to appeal.

Most 504 plans are fairly uncomplicated documents, but informal agreements with your child's school don't carry the same weight. Informal agreements only work as long as the people involved stay the same, and as long as everyone chooses to honor them. If your school gets a new principal or your child's teacher decides to change plans in midstream, you'll be right back where you started. With a 504 plan, you have a document that mandates access to needed services. If your school or district decides not to follow it, you can appeal directly to your district's 504 compliance officer and/or your state office of civil rights.

IDEA and special education

The Individuals with Disabilities Education Act, most recently revised in 1997, revolutionized special education in the US. This set of comprehensive rules and regulations aims to ensure that all children get an adequate education, regardless of disabilities or special needs. This includes children with TS and other neurological conditions.

The special education process starts with evaluation. In most areas, eligibility is determined by a committee of specialists, called the eligibility committee, multidisciplinary team (M-team), child study team, or something similar. As experts on their child, parents also play an important role during the eligibility process. Parents will be asked to fill out forms, but they can also request a personal interview with the team and submit information, such as medical evaluations, to help it make a decision.

The eligibility committee will decide if your child has a condition that qualifies him for special education services. Exact language differs between states, but typical qualifying categories include:

- Autism
- Hearing impaired (deafness)
- Visually impaired
- Both hearing impaired and visually impaired (deaf-blindness)
- Speech and language impaired
- Mentally retarded/developmentally delayed
- Multihandicapped
- Severely orthopedically impaired
- Other health impaired (OHI)
- Seriously emotionally disturbed (SED)
- Severely and profoundly disabled
- Specific learning disability
- Traumatic brain injury

Check your state's special education regulations for the list of labels used in your state.

Most children and teens with TS who receive special education services in the US are classified under the OHI label, if it is available in their state. The US Department of Education has not made an official statement on where TS falls, but it has issued a letter stating that ADHD should be categorized as OHI, along with medical conditions like asthma.[5]

If the main issues that have brought your child to the attention of the special education system are behavioral, the team may seek to use or add the category SED. An SED designation is often required to access day treatment or residential slots; on the other hand, it may prevent your child from being admitted to some alternative school programs without a fight.

The condition that causes the most impairment in school-related activities is called the primary handicapping condition, and any others that coexist with it are called secondary handicapping conditions. For example, a child with TS and dyslexia might be qualified for special education under the primary condition OHI, with specific learning disability as a secondary label. A child with TS and bipolar disorder might qualify as OHI and SED.

Although the eligibility committee will take your child's medical diagnosis and the opinions of Early Intervention evaluators into account when they make their determination, qualifying categories are defined by each school district or state Department of Education in terms of education, not medicine. If your child has a Tourette's syndrome diagnosis from a psychiatrist, neurologist, or other physician, the committee can still say that your child does not meet the educational definition of OHI if it can't see how that diagnosis would impact the child at school. This means that either the committee feels your child does not need special services to take advantage of educational opportunities, or that the committee is unwilling to offer your child needed services. Technically, a medical diagnosis of TS should automatically qualify a child for the label OHI, even if his illness is currently controlled with medication or his symptoms are not prominent.

You have the right to appeal the eligibility team's decision about your child's educational label or any other issue. If its decision prevents your child from receiving special education eligibility or needed services, you should do so. It is helpful to prepare a detailed list of ways your child's problems impact his ability to be educated without the added help of special education services.

Marlene, mother of 8-year-old Billy, says preparation is the key to a successful IEP:

> *These kinds of meetings are not always acrimonious. I had a big fight to get Billy an IEP in the first place (largely due to the outdated philosophy of the principal), but, since then all meetings between school personnel and myself have been great, with all of us on the same side.*
>
> *Usually, at the beginning the school people have little information on what the problem is, and come to the table with a bunch of misunderstandings. They are also afraid that you are going to make their lives more difficult. Once they understand that helping Billy to be less stressed will also make their lives easier, things can start to change.*
>
> *The video "Stop It! I Can't" is an good introductory video about TS, only twelve minutes long, interesting and does not put people to sleep. Ask for a TV and VCR to be available, and show it at the beginning to set the tone for the meeting (if your committee will cooperate). Just say that you realize that they may not have a lot of experience with kids with TS, and that this is the quickest and easiest way to bring them up to date. People*

always feel sympathetic to the kids in the video, who are shown achieving normal kid sort of things.

You are allowed to bring someone with you to the meeting, and it can be helpful to have someone there. If you don't know a professional or someone from the local TSA chapter who can go with you, and your spouse is absent or out of town, even just bringing a friend who isn't going to say anything can help you feel stronger and less isolated, and give you someone to debrief with afterward.

The main thing is having inner confidence. You may feel like all the power is on their side, but it's not, really. You have knowledge, and knowledge is power; and the law is on your side (not that school districts are usually eager to admit this fact). You don't have to be a pediatric neurologist, clinical psychologist, and Ph.D. in special education. You are an expert on the particular issues that your own child faces and struggles with, and what accommodations and interventions are helpful to him in his struggle to succeed. You are strong.

The Individualized Education Plan (IEP)

When completed, your child's special education evaluation will be the basis of a document that's soon to become your close companion: your child's Individualized Education Plan (IEP). The IEP describes your child's strengths and weaknesses, sets educational goals and objectives for her, and details how these can be met within the context of the school system. Unless the IEP team agrees to include it, there will be little information about services from outside programs, services provided by parents, or services provided to parents.

The IEP is created during one or more meetings of your child's IEP team, which has a minimum of three members: a representative of the school district, a teacher, and a parent. The district may send more than one representative, and parents may (at their child's peril) choose not to attend. If your child has more than one teacher, or if direct service providers such as her therapist would like to attend, they can all be present. If it is your child's first IEP and first assessment, one team member is required by Federal law to have experience with and knowledge of the child's suspected or known disabilities. You may want to check this person's credentials in advance. "Specialists" employed by some school districts can have as little as one college psychology course, or even no qualifications other than the title itself.

Both parents should participate in the IEP process if possible, even if they do not live together. Parents can also bring anyone else they would like: a relative or friend, an after-school caretaker, a mental health advocate, or a lawyer, for example. This person may act as an outside expert, or may simply offer moral support or take notes so that you can participate more freely.

The child himself can also be at the IEP meeting if the parents would like—however, it's a good idea to bring a sitter with a young child to avoid disruptions. You want to be able to give the IEP process your full attention, and that's hard if you're also trying to keep a child out of trouble. Most young children find IEP meetings rather boring.

Older teens and self-advocacy

Districts are trying to involve middle school and high school students in the IEP process more often, and this is probably a good trend. Discuss the meeting with your older child and elicit her suggestions in advance. Some adolescents prefer to write up their suggestions rather than (or in addition to) attending the meeting. As with young children, bring someone to take care of your child if she tends to be disruptive, and bring a book or game in case the meeting gets boring. It's not beneficial to force an unwilling child to take part in the meeting.

Recently parents of older teens in special education have reported a disturbing new trend: school districts that try to circumvent IDEA by making teens "self-advocates" at eighteen, regardless of their ability to make wise choices, and regardless of their parents' wishes. If parents agree—and only if parents agree—any child in special education who has reached age eighteen can take full control of all further contacts with the school district. Needless to say, this is often a very unwise thing to agree to. In many cases, the outcome is that the child immediately leaves school and loses all services.

If your district tries this ploy, there is a way back in. As an adult self-advocate, your child can appoint another person to advocate for her. That person can be you, or if your child prefers, a professional advocate.

Special education services should continue until at least age twenty-one, or until the attainment of a regular high-school diploma (not a GED or IEP diploma).

Building an IEP

Usually IEP meetings are held at a school or a district office. However, you can request another location for the meeting if it is necessary—for example, if your child is on homebound instruction, or has severe behavior problems that make caring for him impossible away from the controlled environment of home at this time. The meeting date and time must be convenient to you (and, of course, to the other team members).

Your first IEP meeting, which may be called a Student Study Assessment or something similar, should begin with a presentation of your child's strengths and weaknesses. This may be merely a form listing test scores and milestones, or it can include verbal reports of observations by team members—including you. You can use this time to tell the team a little more about your child, her likes and dislikes, her abilities, and the worries that have brought you all together for this meeting. Even if you're repeating information that the team members already know, this kind of storytelling helps other team members see your child as a person rather than just another case. You'll want to keep it brief, though, so you may want to use a short outline and even practice in advance. This kind of information may also be entered on an evaluation or record summary form.

The document that comes out of this first meeting is not an IEP, but a guide to your child. It might also include information on testing needed before an IEP can be written. Parents need to know that any agreements entered into in this pre-IEP stage are not legally binding.

The IEP itself has two important parts: the cover sheet, usually called the accommodations page, and the goals and objectives pages. Your district may have its own bureaucratic names for these pages, such as a "G3" or an "eval sheet." If team members start throwing around terms you don't understand, ask them to explain.

Accommodations

Parents tend to focus on the goals and objectives pages, and often overlook the accommodations page. That's a mistake. The goals and objectives are all about what your child will do, and if they are not accomplished, there's no one who can be truly held accountable but your child. The accommodations page, however, is about what the school district will do to help make your child able to meet those goals: what services it will provide or pay for, what kind of classroom setting your child will be in, and any other special education help that the district promises to provide.

The accommodations page is where the district's promises are made, so watch out: saying that your child will do something costs the district nothing, but promising that the district will do something has a price tag attached. Be prepared to hear phrases like: "I don't want to commit the district to that" over and over—and to methodically show that the accommodations you're asking for are the only way the goals and objectives the team wants to set can be met.

District representatives tend to see their role in the IEP meeting as being the gatekeeper. They may interpret this as spending as little money as possible, or ensuring that children are matched with services that meet their needs, depending on the person, the district, and the situation. Most representatives struggle to strike a balance between the benefit of each child and the district's resources. As your child's advocate, your job is to persuade the representative to tip the scales in your child's favor.

Accommodations that your child may need include:

- A specific type of classroom

- Provision of other types of environments, such as a resource room setting for certain subjects, mainstreaming for other subjects, or an area for time-outs or self-calming

- A set procedure for allowing the child to take a "self time-out" when overwhelmed, angry, or especially symptomatic—for example, your child might quietly show a green card to the teacher, who could send him on his way to a quiet area (the school nurse's office or the school library, for example) for a predetermined length of time with a nod of her head

- A reduced number of required courses for graduation

- Class schedules adapted to the child's ability to concentrate and stay alert, especially during times of acute symptoms and during medication changes

- Specific learning materials or methods

- Accommodations for testing, such as untimed tests, extended test-taking times, exemption from certain types of tests, or oral exams (this is an especially good idea for those students who have dysgraphia or hand tremor due to medication)

- Grade arrangements that take into account assignments and school days missed due to symptoms or to hospitalization—these might include estimating semester grades based only on the work that was completed; offering the option of an "incomplete" grade to allow the student to finish the course when well; or basing grades on some combination of class participation when present, work completed, and a special oral exam

- A personal educational assistant or aide: either a monitoring aide who simply helps with behavior control, or an inclusion or instructional aide

- Other classroom equipment needed to help your child learn if he has auditory processing or learning disabilities, such as a microphone or sound field system, a slanted work surface, a computer for a student with dysgraphia, or pencils with an orthopedic grip

- Preparation and implementation of a behavior plan

The cover page should also summarize any therapeutic services your child will receive, from whom, where, and how frequently.

The accommodations page should not already be filled out when the IEP meeting begins, as your child's individual goals and objectives should dictate what accommodations are needed.

Goals and objectives

Goals and objectives in the IEP should be as specific as possible. Often each team member will come to the IEP meeting with a list, hopefully with each goal already broken down into steps. This saves a lot of time, and allows everyone to concentrate on the pros and cons of their ideas rather than having to actually come up with the ideas themselves at the meeting. You may choose to meet one-on-one with these team members to talk over IEP ideas before the big meeting.

There is a tendency for the IEP of a child with TS to look more like a behavior plan than an education plan. Goals like "Armando will comply with his teacher's instructions nine times out of ten" are fairly typical—and almost useless. They specify that the student—and the student alone—will do something that has obviously been difficult in the past. For behavior improvements to occur, teachers and parents need to know why misbehavior has happened in the past. This is where a well-researched, well-written behavior plan should come into play.

Behavior goals

Appropriate behavior goals for the IEP can be tied to what you've learned from analyzing the child's problem behaviors, and how the behavior plan addresses them. These two documents can work together. For example, if Armando has often been noncompliant in the past due to having little knowledge of how to get appropriate attention from his teacher or his peers, a better set of goals might be: "Teacher will provide Armando with three appropriate ways to get his teacher's attention," and "Teacher will help Armando identify appropriate and inappropriate times to seek his peers' attention." Other behavior goals might include: "Teacher will help Armando find three unobtrusive ways to deal with tics that could be disruptive," "Teacher will help Armando learn when it is appropriate to take a self-cued time-out for five to ten minutes when he is feeling overwhelmed," and "Teacher will help Armando learn to use two stress-reduction strategies when he is becoming irritated or angry at school."

Although these behavior goals still seem to be all about what the student will do, fulfilling these goals will really require the active participation of teachers and other professionals. Armando is not going to learn these strategies for improving his behavior by osmosis—someone is going to have to teach him, work with him to improve his skills, and reinforce him when he gets it right. To as great an extent as possible, you want to spell out just how that will be done, and by whom, in the IEP and/or the behavior plan.

These goals also have the advantage of being measurable, permitting you to hold teachers and other service providers accountable for meeting them. When it's time for an IEP review, you can find out which three strategies Armando is using to get the teacher's attention, and find out if doing so has reduced inappropriate attention-getting behaviors.

Academic goals

Including academic goals in IEPs is controversial. Schools do not want to guarantee that a student will learn certain material; they usually don't even want to promise that they'll try to teach it. And if most of your child's academic skills are age-appropriate or even superior, it is very hard to have anything written into the IEP about maintaining or developing these skills further. Special education services are about addressing deficits, say the educators.

In reality, the school should not compare a student's achievement against the average or that of other students, but against his own ability as measured by past performance or ability testing. If there is a measurable and significant discrepancy between ability and achievement, you have room to ask for academic goals on the IEP. This is frequently the case for students with TS: related traits such as perfectionism and anxiety-derived procrastination can stymie even brilliant students.

Parents also know from experience that any gifts or islands of competence their child has are essential to his emotional well-being and educational success. Parents and experienced, caring teachers can often show the rest of the team why IEP goals based on strengths can be as important as those based on deficits or discrepancies. For example, your daughter may excel in reading and music. Just as schools often claim that sports programs keep some at-risk kids in school, enhanced opportunities to pursue her special interests may motivate your daughter to attend classes regularly and keep up her GPA, especially if you can tie her ability to participate in a desired activity, such as band or chorus, to maintaining passing grades. As every parent knows, the carrot is often mightier than the stick!

Children in special education programs should be educated to the same standards as all other students whenever that is possible. They should work with the same curriculum and objectives, although specific requirements can be adjusted to fit the child. For example, if third graders in your district are normally required to present a ten-minute oral report about state history, a child with medication-induced fatigue might be allowed to present a shorter oral report, to have her written report read out loud by a helper, or to present her report in two parts.

As a parent, you'll want to talk to your child's teacher about the academic curriculum in use in your child's school and in the district itself. Make sure that your child is being instructed in the skills, concepts, and facts needed to proceed in school. Make sure that he is given appropriate homework, and is also provided with the tools and skills he needs to complete it.

Benchmark testing and special education

If you live in one of the many states with competency standards for all students, make sure that your child (and all children in special education) are not exempted from the same expectations. If your state has set the goal of having all children reading at grade level by fifth grade, for example, your child should be held to the same standard—and offered the special education assistance she may need to achieve it. Sometimes special assistance for students who fall behind benchmarks is actually written into the laws that mandate testing. If this is the case, assistance must be offered to students with known disabilities as well as to those who have fallen behind for other reasons.

If your child must attain certain benchmark standards to move on to the next grade level, to complete high school, or to earn a type of diploma that qualifies him to attend state colleges, you may be able to include a provision in your child's IEP regarding how any standardized achievement tests of this type will be handled. This may range from exempting the child from the testing requirement to insisting that the school provide extra academic help and/or test-taking accommodations. Any accommodations should be geared toward allowing the student with a disability an equal chance of doing well on the test.

Children with TS have varying abilities, from slow to average to gifted. A good IEP doesn't dumb down classes or take away the joy of achieving something difficult, it just ensures that a child with disabilities gets an equal shot. The IEP can provide flexibility while still maintaining appropriate academic standards: for example, permitting your child to audit some courses before taking them for credit, and arranging in advance for using correspondence courses, distance learning (courses taken over the Internet), or independent study to fill in gaps created by hospitalization or flare-ups of TS symptoms.

Socialization goals

Another important area for IEP goals is socialization. Again, you may be told that this is not part of education. However, the school's task is preparing your child to function in the work world, and book learning alone will not help unless he has also mastered the give and take of social interaction. As far as 504 plans are concerned, socialization definitely qualifies as a "major life activity." The best place for children to learn appropriate social skills is in supervised activities with peers, and most schools make a plethora of these available to their students. This makes school an especially appropriate arena for children to work on socialization.

Social skills are used during the school day in classroom conversation, in the lunchroom and library, and in school-sponsored activities, such as student clubs or arts groups. Social skills instruction may be provided in any of these settings, in targeted classroom exercises on social skills, or via non-affiliated community programs. You can write supports into an IEP that will help your child succeed in school social activities despite TS.

Some schools have introduced social skills groups or peer mentoring programs for students who need extra help in socialization. Often these pair younger students with older students, under the guidance and supervision of adults. The older student can show younger kids the ropes, help integrate them into school and after-school activities, and encourage them to feel like they belong at the school. For children entering a new school, returning to school after a long period of hospitalization or homebound education, or suffering from social phobia, peer mentoring and social skills groups are fabulous. Chapter 4 includes a discussion of social skills programs.

Signing the IEP...or not

When the IEP is complete, the accommodations page should include a list of each promise, information about where and when it will be met, and the name of the person responsible for delivering or ensuring delivery. If the complete IEP is acceptable to everyone present, this is probably also where all team members will sign on the dotted line.

You do not have to sign the IEP if it is not acceptable. This fact can't be emphasized enough! If the meeting has ended and you don't feel comfortable with the IEP as it is, you have the right to take home the current document and think about it (or discuss it with your spouse or an advocate) before you sign. You also have the right to set another IEP meeting, and another, and another, until it is truly complete. Don't hinder the process unnecessarily, of course, but also don't let yourself be steamrolled by the district. The IEP is about your child's needs, not the district's needs.

Lee, mom to 13-year-old Joseph, has been around the block enough times to know that she can take her time about approving IEP changes:

> *I never sign an IEP at a meeting. Bringing it home and reviewing it in a low-stress environment always gives me a clearer idea of whether what the district is proposing will work or not.*

Needless to say, you should never sign a blank or unfinished IEP—it's a bit like signing a blank check. Certain school districts ask IEP meeting participants to sign an approval sheet before even talking about the IEP. Others are in the habit of taking notes for a prospective IEP and asking parents to sign an approval form at the end of the meeting, even though the goals, objectives, and accommodations have not been entered on an actual IEP form. This is not acceptable. If they insist that you sign a piece of paper, make sure to add next to your name that you are signing because you were present, but that you have not agreed to a final document.

If your child already has an IEP in place from the previous year, this IEP will stay in place until the new one is finalized and signed. If your child does not, you may need to come to a partial agreement with the district while the IEP is worked out.

If the process has become contentious, be sure to bring an advocate to the next meeting. A good advocate can help smooth out the bumps in the IEP process while preserving your child's access to a free and appropriate education.

Placement decisions

Two factors govern the choice of school for your child: the most appropriate educational program, and the least restrictive environment (LRE). For most children with TS, the least restrictive environment is their neighborhood school, or one very much like it that happens to have an especially good teacher or support services.

This is called inclusion, full integration, or mainstreaming. Inclusion is almost always the best strategy for children and teenagers with TS, assuming that the school is willing to accommodate your child's special needs with a 504 plan and/or IEP.

Characteristics of successful inclusive classrooms include:

- Caring, informed personnel

- Adequate ratio of children to classroom personnel

- Frequent and productive communication between classroom personnel, specialists, and parents

- Availability of appropriate teaching materials

- Individualized educational programming for each child with a disability

- Encouragement of interaction between children with disabilities and their non-disabled peers

- Consistent expectations regarding behavior and academic work, with flexibility built in to allow for changes in the child's symptoms and needs

Full inclusion is not a magical solution to school problems. Too often schools use the concept of full inclusion as a way to deny special education services to the students who need them. That's why many classroom teachers dread having children with mental or physical disabilities in their classes—it's not that they're callous or think these kids don't deserve an equal education, it's that they are not given any additional resources to work with them. Imagine yourself teaching a class of thirty junior high students in which two or three have ADHD, one has TS, and another has a traumatic brain injury. Without help from classroom aides and specialists, administrative support, well-written IEPs, and the resources to help each child meet his goals, you could easily become overwhelmed.

Parents are often the key to making sure their children are properly served in an inclusive setting. Teachers love parents who go to bat with the administration or district to get needed classroom help.

Perhaps the best advice that successful students with TS and their parents can offer is that the people and overall culture of a school count the most, and that one program does not fit all. Some students with TS desire the anonymity and lower social pressure of large public schools, while others thrive in small classes with lots of personal attention. The best school environment is very much an individual thing.

Special classrooms

Some children with TS will not be able to handle the noise, confusion, and demands of a traditional school program. Some troubled schools are, in turn, barely capable of meeting the needs of average students, much less those with special needs. There should be a range of placements available, ranging from staying in the neighborhood school with adjustments in the classroom, to spending part or all of the day in a resource room or special education classroom, to learning at home with one-on-one instruction, to day treatment or residential placement.

Some children will only need a special classroom for part of the day. Perhaps they need special help with math or reading, or maybe their tics or other TS-linked behaviors tend to worsen as the day wears on. A "resource room" can be part of the solution. This is a space in the school where kids can get help from a special education teacher to meet their individual needs.

If you walk into a typical resource room, you'll usually see several activities going on. At one table a group of children are working together on reading skills, in another corner of the room a student with Tourette's syndrome whose tics are flaring up is taking a "time-out" from his regular classroom, and at a third table a speech therapist is doing one-on-one work with a child who stutters. A child whose new medication makes him sleepy might be napping, while another group of kids works with special math software on the room's computers.

Each of these children is in the resource room for only part of the day, either for a scheduled visit with the speech therapist or another specialist, or on an as-needed basis due to symptoms. When children use a resource room for certain types of work, that's called a pull-out. Well-run resource rooms act as a safe haven within a busy school.

Lynette says a well-run resource room was very helpful for her son, giving him a safe place to go when his symptoms were at their height:

> The resource room teacher and the vice principal attended all of Bruce's IEP meetings. At first, I was nervous as to how much information I should give them. Would they treat Bruce as a psychiatric case? Would they think he was a behavior problem? As it turns out, the special ed. teacher has a family member with OCD who calls her frequently. She was very sympathetic, and just a wonderfully warm and caring lady.
>
> We kept in close contact while Bruce was able to attend classes. She would always call me if they noticed he was having particular difficulty at

school. She was Bruce's liaison with his teachers when he was unable to go to class. She asked his teachers for extra time for Bruce to complete assignments (something he didn't always get from teachers), and asked to have his workload reduced. She advised him as to what courses would be better for him to take. For instance, she knew which teachers taught what courses, and how big the classes were, and steered him into classes where there would be flexible teachers. She even tried to secure a commitment from the music teacher that Bruce would be allowed to play the drums should he do music class.

The arrangement was that Bruce attended class, but if he couldn't cope, he could come to the resource room. In the resource room, he could work quietly (he would have his own study carrel if he wanted it) and have access to her and to educational assistants. There was also a couch in the room where he could rest or lay down if he needed to, and there were days that he needed to. There were periods of time when he would be very tired, when we were struggling with dosages of meds. Bruce was allowed to leave and take breaks as needed, the only stipulation was that he needed to let her know where he was at all times.

Eventually, Bruce was not able to stay in class due to his severe symptoms and anxiety. He soon was working in the resource room all the time. The special education teacher would get his work from the other teachers if Bruce couldn't, and assigned him an educational assistant to help him. Actually there were several educational assistants in the resource room, and they all got to know Bruce—it was like a family in there. They were all very supportive, and did their best to help Bruce. They understood that he was overwhelmingly anxious and depressed. He was never accused of malingering or being work avoidant.

Often one or other would phone me to talk about Bruce and ask how hard they should push him—they knew he was barely hanging on by a thread most of the time. They even asked for info on TS and OCD. They understood that he was a very sick boy at the time. The vice principal told me that they would do everything that they could to help Bruce, and they did.

At times the educational assistant would scribe for him, to get him working. Sometimes she would just talk to him and try to encourage him as best she could. The school counselor was in and out of the resource room, so Bruce had access to her, too.

For those students who do need a full-day special education program, there are many types of self-contained special classrooms. Children with TS are most likely to be sent to a behavioral classroom, where their classmates also have disabilities that impact behavior.

Most of these classrooms use some variation of the behavior modification approach. Many use a level system, where children start with no privileges at all and earn each privilege by meeting behavior goals. As their behavior improves (or declines), they work their way through levels that might be numbered or given the name of a color. A child on green level, for instance, would be performing optimally and able to have recess time, eat lunch with peers, and perhaps have a special treat at the end of the week. A child on blue level would be performing badly, confined to the classroom for recess and lunch, and unable to have cookies with the green-level guys on Friday.

Level systems and behavior modification techniques work very well with children who are deliberately misbehaving. Level systems do not work well with children whose behaviors are due to neurological dysfunction. These kids may simply feel humiliated when symptom exacerbations prevent them from reaching behavior goals. Their teachers are mystified when techniques that worked so well when the child's symptoms were well controlled by medication suddenly become useless when the medication no longer works.

Colleen Wang, RN, medical liaison for the Tourette Spectrum Disorder Association, offers the following view of level systems:

> Because of inconsistent brain function, children with neurobiological disorders find the standard behavior modification programs very negative.
>
> Why? Because on the days when their function is good, the brain is turned on, everything is falling into place, and they are cruising. They are just having a good day. They aren't "trying" and so thus having a good day. Their brain function is simply better today (which is not to say they aren't working the level system) but, ultimately, they know how much effort they are putting forth to meet required behavioral expectations. On these days, they are rewarded for "being on task" as if it was a function of effort.
>
> On the day they wake up with their brain off, they know it is going to be a bad day. It is not something they wish, it just is. However, they are good kids, so they go to school and try to work the level system. But the brain is just short-circuiting. They try really hard, but they keep screwing

up. On these days, they are debited. They lose points or levels. The failure on their part is brain function, not effort; it is not voluntary.

The message the child gets is: When I'm cruising but not really trying...REWARD.

When I'm trying really hard...DEBIT.

Since the kid knows how much effort they are putting forth, they can't miss the message.

However, you can use the same reward system that behavior modification uses, without the negativity, by saying to the child: "When you finish the hard stuff, you get to do the fun stuff." The child is then not being rewarded for brain function, but rather effort. They don't miss the difference!

Sound reasonable?

Despite the drawbacks of the level system/behavior mod approach, some behavioral classrooms are excellent learning environments for kids with TS. Successful behavioral classrooms are usually small (no more than fifteen children, sometimes as few as six), they often have aides and support staff in place to meet the children's needs, and they are headed by teachers with training and, hopefully, expertise in working with kids who have special needs.

The curriculum in a behavioral class should be identical to that used in regular classrooms, with adaptations as needed for each student. Many of these classes mix students who are in several grades, however, and it takes a skilled teacher to ensure that each child learns what he needs to know.

In most school districts, behavioral classes are seen as a short-term placement—like a boot-camp class for kids who behave badly. For children with severe TS symptoms or difficult behaviors, this view is neither realistic nor wise. If a particular behavioral class is working well for your child, see what you can do to hold onto that placement.

Some school districts do have special classes for "seriously emotionally disturbed" students. Unfortunately, many of these classes also use level system/behavior mod techniques exclusively, without the level of support that most of the kids they serve really need. If your child is offered placement in a classroom that does happen to have a good therapeutic support program, however, grab it!

Most districts have special classes for children with moderate to severe developmental delays (mental retardation, autism, etc.). In small districts, this may be the only special education classroom available. Such a placement might seem like a terrible idea for your child—and it might well be a mistake. However, if the classroom happens to have a very good teacher and will make other needed supports available to your child, it could be worth considering. There may be a stigma attached for your child, of course, especially if the class is in his neighborhood school. Insensitive neighbor kids may tease him about being in the "retarded kids class." Many of these classes are actually quite good, with a caring and individualized approach that some of the behavioral classes would do well to emulate. For some kids with TS, especially the very youngest students, there will be times that being the "smart kid" in a developmental delay class is a great solution to a difficult education problem.

The law mandates that children be educated in the most inclusive environment possible, and that's an important value. However, recognizing that the best environment for an individual child may not always be fully inclusive is of equal importance.

Parents must also remember that the school's classrooms, computers, and books are often of secondary importance when compared to the value of caring teachers and administrators. If your child has an ally in his school—a favorite teacher, a super counselor, a teacher's aide who bends over backwards to help her—that person can often do more to help her get through school than the best-designed special education program. Parents should try to identify and develop allies within their child's school, wherever he or she is placed.

Alternative schools

For some students with TS, alternative schools (including the charter schools that are springing up in some parts of the country) offer a good mix of high academic expectations, strong behavioral supports, and flexibility. Of course, that depends on the alternative school program itself. Large urban districts may offer all sorts of public alternative schools, ranging from special schools for at-risk or gang-affected youth, to arts magnet schools. Small, rural districts may have no choices at all. Suburban areas may have only alternative schools that emphasize behavior modification rather than academics, and they often use them as a dumping ground for problem students with little regard for these children's actual needs or abilities.

If your district does offer alternative programs, be sure to look before you leap. Visit the site with your child, and ask for a guided tour. It may help your child to talk to other students about the school. Sit in on a typical class. If you can, talk to other parents whose children attend the school, and meet the teachers that your child would be working with. Make sure you feel comfortable with the alternative school's philosophy, methods, and objectives. Find out what typical outcomes are for students at this school—how are they performing on standardized tests? What's the graduation and dropout rate? How many return successfully to a neighborhood school, if that's your goal? Talk to the teacher whose classroom your child would be in. Is she a new graduate, an old pro, or burned out? Organized or disorganized? Flexible and creative, or rigid and doctrinaire?

Take your time—if your child has had difficulty in handling school in the past, you don't want to set him up for additional failure by making a hasty decision. Finding the right fit will make school success more likely.

Alternative schools and, in most cases, charter schools will still need to abide by your child's IEP. Often these schools are much more flexible, but occasionally they have been set up with a very specific program in mind, such as a levels-based behavior modification system or an arts-centered program designed for self-directed learners. If you sense that the alternative school is rigid in its format, make sure that format is already a good fit for your child. Like a regular public school that has a one-size-fits-all mentality, alternative schools with a specific mission are unlikely to change their approach, even to meet your child's IEP objectives.

Diagnostic classroom

If your child's diagnosis is still not set in stone, your district might suggest placement in a diagnostic classroom. This classroom might be a joint project of the school district and a regional medical center or medical school.

Diagnostic classrooms are used for long-term medical or psychiatric observation and evaluation of children whose behavior and abilities don't seem to fit the profile of any typical diagnosis. This is not a permanent placement, but if your child's case is especially unusual, she may stay in the diagnostic classroom for quite some time.

A well-run diagnostic classroom offers your family a unique opportunity to have your child seen at length by experts, and to try new medications, therapies, and treatments in a medically savvy setting. Make sure that the classroom staff and doctors involve your whole family in the diagnostic and treatment process. Parents report that some diagnostic classrooms are so patient-centered that they forget to talk to parents after the initial interview process.

Special schools

There are very few public schools specifically created for children with TS. Some private schools do exist that serve "emotionally troubled" or "behaviorally challenged" youth, who may or may not have an actual clinical diagnosis. Some of these special schools are excellent, and some are not.

If your child is unable to attend a regular school, either in an inclusive situation or in a special education classroom, and if she is not able to meet the entry requirements for alternative schools (many of which exclude children with the SED label), she may be able to go to a special school. If it's public, it will be very much like going to alternative school, but with a special education basis. However, they may not be required to follow your child's IEP, so beware.

Many districts contract with private schools that work with certain types of students. For example, they might contract with a private school that uses the Orton-Gillingham method to teach students with dyslexia, or with a private school that specializes in educating deaf and blind students. A very few areas in the US offer programs that are TS-specific, such as the BOCES Tourette's syndrome program in New York state.

One would expect a special school to have a psychiatrist, therapist, and other specialists on staff in addition to having fresh approaches to academic work. This type of contract program might be called a day treatment center. It may be attached to or affiliated with a residential school or hospital. At the end of the school day, children in day treatment go home to their families.

Placement at a day treatment center is usually reserved for children with very difficult behaviors, such as self-injurious or aggressive behavior, that make even a self-contained special education classroom inappropriate. Good day treatment centers provide medical and psychiatric support, specially trained staff, a very secure environment, and intensive intervention. However, many specialize in the treatment of behavior disorders that occur as a result of child abuse or other non-neurological reasons, and may not have a full understanding of TS.

The other problem with many current day treatment programs is that they are usually short-term interventions. The normal length of stay is short: one school year, or even as little as three months. Students cycle in and out, and staff turnover may also be high. Since most children with TS do not deal well with constant upheaval, this can present a problem. Your child may also end up in class with children whose behaviors are even more unmanageable than her own.

As with any other placement, tour the facility, meet the staff, and ask lots of questions before you agree to a day treatment placement.

If the district sends your child to a special school or day treatment center, it will pay the full costs.

Residential schools

In some cases, residential programs are your only option. Appropriate placements are hard to find if you live in a small, rural school district, assuming that homebound instruction would not be appropriate for your child or your family situation. If your child is dangerously self-abusive or actively suicidal, residential settings may be able to offer a safer setting than your home. Unlike hospital in-patient programs, their offerings usually include a strong educational component, not just psychiatric treatment.

Residential schools offer educational programming and 24-hour care for the child. If your school district asks to send your child to a residential program, the district will pay his tuition and all associated costs, usually with help from county mental health and/or the Federal government's SSI program (see Chapter 9, *Healthcare and Insurance*, for more information about SSI). Of course, you also have the option to choose a residential program for your child and pay for it yourself, if you have the financial means.

The best residential programs have staff with a strong medical/psychiatric background, a high level of employee retention, and a commitment to communicating with and working with students' families. As with any other type of school program, you'll want to proceed with caution. Visit the campus, observe a classroom, see the living quarters, talk to staff and (if possible) students, and try to talk to other parents whose children have attended the school. No place is perfect, but some residential schools have deservedly bad reputations.

If your child needs a residential setting, security is probably a major concern. Make sure security measures are more than adequate to prevent students from self-harm, assault, and running away. Also find out how they manage difficult behaviors. Avoid schools that rely on isolation rooms, restraints, or excessive medication. Schools that involve families in their child's care have a strong understanding of how your child's diagnosis impacts his behavior, and that employ flexible solutions to challenging behaviors are most likely to have success.

Ask how the residential program handles returning students to the community, whether it's preparing your child for coming home and going back to his former school after he stabilizes, or simply moving him into a less-restrictive residential setting. Some children with very complicated psychiatric problems leave residential schools for a therapeutic group home rather than returning to the family home, either as a permanent placement or as a transitional measure.

Hospital-based education

If your child needs to be in an in-patient in a psychiatric hospital, or if he has a medical problem that requires a stay in a regular hospital for more than a week or so, you'll need to ensure that his education is continued. With the trend toward short hospitalizations for crises only, child or adolescent psychiatric wards may not have built-in resources for continuing your child's education. Regular hospitals do tend to have established education programs for long-term pediatric patients, but they may need to be adapted for a student with TS.

If your child is going to have a lengthy or planned hospitalization, contact the hospital program and find out who's in charge of communicating with patients' schools. There may be a formal school-hospital liaison. Make sure this person is in contact with your child's teacher (or in the case of a high school student who has many teachers, a homeroom teacher, school counselor, or other person who can be a go-between) before your child's scheduled entry date, and that they have set up an educational program in advance. This might include providing lesson plans and reading lists, sending your child's homework assignments to the hospital, and returning graded papers to you, for example.

If the hospitalization is sudden, you will probably need to act as the go-between yourself. Call your child's teacher or teachers and make arrangements for what they feel would be appropriate work to complete during her illness. Before her release, make plans for what she should be doing at home while she recuperates, or how to plan her school reentry. You can then make arrangements with hospital staff to ensure that she has the tools and time she needs to do the work. Staff can also let you know if the teacher's plans are too ambitious, and can provide medical documentation for reducing or even eliminating schoolwork for awhile if needed.

Some general tips on evaluating and working with hospitals are covered in Chapter 6, *Medical Care*.

Homebound instruction

Homebound instruction is considered the most restrictive school environment, because it involves sending someone to teach your child individually. However, children may prefer homebound instruction to attending a special school or entering a residential program because it keeps them in the company of their parents and siblings, even though it does restrict their ability to interact with same-age peers.

Homebound instruction can be delivered in person, via correspondence courses or distance learning arrangements, or with any combination of methods. If your child is in high school, you'll probably need to make sure his homebound program will help him meet the requirements for graduation. This may mean having the instructor follow specific lesson plans, use certain textbooks, or help your child complete required projects.

You'll also want to meet with the homebound instructor privately to explain your child's symptoms, go over her IEP, and talk about grading arrangements.

Although homebound instruction sounds ideal for students with severe TS, especially if it is accompanied by school phobia, severe anxiety, or OCD, therapists and many parents note that the reality is often not so rosy. Homebound instruction is usually available for only a few hours each week, and can reinforce avoidance and behavioral symptoms if therapy to combat them is not taking place at the same time.

Jean says her son Josh benefited greatly from a program that combined homebound instruction and regular high school classes:

> At the time that Josh started high school, it was obvious that he could no longer tolerate a full day of classes. While looking for alternatives that would still allow him to graduate in four years, we came across the district hospital/homebound program. With the help of our family doctor, we were able to arrange for him to take half of his classes through the program, and half at the high school for the freshman and sophomore years.
>
> Due to scheduling problems, Josh ended up full-time homebound the junior and senior years. There were several very big pluses to this program. Except for the last semester, all of the classes were done over the phone, which meant much more oral work and much less written work. For someone with handwriting issues, this was great. The class size was very small, which gave each student more individual attention, and there were a lot of modifications to suit the student's needs. In addition, the courses were set up in block scheduling, with each one taking half a school year to complete. If Josh failed a class, he would still have time to retake it without falling a year behind. It also gave him an opportunity to get ahead on his credits and finish a half a year early.
>
> The teachers, administrators, and guidance counselor are used to dealing with special kids and special circumstances, and were very

accommodating. When it became clear that Josh was not doing well in his senior year, the principal and guidance counselor decided to hire a one-on-one teacher for him to get him through, and this was the incentive that he needed to finish. His father and I doubt that he would have gotten through high school without this program.

The big minus to the hospital/homebound program is the lack of social contacts. A half homebound and half regular school schedule can take care of this, however.

Homeschooling

Educating your children at home is legal in most US states. Each state has its own regulations about who can homeschool, what (if anything) must be taught, and how (or if) children's educational achievements will be tested. If your state mandates standardized testing for homeschooled students, exceptions to the testing requirements for disabled children are usually not written into the law. You will want to be very careful about doing baseline testing, and about documenting any reasons that your child may not do well on required standardized tests, or may have regressed due to his illness or medication.

Eligible homeschooled children are entitled to special education services. These services may be delivered in the child's home, at a neutral site, or in a nearby school or clinic. This means that even if you choose to teach your child at home, you can still have an IEP with the school district that provides your child with speech therapy, counseling, and other needed services. Homeschoolers can choose to take part in extracurricular activities at their neighborhood public school, and may even be able to take some classes at school (advanced math, for example) while doing the bulk of their schoolwork at home.

Some districts have programs to help homeschooling parents create good programs for children with disabilities, while others go out of their way to make it difficult.

When home learning opportunities are well planned, it isn't necessary for children to spend an eight-hour day doing schoolwork. Consider how much of a typical school day is taken up with lunch, recess, waiting for the teacher's help, filling out ditto sheets, and other relatively non-productive activities, and its easy to see how a few hours of structured learning activities each day with one-on-one attention can provide equal educational benefits. Add in unstructured learning opportunities, like impromptu math lessons while measuring ingredients in the kitchen, and the "school" day at home looks rather inviting. For children whose symptoms make attending school for long periods too difficult, homeschooling offers an especially flexible option.

It's important to set up socialization opportunities if you are homeschooling, because as with homebound instruction, social avoidance and other problems may otherwise be reinforced. Many homeschooling families share teaching duties with other parents, bringing several children together for certain lessons or activities.

If your district forces you to homeschool your child because it cannot or will not provide a free and appropriate education program, it may be required to pay you for providing this service. This option has worked for parents in very rural areas, as well as for some in districts that could not provide a safe setting for a child with assaultive behaviors.

Homeschooling is not for everyone, even if you can get help from other parents who are in the same boat. Parents are a child's first teacher, but they're not always the best teachers for all topics. There's also the issue of burnout. Parents don't like to bring it up, but spending all day with your child can be exhausting. There are many parents who send their child off to school each day knowing that he will learn little, but also knowing that getting a break will make it possible for the parent to help him after school. You don't have to feel guilty if you are not emotionally or financially able to homeschool your child.

If you do homeschool, decide in advance whether your child will be working toward a high-school diploma (this is possible if you use certain homeschooling curricula), a GED, or a portfolio of work. Experienced homeschooling parents can help you learn about your options, and can be contacted through local groups or online.

Private schools

As noted earlier in this chapter, school districts sometimes contract with private schools and programs to provide services that they do not. These programs are usually not religious in nature (there are a few exceptions, such as residential programs that are affiliated with a religious denomination), and they must be willing to comply with district regulations.

Sometimes parents opt for private school placement directly, at their own cost. Perhaps daily religious instruction is very important to you, or your child's siblings already attend a private school. Luckily, choosing a private school does not automatically disqualify your child from publicly funded special education services, although in some areas the school district will place limits on what services you can receive, and how they will be delivered.

For 13-year-old Joseph, a private school has proved to be the best choice:

> Joseph is in a regular classroom in a small private school this year. He needs small classes. He needs few changes. He needs creative, flexible staff to work with him. The last evaluations we had done pinpointed about forty different things he needs to be successful in school—the public school offered us about five of those things, and said that was enough to start with.
>
> They wanted him to be isolated in a room with just an aide part of the day to start with, but Joseph loves being with other kids. He learns best with others.
>
> The small school he is in works really well with us and Joseph's doctor to provide what Joseph needs. They are flexible. His classes are small and he is in with kids of different ages. They teach him at his pace.
>
> He is learning and doing well: he had all As for the first nine weeks. The hard part is he has to have an aide to attend school. Finding the right aide was really hard, but I think we have one now. Paying for all of this is another story!

In a few areas, parents may be able to use school vouchers to lower the cost of private schools, making this educational option more accessible. Depending on local regulations (and on the mood of the courts) vouchers may be used at some parochial schools.

When looking at private school programs, give them the same level of scrutiny as you would a public program. The private school that served your other children well may be horribly wrong for a child with TS. Educational programming for children with TS requires a certain level of knowledge and flexibility that not all schools have, public or private. You can advocate until you're blue in the face, but in the end, private schools do not have to work with your child.

To receive public special education services while your child is in private school, you must have your child evaluated and qualified within the public system. Then you'll use an IEP to determine which services will be delivered, where they will be delivered, and by whom.

Delivery of public services in a parochial school can get especially sticky, depending on your state or local district. Some districts are so cautious about maintaining separation of church and state that if several children in a parochial school need speech therapy they will park a "speech van" outside the school, and then have children receive speech therapy in the van rather than allowing a public employee to help children inside the walls of a parochial school. Other districts have no qualms about sending employees to private school sites.

Unlike a public school, your private school itself will not be required to fulfill any academic promises made in an IEP. The IEP is a contract between you and the school district only. However, enlightened private schools that wish to better serve students with disabilities are aware of a well-written IEP's value. Some private schools encourage their teachers to attend IEP meetings as a guest of the child's parents. In some cases, these representatives have been treated as full team members, able to help determine meeting agendas and propose IEP goals.

Private schools that accept any form of public funding may be subject to additional regulations. Most are also subject to the Americans with Disabilities Act, which prevents a school from discriminating against your child due to his disability. However, unlike Section 504 and IDEA, it does not normally require the school to take specific action, unless there are issues concerning physical access, such as the need for a wheelchair ramp.

Let the setting fit the child

In between the placement options presented in this chapter are combination settings created to meet a student's specific needs. As noted, one student might be able to handle a half-day inclusion program in the morning, then have home-based instruction for other subjects in the afternoon. Another child might be placed in a special class for everything but art and music.

The setting(s) listed in your child's IEP should be reviewed every year (or more often, if you request it) to ensure that the educational program is still meeting his needs, and that he is still in the least restrictive setting. As his symptoms improve, the setting may change with them.

Andrea, mother of 17-year-old Robbie, has been pleased with how his schools have responded to his changing needs:

> Robbie is dysgraphic. Other than that he has no difficulties
> academically. Encouraging the teachers to take the pressure off Robbie
> helped. With pressure he becomes overwhelmed and has difficulty.
> Without it he can achieve more than most other students.

His elementary schools provided the accommodations he needed, first through special ed, then through their gifted program. He does not need accommodations now that he is in high school, other than occasional reminders to his teachers to allow him to submit word-processed work rather than handwritten work, but we are watching him closely to see if the special ed services need to be reinstated.

Whenever possible, the current movement in US schools is toward full inclusion. Although this is the best choice for the majority of students with TS, sometimes it is not appropriate. If the district proposes a setting, be open-minded enough to check it out, but don't say yes unless you're sure it's right. Inquire about supports, such as personal or classroom aides, that can make inclusive settings more realistic.

It's important to remember that because your child's symptoms may wax and wane drastically, a school setting that once worked well may not work forever. And even though you may want your child to finish high school on time, take college prep courses, or be in a special magnet program, she may not be able to handle it. At the same time, be a fierce advocate for your child's educational opportunities. Far too many kids with TS are pushed out or sent to get a GED or an IEP diploma, when with appropriate support they could have made it through.

Monitoring school progress

Once you have an educational program in place, your next job is monitoring the program. You can't rely totally on the school or the school district to monitor your child's progress, or to ensure compliance with his IEP. Keep a copy of all documents on hand, and check them against communications notebooks, progress reports, report cards, and assignments that come home from the school.

Of course you'll want to attend all official meetings, but make a point of just dropping by occasionally on the pretext of bringing your child her coat or having paperwork due at the school office. It's even better if you can volunteer an hour a week or so in the school (not necessarily in your child's classroom).

If the school is not complying with IEP, start by talking to the teacher, and work your way up. Most compliance problems can be addressed at the classroom level.

One area that can be especially difficult is monitoring the delivery of therapy and other pull-out services. It seems like a relatively simple task, but parents across the country report that their school district refuses to provide any type of checklist that lets parents see if their child is receiving the services listed in the IEP.

If your child's IEP includes academic goals, see if there are standardized ways to monitor progress—letter grades aren't always enough. Too often parents are told that their child is participating well and "making satisfactory progress," only to discover that he has not gained new skills when an objective measurement system is used. Ask that your child be tested every year if you can—if possible, have this written into your IEP. You are entitled to see the results of any standardized tests your child may take. Check the scores against his grades to make sure your child is progressing—sometimes "grade inflation" obscures the truth about a student's performance.

Many parents have found that their children are actually regressing due to inadequate classroom support or curriculum. Lack of progress or regression give you firm grounds for demanding that your child's academic needs be included in the IEP.

GED programs

Because of the high dropout rate among children with disabilities, and because of many school districts' unwillingness to serve these children, there is a possibility that your child may end up pursuing a General Equivalency Diploma (GED) rather than a regular high-school diploma. The GED is earned by passing a test. The test includes a short essay and questions on a variety of topics. In most states, you must be 16 to take the GED exam.

If the school district suspends or expels your child, or simply allows him to drop out, the very least he should receive is assistance to help him pass the GED exam. This might mean homebound instruction focusing on skills needed to pass the test, an alternative school program that has earning a GED as its goal, or study materials. There are books, videos, and software programs available to help people be successful on the GED. Most community colleges offer tutoring or classes to help adults pass the GED, and sometimes these are made available to teens as well.

Frankly, the GED is not a difficult test. If your child has successfully completed junior high and can apply a simple formula for writing a short essay, he can probably pass it already.

A GED is legally equal to a high-school diploma. You can get a job, attend any community college, enter a trade school or apprenticeship program, or join the military with a GED. If your child wants to pursue a degree at a four-year college, he will probably be able to get in with a GED if he meets the school's other requirements, such as having an adequate score on college placement exams like the SAT and ACT. His chances of admission will be best if he can also write a persuasive admissions essay and show a high-quality portfolio of work. He may also want to complete a year or two of community college before applying, as this will demonstrate his ability to handle college-level work.

Taking on the school system

If your child's school persistently refuses to comply with her IEP, what can you do? A lot—the IEP is a type of legal contract, although some schools treat it like a nuisance that they can ignore at their leisure. Your options include:

- Sitting back and letting it happen (obviously not recommended)
- Advocating for your child within the classroom and the IEP process
- Bringing in an expert to help you advocate for your child
- Requesting a due process hearing
- Filing a complaint with your state department of education
- Organizing with other parents to advocate for a group of students with similar problems
- Working with other advocates at a legislative level
- Going to court

While some schools and school districts have a well-deserved reputation for venality, most are simply hamstrung by low budgets and a lack of knowledge. These are areas where an informed parent can make a difference. You can provide the teacher and administrators with information about educational possibilities, and brainstorm ideas on how to best meet your child's needs.

Remember that as a full member of the IEP team, you have the power to call an IEP meeting whenever one is needed. This will bring together all of the team members to review the document, and to compare its requirements with what your child is receiving.

There are times when you may need to bring in an expert. Special education advocates and self-styled IEP experts are available all over the country. Some of these people work for disability advocacy organizations or law firms. Others are freelance practition ers. Some are parents of children with disabilities who have turned their avocation into a vocation.

You will probably have to pay for expert services, unless they are available through your local TSA chapter, another advocacy group, or your state's protection and advocacy system (for details, see the listing for the National Association of Protection and Advocacy Systems in Appendix A). Expert services can include researching programs available in your area, connecting you with appropriate resources, helping you write a better IEP, and advocating for your child at IEP meetings and due process hearings.

Due process

The words "due process" make schools very nervous. This term refers to the processes that a child and his family are supposed to have access to while being evaluated for special education or provided with special education services. If any step in this process is skipped, you can formally request a due process hearing to fix the problem. If you or the school has requested special education evaluation or services for your child, whether or not they have been approved, you are entitled to due process.

When parents start talking about due process, they're usually referring to a due process hearing: an internal appeals procedure used by school districts to determine whether or not procedures have been handled properly. Due process hearings hinge on whether the district has followed federal and state-mandated procedures for evaluating a child for special education and setting up a program for that child. Violations can include small things, like notifying parents of a meeting over the phone rather than in writing; or major issues, like using untrained or incompetent personnel to evaluate children, or deliberately denying needed services to save money.

Issues that tend to end up in due process include disagreements over evaluations or educational labels, provision of inadequate therapeutic services, placement in inappropriate educational settings, noncompliance with the IEP, lack of extended school year services when appropriate, and poor transition planning.

Obviously, every due process case is unique. Each state also has its own due process system. Regulations that all of these systems have in common are:

- Parents must initiate a due process hearing in writing

- The hearing must take place in a timely fashion

- Hearings are presided over by an impartial person who does not work for the district

- Children have the right to stay in the current placement until after the hearing (this is called the "stay put" rule)

- Parents can attend due process hearings and advocate for their child

- Parents can be assisted by an educational advocate or represented by a lawyer at the due process hearing

- If the parents use a lawyer and they win, they are entitled to have their legal fees paid by the district

Due process hearings resemble a court hearing before a judge. Each side argues its case and presents evidence. Each side can call on experts or submit documents to buttress its statements. However, experienced advocates know that despite the veneer of impartiality, if it comes down to your word against the district's word on educational or placement issues, the district will probably have an edge.

Some districts offer arbitration or mediation, which are not as formal as a due process hearing. In an arbitration hearing, both parties agree in advance to comply with the arbitrator's ruling. You can't recover your legal fees in arbitration, and your rights are not spelled out in the law. Be very cautious before agreeing to waive your right to a due process hearing in favor of mediation.

However, you can try mediation without waiving your right to due process while you're waiting for your due process hearing date to come up. If mediation works, you're done; if it doesn't, you can continue with the due process proceeding.

Section 504 actions

You can bypass the cumbersome due process procedure if your child has a 504 plan rather than or in addition to an IEP. Assuming that the school and then the district 504 compliance officer do not respond to your written complaints, take your case directly to your state office of civil rights. This office is responsible for enforcing the Rehabilitation Act.

The state office of civil rights is also charged with enforcing the Americans with Disabilities Act (see the section "The ADA and the schools," later in this chapter).

Public advocacy

If your child is denied special education services, you'll soon find out that you have a lot of company. Some problems in special education are systemic. Parents in several states have banded together effectively to get better services for their children. You may choose to get your local TSA chapter involved or work with a larger group of special education parents. You may also find allies in teacher's unions and organizations, the PTA and other parents associations, and elsewhere in your community.

Parents can personally help improve school funding for special education by lobbying their local school board or state legislature. They can help write and press for laws that require adequate support for these students, and for others in the special education system.

If you're not the kind of person who enjoys conflict, advocacy and due process can be very draining. School district lawyers count on endless meetings, criticism of your parenting skills, and constant references to their superior knowledge to wear down your defenses. You must always stay on guard, and yet be open to logical compromises and the possibility of beneficial alliances. It's not easy, but it's necessary.

Going to court

Going to court is time-consuming, exhausting, and expensive. The outcome is uncertain, and while the case drags on, your child may languish in an inappropriate setting. But if you've exhausted every other avenue, it may just have to happen.

Most special education court cases involve school districts that have lost a due process hearing, yet persist in denying the services mandated for a child. A 1994 case, W. B. v. Matula, also established the right of parents to sue a school on constitutional grounds. The parent of a grade-schooler who was eventually diagnosed with ADHD, OCD, and Tourette's syndrome took her district to court over violation of her child's due process rights and invoked the Fourteenth Amendment of the Constitution, which entitles all citizens to equal protection under the law.[6] To the consternation of school districts everywhere, she won her case, which included a substantial financial judgment. (She used the money to pay her massive legal bills and to get her son an appropriate education.)

Since the Matula case, school districts have been put on notice that parents of special-needs children can successfully pursue them beyond the due process hearing. Besides the grounds used in the Matula case, parents may be able to ask the courts for redress under state education laws, or even contract law. There are few legal precedents as of yet, but the number of successful legal challenges is growing. Court battles are underway in almost every state over unavailable, inadequate, or even harmful special education services.

The ADA and schools

The Americans with Disabilities Act (ADA) was patterned on civil rights laws that bar discrimination based on race, ethnicity, or gender. It mandates access to all public and most private facilities for disabled citizens. It's usually invoked to make sure people with physical disabilities have access to wheelchair ramps, elevators, grab bars, and other aids to using public or private accommodations. It also protects handicapped people from most forms of job discrimination.

In schools, the ADA does more than force the district to install handicapped-accessible restrooms and wheelchair ramps for physical access. It mandates that children with disabilities have the right to be involved in all school activities, not just classroom-based educational activities. This includes band, chess club, chorus, sports, camping trips, field trips, and any other school-sponsored or school-affiliated activities of interest to your child.

If your child will need accommodations or support to take advantage of these activities, the IEP should list them. If you do not have an IEP, use a 504 plan.

It's another issue if your child's behavior is actually dangerous to himself or others. However, under the ADA the school cannot discriminate based simply on his diagnosis or on assumptions it might have about his behavior.

Extended school year services

Most school districts only provide services during summer vacations and other long breaks if you can document his need for extended school year (ESY) services. This requires special attention to monitoring how your child copes with breaks in the school routine. Teachers and your child's psychiatrist or therapist can help you gather the evidence you need to show that your child loses skills or regresses behaviorally after being out of school for more than a weekend. During breaks from school, keep your own log of behaviors and regressions, if any.

Some parents gain ESY services for their child by showing that services made available during breaks can satisfy parts of the IEP not addressed adequately during the school year. For example, a student might be able to get ESY funding approved for a special summer program geared toward teaching social skills or independent living skills.

Education in Canada

The Canadian special education process is fairly similar to that used in the US. Some very basic guidelines are governed by the national Education Act, but almost all education policy is set at the provincial level.

Special education evaluations may be done by a team, which might include a school psychologist, a behavior specialist, a special education teacher, other school or district personnel, and in some cases a parent, although inviting parents to participate is not required by law in all provinces. Parents must request this type of evaluation, however. Alternatively, evaluation may be done privately, at the parent's expense.

The evaluation is used as a basis for a document setting forth the student's needs, which is usually called an IEP. Almost identical to the American IEP, this document is usually updated yearly, or more frequently if needed. A formal review may be required every three years. In most provinces, parents must sign a statement that says they have been consulted during the IEP process; students aged 16 or older may also need to sign. The level of parental participation varies greatly between provinces and between individual school boards.

Placement options for Canadian students vary based on provincial policy. Inclusion is the most common setting for children with TS, although behavioral classes are springing up around the country. Other options are also available, including home-based instruction and residential schools, in certain cases. Partial inclusion is increasingly common, as is supported mainstreaming. Students from rural or poorly served areas may be sent to a residential school, or funding may be provided for room and board to allow the student to attend a day program outside of their home area.

If disputes arise between the school or the school board and the parents, there is a School Division Decision Review Process available for adjudicating them. The concept known as due process in the US is usually referred to as "fundamental justice" in Canada. Parents also have recourse to informal arbitration or the regular provincial justice system. The rights of persons with disabilities are protected by the Charter of Human Rights, which may be invoked in certain kinds of education disputes.

As in the US, many families feel that the system is hard to navigate. Brenda, grandmother of 10-year-old Charisse, says:

> *Charisse's tics have included blinking, smelling, and sniffing everything and anything; cartwheels and headstands; twirling; tossing things in the*

air; twirling fingers; pressing the fingers of both hands in a specific pattern; stretching her chin to touch her chest; banging her knees together; licking her lips until they are chapped; some vocal noises, grunting, "hmm hmm" noises, and little squeals; and occasional full body jerks. Her behaviors have been more of a problem than tics, though. Charisse is often impatient and quite assertive—she likes to lead and have things her way. She can be confrontational and argumentative, although maturity is helping her to understand her disorders better, and to learn strategies to better deal with problems and frustrations caused by her disorders.

It has been an ongoing struggle, and very frustrating. The school is not cooperative generally in making accommodation for Charisse's disorders. They resist accepting the disorders, in fact. We have suffered much grief and worry for her with the school system. Because Charisse is extremely bright, the school and teachers often discount her disorders, and have expectations that are unrealistic.

Education in the UK

When a child in the UK is judged eligible for special education services, he is said to be a Special Educational Needs (SEN) student or *statemented*. The latter term refers to an IEP-like document called a Statement of Special Educational Needs, also known as a Record of Needs. This document is developed at the council level by the Local Educational Authority (LEA), and lists the services that a statemented child needs. Usually the team that creates the statement includes an educational psychologist, a teacher, and the parents. It may also include the family's health visitor or other personnel, such as a psychiatrist or child development specialist. Each child's statement is reviewed and updated annually. Disability advocates strongly urge parents to get expert help with the statementing process.

Your LEA can limit services according to its budget, even if those services are listed as necessary on your child's statement. Service availability varies widely between LEAs. Some therapeutic services that would be delivered by schools in the US, such as psychiatric care and speech therapy, may be made available through National Health instead.

School placements in the UK run the gamut from residential schools to specialist schools to full inclusion in mainstream schools. There are more residential options available than in the US system due to the English tradition of public schools. (American readers may be confused by this term: in the UK, "public" schools are privately owned and run; schools run by the LEAs are called government schools.)

Schools working with SEN students operate under a government Code of Practice that is analogous to, but much weaker than, IDEA in the US. Parents and disability advocates can insist that LEAs follow this code when devising programs for statemented students, and the code allows a formal appeals process.

Seventeen-year-old Keith spent time in both day and residential schools without success, says his mother, Grace:

> From ages 5 to 10, he attended normal local day schools, from age 7 onwards with help from a classroom assistant. From ages 10 to 13, he attended a school in a nearby town for children with moderate learning difficulties. From ages 13 to 15, he was at residential school about a half hour's journey away, but came home at weekends. The latter school was for children with significant to severe learning difficulties and supposedly specialized in autism.
>
> None of these schooling situations were in any way successful for him, and each in their own way caused a lot of damage.
>
> From age 15 until the present day he has been homeschooled, which has been very successful in terms of both educational and emotional progress.
>
> He is said to have generalized learning difficulties. His reading, writing, and math are at a 5- or 6-year-old level, whereas in other respects he is handling studies appropriate to an 11- to 14-year-old, and in many instances understanding adult literature and materials. I feel he has a specific learning disability in literacy and numeracy, but in the UK you cannot be labeled as, say, "dyslexic" unless you are assessed as having a normal IQ or above. Keith's is assessed in the 60 to 70 range, although one test showed verbal IQ into the 80s.

Parents report that homeschooling a child with a disability is particularly hard in some parts of the UK. Regular inspection by an Educational Welfare Officer is required, and some of these bureaucrats are not very knowledgeable about neurological issues. Parents need to provide detailed documentation of what they are teaching, and of how well their child is progressing.

Education in Australia

Australia's system is paradoxically looser and yet more accommodating to students with disabilities of all sorts. There is only a thin legal framework for the provision of special education services, but in the urban areas where most Australians live, these services are apparently no harder to obtain than they are in the UK.

Placement options include residential schools (including placement in residential schools located in the UK, for some students), special schools for children with moderate to severe developmental delay or severe behavior disorders, special classrooms for disabled children within regular schools, and the full range of mainstreaming options. "Mix and match" placements that allow students to be mainstreamed for just part of the day are still rare, however. For students in rural areas, there is a Traveling Teacher service that can provide special education services and consultation to children learning in "outback" schools or at home.

According to Gabrielle, mother of 13-year-old Dion, location matters a lot when it comes to services in Australia:

> We live in rural Australia, which almost by definition means we have reduced access to any services. We have a home-built shack in the rainforest with solar panels and rainwater tanks, and take "pot luck" at the local high school, there being little other choice.
>
> Accessing Special Ed in rural New South Wales, the state in which we live, has been a long and frustrating process. There is a limited bucket of funds, and this year there has been a budget freeze. I don't know yet if Dion's application for a teacher's aide for next year has been approved. He has had an aide for four years now, and before that he had behavioral support and other desultory intervention programs.
>
> Trouble is, TS is such an esoteric complaint that most people have only the most rudimentary of ideas about it, and are not aware of its subtle and bizarre manifestations. I've made a lot of fuss in Dion's schools, as they kept on excluding him, and suspending him. I am holding a (fairly friendly) threat of a complaint to the Human Rights and Equal Opportunities Commission over the head of the new school principal if Dion is suspended again for symptoms of his disability.

Australia has Federal special education regulations, but each state's Department of Education, Training and Employment (DETS, formerly called the Department of Education and Children's Services) is more important. Each DETS provides information, parent services, assistive technology, augmentative communication, special curricula, and many more services for students with disabilities. Individual school districts and schools themselves may also apply different rules, or offer special programs.

As Gabrielle notes above, national disability rights laws also apply to schools and students.

Education in New Zealand

The Ministry of Education sets qualifying guidelines for special education services in New Zealand. Students who qualify are called "section nined" (old terminology) or "qualified for the Ongoing Resourcing Scheme" (ORS). ORS qualification is currently reserved for those children whose impairment is judged to be "high" or "very high," with the most resources going to the latter group. Recent news reports indicate that limited local resources and a move to push for full inclusion under the Special Education 2000 program has eliminated many special education resources that were once available in New Zealand's schools. According to New Zealand parents, children with neurological disorders were never particularly well served by the system anyway. Advocates hope that a corresponding move to community-based services will eventually fill in the gaps, but as of yet services are neither widespread nor easy to obtain.

School placements include a few special schools, attached special education units within regular schools, and a range of inclusion options in mainstream settings. Some students are in residential settings. Under Special Education 2000, many more schools will have a resource-room-like arrangement rather than self-contained special education units.

Graduation and beyond

Most students with TS are headed for a regular high school diploma. This usually requires passing a certain number of specified courses. If the student needs changes in the graduation requirements—for example, if your child has been unable to develop proficiency in a foreign language due to cognitive deficits caused by medication, or if he was hospitalized during a required course and needs a waiver—arrange for these changes early in the high school years.

Some students will need extra coursework to make it through high school, such as special instruction in keyboarding or study skills. These abilities will also help with higher education or work later on, and you can make them part of your child's IEP.

Some students need more than the usual four years to complete diploma requirements. This can be a problem—most teens have a strong desire to graduate with their class. It is sometimes possible for a student who is still short some requirements for graduation to participate in the commencement ceremony with her class, if a plan has been made to remedy the deficits over the next few months.

Some students are not able to earn a regular diploma. They may choose (or be forced) to pursue a GED, as noted earlier in this chapter. A special form of graduation called an IEP diploma or modified diploma is also available. If a student earns an IEP diploma, she has completed all of the objectives set out in her IEP for graduation. This option is usually reserved for students who are unable to master high-school–level work, such as students with severe mental retardation. However, it could be the route to a creative graduation option for your child.

Students who are headed for college may want or need to go beyond the basic high school diploma. If your state has a special diploma for advanced students, such as Oregon's Certificate of Advanced Mastery or New York's Regents Diploma, check early on about any accommodations that may be needed for the examination or portfolio process. Some states have refused to permit accommodations on these tests, such as extended time limits or alternate examination formats. This is patently illegal, and already the subject of court challenges. For now, you can ask for special tutoring in advance of the test if accommodations are not available during the exam.

In the UK, Australia, New Zealand, and Ireland, special help may be available to help teens pass their level exams, including modified exams in some cases. Talk to your LEA or education department for more information about options in your area.

Transition to adulthood

The period of transition that begins around age fifteen can be a minefield for young people with TS. School starts getting serious, with college and careers becoming less of an abstract proposition. Grades matter, missing school can have a major impact, the social scene becomes more cliquish, and the pressures of teenage romantic and sexual yearnings add stress.

It's during this period of high anxiety that parents and teenagers take crucial steps toward becoming independent of each other. Transition planning is the formal name given to these steps. There are two kinds of transition planning: a formal process that is part of your child's IEP and that concentrates on school and employment issues, and a family process that covers legal, financial, and personal concerns.

For most students, high school graduation marks a jumping-off point: some go straight to work, some to apprenticeships, some to community college, and some to college. But there's nothing magical about the number 18. When your child reaches the age of legal majority, he may still need your assistance. How much help he'll need will depend entirely on the severity of his symptoms, and on how well you have been able to plan for the future.

Within the special education system, transition planning should begin by age 13 or 14, when your child's peers are beginning to gain basic work skills and amass credits toward high school graduation. Special education students have a right to prepare for graduation, higher education, and work in ways that fit their needs. Many need extra support.

Your teenager's transition plan should address high school graduation, higher education, and work skills and opportunities. It may also include preparing the young adult to apply for public assistance, supported housing, and other necessary benefits; helping her learn how to self-manage medical and psychiatric care; and instructing her in life skills such as budgeting, banking, driving, and cooking.

A high school student's IEP must include an area for transition planning. Because this is an area that has received little emphasis in the past, you may need to keep the IEP team on track. Make sure your child's transition plan involves all relevant life areas, not just education.

Preparing for work

Preparing for the world of work means gaining appropriate basic skills, such as typing, filing, driving, filling out forms, writing business letters, using tools, or cooking. Students can get these skills in school-based vocational-technical classes, in classes taken at a community college or vocational school while the student is still in high school, in a union- or employer-sponsored apprenticeship program, through job shadowing arrangements or internships, or on the job. Vocational planning is mandatory for special education students in the US by age 14 or 16, depending on the state, and should start much earlier.

Transition-to-work services may include moving into the public Vocational Rehabilitation system, which trains and places adults with disabilities into jobs. However, in many states the Vocational Rehabilitation system is severely overloaded, with wait times for placement ranging from three months to as much as three years. Typical opportunities range from sheltered workshop jobs (splitting kindling wood, sorting recyclables, light assembly work) under direct supervision, to supported placement in the community as grocery clerks, office helpers, chip-fabrication plant workers, and the like. Often the person works with a job coach, a person who helps them handle workplace stresses and learn work skills. In some cases, the job coach actually comes to work with the person for a while.

School districts may sponsor their own supported work opportunities for special education students, such as learning how to run an espresso coffee cart or working in a student-run horticultural business. Many schools have vocational programs that give students a chance to have a mentor in their chosen field, possibly including actual work experience with local employers. Not all vocational programs are for low-wage or "blue-collar" jobs. Vocational options in some urban districts include health and bio-technology careers, computing, and the fine arts.

Some public and private agencies also help with job training and placement. These include state employment departments; the Opportunities Industrialization Commission (OIC); the Private Industry Council (PIC); and job placement services operated by Goodwill Industries, St. Vincent de Paul, and similar service organizations for people with disabilities.

All students with disabilities should receive appropriate vocational counseling, including aptitude testing, discussion of their interests and abilities, and information about different employment possibilities. Parents need to ensure that capable students are not shunted into dead-end positions that will leave them financially vulnerable as adults.

Higher education

If your child has been evaluated and judged eligible for special education services, the school district's responsibility for his education does not end with the GED or high school diploma. Students planning to attend trade school, a two-year community college program, or a four-year college program need information far in advance on which high school courses are required for entry. This is especially important for those students with disabilities who carry a lighter course load, as they may need to make up some credits in summer school or through correspondence courses.

Transition programs should address the move from high school to higher education with specific assistance, including financial help if needed. Disabled students are eligible for publicly funded education and/or services until age 22 if needed. In some cases this assistance will include tuition; in all cases it should include setting up mentoring and counseling services in advance at the student's new school. Special education services and help for students with learning disabilities are available on campus and in the dorms at many colleges.

It's against the law to deny admission to a student just because he has a disability, but other college admission criteria generally must be met. Public universities and community colleges may waive some admission criteria for disabled students on a case-by-case basis if the student can show that they are capable of college-level work. Standardized test requirements might also be set aside if high school grades or the student's work portfolio look good.

Schools that normally require all freshmen to live on campus may waive this requirement for a student with special needs. If living at home is not an option, a group home or supervised apartment near campus might be. Before your child leaves for college in another city, make sure that you have secured safe and appropriate housing, and found competent local professionals to provide ongoing care. You'll also want to work out a crisis plan with your child, just in case things go wrong. She will want to know who to call and where to go. The freshman year of college is a very common time for symptoms to flare. The stress, the missed sleep, and the attractions of newfound freedom (such as drug and alcohol use) all play a role.

Healthcare

Family therapy is a useful venue for teens and parents who are working to balance issues of health and independence. The ultimate goal is ensuring that your teenager is well informed about his diagnosis and treatment options, and capable of self-care by young adulthood.

Parents need to start teaching their children as early as possible about using public transportation or driving, picking up prescriptions and reading their labels, making and keeping medical appointments, paying medical bills, and knowing where to go for help.

You'll also need to identify adult health-care providers in advance as your child nears the end of adolescence. Young women will need to see a gynecologist, for example, and both boys and girls will be leaving their pediatrician for a general practitioner.

If your teen will be transitioning from private health insurance to Medicaid or leaving your family health plan, help him prospect for knowledgeable doctors in the unfamiliar medical bureaucracy.

Hopefully you've been providing your child with reminders all along about symptom triggers and "early warning signs" that should send him in search of help. You might want to go over this information more formally with your teenager and his psychiatrist at this time. Sometimes getting the word from a doctor is more effective than parental advice, which many teens think of as nagging.

Case management

Most adults with TS are able to manage their own healthcare and personal needs. However, some (particularly those who have additional psychiatric diagnoses or developmental delay in addition to TS) need day-to-day support. Case management can take some of the long-term care burden off of the person's family, and ensure delivery of services after a parent's death.

Case management services can encompass arranging for healthcare, connecting the client with community services, a certain amount of financial management (such as being the client's payee for Social Security benefits), and more.

You may continue to act as your adult child's informal case manager for many years, or you may wish to give this job to a professional. You can hire a case manager privately, find one through a government mental health or community services department, or access one through an advocacy agency for the mentally ill or developmentally disabled. Some health insurance plans provide case management services as part of their behavioral health package, including coordination of outside services as well as managing the person's medical needs.

CHAPTER 9

Healthcare and Insurance

HEALTHCARE FOR NEUROLOGICAL DISORDERS can be difficult to get and manage. The main problem is gaining access to knowledgeable practitioners at an affordable cost. There is a limited supply of doctors with expertise in caring for people with Tourette's syndrome, particularly when the person is question is a child. Insurance coverage limits based on misclassifying TS as a psychiatric disorder can also be a vexing issue.

This chapter will explain how to access the best care through your existing health plan, as well as how to get medical care if you do not have insurance coverage. It covers private insurance, including health maintenance organizations (HMOs) and other forms of managed care, as well as public health insurance plans. It describes typical insurance roadblocks and shows you how to get around them. It also explains how service and coverage denials can be handled.

Both US options and the healthcare systems of other countries in the English-speaking world are covered.

Public assistance in the US and some other countries is closely tied to eligibility for public health benefits. This chapter also covers SSI disability income and other benefits that may be available to people whose severe tics prevent them from working, and to families caring for children with severe TS or multiple disabilities.

Private insurance: the American way

In the US and other countries where private medical insurance is the norm, the system can be hard to deal with under the best of circumstances. Each insurance company offers multiple plans with various rates and benefits, and there's no central oversight. As a result, your diagnosis may come with an unpleasant surprise: the healthcare services you need aren't covered, even though you have paid your insurance premiums. Some insurance plans specifically refuse to cover any neurological or psychiatric disorder, and in many cases it's legal for insurers to make that choice.

Some companies try to serve people with Tourette's syndrome within mental-health programs, which may or may not be appropriate to their needs, and limit access to neurologists, psychiatrists, and other specialists. Others may have no qualified "in-plan" practitioners but refuse to make outside referrals, or they may limit plan members to a certain number of outpatient visits or in-patient hospital days each year, regardless of what they actually need. In other cases, your plan may cover all of the medical services you need.

Lee, mother of 13-year-old Joseph, says her insurance company's insistence on covering her son's diagnoses as mental health cost them dearly:

> Our former health insurance company decided that Tourette's syndrome, OCD, and ADHD were all "Mental/Nervous" conditions, and were only covered at 50 percent up to $1000 per year. This lasted until we got rid of the policy in May of 2000. The premiums at that time were up to $960 a month.
>
> They also only covered his medications at 50 percent up to the $1000. When Joseph was on Depakote, the blood tests the doctor ordered every month cost $500, which the insurance called "Mental/Nervous." One year our medical costs were 40 percent of our income.
>
> Later the high cost of the insurance and limited benefits kept us from being able to afford to get Joseph to the doctors and therapists.

Making insurance choices

Whenever you are in the position of choosing between new insurance plans, try to find out about each plan's coverage of treatment for neurological disorders in general, and for Tourette's syndrome specifically. If there is a local treatment center with expertise in Tourette's, does it accept one or more of the plans you're considering? How about the neurologist or psychiatrist you would most like to see?

Maria, mother of 5-year-old Jesse, says a plan that offers a choice between many doctors has worked best for her child's care:

> We have a preferred provider organization (PPO), and that has been okay. I understand that hospital stays would be very brief and for "medical necessity only," but we haven't had any. The organization that does Jesse's occupational therapy has had to do a lot of precertification, but we have gotten everything we have asked for so far. The best way to save money is to see the most highly trained Tourette's syndrome specialist

*first. Otherwise you waste a lot of money on doctors who know little
about TS, and a lot of money on the wrong medications, or medications
that are not likely to work.*

Because most insurance plans will limit your choice of physicians, and may also control the type and frequency of care you receive, you should interview the companies you are considering as if you were hiring one—because you are. Here are just some of the questions you may want to ask, as adapted from *Working With Your Doctor: Getting the Healthcare You Deserve* (Nancy Keene, O'Reilly & Associates, 1998):

- How many subscribers does the plan have in your area?

- How many primary care doctors are on its provider list? Are they all board certified? If you already have a doctor with whom you feel comfortable, make sure he is on the primary care provider list, or you will have to change doctors if you sign up. If your doctor is a specialist, most likely you will have to see a primary care doctor, known as a gatekeeper, who will decide when and if you need to see a specialist.

- What criteria does the insurer use when selecting providers? Are they still accepting additional providers?

- How are the doctors paid? Are they paid a flat monthly fee per patient, an arrangement called capitation? Do they get a bonus or penalty based on referrals to specialists, number of office visits, hospital admissions, prescriptions written, or any other action?

- Is there a maximum lifetime cap on medical payments? Are there annual limits on the length of hospital stays?

- Must all referrals first have the approval of the primary care doctor? Can the PCP be financially penalized for referring you to a specialist, emergency room, or diagnostic test? Are there economic incentives for the doctors to limit these types of services?

- What hospitals, radiological services, home-health agencies, nursing homes and other facilities does the managed-care agency use? Are these facilities located close to your home?

- Is the plan accredited by the National Committee for Quality Assurance (NCQA)? This organization reviews more than 330 managed-care organizations annually and gives them one of four ratings: full accreditation (good for three years), one-year accreditation (if the organization is equipped to make recommended changes within one year), provisional accreditation (for organizations with potential for improvement), and denial for accreditation (does not meet NCQA standards). In addition to accreditation status, you can also get a report from NCQA summarizing their findings for an individual HMO. Call the NCQA Accreditation Status Line at (888) 275-7585 or order a list of accredited HMOs by calling (800) 839-6487. The same information is available at the NCQA's web site at *http://www.ncqa.org*.

- Does the plan pay for a second opinion if you request one?

- Can you change doctors anytime?

- Are the doctors bound by a "gag order" or other contractual provisions that prevent them from fully informing you of all treatment options? Are they barred from disclosing bonuses they receive from the plan if they limit care, referrals, or prescriptions? Ask for a copy of the HMO policy regarding gag clauses, and refuse to sign up until you get one. Some states now have laws that prohibit gag clauses for HMO doctors.

- Will you see a doctor at each appointment? How often and in what capacity are nurse practitioners and physician's assistants used? How long will you have to wait to get an appointment?

- Does the plan offer a point-of-service (POS) option to enable you to go outside the network if you think it is necessary to get the best care?

- What is the plan's coverage for pre-existing conditions? If you have a pre-existing condition, Federal Law (H.R. 3103—effective date: July 1, 1997) restricts group health plans, insurers, and HMOs from denying coverage because of pre-existing conditions if you already have coverage from another health plan. The law has several restrictions, so be sure to check it out if you have a pre-existing condition.

- Is treatment for Tourette's syndrome covered as mental health care, as medical care but within a special "neurological condition" category, or simply as medical care?

- If it is treated differently from general medical care, will services be accessed through a different provider—an arrangement called a mental health "cut-out" or "carve-out"? If so, will your primary care physician have to approve each mental health service, or will the mental health provider be empowered to create a treatment plan, prescribe and manage medications, and make needed referrals?

- Are there coverage limits for mental health care, and if so, are they lower than for regular medical care? Are you restricted to picking a mental healthcare provider from a list? How many visits per year are authorized?

- Does the plan have a formulary for prescription drugs, and if so, are your drugs or those you are considering on it? Is there a way for physicians to make exceptions?

- Are providers required to use cheaper drugs first, before being allowed to use newer, more expensive drugs? This is a particular concern for people with TS— older, cheaper neuroleptics like Haldol have a much higher potential for serious side effects than newer ones like Risperdal.

- Will you be limited to selected pharmacies? Is there a monthly drug budget, and are doctors penalized or rewarded for restricting prescription drugs?

- What are the plan's complaint and appeals policies? Who is on the appeals board? How quickly are complaints usually resolved?

To find answers to these questions, get a copy of the actual contract (not the glossy promotional material) and read it thoroughly. You may also want to ask your benefits manager at work, and talk to your doctor. Do not rely on a salesperson's verbal answers. To see how 150,000 HMO members rate their HMOs, get the *Consumer's Guide to Health Plans,* which is published by the nonprofit Center for the Study of Service (800-475-7283).

If an employer provides your coverage through a group plan, it is required to provide you with a Summary Plan Description (SPD) that outlines both the benefits and restrictions of the plan. The SPD must be written in easy-to-understand language, not legalese.

Although doctors are rarely willing to speak ill of specific insurers, their office staff may not be as circumspect. Ask about whether the firm you're thinking of cooperates with them at billing time, buries them in unnecessary paperwork, or has a reputation for denying services the doctor requests. You can tell a lot about an insurance company or HMO by how it treats its business partners—and that's what doctors and their staff members are when it comes to healthcare plans.

In the absence of a plan that definitely covers the practitioners and facilities you want, your best bet is one with an out-of-network clause. These plans allow you to choose your own providers if you can't find the right professional on the company's list of preferred providers or HMO members. You will generally pay more for out-of-plan visits, but you also won't have to run the referral gauntlet as often. The cost of using these providers regularly may be more than your budget will bear, however.

If your employer does not offer insurance that covers out-of-network providers or other needed services, take up the issue with the human resources or benefits department (or in small companies, the boss). When the cost is spread over a group, expanded benefits may not be very expensive. You can also make a very persuasive case that providing better coverage will keep employees on the job more days, because they will be less likely to need long periods off work due to health problems or caring for a sick family member.

COBRAs and individual plans

Insurance for families or individuals affected by any long-term disability is very hard to get in the private market (i.e., without going through an employer). It's available, but premium costs can be extraordinarily high.

If you are leaving a job that provides you with health insurance for one that does not, pursue a COBRA plan. These allow you to continue your coverage after leaving employment. You will pay the full rate, including the contribution previously made by your employer plus up to a 2 percent administrative fee, but it will still be less than what you'd pay as an individual customer. If you do choose a COBRA, be sure you pay all of your premiums on time. COBRA plans generally have a higher claims ratio, so COBRA administrators are not lenient with late premiums.

The COBRA plan is not a permanent arrangement, but it can help you maintain your coverage for eighteen months if the Social Security Administration finds your child with TS or another covered member of your family disabled (see the section "SSI" later in this chapter). For this reason, it may be wise to apply for Social Security Income on the basis of that person's disability even if you are quite sure that your family income would prevent him from actually receiving SSI or SSDI benefits. Once the Social Security Administration informs you in writing that the person has been found to be disabled, you must send a copy of that letter to your COBRA administrator within sixty days to arrange for an eleven-month extension of your COBRA coverage. This extension will apply to the entire family, not just the person with a disability.

If your COBRA is about to run out and cannot be extended, call your state insurance commission to see what your options are. Some states sponsor an insurance pool for people whose COBRA plan has expired. To qualify, you will have to show proof of state residency and COBRA status. It's best to apply at least a month before your plan is due to expire.

Maintaining continuous health insurance coverage is critical to prevent being locked out of healthcare by pre-existing conditions. If a COBRA plan is not available, other lower-cost possibilities include group plans offered by trade associations, unions, clubs, and other organizations. You may also want to look into public health insurance options, which are discussed later in this chapter.

If you can't find a group plan, you can sometimes obtain insurance directly from an insurance company. An insurance broker that works with many different individual plans can usually help you find the widest selection of options, and assist you in making a choice that ensures the best possible quality of care.

If your family is rejected for health insurance coverage because of your child's diagnosis, call your state insurance commission to see what your options are. Some states sponsor an insurance pool for persons who cannot get individual insurance due to health problems. To qualify, you will need to supply documentation showing state residency and proof that you were denied insurance coverage for health reasons.

Several states also have income-based state plans for adults on public assistance or in low-wage occupations.

You can also appeal the insurance coverage denial to the insurance company itself. Call the insurer's business office to find out what its procedures are for formally appealing denial of coverage. Ask to receive this information in writing. Healthcare for people with Tourette's syndrome is not usually an expensive proposition. Your appeal should stress that if appropriate routine medical and preventative care is provided, it is highly unlikely that your child will require expensive services, such as hospitalization.

Managing managed care

In most HMOs and other managed healthcare insurance companies, doctors earn more if their patients stay healthy. In many ways, this makes more sense than rewarding doctors for keeping their patients sick. It removes the financial incentive for ordering unnecessary tests or padding the bill with extra office visits—at least, that's the theory.

For patients with long-term conditions, however, the reality of managed care is that sometimes you may be perceived as an obstacle in the way of your physician's profits.

There are four basic rules for managing your insurance affairs, whether you're dealing with an HMO, another type of managed-care organization, an old-style "fee for service" arrangement, or a public health agency. Following these steps can help you obtain maximum benefits when dealing with care providers and insurers.

Learn how the system works

Informed insurance consumers are a rarity. Most people look at the glossy plan brochure and the provider list when their insurance first kicks in, but unless something goes wrong, that's about as much as they want to know. If you suspect that you may need to advocate for services, however, you'll need a copy of the firm's master policy.

You can obtain this document, which specifies everything that is and isn't covered, through your employer's human resources office (for employer-provided insurance or COBRA plans administered by a former employer), or from the insurance company's customer relations office (for health insurance that you buy directly from the insurer). Read it. It will be tough going, but the results will be worthwhile. If you need help interpreting this document, disability advocacy organizations and insurance-related sites on the Web can help. For a list of some helpful organizations, see Appendix A, *Resources*.

Find out in detail what the chain of command is for your health-care provider and your insurer. You'll need to know exactly who to call and what to do if you need hospitalization, emergency services, or a referral to a specialist.

If your employer provides your insurance plan, find out if it is self-funded through your employer or if the employer is paying premiums to the insurer. If the plan is self-funded, discuss any concerns with your company's benefits manager first, before contacting the insurer. Since the employer is, in effect, paying the benefits, it may be more generous than the insurer.

Ask whether there is a medication formulary in place, and find out in advance how you can appeal prescription denials for "off-formulary" medications. A formulary is a list of medications that are automatically approved for prescription by participating physicians. Unfortunately, some formularies don't include the latest medications, which may cost more than older medications. If the two drugs work equally well, that's fine, but many newer medications for Tourette's have far fewer side effects than their older counterparts.

Formularies may also restrict you to generic versions whenever they are available, preventing you from getting certain formulations you need. For example, generic clonidine does not come in patch form, but the patch is often preferable for children who have a hard time taking pills or who are falling asleep in school because of increased sedation that can occur with the pill.

Linda, mother of 10-year-old William, successfully appealed for a formulary exception:

> When our doctor prescribed clonidine for William, it came in pill form.
> It was much too sedating, and caused him to sleep in school. We tried
> reducing the dose, but that reduced the positive effects too much. Our
> doctor then prescribed it in patch form, which he said should eliminate
> the sedation problem. At first the insurance company balked, but we
> wrote a letter explaining that William's doctor had decided that the

> *Catapres patch would be more appropriate because the sedation was interfering with "an activity of daily living," attending school. The letter worked—and so did the patch.*

You will also need to find out about your plan's procedures for grievances and appeals, just in case (see the section "Fighting denial of care," later in this chapter).

Document everything

You should keep copies of all your bills, reports, evaluations, test results, and other medical records. You should also keep records of when and how your insurance payments were made. This information will be essential if you have a dispute with your healthcare provider or insurer.

It's also helpful to document personal conversations and phone calls. You needn't tape-record these, although if a dispute has already begun this can be a good idea (make sure to let the other party know that you are recording, of course). Simply note the date and time of your call or conversation, whom you spoke with, and what was said or decided. If a service or treatment is promised in a phone conversation, it's a good idea to send a letter or fax documenting the conversation. For example:

> *Dear Dr. Hippocrates:*
> *When we spoke on Tuesday, you promised to authorize a referral to Dr. Pauling at the City Hospital Neurology Center for my son's neurological exam. Please fax a copy of the referral form to me at xxx-xxxx when it is finished, as well as to Dr. Pauling at xxx-xxxx. Thanks again for your help.*

Referral forms are especially important. Most managed-care firms send a copy to both the patient and the provider. This document usually has a referral number on it. Be sure to bring your referral form when you first see a new provider. If the provider has not received his or her copy of the form, your copy and the referral number can ensure that you'll still be seen, and that payment can be processed. Without it, you may be turned away.

Form a partnership with your healthcare providers

Most doctors and other healthcare providers care about helping their patients, and they are the most powerful allies you have. Make sure they know your case well. Give them additional information about Tourette's syndrome if they need it. Let them know how important their help is. Your child's pediatrician may not be providing treatment related directly to Tourette's, but he does have the power to write referrals, to recommend and approve certain treatments suggested by specialists, and to advocate on your behalf within the managed-care organization.

Rindy, mother of 14-year-old Shawn, says her son's pediatrician not only made the initial TS diagnosis, but has also helped them access services as needed:

> She and other practitioners have written letters to his schools at my
> request to advocate specific positions and environments. Any care needed
> that has not been available within the HMO has been referred out without
> any hassle at all, and we've never had to pay for anything.

Don't rely on your providers completely, however. They have many patients, some of whose needs will likely take precedence over yours. A life-or-death emergency or a large caseload may cause paperwork or meetings on your behalf to be overlooked temporarily or even forgotten.

Another staff member, such as a nurse or office assistant, may help keep your provider on track, but you will have to be persistent. Make sure that you return calls, provide accurate information, and keep the provider's needs in mind. For example, if you have information for your doctor about a new medication, summarize it on one page, and attach the relevant studies or journal articles. The doctor can then quickly scan the basics in her office, and read the rest when time permits.

Semi-sneaky tips

Some people are better at managing managed care than others. The following suggestions may be a little shady, but they have worked for certain managed-care customers:

- Subvert voicemail and phone queues that present problems. If you are continually routed into a voicemail system and your calls are never returned, or if you are left on hold forever, don't passively accept it. Start punching buttons when you are stuck in voicemail or on hold, in hope of reaching a real person. If you get an operator, ask for Administration (Claims and Marketing never seem to have enough people to answer the phone). Nicely ask the operator to transfer you directly to an appropriate person who can help, not to the department in general. The old "gosh, I just keep getting lost and cut off in your phone system" ploy may do the trick.

- Whenever you speak to someone at your HMO, especially if it's a claims representative, ask for her full name and direct phone number, and keep it on file. It will make her feel more accountable for resolving your problem, because she knows you'll call her back directly if she doesn't.

- If you can't get help from a claims or customer service representative, ask for his supervisor. If you're told that he isn't available, get the supervisor's full name, direct phone line, and mailing address. Simply asking for this information sometimes makes missing supervisors magically appear.

- Use humor when you can. It defuses situations that are starting to get ugly, and humanizes you to distant healthcare company employees.

- Explain why your request is urgent, and do so in terms that non-doctors can understand. For example, if receiving a certain treatment now could mean avoiding expensive hospitalization later, that's an argument that even junior assistant accountants can comprehend.

- Whatever you do, stay calm. If you yell at managed-care people, they'll be angry instead of sympathetic. That doesn't mean being unemotional. Sometimes you can successfully make a personal appeal. You can act confused instead of angry when you are denied assistance for no good reason. You may also want to make it clear that you're gathering information in a way that indicates legal action—for instance, asking how to spell names, and asking where official documents should be sent.

Some plans have a special-needs liaison, an employee whose job is making sure that members with disabilities are cared for properly. Most special-needs liaisons act more like a resource person than an ombudsman, but the best of them can help you strategize to get what you need.

Linda, William's mother, explains how her insurance company's liaison helped:

> William is now on a public insurance plan, based on a Medicaid waiver that gives us a choice of five HMOs. We were having real problems getting to see a child neurologist. I called the special-needs coordinator, and she walked me through the process of how to get a referral, making sure we didn't have to wait any longer than we already had. She also made some phone calls on our behalf. I'm not great at dealing with bureaucracy, so her help was really appreciated.

Fighting denial of care

Would you believe that most insurance coverage and claims denials are never appealed? It's true. Most healthcare consumers are so discouraged by the initial denial that they don't pursue it further. However, all insurance companies and managed-care entities have an internal appeals process, and it's worth your while to be persistent.

The appeals process should be explained in the master plan. If it's not, call the insurance company's customer service office or your employer's human resources department for information.

Grievances

A formal appeal is not the same thing as a grievance. Grievances are complaints about the quality of services you receive: for example, complaints about rude doctors, overly long waits, or lost paperwork.

These conflicts can usually be resolved person-to-person, by talking with your provider or the office staff. If this doesn't work, you may want to ask the insurance company or HMO to investigate your grievance, and help to mediate a solution.

Sandi, mother of 14-year-old Brian, says:

> The biggest suggestion I can make when dealing with health insurers is to talk to someone in a decision-making capacity—not a trained customer service robot who just gives you scripted answers and doesn't hear your concerns.
>
> To illustrate, shortly after Brian was diagnosed with TS, our HMO decided they would cut their cost of sending out bills by reducing the number of mental health professionals they allowed in their plan. Fewer doctors and fewer bills equal less postage. Brian's psychologist was one of the people they cut. They gave us 90 days to find a new psychologist.
>
> To make a long story short, I ended up speaking to the person who was the HMO's clinical director for the state of Pennsylvania. I asked her if she was willing to risk the health and well-being, and possibly the life, of a child who was struggling with a new diagnosis, had just become comfortable with his psychologist, and was borderline suicidal to save .32 every few months (that was the postage rate at the time). When put in those terms, a reasonably intelligent person could easily see how stupid it sounded. So she told me if the psychologist was willing to continue to see Brian, even though he would be the only patient through this HMO, they would be willing to continue paying for it. And they did.
>
> I think the reason I was so successful in getting a positive response is because I spoke to someone at the proper level who was allowed to make decisions.

Appeals

Appeals are formal complaints about healthcare decisions made by insurers and providers. They have legal status, and healthcare consumers are entitled to have appeals addressed in a specific and timely manner.

The appeals process begins by addressing the issue directly with the provider or office in question. For example, if your provider refuses to give your child a needed referral to a neurologist, set up a meeting with the provider to find out why, and to let the provider know that you need to have a copy of this refusal in writing. Often this request will lead to a change of heart.

If it doesn't, make sure that you receive a written denial. If you do not, request it again, asking that specific reasons for denial be included, as well as the names of all persons who took part in the decision. You should also ask for articles from the medical literature that support the plan's position. If the administration can't or won't provide any, your case is strengthened. In the meantime, do your own medical literature search—your local TSA chapter may already have many of the basic documents you need on file, or may be able to order supporting material from the national office. You can also use Web-based services like Medscape (*http://www.medscape.org*) to look up journal articles, "best practices" statements from medical boards, and other useful literature.

When you do receive a written denial of care, make sure that the reason you were given verbally is also the reason given in this document.

If your primary care provider disagrees with the decision involved in your appeal, it's very effective to have him appeal that decision directly. Ask if he will write a letter of appeal to the appropriate employee, office, or committee. If he will not, ask if you can get a second opinion from another doctor. If he cannot refer you for a second opinion, you may want to take the step of arranging to pay privately for a second opinion from another physician.

If you have already seen a neurologist or psychiatrist, he may be able to help plead your case by providing hard evidence of your condition, such as test results and examination reports. These experts can also explain how much more cost-effective consistent treatment for tic disorders and associated symptoms is—particularly by showing the insurance company what the financial risk is of going without the treatment. Hospitalization, for example, is far more expensive than adequate medication and case management.

At this point you should also enlist the help of your company's benefits department or union benefits manager, if you have one. If the same problem has occurred before, he may know how it was resolved. He may also be able to support your position or, if such problems are happening often, to threaten the insurer with loss of its contract.

If your person-to-person efforts are unsuccessful, it's time to make a formal appeal to insurance company or HMO management. This type of appeal should be made in writing, and clearly marked "appeal" at the top of the document. Send it by certified mail with return receipt. This will provide you with documentation of what date the letter was received, and who signed for it. The letter should contain a clear and concise definition of the problem, as well as your name, insurance policy number and/or patient ID number, as well as any statements from your doctor, lab reports, and other pertinent materials. Make sure to state in the letter what action you want the group to take to resolve the problem. Don't delay writing this letter: your right to start an appeal may expire in as few as 30 days after the original decision was made. Keep a copy of this letter and all other correspondence for your records.

Every company, and every state, has slightly different procedures for handling appeals. In most cases, the company must complete its reconsideration of the decision you have appealed within sixty days of receiving your letter. If you need an expedited appeal because waiting this long could endanger your child's health, say so in writing, and enclose supporting documentation from a doctor.

When you file a formal appeal, the managed care entity should convene a committee made up of people not involved in your problem. This committee will meet to consider the matter, usually within 30 days of receiving your written appeal. Particularly in HMOs, where the committee is usually made up mostly of physicians, your medical arguments may fall upon receptive ears.

You usually can't attend an insurance company or HMO appeal. You can send written material to support your appeal, such as medical studies that support your position.

Some companies have more than one level of appeal resolution; so if you are denied at first, check your plan to see if you can appeal the committee's decision to a higher body. You may have the right to appear in person at this higher-level hearing, to bring an outside representative (such as a disability advocate, outside medical expert, or healthcare lawyer), and to question the medical practitioners involved. In other words, if a second-level procedure is available, it will be more like a trial or arbitration hearing than an informal discussion.

To prepare your appeals "case," look first at the insurance company's own documents. Somewhere in the fine print of the master policy that you should already have in your files, you will probably find a provision stating that if any of the company's policies are unenforceable based on state law, state law supercedes them. Most insurance company claims adjusters know very little about state insurance law. Your job is to educate yourself, and then educate them.

Now you need to find out what your state says about coverage in general, and about neurological disorders or Tourette's syndrome in particular. The answer may be found in actual legislation. Tourette's syndrome is not normally included in the list of conditions covered under the mental health parity laws now found in some states, but the rationale behind those laws is that any brain illness deserves equal treatment. Laws protecting the disabled against discrimination may also have bearing. Both of these types of laws were written to ensure that people with disabilities or health problems get equitable treatment. Your state's protection and advocacy (P&A) office can help you find out about what laws in your state apply to your insurance or healthcare problems. Sometimes P&A representatives, many of whom are lawyers, can resolve problems for you; in other cases, they can provide you with advice and referrals to other resources in your area (see the listing for the National Association of Protection and Advocacy Systems in Appendix A).

If you can show your insurance company that it is trying to assert a provision that violates a state or Federal Law, it should back down and provide treatment. Legal arguments of the sort needed to secure coverage can be hard for a layperson to craft. Advocacy groups may help you write a persuasive letter of appeal on legal grounds.

Your state's insurance commission—every state has its own, there's no federal insurance commission—will also have written policies about coverage. These policies are available in printed form from the insurance commission, and may even be available on the Web in some states. Remember, actual state law trumps state policy statements every time. State laws may be more restrictive than federal regulations, in which case the state prevails. If state laws are less restrictive than federal mandates, the federal government prevails. Insurance commission staff members should also be able to help you with general questions about what your state requires coverage for, and can tell you about any protections written into state insurance, healthcare, or consumer protection laws.

Your local TSA chapter or another advocacy group may already have a file of information about appealing insurance decisions in your state: call the national office, listed in Appendix A, if you need contact information.

If you are still denied after all this time and trouble, you may be able to take the matter directly to your state's insurance commission. If your managed-care plan is part of a public insurance program (for example, if you receive Medicaid or state medical benefits but you have been required to join an HMO), you can also appeal through a state agency, such as the county health department or the state children's services agency.

If your insurance company or healthcare provider cites state or Federal Law as the basis for its decision, if you believe it is acting in violation of a law (such as the Mental Health Parity Act or the ADA), or if your dispute is with a public healthcare program, you may want to send a copy of your appeal to your state representative or senator, or your US representative or senator. These elected officials have staff members who try to help their constituents.

Sometimes going to the press (or at least threatening to) also gets results.

Arbitration

Formal arbitration is another possibility when appeals fail, although experienced advocates warn that since arbitrators are paid by the healthcare plans, it's a tough arena for consumers.

In most cases, you can't recover your legal costs in arbitration, although they can reach $50,000 or more. Most consumer-law cases in the courts are taken by lawyers who work on contingency, meaning that you don't pay unless you win a financial settlement, which makes it hard to secure legal help for arbitration. Arbitration can actually cost consumers more than a court trial, and if it is "binding arbitration," it may prevent you from pursuing help through the court system if the decision goes against you.[1]

Legal action

Taking your insurance company to court is something that you should consider only as a last resort. It's expensive, and it takes so long for a decision to come down and then be implemented that your current healthcare crisis may have passed long before the gavel bangs. If you have the means and the gumption, don't be dissuaded from making things better for others. Just don't pin all your hopes on a quick resolution by a judge.

In some cases your state disability protection and advocacy group (see the listing for the National Association of Protection and Advocacy Systems in Appendix A) can provide legal advice or even representation, and there are lawyers willing to take insurance cases on contingency.

Getting coverage for new treatments

Almost all insurance plans bar coverage for experimental treatments. Some do have a "compassionate care" exception, which comes into play when regular treatments have been tried unsuccessfully and the plan's medical advisors agree that the experimental treatment might work.

So what do you do to pay for promising new treatments, such as newly developed medications that aren't on your insurance company's formulary? You either pay out of pocket, or you work closely with your physician to get around the experimental treatment exclusion.

Your physician may have to prepare a "letter of medical necessity" to support your request—or this task may fall to you. This letter must include the following items:

- The diagnosis for which the service, equipment, or medication is needed

- The specific symptom or function that the service, equipment, or medication will treat

- A full description of the service, equipment, or medication and how it will help the patient

- Evidence (medical studies, journal articles, etc.) to support your request, if the service, equipment, or medication is new or experimental; if there are less expensive or traditionally used alternatives to the new or experimental service, equipment, or medication, well-supported reasons that these alternatives are not appropriate for you

If your letter of medical necessity is not successful, you can then launch an appeal of the insurance company's decision (see the section "Appeals," earlier in this chapter).

Public healthcare in the US

Some people in the US have an extremely serious health insurance problem: they just can't get any. If this ever-growing group includes you, the main publicly funded option is Medicaid, with or without a waiver program.

The federal government also offers the Tricare plan for those in current military service and their dependents and, through the Veterans Administration, coverage for former military personnel.

Medicaid

Medicaid is the federal health insurance program for eligible individuals who are not senior citizens. It will pay for doctor and hospital bills, including consultations with neurologists and psychiatrists; six prescription medications per month; physical, occupational, and speech therapy; and adaptive equipment. You can get Medicaid by becoming eligible for SSI (see below). In some states, such as Hawaii and Oregon, Medicaid may also be delivered through a statewide healthcare system based on state funds plus a Federal Medicaid waiver. Medicaid is one of the few insurance plans that will pay for in-home therapy services, therapeutic foster care, partial hospitalization or day treatment, crisis services, and long-term hospitalization or residential care for people with disabilities. Although it is excessively bureaucratic, it is in many ways superior to private insurance coverage for people who have disabilities.

SSI

Supplemental Security Income (SSI) is a benefit program available to severely disabled children of low-income families and to low-income adults with disabilities. In all states, Washington DC, and the Northern Marianas Islands, disabled people who qualify for SSI may be able to qualify for healthcare coverage through the Federal Medicaid plan.

Mild to moderate Tourette's syndrome is not likely to qualify a person for SSI. However, for those whose tics are severe or unresponsive to medication, and for those who have TS in addition to other disorders, SSI may be an option.

SSI benefits range from around $300 to $500 per month for children or for adults living in another person's household, to just over $500 per month for adults living independently. A dependent child's grant depends on family income, while a dependent adult's grant may be debited for such things as free room and board. Some states also supplement SSI to allow for higher living expenses.

This money is only to be used for the direct needs of the disabled individual: it is not family income per se. You should keep receipts for all your expenditures.

To apply for SSI and/or Medicaid, go to your nearest Social Security office or call the Social Security hotline at (000) 772 1213 for an eligibility pre-screening. If you are given a green light by the eligibility screener, your next step is making an initial interview appointment and filling out a long form. This form asks dozens of difficult questions, including information about every physician or clinic that might have your medical records or test results, and information about your previous contacts with public health agencies. Provide copies of as many of your health records as you can—this may make the difference between winning or losing your claim.

If you need help in completing this form (and many people do) a social worker or someone from a disability advocacy group may be able to assist you. Some law firms specialize in helping people with new or pending SSI claims. Others can help only after a claim has been rejected one or more times.

Make sure your forms and records are complete when your initial interview takes place. You can be interviewed in person or over the phone. Most experienced applicants say in-person interviews are best, but they aren't always possible. Careful record keeping and having phone numbers and addresses for your doctors and (for parents) school personnel handy are very important if you choose a phone interview. During the interview, the Social Security representative will go over your application with you.

The Social Security caseworker will send your documentation and application to a state agency that can make a decision about your claim. This agency may order a review of your medical documentation, sometimes including interviews and observation by doctors who contract with Social Security. Social Security is actually supposed to arrange for any "consultative exam" to be with your treating physician, if possible, although this rule is routinely ignored. It can't hurt to ask—because doctors contracting with Social Security are poorly paid, some on the agency's list may not be very good.

Most applicants for SSI are rejected on their first try. You do have the right to appeal this denial, however—and you should, because a high percentage of appeals succeed. In addition, successful appellants get a lump sum equal to the payments they should have received, had their original application been properly approved. You must appeal the decision within sixty days, a process known as "reconsideration." You have a right to a hearing before an administrative law judge.

If your application is denied, contact a disability advocacy agency through the National Association of Protection and Advocacy Systems, which is listed in Appendix A. These publicly funded agencies can help you through the application process, and most can provide legal assistance if you need to appeal.

If you would prefer to work with a paid legal representative, you can find an SSI specialist through the National Organization of Social Security Claimants Representatives (NOSSCR) at *http://www.nosscr.org*. If you win, a lawyer can charge a fee of 25 percent of your back due benefits, up to a maximum of $4000. If you lose, you will be liable only for the cost of obtaining your medical records, copying fees, and possibly some other minor expenses.

Additional information about the SSI program for children is available online at *http://www.ssas.com/ssikids.html*.

Medicaid waivers

The reason one might need a Medicaid waiver is that SSI is an income-dependant program. A waiver sets aside the income limits. If you or your spouse earns more than the regulations allow, a disabled spouse or child will not be eligible for SSI. In some cases, family income will reduce the amount of SSI received to as little as one dollar per month, but the beneficiary will get full medical coverage. Others must apply for a special income-limit waiver—those for disabled children are colloquially known as "Katie Beckett waivers," named after a severely disabled child whose parents' pleas inspired the program.

The Katie Beckett waiver program is part of a larger category of Medicaid waiver permissions for the states under the general title of Home and Community-Based Services, or 1915(c), waivers. These waiver programs are administered at a state level. Some states have severely limited the number of waivers they will allow; some have created their own disability-specific waiver pools for conditions like cerebral palsy and autism; and a few do not offer any waivers at all. Contact your county's Child and Family Services (CFS) department and ask for an appointment with a Medicaid worker, who can help you learn about and apply for waiver programs that may be available in your state.

The appointment to apply for a waiver will be long, and the questions will be intrusive, so be prepared. You will need copious documentation, including:

- In most states, a rejection letter from SSI citing your income as the reason for rejection
- Your child's birth certificate and Social Security number
- Proof of income (check stubs or a CFS form filled out and signed by your and/or your spouse's employer, and possibly income tax forms)
- Names, addresses, and phone numbers of all physicians who have examined your child
- Bank account and safety deposit box numbers, and amounts in these accounts
- List of other assets and their value, including your house and car
- A DMA6 medical report and a physician referral form signed by the doctor who knows your child best (CFS will provide you with these forms)

If you have a caseworker with your county's Mental Health offices, or if you regularly work with someone at a Regional Center or in an Early Intervention program, this person may be able to help you navigate the SSI, Medicaid, and waiver process. State-by-state information about waiver programs is available online at *http://www. hcfa.gov/medicaid/hpg4.htm.*

If you have specific problems accessing appropriate medical benefits under Medicaid, state health plans, or other public healthcare plans, your caseworker or an advocate may be able to help. If your problems are of a legal nature, such as outright refusal of services or discrimination, call your state Bar Association and ask for its pro bono (free) legal help referral service, or contact the National Association of Protection and Advocacy Systems (see Appendix A). This national organization can put you in touch with your state's protection and advocacy agency, which provides free advice and legal help for issues related to disability. You can also consult the Health Law Project at (800) 274-3258.

Lee, whose son Joseph has an autistic spectrum disorder as well as Tourette's syndrome, was able to obtain a Medicaid waiver in her state. She says it helped get her son to appropriate care, although managing its bureaucratic details has been difficult:

> In Ohio, the Katie Beckett waiver program seems to have evolved into something called the Ohio Home Care Waiver Program. This is run through the Department of Job and Family Services. It took a lot of digging to get to this information—I finally found it through the Autism Society. A person there had a child on it, and coached me through applying.
>
> This program is for children who would be institutionalized without support. It comes with a medical card, respite care and therapies. It has been a great program for Joseph. We have been able to see his psychiatrist once a month or so, and totally revamp his medication plan, which has helped. We were able to find a wonderful psychologist and afford for Joseph to see her as often as necessary. This is the first doctor that Joseph has been able or willing to work with, and the benefits have been great. The program also pays for all other medical costs, and for medications, occupational therapy, and speech and language therapy.
>
> In Ohio they don't give you enough information to understand the program, its uses and restrictions, and the agency administrating it for our area is pretty poor. I finally found out what is covered by reading the state Administrative Code! Seems like a pretty extreme thing for a parent

who is already dealing with all that goes along with a special-needs child to have to take on, but it worked.

After I read the code, I found that they had denied us several services that were clearly covered. I just filed for a due process hearing on this because they recommended disenrolling Joseph! I was pretty sure they were off base and we would be able to keep the coverage. It was really hard to get straight information from the state on whether Joseph was even being disenrolled or not. I finally contacted our state senator's constituent services office, and they helped us out. When we had our hearing, Joseph was retained on the program. We even got a verbal apology from the state for the difficulty they had put us through.

There is another program in Ohio that is very useful. It is the Bureau for Children with Medical Handicaps. It provides diagnostic testing and then neurologist, pediatrician visits, and medication. Tourette's is a covered condition for this agency. However, it is behind the times, and only covers what they determine is "medical." It does not cover psychology or psychiatry visits.

State and local public health plans

All fifty US states, Puerto Rico, Guam, and several US holdings participate in the federal program known as State Children's Insurance Plans (SCHIP, also known as Title XXI), which offers uninsured children the same or similar benefits as Medicaid does. Each state's plan is slightly different, and some may not be fully operational as of this writing in spring 2001. For updated information about some state programs, see the national SCHIP web site at *http://www.hcfa.gov/init/children.htm*. You can also call your state health department.

Linda, mother of 10-year-old William, says her state's insurance plan has been an excellent match for her son's medical needs:

Because my son was on SSI and Medicaid while my husband was out of work for several months, our state approved my son for continuing coverage through the Oregon Health Plan even after our income went up too much for SSI. This state health insurance plan is funded with state tax money and Federal Medicaid money through a different kind of waiver program—it's a waiver for the whole state to do something special with its Medicaid money, not the same as a Katie Beckett waiver for individuals.

> *We had our choice of about six HMOs. I have not been thrilled with the one I chose, but it's still better than the private insurance we had through my husband's former employer, and I can switch anytime. There is a disability coordinator who can help you "work the system," and there are no lifetime limits imposed on services like speech therapy. It has also been a little easier to access specialists.*
>
> *William's medication costs are covered in full, and this has made a big difference in our monthly budget.*

In some areas, city or county health programs are available, either in the form of insurance or simply via access to a network of public clinics that operate on a sliding-scale fee basis.

Tricare

Tricare Standard is the health insurance program provided to active duty and retired members of the US military under the age of sixty-five and their families. A special service within Tricare, the Program for Persons with Disabilities, can help you with special medical needs, including care for a family member with a disability or developmental delay. Tricare also includes dental benefits and access to Department of Defense pharmacies. A second program called Tricare Extra offers more benefits.

Retired service members over age sixty-five may move into a special Medicare program (Tricare Prime) operated by the Department of Defense, although this area of benefits is changing.

The problem with public health plans

Coverage is a fine thing, but what happens when no one will accept you as a patient? This is the situation faced by millions of Americans who have government-provided healthcare. You may find yourself limited to using county health clinics or public hospitals, and those private providers who are willing to work for cut-rate fees. Medicaid and its cousins pay healthcare providers less than private insurers do, and there's no law that says a given provider must take patients with public insurance.

The latest wrinkle in some states is that even public health clinics are refusing the uninsured unless it's an emergency situation. Some public facilities are run-down, understaffed, and hectic as a result of high demand and low budgets. In fact, the emergency rooms of some public hospitals are downright frightening on weekend nights!

If you familiarize yourself with all of the options covered by your public healthcare plan, you may have more choices than you originally thought. In some cases you may have the option to join one or more HMO plans, receiving the same benefits as non-subsidized HMO members. Check with other recipients or local advocacy groups if you are offered this choice—some of these plans do a good job of caring for disabled clients, while others are not preferable to plain old Medicaid or state healthcare.

Sadly, there is also an "anti-Welfare" attitude abroad amongst some healthcare workers, who may not know or care what financial and medical troubles drove you to need public healthcare or income help. You shouldn't have to tolerate substandard or un-businesslike treatment from providers. If it happens and you can't work things out with the provider directly, ask your caseworker about complaint options.

Other public assistance for the disabled

While all western European nations and many other countries provide family support allowances to encourage one parent to stay home with young children, the US government has cut support even to single parents, and provides extraordinarily low allowances when they are available. This policy affects the parents of children with disabilities particularly harshly.

Between the 1950s and the 1980s, single, low-income parents of children with disabilities tended to receive Aid to Families with Dependent Children (AFDC, "welfare") and SSI. When put together, income from these two programs permitted them to eke out a living. While they remained well below the poverty line, they could generally obtain housing and adequate food. For many of these families, the most important benefit of receiving public assistance was access to Medicaid.

Welfare reform has changed this picture drastically. The Temporary Assistance for Needy Families (TANF) program, a system of short-term emergency supports, has replaced AFDC. All states have now imposed stringent rules, such as limiting assistance to once in a lifetime, requiring that parents work for their grants, or forcing parents into job-training schemes geared toward a rapid transition to low-wage employment. Although most states have also added childcare services to their offerings to help parents receiving TANF grants transition to the workplace, affordable childcare slots for children and teens with disabilities are almost nonexistent. This leaves even the most determined low-income parent at a severe disadvantage.

Federal Law permits exceptions to TANF regulations be made for some—but not all—parents caring for disabled children, and for parents who are themselves disabled.

However, caseworkers are responsible for holding down the number of exemptions to a small percentage of their clients, even though as many as half of families remaining on welfare now include either a mother or a child with a serious disability.[2] You can apply for TANF at your county's Child and Family Services department. The program is primarily for single parents, but two-parent families are eligible in some areas and under some circumstances.

The amount of the monthly grant varies. It is determined by the county government, which administers TANF programs at the local level. If you are parenting a child with any type of difficult health condition, you'll need to provide very complete documentation to get and retain benefits on the basis of needing to provide full-time home care. You can expect to have an eligibility review at least every three months, during which all of your documents will be reviewed and you will be re-interviewed. Generally speaking, you cannot have savings or possessions worth over $1,000, although you may own a modest home and car. You may need to sell a late-model car and other valuables before you can receive benefits. Your grant may be reduced by the amount of other financial assistance you receive. If you find part-time work, your pay or a portion thereof may also reduce your grant. Some states have work incentive programs, however. Court-ordered child-support payments to TANF recipients are paid to the county rather than directly to the parent, to offset the cost of the grant.

You may be eligible for Food Stamps, "commodities" (free food), and other benefits, such as job training, if you receive TANF.

People leaving TANF programs may be eligible for certain short-term benefits, such as subsidized childcare and continued health insurance. Until recently, child-support checks received after leaving the TANF program were also taken by the state until grant money was repaid, but this policy changed in fall 2000.

If you need help in obtaining or keeping public assistance, contact a local welfare rights organization or advocacy group, or contact the National Welfare Monitoring and Advocacy Partnership (NWMAP) for national information and referrals (see Appendix A).

Indirect financial help

In the US, tax deductions have replaced direct financial assistance to the poor in many cases. These benefits are provided just once a year, but families coping with the high cost of caring for a disabled child should take advantage of them.

One of the most important tax benefits is the ability to itemize medical deductions on your Federal income tax. You can write off not only the direct cost of doctor's visits not covered by health insurance, but also health insurance co-pays and deductibles, out-of-pocket expenses for medications, travel costs related to medical care, and at least some expenses related to attending medical or disability conferences and classes. Self-employed people can deduct most of their health-insurance premiums, even if they don't itemize.

Because itemized deductions limit your Federal tax liability, they also reduce your state income taxes, if any. (State taxes are usually based on taxable income figures taken from your federal form.) Some states have additional tax benefits for the disabled. In Oregon, for example, each disabled child counts as two dependents.

Another important Federal tax benefit is the Earned Income Credit (EIC) program. This benefit for the working poor can actually supplement your earnings with a tax rebate, not just a deduction. You can file for EIC on your Federal 1040 tax form.

Participate in a Health Care Flex Spending Account (FSA), if your employer offers this opportunity. An FSA allows you to elect an amount that will be deducted from your paychecks on a pre-tax basis to pay for uncovered medical expenses. To participate in an FSA, you would elect an amount at the beginning of the calendar year. As you accrue expenses, you can be reimbursed for those medical expenses, even if your paycheck deductions have not yet totaled the amount of the reimbursement. The one disadvantage of an FSA is that if your expenses do not total your election amount, you would forfeit the difference. Accordingly, it's important to accurately estimate your anticipated uncovered expenses. Expenses recovered through a Health Care FSA cannot be deducted on your federal taxes, so this option works best if your combination of income and medical expenses do not allow you to itemize your medical deductions.

Mortgage interest is also tax-deductible in the US, as most people are aware. Since your home is usually not considered as an asset when determining eligibility for direct financial assistance, such as SSI, this makes home ownership particularly attractive to families coping with disability. Some banks and credit unions have special mortgage programs for low- and moderate-income families. Given the strong financial benefits of home ownership, including the opportunity to keep your housing costs from going up in the future, purchasing a house is very advisable.

Very low-income families may be able to get additional help in reaching the goal of home ownership from organizations like Habitat for Humanity. Disability advocacy and social service organizations have recently begun to push to increase the level of home ownership among disabled adults, and some can help you with planning for a teen's future as well. In some cases a home can be part of a special trust that provides professional management services.

Health Canada

In Canada, the Canada Health Act ensures healthcare coverage for all Canadian citizens, landed immigrants, and for non-citizens who need emergency care. How healthcare is actually delivered is a provincial matter, however, and qualified providers can be hard to find in the less-populated northern provinces.

To initiate an evaluation for Tourette's syndrome, see your general practitioner, who can then make a referral to an appropriate specialist. A wide variety of specialists are available through provincial health plans. Most of the best specialists are affiliated with university hospitals. Waiting lists are a reality, but reports indicate that calls and letters (especially if they come from a pediatrician or general practitioner) can often open doors.

If there is no qualified provider nearby, public assistance programs are available to help patients get expert care elsewhere. This help may include covering transportation costs, housing the patient during evaluation and treatment, and providing regular consultations later on with a doctor closer to home. As each province has its own provincial insurance scheme, however, going out-of-province for care may mean paying up front and applying for reimbursement, which can be difficult to obtain.

Canadians also report that privatization and other changes are starting to limit their access to healthcare. Some families are now carrying private insurance to ensure timely access to care providers of their choice, although it is still rare.

Canadians in border areas may wish to consult with specialists in the US. Except for rare and pre-approved cases, public health insurance will not cover these visits.

Brenda, grandmother of 10-year-old Charisse, said they lack appropriate services in their area:

> Getting a diagnosis was a struggle, but since then we feel we have good basic healthcare for Charisse.
>
> As for direct services…well, I don't know. Our province does not consider TS or ADHD a disorder for which you are eligible for services paid by government. The school doesn't accommodate special needs readily, and we receive no service from any agency. There isn't much available. The only place you can go for help is the local Tourette Syndrome Foundation, and this is mostly meetings, with a few activities throughout the year. The TSF is operated by volunteers.

We do feel extremely fortunate that we were able to get Charisse taken on as a patient at the Tourette clinic at Toronto Western Hospital. This has been one of the few successes with the health system that we have achieved, and the experience has been beneficial for Charisse. There is a long waiting list, because this is the only clinic of its kind in Ontario with expert doctors in the field.

Welfare is available in Canada for people with disabilities, single parents, and unemployed adults with or without children. The amount of the monthly payment is set at the provincial level. The disability payment varies from a low of about $580 per month in poor provinces like New Brunswick to around $800 per month in more expensive Ontario and British Columbia. Under the Canadian system, parents caring for children, single or otherwise, receive higher payments than disabled adults do.

To apply for welfare benefits, visit your nearest Ministry or Department of Social Services. For disability benefits, regulations vary by province. Typically, you must be 18 years of age or older and have confirmation from a medical practitioner that the impairment exists and will likely continue for at least two years or longer, or that it is likely to continue for at least one year and then reoccur. In addition you must require, as a direct result of a severe mental or physical impairment, one of the following:

- Extensive assistance or supervision in order to perform daily living tasks within a reasonable time

- Unusual and continuous monthly expenditures for transportation or for special diets or for other unusual but essential and continuous needs

There are limits on the amount and kinds of savings and other property that a person or family receiving benefits can have.

As in the US, welfare reform is a growing trend in Canada. Some provinces have introduced mandatory workfare programs for single adults and for some parents on welfare. These provisions generally do not apply to people receiving disability benefits, and parents caring for disabled children can usually have welfare-to-work requirements waived or deferred.

Canadians who are denied benefits or who have other problems with the benefits agency can appeal its decisions to an independent tribunal. Some assistance for people with disabilities may also be available at the federal level, or from First Nations (Native Canadian) agencies.

Other direct and indirect income assistance is available to Canadians, including income tax benefits. Some provinces provide a healthcare tax credit, which can be used to cover medical costs not covered by public health insurance. College students with permanent disabilities can have their student loans forgiven, and are also eligible for special grants to pay for hiring a note-taker, school transportation, and other education-related expenses.

Benefits in the UK

The National Health system in Britain and Scotland has undergone tremendous upheaval over the past three decades. Public services have since been sharply curtailed, and co-pays have been introduced. Nevertheless, services for people with neurological disorders are much better now than they were in the past.

Specialists are accessed through your general practitioner (GP). Referrals to specialists are notoriously difficult to obtain, even for private-pay patients.

Grace, mother of 17-year-old Keith, said she's glad that regular medical care is always there, but getting specialized help has been a struggle:

> *Under the National Health Service, we have found great difficulty getting appropriate advice, help, and diagnosis. He was a very difficult baby, fretful and hard to feed. He grew into a toddler who seemed very behind, had speech difficulties and delay, and was stunningly hyperactive and tantrum-my. Although it was acknowledged that he was delayed developmentally, everything else was more or less shrugged off, and we were told he would "grow out of it" and catch up. It was not until he was seven that he got his first "statement" (IEP) which was very vague and merely stated mild to moderate learning difficulties. We have been continually pushed from pillar to post until we found Keith's current pediatric neurologist when he was in his mid teens. Unfortunately, he will not be able to see the same doctor once he turns 19 and so the whole game will start again.*

In the UK, people with disabilities have access to three major types of direct state benefits. You can apply for these programs at your local Benefits Agency Office:

- The Disability Living Allowance (DLA) is for adults or children with a disability. Parents or caregivers can apply on behalf of a child. Payment ranges from 15 to 35 pounds sterling per week. The DLA forms are relatively complex, so find an experienced disability advocate to help you fill them out if possible. Your local council may also have staff members who can help you apply.

- Parents and others caring for a child who receives DLA can apply for the Attendants Allowance (also called the Carers Allowance) program as well.

- Any person over five years old who receives DLA can also get a Mobility Allowance, a small sum of money to help them get to medical appointments and meet general transportation needs.

Your local council may also have its own benefits scheme. These may be direct payments, such as a supplemental housing benefit, or tax offsets.

A number of supported work schemes are available for people with disabilities and adults receiving other forms of public assistance. In some cases, these programs are mandatory. If you are parenting a child whose severe tics may impact his ability to find work, he should start learning about these programs before school-leaving age.

Teens and young adults attending college or trade school may find themselves in a "Catch 22" situation: on some occasions benefits officers have decided that if they are well enough to go to college, they're well enough to work, and canceled their benefits. You can appeal these and other unfavorable decisions to a Social Security Appeals Tribunal.

Help with disability benefit issues is available from UK groups listed in Appendix A.

Benefits in the Republic of Ireland

Disability Allowance and Disability Benefit are available in Ireland, but are far from generous. The Department of Social Welfare administers both. Disabled students can continue to receive these benefits while attending third-level courses, although they may lose other types of public assistance, such as rent allowance. Maintenance grant (a general benefit for poor families) is not affected by these benefits.

Supported work schemes are available, although your earnings may make you lose your disability benefits. The exception is work that the local welfare officer agrees is "rehabilitative" in nature.

Some direct healthcare is available from public or charitable hospitals and clinics in Ireland at low or no cost. A number of scholarship and grant programs are available to assist students with disabilities in Northern Ireland. An online report at *http://www. ahead.ie/grants/grants.html#toc* offers more information.

Benefits in Australia

Medicare, the Australian health plan, pays 85 percent of all doctor's fees. It also qualifies Australian citizens for treatment in any public hospital at no cost. Many general practitioners and pediatricians "bulk bill": they charge the government directly for all of their patient visits and let the 15 percent co-payment slide. Specialists usually won't bulk-bill. Once a certain cost level has been reached, Medicare pays 100 percent of the bill.

Patients can see the physician of their choice without getting a preliminary referral, but many specialists have long waiting lists. Access to qualified practitioners is especially difficult in rural areas, although the emergency healthcare system for rural Australia is enviable. In some situations, patients may be able to access professionals for advice or "virtual consultations" over the Internet, telephone, or even radio.

Medicaid does not cover some prescription medications, and there is a sliding-scale co-payment for those that are.

Kerry, mother of 12-year-old Kim, explains how the system works:

> In the past, the government used to provide a free screening for all children at age 4, and again at around age 6. This would be conducted in kindergartens, some daycare centers, and in schools. This was mainly a medical screening, but basic developmental and behavioral differences were sometimes picked up at this stage. Nowadays the screening is no longer universal.... Either the parent or teacher/childcare worker has to request it. Many children who would benefit from intervention thus slip through the net.
>
> In Australia, some pediatricians specialize in behavioral issues (the specialty of "ambulatory pediatrics"), and at the present time children with neurological issues end up being sent to one of these. Neurologists and psychiatrists are not involved in the care of children, except in cases of clear physical signs (e.g., epilepsy) or adolescent depression.
>
> Psychologists and non-medical providers are generally not covered by Medicare. However, the school system provides limited services of this sort (free) and the public hospital system is also involved, but overcrowded and under funded.

A variety of income support programs are available to Australian citizens, including direct financial assistance for adults with disabilities, parents caring for children with disabilities, single parents, unemployed single adults, youth, and students. Programs related specifically to disabled citizens and their families include Disability Support Pension, Related Wife Pension, Sickness Allowance, Mobility Allowance, Carer Payment, and Child Disability Allowance.

Employment programs for Australians with disabilities are many and varied, including the Supported Wage System (SWS), which brings the earnings of disabled workers in sheltered workshops or other types of supported or low-wage employment closer to the livability range.

Indirect benefits may also be available under the Disability Services Act in the areas of education, work, recreation, and more.

You can find online information about all of Australia's benefit plans at the Centrelink web site (*http://www.centrelink.gov.au*). To apply for benefits or disability services, contact your local Department of Family and Community Services.

You can get help with disability income and health benefit issues from the support and advocacy organizations listed in Appendix A.

Benefits in New Zealand

About 75 percent of all healthcare in New Zealand is publicly funded. Care is delivered through private physicians who accept payment from the public health system. Treatment at public hospitals is fully covered for all New Zealand citizens, and also for Australian and UK citizens living and working in New Zealand. Privatization is a growing trend in New Zealand. Public hospitals and their allied clinics have been re-created as public-private corporations. However, the government still provides most of the funding and regulations for healthcare.

Healthcare and disability services are both provided through a central Health Authority, which has for the past few years been making special efforts to improve delivery. To start an assessment, patients should first talk to their pediatrician or family physician about a specialist referral. Self-referral is also possible.

Urban patients may have access to group practices centered around Crown (public) hospitals, which often have excellent specialists. Māori patients may access healthcare and assessments through medical clinics centered around traditional *iwi* (tribal) structures if they prefer.

About 40 percent of New Zealanders carry private insurance, usually for hospitalization or long-term geriatric care only. This insurance is helpful when you need elective surgery and want to avoid waiting lists at public hospitals. It is not needed to access psychiatric care or other direct health or disability services.

New Zealanders complain that waiting lists for assessments and major medical treatments can be excessive. For many years, patients on waiting lists were not given a firm date for their visits, and were expected to be available immediately should an opening occur. A new booking system instituted in 1999 is said to be more reliable.

For patients in need of temporary or permanent residential care, volunteer organizations (particularly churches) are heavily involved in running long-term care facilities in New Zealand. These facilities are usually free of charge to the patient or family, although some are reimbursed by public health.

The social safety net in New Zealand is currently being revamped, and services for people with disabilities are expected to expand.

Direct benefits in New Zealand are similar to those provided in Australia, although the payments have historically been much lower. Domestic Purposes Benefit is for single parents, including those with disabled children. There are also a number of additional services available to the disabled and their caregivers, including training schemes, supported employment, and recreational assistance.

To apply for benefits or services, contact your local Ministry of Social Welfare office, which runs the Income Support program. If you need help with paperwork or appeals, Beneficiary Advisory Services (*http://canterbury.cyberplace.org.nz/community/ bas.html*) in Christchurch provides assistance and advocacy, as do a number of disability advocacy groups, particularly the information clearinghouse Disability Information Service (*http://canterbury.cyberplace.co.nz/community/dis.html*).

Alternatives to insurance

No matter where you live, there are alternatives to expensive medical care. Those who don't have insurance, or whose insurance is inadequate, may want to investigate these resources.

In some cases, creative private-pay arrangements may be possible with care providers. Parents have traded services or products for care, and others have arranged payment plans or reduced fees based on financial need. The larger the provider, the more likely it is to have a system in place for providing income-based fees. The smaller the provider, the more receptive an individual might be to informal arrangements, including barter.

Hospitals and major clinics usually have social workers on staff who can help you make financial arrangements.

Sources of free or low-cost healthcare or therapeutic services may include:

- Public health clinics, including school-based health clinics
- Public hospitals
- Medical schools, and associated teaching hospitals and clinics
- Hospitals and clinics run by religious or charitable orders, such as Lutheran Family Services clinics
- Charitable institutions associated with religious denominations, such as Catholic Charities, the Jewish Aid Society, and the Salvation Army
- United Way, an umbrella fund-raising organization for many programs that can often provide referrals
- Children's Home Society, the Boys and Girls Aid Society, and similar local children's aid associations
- Grant programs, both public and private

Medical savings accounts

Medical savings accounts are a new healthcare payment option in the US that may benefit some children and adults with Tourette's syndrome. A medical savings account (MSA) allows families to put away a certain amount of money specifically for healthcare costs. This income is then exempted from Federal (and in some cases state) income taxes. Unused funds continue to gain tax-free interest. These accounts can be used to pay for insurance deductibles, co-payments, prescriptions, and medical services not covered by insurance.

Families faced with paying out-of-pocket for an expensive residential program or experimental medication are sometimes able to use an MSA to reduce their costs by an impressive percentage. You'll need to check the regulations of the specific MSA plan to see what expenses qualify.

Medical savings accounts are currently available through a wide variety of investment firms, as well as some banks. They are governed by rules similar to those for an Individual Retirement Account (IRA), except that you can make withdrawals as needed for qualified medical expenses. There are limits to how much you can place in an MSA, what expenses it can be withdrawn for, and who can have an MSA. Talk to a financial advisor at your bank or an investment firm for more information about MSAs.

Help with medications

Low-income patients are sometimes able to get their medications for free by providing documentation to charitable programs run by pharmaceutical companies. In the US, the Pharmaceutical Research and Manufacturers of America Association (PhRMA) publishes a directory of medication assistance programs at *http://www.phrma.org/patients*. Alternatively, you or your doctor can call the company that makes your medication to find out about its indigent patient program. Individual company programs are listed in Appendix A.

Most pharmaceutical companies require that you have no insurance coverage for outpatient prescription drugs, that purchasing the medication at its retail price is a hardship for you due to your income and/or expenses, and that you do not qualify for a government or third-party program that can pay for the prescription. An organization called The Medicine Program at (573) 996-7300 and *http://www.themedicineprogram.com* can help you apply to indigent patient programs.

Doctor's samples

Another source for free medications is your physician's sample cabinet. All you have to do is ask, and hope that the pharmaceutical rep has paid a recent visit. Samples can help tide you over rough financial patches, but you can't rely on getting them monthly.

Mail-order medications

In some cases, you can reduce the cost of your monthly medication bill by using a mail order or online pharmacy. These pharmacies can fill your prescription and mail it to you, sometimes at substantial savings. Medications may be available via mail order within your country, or from overseas. The latter option can be surprisingly inexpensive, and may provide you with access to medications that normally are not available where you live.

Jackie, age 60, obtains a medication she needs through mail order:

> *Because I spent too many years on antipsychotics due to misdiagnosis,
> I now have the movement disorder tardive dyskinesia. My doctor helped*

me find a medication that helps, tetrabenezine, but isn't available in the
US. I have to buy it from England. My doctor does all of the prescription
legwork, but boy, is it expensive. I just ordered some more from a
pharmacy in London, and it will come to me in the US by mail.

Your doctor may have to fill out some paperwork before you can use these mail-order services. As with any other transaction by mail or over the Internet, you should check out the company's reputation and quality of service before sending money or using your credit card.

These firms can usually send you a three-month supply in each order. If you are doing business with an overseas pharmacy, check Customs regulations that might prohibit you from importing medication before ordering, especially if the drug is not approved for use in your country.

Some mail order and online pharmacies were initially created to serve the market for AIDS medications, but have since expanded to provide a wide selection of drugs. Many will accept health insurance if you have a drug benefit—some will actually cover your medication co-payment as part of the deal.

If you have US military health benefits, contact your Tricare representative about mail-order arrangements. The main Tricare-approved mail-order service is Merck-Medco at (800) 903-4680 and *http://www.merck-medco.com/medco/index.jsp*.

Mail-order pharmacies that some people with Tourette's have worked with successfully are listed in Appendix A.

Clinical trials

Some people receive excellent medical care by taking part in clinical trials of new medications or treatments. Others have suffered unpleasant side effects or felt that they were treated like guinea pigs.

Before enrolling in a clinical trial, make sure that you feel comfortable with the procedure or medication being tested, the professionals conducting the study, and the facility where it will take place.

An international listing service for current clinical trials is available at *http://www. centerwatch.com*. You can reach CenterWatch by phone at (617) 247-2327. You can also find listings online at *http://www.clinicaltrials.gov*, a site maintained by the National Institutes of Health.

Miscellaneous discounts

There are a number of programs around the world that help disabled people get access to computers and the Internet. One that offers free computers is the Center for Computer Redistribution at PO Box 70001, Richmond, VA 23255, or online at *http://www.freepcs.org*.

If you or your child needs medical care in a location far from home but you can't afford the cost of a flight or hotel, Appendix A lists resources in the US or Canada that may be able to help.

Similar corporate programs may be available in Europe, Australia, and New Zealand: contact the public relations office of your national airline to find out more. Social service agencies may be able to give you an emergency travel grant to cover these needs.

Advocating for change

Advocating for changes in the insurance and healthcare systems is a big job. Unless you want to make it your life mission, it's probably too big for any one person. But by working together, individuals can accomplish a lot.

The Tourette Syndrome Association in the US, and similar organizations elsewhere, have made great strides over the years. They have helped TS be recognized as a medical illness rather than a psychological problem, educated healthcare and social-services providers, and pushed public and private insurance companies to adopt non-discriminatory practices. Advocacy organizations like TSA can be the point of contact between healthcare consumers, insurers, HMOs, and public health.

In the US, most insurance regulation takes place at the state level, so that's probably where the most effective efforts for change will be made. There's still a need for education, for public advocacy, for legislative action, and in some cases for legal action. If you choose, you can make a big difference in these efforts.

By working closely with practitioners and with allies in the public, private, and volunteer sectors, change can happen. Even insurance companies and managed-care entities can be brought on board if you show them the positive benefits (financial and otherwise) of helping people avoid hospitalization, medication side effects, and worsening symptoms. Alternative models for delivery of care are evolving, and with hard work these new systems can be both more humane and more cost-efficient.

Afterword

WHEN I BEGAN MY JOURNEY to find help for my son, one of the very first people who offered me expert advice and support was Jackie Aron. At first, I thought of her as a professional, an experienced psychiatric nurse whose personal experience with TS gave her an insider's view. Over the years, she has become a friend.

I eventually learned that she had gained her expertise at a high personal cost. Her story lets people with Tourette's syndrome and their family members know what once was—and what can be when today's advances in medical knowledge are made available. I share her story here to let adults with TS know that their lives can change, no matter what the past has been like, and to let parents know why an appropriate diagnosis and the right treatment can make a huge difference in their child's life.

—Mitzi Waltz
June 2001

· · · · ·

MY NAME IS Jackie Aron, and I will be 60 years old when you read this. I have spent my adult life working as a registered nurse and raising a son. I also lived with undiagnosed Tourette's syndrome and severe OCD until just ten years ago.

This is the story of what happened to me. It's also the story of what happened to many people with Tourette's in my generation, before there were effective treatments and knowledgeable doctors. Unfortunately, similar things still happen despite these advances. I warn you now: it's an awful story. But it's my story, and I want you to know it.

I always knew that I was different than the other kids. I used to fool with my hair a lot—as a matter of fact, I still do that. I used to pick at myself. I seemed to have very little self-control, especially over the things I said. I would listen to myself, and think, "Did I really say that?"

But this wasn't the big thing. The big thing was this terrible feeling that was inside me. I used to call it my monster. The monster inside me. For as long as I can remember, I have been really terrified of everything. I felt like there was a vise around my chest. Often I was literally so afraid of this overwhelming feeling, and of my lack of control over this feeling and my body itself, that I begged to be put in a hospital. Instead, I was laughed at.

I couldn't explain why I did things like push my hair out of my face twenty times an hour or bite my lip all the time—I can still remember my father saying, "Jackie, don't do that, it's not attractive." People kept telling me to "Just stop it." I couldn't, and I didn't know why.

By the time I was 17, I had just about given up on this world that I didn't fit into. I took an overdose of drugs, and landed in the hospital. They sent me to a mental hospital, where I spent two years.

"Anxiety," they said. "She has the worst anxiety we have ever seen."

When I got out, the hospital referred me to a prominent psychiatrist in New York. He treated me for anxiety and for recurrent depression. He told me that I was terribly sick, that without him I would be dead, that there was no cure or treatment for what I had.

It seems unbelievable, but this doctor treated me for 30 years for anxiety and depression. He put me on antipsychotic medications, and kept me on them for over 20 years. He also put me on several other drugs that did me a lot of harm. One or two of them landed me in the emergency room, and one put me into congestive heart failure.

I couldn't understand why I kept going to therapy and doing everything he said, and I kept getting sicker and sicker. I was still frightened of everything. He told me that I was going to be scared—that was my anxiety again. I started doing strange things to try to decrease the constant terror I felt.

One day I was online, and I read something that had been written by a person with OCD. I knew immediately that this was exactly how I thought. I went to see my famous psychiatrist and said to him, with the print-out in hand, "Why didn't you tell me I had OCD?"

"You don't," he said, "You're just a hypochondriac, and this is another one of your hysterical illnesses."

About that time, I became really close friends with a family in which three of the four members had Tourette's syndrome. It quickly became apparent to them, even before I noticed, that I was doing all the same things that they were, and that I had always done these things. One day my friend asked me if I knew I had TS and OCD. I said I couldn't possibly. But I started watching her husband and her kids, and deep down a doubt began to grow. I began to wonder if she was right.

I asked my famous psychiatrist again if he thought I had TS or OCD. "No," he said, "You're a hypochondriac. Just stop this stuff." Different things transpired, and I left this psychiatrist.

I was beginning to smarten up. My friend made sure I saw the 1994 PBS documentary about a person with Tourette's, "Twitch and Shout," and I joined a list called POV-Twitch about the film and its topic. I read more, and saw some other videos that made me question what I thought I knew about tics and Tourette's.

Although still unbelieving, I finally asked my friend to point me toward a Tourette's syndrome specialist. She sent me to Dr. Ruth Bruun, who is probably the top TS expert in the US. Dr. Bruun wrote one of the very first modern books about Tourette's, *A Mind of Its Own,* and has seen hundreds of patients.

I had to wait three months to see Dr. Bruun, but it was worth it. First, she looked at the list of medications I was taking. "Why are you on this antipsychotic? This is a powerful drug in a huge dose," Dr. Bruun asked me. I replied that it was for my "anxiety." She asked me to describe this anxiety, and I did. She said what I was experiencing was not "anxiety" at all; it was a typical symptom of Tourette's syndrome.

Before our first appointment was over, I found out that so many of the things I had been experiencing for years—the symptoms that in the eyes of my former psychiatrist made me a hypochondriac—turned out to be symptoms of Tourette's syndrome.

Another clue was the response I had to clonidine, which had been prescribed to me for high blood pressure. When I started taking it, suddenly I felt so much better. When the dose was reduced, I started having odd symptoms that two doctors told me I just couldn't be having. Dr. Bruun said, "Of course you felt that way. It had been helping your Tourette's symptoms, not just your blood pressure."

I told her about my hypersensitivity to sounds and my focus problems. For example, if there's the sound of a dripping faucet or something like that in the background, it seems to me like it gets louder until I can't hear anything else. All she said was, "Oh, yes, that's common."

She said there was no question at all about what was wrong with me. Her diagnosis was Tourette's syndrome, severe OCD, and tardive dyskinesia—permanent neurological damage from the drugs I never should have been given.

I had always taken for granted that I was crazy, so it seemed too good to be true. Here was an explanation for everything. Things that I never even thought were related, this explained. It was the most exciting thing that ever happened to me.

In one hour with Dr. Bruun, I went from thinking of myself as an incurable psychiatric patient, a hypochondriac, and the sickest person anyone had ever seen, to just having a treatable neurological condition. I was just another person with Tourette's.

There are not enough thanks in the world for me to express to my friend, Dr. Leslie Packer, and to Dr. Ruth Bruun, for finally diagnosing me after a life of misery.

Now I'm finally on the proper medications, and I am really alive for the first time in my life. When I started taking an SSRI, "the monster inside me," that anxiety that was supposedly incurable, went away. When I wake up in the morning, I have something to get up for. I don't lie in the bed in the morning and calculate how long I will have to drag along until I get back there. I have purpose and meaning in my life now, and the fact that I'm not OCDing all over the place helps a lot.

Part of my purpose is to spare others what I've gone through. We've got to stop kids with Tourette's syndrome from getting "referrals" to ophthalmologists, barbers, and allergists. People have got to start knowing that these are tics and helping kids get appropriate treatment.

Eventually I started running the POV-Twitch list, which has since become Sunrise Tourette, a moderated online discussion group for about 115 families. I have always been very careful about who comes on the list and who posts there. Sunrise is going to be the safe place that I never had, with no marketing or meanness. "Newbies" who come in asking questions and absorbing things are just a joy to me.

When people say to me that Tourette's is horrible, I sometimes reply, "No, it's wonderful." They look at me strangely then. Now you know why I say that. Knowing you have Tourette's is a lot better than being considered crazy and a fake. This is what your children have been spared, this thinking that they are crazy and incurable.

—Jackie Aron

Resources

THIS APPENDIX LISTS support and advocacy organizations, books, and online resources related to Tourette's syndrome. It also includes contact information for prominent diagnostic and treatment centers, national and state agencies in charge of mental health care, links to information about related health conditions, and general resources for managing your own health care.

Tourette's syndrome support and advocacy groups

Support and advocacy groups are the primary resource for information and direct support. Their services and goals vary, but range from coordinating local, in-person support groups to hiring lobbyists to influence national legislation related to TS.

United States

Tourette Syndrome Association Inc.
42–40 Bell Blvd.
Bayside, NY 11361
(718) 224-2999
Fax: (718) 279-9596
ts@tsa-usa.org
http://tsa-usa.org

The national TSA publishes articles, newsletters, videotapes, and other materials for families, educators, and professionals. It also organizes a bi-annual national conference on TS. State and local chapters provide direct support for people with TS and their family members.

Tourette Spectrum Disorder Association Inc.
30733 East Sunset Dr. South
Redlands, CA 92373
(909) 794-3000
http://www.tourettesyndrome.org

The TSDA operates primarily in California. It offers local support groups, help with in-services for schools and health care providers, publications, and the excellent video on discipline strategies for kids with TS, "Bending the Rules."

Canada

Tourette Syndrome Foundation of Canada
194 Jarvis Street, Suite 206
Toronto, Ontario M5B 2B7
(416) 861-8398 or (800) 361-3120
tsfc.org@sympatico.ca
http://www.tourette.ca

This is the primary national TS organization in Canada.

United Kingdom

Tourette Syndrome (UK) Association
P.O. Box 26149
Dunfermline KY12 9WT
enquiries@tsa.org.uk
http://www.tsa.org.uk/

TS (UK) sponsors an annual conference, local support groups, and an excellent web site. It produces and sells literature on TS, and can help with school and medical issues.

Ireland

Tourette Syndrome Association of Ireland
39 Elderwood Road
Palmerstown, Dublin 20
(00) 353 01 626-4564

TSA-Ireland has a Helpline available every Wednesday from 9:30 A.M. to 1:30 P.M., and also sponsors support groups.

Australia

Tourette Syndrome Association of Australia
ABN 76 104 434 459
P.O. Box 1173
Maroubra, NSW 2035
(02) 9382 3726
Fax: (02) 9382-3764
info@tourette.org.au
http://www.tourette.org.au

New Zealand

TS support group
c/o David and Caroline Ashby
258 Kennedy Road
Napier, N.Z.
(06) 843-0024

General mental health support and advocacy

If there is not a Tourette's syndrome support group in your area, or if you are coping with other mental health issues in addition to TS, these support and advocacy groups are an excellent resource.

United States

Federation of Families for Children's Mental Health
1021 Prince Street
Alexandria, VA 22314-2971
(703) 684-7710
Fax: (703) 836-1040
http://www.ffcmh.org

This group serves families, especially low-income families, who are caring for a child with a mental illness. The web site is available in both English and Spanish.

National Alliance for the Mentally Ill (NAMI)
200 North Glebe Road, Suite 1015
Arlington, VA 22203-3754
(703) 524-7600
Fax: (703) 524-9094
TDD: (703) 516-7227
(800) 950-NAMI (Helpline)
http://www.nami.org

NAMI is the largest organization for mentally ill people and their families in the US. It has state and local chapters around the country, sponsors legislation, advocates for mentally ill people, and provides excellent information through its web site and publications.

Canada

Canadian Mental Health Association
2160 Yonge Street, Third Floor
Toronto, Ontario M4S 2Z3
(416) 484-7750
Fax: (416) 484-4617
cmhanat@interlog.com
http://www.cmha.ca

This is a group for Canadian families coping with a mental illness. The web site is available in both English and French.

United Kingdom

SANE
Second Floor
Worthington House
199–205 Old Marylebone Road.
London NW1 5QP
(0171) 724 6520 (office)
National Helpline: 0345 678000 (daily from 2 P.M. until midnight)

Young Minds
102–108 Clerkenwell Road, Second Floor
London EC1M 5SA
(0171) 336 8445 (office)
(0345) 626376 (Parents' Information Service hotline)

Ireland

Mental Health Association of Ireland
Mensana House, 6 Adelaide Street.
Dun Laoghaire, County Dublin
(01) 284-1166
Fax: (01) 284-1736
http://mhai.healthyirish.com/index.html

Australia

Association of Relatives and Friends of the Mentally Ill (ARAFMI)
http://www.span.com.au/mhrc/arafmi.html

ARAFMI has chapters in most Australian states.

SANE Australia
P.O. Box 226
South Melbourne 3065
(61) 3 9682 5933
Fax: (61) 3 9682 5944
http://www.sane.org
info@sane.org

New Zealand

Richmond Fellowship
249 Madras Street, Level Three
Christchurch, N.Z.
(64) 3 365-3211
Fax: (64) 3 365-3905
national@richmond.org.nz
http://www.richmondnz.org/

The Richmond Fellowship provides mental health services, information, and referrals in New Zealand.

General disability support and advocacy

The resources listed in this section provide legal information and, in some cases, practical help and advice, on matters connected with disability.

Exceptional Parent
555 Kinderkamack Road
Oradell, NJ 07649-1517
(201) 634-6550
Fax: (201) 634-6599
http://www.eparent.com

This magazine for parents of children with any disability is an invaluable resource. Most issues are constructed around a theme, such as transition planning, mobility, or special education. The parent-to-parent letters section is especially useful for families trying to identify or find others with a rare disability. The web site includes collected articles from past issues.

United States

Disability Rights and Education Fund
2212 Sixth Street
Berkeley, CA 94710
Phone/TTY: (510) 644-2555
Fax: (510) 841-8645
dredf@dredf.org
http://www.dredf.org

FindLaw
http://www.findlaw.com/01topics/36civil/disabilities.html

FindLaw has a legal research search engine, as well as a wealth of specific information about disability law.

The National Welfare Monitoring and Advocacy Partnership (NWMAP)
(202) 662-3556
info@nwmap.org
http://www.nwmap.org/index.htm

The NWMAP is a project of the Children's Defense Fund.

National Association of Protection and Advocacy Systems
900 Second Street NE, Suite 211
Washington, DC 20002
(202) 408-9514
http://www.protectionandadvocacy.com

Every US state has a federally funded Protection and Advocacy system. Call this group or check its web site to find a referral to your state's P&A organization. These organizations provide legal advice, and in some cases legal representation, to people with disabilities and their family members who have disability-related needs. This may include assistance with securing federal or state benefits, advocacy in the special education system, and helping with Americans with Disabilities Act compliance issues, among other areas.

National Information Center for Children and Youth with Disabilities (NICHCY)
Box 1492
Washington, DC 20013
(202) 884-8200 or (800) 695-0285
Fax: (202) 884-8441
http://www.nichcy.org
nichcy@aed.org

NICHY provides free information on disabilities. Spanish-language resources are available.

National Organization of Social Security Claimants
6 Prospect Street
Midland Park, NJ 07432
(800) 432-2804
http://www.nosscr.org

United Kingdom

Disability Rights Commission
DRC Helpline
Freepost, MID 02164
Stratford-Upon-Avon CV37 9BR
(08457) 622633 or (08457) 622633
Fax: (08457) 622611
http://drc-gb.org
ddahelp@stra.sitel.co.uk

UK Advocacy Network
Volserve House
14–18 West Bar Green
Sheffield SI 2DA
(0114) 272 8171

Australia

Disability Action Inc.
62 Henley Beach Road
Mile End, SA 5031
(08) 8352 8599 or (800) 805 495
Fax: (08) 8354 0049
TTY: (08) 8352 8022
brad@disabilityaction.in-sa.com.au

Online Tourette's syndrome resources

If you need information about TS fast, the Web and email discussion groups are just the ticket. Here's a list of some excellent places to get started (see also the web sites listed under "Tourette's syndrome support and advocacy groups," earlier in this appendix).

Web sites about TS

Tourette Syndrome Fact Sheet
http://www.ninds.nih.gov/health_and_medical/pubs/tourette_syndrome.htm

This fact sheet on TS is provided by the National Institutes of Health's National Institute of Neutological Disorders and Stroke (NINDS) division.

Tourette Syndrome—Now What?
http://members.home.net/tourettenowwhat/

This mom-run web site is an upbeat, reassuring oasis of information about TS. It accentuates the fact that for the majority of people with TS, tics are "no big deal." It also includes web-based discussion groups.

Tourette Syndrome "Plus"
http://www.tourettesyndrome.net

A very good site covering issues involved in having Tourette's syndrome with one or more comorbid disorders, such as OCD.

TouretteHelp.com
http://www.tourettehelp.com/

Sponsored by Layton BioScience Inc., which makes the nicotine-based drug mecamylamine that's currently being tested for use in TS, this is a slick but informative site. Helpful items include handouts and illustrations you can print out to use for in-service presentations. There are sections for patients and families and also for health care professionals.

Life's a Twitch
http://www.lifesatwitch.com

Duncan McKinlay is a Canadian psychologist-in-training who just happens to have TS. His web site is both informative and entertaining. It includes a web-based chat room and The Haven, an area for kids and teens with TS.

Tourette Syndrome Support UK
http://www.tourettesyndrome.co.uk/

Check in here for information and links related to TS in England, Scotland, and Northern Ireland. It includes a regularly scheduled web-based chat room. Some information is available in French as well as English.

WE MOVE: Worldwide Education and Awareness for Movement Disorders
http://www.wemove.org/

The WE MOVE site includes a well-written primer on TS, and also features information on other major movement disorders.

Online TS discussion groups

Online discussion groups provide an easy way to discuss issues. Read the privacy statement of any group you join before posting, however—with the exception of Sunrise Tourette, past posts from all of these groups can be accessed through the Web, and no one who wishes to join or post is refused entry. You can post anonymously and/or use an email address that is not linked with identifying information if you wish.

Sunrise Tourette

To subscribe, send email to: *sunrise-tourette-subscribe@igc.topica.com*
http://igc.topica.com/lists/sunrise-tourette

This is a members-only online mailing list for parents of children with Tourette's syndrome and adults with Tourette's syndrome. It is moderated by Jackie Aron.

alt.support.tourette

If you have a newsreader application (many are available free), direct it toward *alt.support. tourette* to join this unmoderated discussion about TS. You can also use a web-mail interface, such as *http://www.news2mail.com/Alt/Support/Tourette.html*.

Neurology WebForums at Massachusetts General Hospital
http://www.braintalk.org

This collection of web-based, unmoderated discussion forums includes a section for talking about TS, as well as forums for discussing many other neurological conditions.

Tourette Syndrome at Yahoo.com
http://groups.yahoo.com

Use the Yahoo search engine to see a list of over thirty TS-related groups, including several in languages other than English. Options include AdultsWithTourettes, TSKids, aussietourettes, and more.

Books about Tourette's syndrome

Beurhens, Adam, and Carol Buehrens. *Adam and the Magic Marble.* Duarte, CA: Hope Press, 1991. This book and the book below were written especially for children by a teenager who has TS.

Beuhrens, Adam. *Hi, I'm Adam.* Duarte, CA: Hope Press, 1990.

Bruun, Ruth Dowling. *A Mind of Its Own: Tourette's Syndrome: A Story and a Guide.* Oxford (UK): Oxford University Press, 1994.

Comings, David, MD. *Tourette Syndrome and Human Behavior.* Duarte, CA: Hope Press, 1990. A huge, rather technical book covering Dr. Comings' work on the genetics of TS.

Hamer, Sheryl, RN. *Raising Joshua: One Mother's Account of the Challenges of Parenting a Child with Tourette Syndrome.* Duarte, CA: Hope Press, 1997.

Handler, Lowell. *Twitch and Shout: A Touretter's Tale.* New York: N.A.L., 1999. Memoir by a well-known photojournalist who has TS.

Haerle, Tracy (editor.) *Children with Tourette Syndrome: A Parents' Guide.* Rockville, MD: Woodbine House, 1992.

Hughes, Susan. *Ryan: A Mother's Story of Her Hyperactive/Tourette Syndrome Child.* Duarte, CA: Hope Press, 1990.

Hughes, Susan. *What Makes Ryan Tick?: A Family's Triumph Over Tourette Syndrome and Attention Deficit Hyperactivity Disorder.* Duarte, CA: Hope Press, 1996.

Kushner, Howard I. *A Cursing Brain?: The Histories of Tourette Syndrome.* Cambridge, MA: Harvard University Press, 1999.

Leckman, James F., and Donald J. Cohen. *Tourette's Syndrome: Tics, Obsessions, Compulsions: Developmental Psychopathology and Clinical Care.* New York: John Wiley & Sons, 1999

Shimberg, Elaine Fantle. *Living With Tourette Syndrome.* New York: Simon & Schuster, 1995.

Wilensky, Amy. *Passing for Normal: A Memoir of Compulsion.* New York: Broadway Books, 1999.

Videos about Tourette's syndrome

These are just three of the videos available from the Tourette Syndrome Association Inc. (See "Tourette's syndrome support and advocacy groups," earlier in this appendix.) "Bending the Rules," a video on discipline strategies for kids with TS, is available from the Tourette Spectrum Disorder Association, listed in the same section.

Tourette Syndrome: A Guide to Diagnosis of TS

This 30-minute film is intended for professionals. It features patients with a full range of TS symptoms, plus video of patients with other movement disorders to make differential diagnosis easier.

"Stop It! I Can't"

This thirteen-minute documentary is a great way to start a discussion or in-service about TS for your child's classmates.

"A Regular Kid, That's Me"

This 45-minute video was designed for teacher in-service presentations. It explains classroom strategies for kids with TS.

"Be My Friend"

This short video for elementary school children explains TS in simple langauge, and can be used to educate a child's classmates. It was created by the Minnesota chapter of TSA, which can be reached at (952) 918-0350 or via email at *lbulger@scc.net,* and is also available from some other TS advocacy groups.

TS information in other languages

If you need basic information about Tourette's syndrome in a language other than English, you may want to check *http://groups.yahoo.com,* which houses TS discussion groups in Spanish, Dutch, German, and other languages, and *http://www.tourette-syndrome.com/tourette-syndrome-association.htm,* which features a list of TS support groups around the world.

The US-based Tourette Syndrome Association Inc. offers some materials in Spanish (see "Tourette's syndrome support and advocacy groups," earlier in this appendix).

El Síndrome de Tourette
http://www.ciudadfutura.com/hospital/tourette.html

This very complete Spanish-language resource includes information on history, diagnosis, and treatment.

Association Québécoise du Syndrome de la Tourette
222 Boul. Henri Bourassa Est, Suite 38
Montréal, Québec H3L 1B9
(514) 345-0251

L'AFTOC
afsgtjfm@aol.com
http://esstourette.ifrance.com

This email address and web site can put you in touch with l'Association Française de Personnes Souffrant de Troubles Obsessionels et Compulsifs, an OCD advocacy group that also has information about TS on its web site.

Diagnostic and treatment centers

The following list includes many, but not all, of the best-known centers for diagnosis and treatment of Tourette's syndrome. Most people with TS do not need the specialized level of care available through these facilities, but for those who do, their expertise can be invaluable. Your closest TSA chapter can help you with referrals and information about local physicians as well.

United States

California

Tourette Syndrome Clinic
City of Hope National Medical Center
1500 East Duarte Road
Duarte, CA 91010
(818) 359-8111

M.I.N.D. Institute Clinic
Ellison Ambulatory Care Center
UC Davis Health System
4860 Y Street
Sacramento, CA 95817
(916) 734-5153 or (888) 883-0961
http://mindinstitute.ucdmc.ucdavis.edu/index.htm

As of this writing in spring 2001, the Medical Investigation of Neurodevelopmental Disorders (M.I.N.D.) Institute clinic is quite new, and serving a limited number of patients. It provides services to children with TS and other neurological disorders.

UC-Irvine Movement Disorder Clinic
UCI Gottschalk Medical Plaza
Irvine, CA 92697
(714) 456-7002 or (888) 456-7004
http://ucihealth.com/healthcareservices/movdisorder.htm

UCLA Neuropsychiatric Institute (UCLA-NPI)
University of California, Westwood Campus
300 Medical Plaza
Los Angeles, CA 90024
(310) 825-9989 or (800) 825-9989
http://www.mentalhealth.ucla.edu

UCSD School of Medicine
University of California, San Diego
Department of Psychiatry
La Jolla, CA 92093-0804
(619) 543-6270 or (800) 926-8273

UCSD does not have a TS specialty clinic, but there are doctors on staff with expertise in TS who do both clinical research and patient care. UCSD does have a well-known OCD specialty clinic.

Connecticut

Tourette's Syndrome/Obsessive Compulsive Disorder Specialty Clinic
Yale Child Study Center
230 South Frontage Road
New Haven, CT 06520-7900
(203) 785-5880
http://info.med.yale.edu/chldstdy/tsocd/

Florida

Psychiatric Specialty Clinic
Shands Health Care at University of Florida
University of Florida Health Science Center
1600 SW Archer Road
11th Floor, Room 11-43
Gainesville, FL 32610
(352) 265-8000 or (800) 633-2122

Illinois

Parkinson Disease and Movement Disorders Clinic
Southern Illinois University School of Medicine
SIU Dept. of Neurology
751 North Rutledge Street, Room 2030
Springfield, IL 62794
(217) 524-8417

Pediatric OCD and Tic Disorders Clinic
University of Illinois at Chicago
UIC Institute for Juvenile Research
907 South Wolcott
Chicago, IL 60612
(312) 335-3000

This clinic also has a satellite office in suburban Deerfield, IL.

Maryland

Tic and Anxiety Disorders Clinic
Johns Hopkins Hospital
Division of Child and Adolescent Psychiatry
600 North Wolfe Street
Baltimore, MD 21287
(410) 955-1925
http://www.med.jhu.edu/jhhpsychiatry/childmain.htm

National Institutes of Mental Health (NIMH)
Biological Psychiatry Branch
Building 10, Room 3N212
9000 Rockville Pike
Bethesda, MD 20892
(301) 496-6827
Fax: (301) 402-0052
http://www.cc.nih.gov
NIMH Patient Recruitment and Referral Service
(800) 411-1222
prcc@cc.nih.gov

Massachusetts

Movement Disorders Unit
Massachusetts General Hospital East
Department of Psychiatry
Building 149, 13th Street
Charlestown, MA 02129
(617) 726-5532
http://neuro-www.mgh.harvard.edu/units/movement.html

MGH also has clinics focused on trichotillomania, OCD, and other related conditions.

Tourette's Clinic
McLean Hospital
115 Mill Street
Belmont, MA 02478
(800) 333-0338

New York

Compulsive, Impulsive, and Anxiety Disorders Program
Mount Sinai Medical Center
Box 1230
1 Gustave Levy Place
New York, NY 10029
(212) 241-8185

Tourette's Clinic
Children's Hospital of Buffalo
219 Bryant Street
Buffalo, NY 14222
(716) 878-7840

Ohio

Tourette Syndrome Clinic
Children's Hospital Medical Center of Cincinnati
Neurology Dept.
3333 Burnet Avenue
Cincinnati, OH 45229-3039
(513) 636-4222 or (800) 344-2462
tics@chmcc.org
http://www.cincinnatichildrens.org/programs_services/396

The Cleveland Clinic
Child and Adolescent Psychiatry
9500 Euclid Avenue
Cleveland, OH 44195
(216) 444-5812
TTY: (216) 444-0261

South Carolina

Tourette's and Tic Disorders Clinic
Medical University of South Carolina
Institute of Psychiatry
67 President Street
P.O. Box 25061
Charleston, SC 29425
psych@musc.edu
(843) 792-2300

Texas

Blue Bird Circle Clinic for Pediatric Neurology
Baylor College of Medicine
Dept. of Neurology
6565 Fannin Street, Suite NB100
Houston, TX 77030
(713) 790-5046
http://www.bcm.tmc.edu/neurol/struct/blueb/blueb2.html

Wisconsin

Tic Disorders Specialty Clinic
University of Wisconsin-Milwaukee
Pearse Hall, First Floor
2513 East Hartford Avenue
Milwaukee, WI 53201
(414) 229-5521
http://www.uwm.edu/~dwoods/newpage11.htm

The Tic Disorders Specialty Clinic at UW is part of the school's Psychology Clinic. Referrals can be made for medication, but its specialty is cognitive behavioral techniques, including habit reversal.

Movement Disorders Center
The Marshfield Clinic
1000 North Oak Avenue
Marshfield, WI 54449-5777
(715) 387-5511
(800) 782-8581
http://www.marshfieldclinic.org

Canada

TTH Tourette Syndrome Clinic
The Toronto Hospital, Western Division
399 Bathurst Street
Toronto, Ontario M5T 2S8
(416) 603-5794
Fax: (416) 603 5292
http://www.uhealthnet.on.ca

Dr. Paul Sandor's program at TTH is highly recommended to patients with Tourette's syndrome in addition to OCD.

Tourette Syndrome Clinic
St. Boniface General Hospital
409 Tache Avenue
Winnipeg, Manitoba R2H 2A6
(204) 237-2690

Neuropsychiatry Clinic
British Columbia's Children's Hospital
4480 Oak Street, Room C4
Vancouver, BC V6H 3V4
(604) 875-2345
http://www.cw.bc.ca/childrens/mhrev05/srvnp2.html

United Kingdom

Prof. Mary M. Robertson
National Hospital for Neurology and Neurosurgery
Queen Square
London, WC1N 3BG
(02) 7837-3611
Fax: (020) 7829-8720

Dr. Robertson also holds clinic hours at St. Luke's Woodside Hospital in London.

Dr. Helen Garrett
Wythenshawe Hospital
Clay Lane
Wythenshawe, Manchester M23 9LT
(0161) 998-7070
Fax: 0161-946-2603

Dr. Garrett also holds clinic hours at Withington Hospital in Manchester.

Australia

Neuropsychiatric Institute
Prince Henry Hospital
University of New South Wales
Sydney, N.S.W. 2052
(02) 9382-2645

Related health conditions

When any of the following neurological or mental health problems occur with Tourette's syndrome, it can complicate diagnosis and treatment. These resources can help you learn more.

ADHD

Hallowell, Edward, MD. *Driven to Distraction: Recognizing and Coping with Attention Deficit Disorder from Childhood Through Adulthood.* Reading, MA: Addison-Wesley, 1994. The classic book on ADD/ADHD.

Hallowell, Edward, MD, and John Ratey. *Answers to Distraction.* New York: Bantam Books, 1996. A companion to *Driven to Distraction,* this book provides behavior management and learning strategies to help the ADD/ADHD child.

Children and Adults with Attention Deficit Disorder (CHADD)
8181 Professional Place, Suite 201
Landover, MD 20785
(301) 306-7070
Fax: (301) 306-7090
http://www.chadd.org/

ADDO Foundation
Station R, Box 223
Toronto, Ontario M4G 3 Z9 Canada
(416) 813-6858
ADDO@addofundation.org

ADDnet UK
http://www.btinternet.com/~black.ice/addnet/addnetmain.html
44 (0) 181 269-1400 or 44 (0) 181 516-1413

Anxiety disorders

March, John (editor.) *Anxiety Disorders in Children and Adolescents.* New York: Guilford Press, 1999.

Hallowell, Edward, MD. *Worry: Controlling It and Using It Wisely.* New York: Ballantine Books, 1998.

Anxiety Disorders Association of America
Dr., Suite 100
Rockville, MD 20852
(301) 231-9350
Fax: (301) 231-7392
AnxDis@adaa.org
http://www.adaa.org

The Anxiety Network/La Red de la Ansiedad
http://www.anxietynetwork.com

The Anxiety-Panic Internet Resource (tAPir)
http://www.algy.com/anxiety/index.shtml

Obsessive-compulsive disorder

OCD frequently accompanies Tourette's syndrome. These resources can help you learn more about how it is diagnosed and treated.

March, John, MD, and Karen Mulle. *OCD in Children and Adolescents: A Cognitive-Behavioral Treatment Manual.* New York: Guilford Press, 1998.

March, John, MD, and Karen Mulle. *How I Ran OCD Off My Land: A Guide to Cognitive-Behavioral Psychotherapy for Children and Adolescents with Obsessive-Compulsive Disorder.* 1994. Currently distributed by the OC Foundation, this is a cognitive behavioral therapy protocol for use with children. While designed for professionals, it has also been successfully used by families who do not have access to a trained CBT therapist.

Osborn, Ian. *Tormenting Thoughts and Secret Rituals: The Hidden Epidemic of Obsessive Compulsive Disorder.* New York: Pantheon Books, 1998. Who would have thought a book about OCD could be entertaining as well as informative? Osborn offers up medical facts, hundreds of years of history, and personal observations.

Rapoport, Judith L., MD. *The Boy Who Couldn't Stop Washing: The Experience and Treatment of Obsessive-Compulsive Disorder.* New York: Signet, 1991. A classic introduction to OCD. Includes some case studies involving children and teenagers, and has a particularly good section on spiritual help for people with scrupulosity from both Catholic and Jewish perspectives.

Schwartz, Jeffrey M., MD, and Beverly Beyette. *Brain Lock: Free Yourself from Obsessive-Compulsive Behavior.* New York: Regan Books, 1996. Dr. Schwartz' book offers a four-step model for dealing with OCD symptoms. While written as an adult self-help book, it may be helpful to some teenagers and parents as well.

Waltz, Mitzi. *Obsessive-Compulsive Disorder: Help for Children and Adolescents.* Sebastopol, CA: O'Reilly & Associates, 2000. Written by a parent who is also a medical journalist, this book provides practical information about diagnosing, treating, and living with childhood-onset OCD.

Obsessive-Compulsive and Spectrum Disorders Association (OCSDA)
18653 Ventura Boulevard, Suite 414
Tarzana, CA 91356
(818) 990-4830
Fax: (818) 760-3784
Jill@ocsda.org
http://www.ocdhelp.org/

Obsessive-Compulsive Foundation Inc. (OC Foundation)
337 Knotch Hill Road
North Branford, CT 06471
(203) 315-2190
Fax: (203) 315-2196
info@ocfoundation.org
http://www.ocfoundation.org

Obsessive Compulsive Information Center
Madison Institute of Medicine
7617 Mineral Point Road, Suite 300
Madison, WI 53717
(608) 827-2470
Fax: (608) 827-2479
http://www.miminc.org/

OCD-L
For more information, send email to *OCD-L-request@VM.MARIST.EDU*
To subscribe, send email to *listserv@VM.MARIST.EDU* with the message body "subscribe ocd-l".

OCD-L is probably the largest OCD-related discussion group on the Internet. Members include adults and some teens with OCD, as well as family members and excellent medical professionals. Moderated by Chris Vertullo.

Autistic spectrum disorders

Cohen, Shirley. *Targeting Autism: What We Know, Don't Know, and Can Do to Help Young Children With Autism and Related Disorders.* Berkeley, CA: University of California Press, 1998.

Gerlach, Elizabeth. *Autism Treatment Guide.* Eugene, OR: Four Leaf Press, 1996. This book provides hundreds of practical suggestions for addressing autistic symptoms.

Waltz, Mitzi. *Pervasive Developmental Disorders: Finding a Diagnosis and Getting Help.* Sebastopol, CA: O'Reilly & Associates, 1999. This book focuses on PDD-NOS and atypical PDD as well as classical autism, providing the latest information on treatment, education, and other aspects of living with PDDs.

Autism Research Institute
http://www.autism.com

See the ARI Publications List for a wide variety of ARI pamphlets, papers, books, and video-tapes on subjects related to autistic spectrum disorders.

Center for the Study of Autism
http://www.autism.org

This web site covers the latest information, including diet, vitamins, and other alternative therapies. Some information is available in languages other than English (Chinese, Italian, Japanese, Korean, Spanish).

O.A.S.I.S.: Online Asperger's Syndrome Information and Support
http://www.udel.edu/bkirby/asperger

O.A.S.I.S. is Information Central for issues related to Asperger's syndrome or autism in general.

The National Autistic Society
http://www.nas.org.uk

The NAS offers UK publications on autism and related topics, support schools and other service providers, and has basic information on autism available in several European languages as well.

Autism-L
To subscribe, send an email to *listserv@sjuvm.stjohns.edu,* and in the body of the message, type: "subscribe autism-l" and nothing else.

Bipolar disorders and depression

The Child and Adolescent Bipolar Foundation (CABF)
1187 Wilmette Avenue, PMB 331
Wilmette, IL 60091
(847) 256-8525
Fax: (847) 920-9498
cabf@bpkids.org
http://www.cabf.org

This parent-led group provides education, support, and advocacy for children, adolescents, families, and professionals.

National Depressive and Manic-Depressive Association
730 North Franklin Street, Suite 501
Chicago, IL 60610-3526
(312) 642-0049 or (800) 826-3632
Fax: (312) 642-7243
http://www.ndmda.org

This support and advocacy group specifically for people with depression or bipolar depression has chapters throughout the US, and an informative web site.

Canadian Network for Mood and Anxiety Treatments (CANMAT)
http://www.canmat.org

This is a consortium of university medical schools and other research organizations concentrating on depression, bipolar disorders, and anxiety disorders. Its web site can link you with a CANMAT center near you, and also provides information about diagnosis and treatment options.

Manic Depression Fellowship
21 St. Georges Road
London SE1 6ES
020 7793 2600
Fax: 020 7793 2639
mdf@mdf.org.uk
http://www.mdf.org.uk

This organization has regional offices in Wales, Greater London, and Manchester, as well as 125 local groups throughout the UK. It provides support, advice and information for people with manic depression, their families, friends, and caregivers.

Mood Disorders Association (SA) Inc./Self-Help (MDP) Inc.
MHRC Building, 1 Richmond Road
Keswick, S.A. 5035
(08) 8221-5170
Fax (08) 8221-5159
http://homepages.picknowl.com.au/mda

The MDA sponsors support groups, a center with trained volunteers, and a library.

Body dysmorphic disorder

Phillips, Katherine A. *The Broken Mirror: Understanding and Treating Body Dysmorphic Disorder.* Oxford: Oxford University Press, 1996.

BDD (Body Dysmorphic Disorder) list
http://www.onelist.com/subscribe/BDD

Moderated by Emma Broughton (*emmab@netspace.net.au*), this list is open only to people with BDD.

ODD/Conduct disorders

Oppositional Defiant Disorder: What is it?
http://www.klis.com/chandler/pamphlet/oddcd/about.htm

A Place for Us
http://www.conductdisorders.com

This web site includes a parent message board, information, and links about conduct disorders, ODD, and related problems.

Eating disorders

BODYWHYS
P.O. Box 105
Blackrock, Dublin 7 Ireland
(01) 283-4963
Helpline: (01) 283-5126
bodywhys@clubi.ie
http://www.mensana.org/Alliance/BODYWHYS.htm

Anorexia Nervosa and Related Eating Disorders Inc. (ANRED)
http://www.anred.com/

This site includes links to US and Canadian support and informational sites on anorexia and bulimia.

Eating Disorders Association
103 Prince of Wales Road
Norwich NR1 1DW UK
Helpline: (01603) 621414
Youth helpline: (01603) 765050
info@edauk.com
http://www.edauk.com

Self-injurious behavior

Strong, Marilee. *A Bright Red Scream: Self-Mutilation and the Language of Pain.* New York: Penguin USA, 1998.

Favazza, Armando R. *Bodies Under Siege: Self Mutilation and Body Modification in Culture and Psychiatry,* Second Edition. Baltimore, MD: Johns Hopkins University Press, 1996.

Bodies-Under-Siege mailing list
To subscribe, send email to *majordomo@majordomo.pobox.com* with the message body: "subscribe bus".
http://www.palace.net/~llama/psych/busfaq.html

Bodies-Under-Siege is an online support group for people with self-injurious behavior. May not be appropriate for teens with SIB

Secret Shame
http://www.palace.net/~llama/psych/injury.html

This web site is about self-injury, offering information and support to people with SIB and their families.

Sensory integration dysfunction

Kranowitz, Carol Stock. *The Out-of-Sync Child: Recognizing and Coping with Sensory Integration Dysfunction.* New York: Perigee, 1998.

Williams, Mary Sue and Shelley Shellenberger. *How Does Your Engine Run?: A Leader's Guide to the Alert Program for Self-Regulation.* Albuquerque, NM : Therapy Works Inc., 1996.

The Alert Program also has a web site (*http://www.alertprogram.com*), where more information and addition materials on sensory integration can be found.

Sensory Integration International (SII)
1602 Cabrillo Avenue
Torrance, CA 90501
(310) 320-9986
Fax: (310) 320-9934
http://home.earthlink.net/~sensoryint

This national organization offers referrals to SII-qualified occupational therapists, books, and other materials for sensory integration.

Sleep problems

Durand, V. M. *Sleep Better: A Guide to Improving Sleep for Children with Special Needs.* Baltimore, MD: Paul H. Brookes Publishing Co., 1998.

SleepNet.com
http://www.sleepnet.com

Speech disorders

Myers, Florence L., and Kenneth O. St. Louis (editor.) *Cluttering: A Clinical Perspective.* Florence, KY: Singular Publishing Group Inc., 1995.

Net Connections to Communication Disorders and Sciences
http://www.communicationdisorders.com

Cluttering and Other Fluency Disorders
http://www.mankato.msus.edu/depts/comdis/kuster/related.html

Substance abuse

Babbit, Nikki. *Adolescent Drug & Alcohol Abuse: How to Spot It, Stop It, and Get Help for Your Family.* Sebastopol, CA: O'Reilly & Associates, 2000.

Adolescent Substance Abuse and Recovery Resources
http://www.winternet.com/~webpage/adolrecovery.html

This web site includes links to AA, NA, and many other groups that can help people stop using drugs and alcohol.

Canadian Centre on Substance Abuse
75 Albert Street, Suite 300
Ottawa, ON K1P 5E7 Canada
(613) 235-4048
Fax: (613) 235-8101
http://www.ccsa.ca/default.htm

Drugline Ltd.
9A Brockley Cross
Brockley, London SE4 2AB UK
(0181) 692-4975

Dual Diagnosis web site
http://users.erols.com/ksciacca/

Trichotillomania

Amanda's Trichotillomania Guide
http://home.intekom.com/jly2

Trichotillomania Learning Center
1215 Mission Street, Suite 2
Santa Cruz, CA 95060
(408) 457-1004
trichster@aol.com

General medical resources

Books

Glanze, Walter, et al. (editors). *The Signet Mosby Medical Encyclopedia,* Revised Edition. New York: Signet, 1998. This book is a condensed, paperback version of *Mosby's Medical, Nursing, and Allied Health Dictionary* for health consumers.

Andreasen, Dr. Nancy C. *The Broken Brain: The Biological Revolution in Psychiatry.* New York: HarperCollins, 1985. Although it concentrates on the biology of psychiatric illness, *The Broken Brain* also does an excellent job of explaining neurochemistry concepts in accessible language.

Beers, Mark H., MD, Robert Berkow, MD, and Andrew J. Fletcher (editors). *The Merck Manual of Medical Information: Home Edition.* Whitehouse Station, NJ: Merck Research Laboratories, 1999. This is a consumer version of the standard medical reference book.

Diamond, M. C., A. B. Scheibel, and L. M. Elson. *The Human Brain Coloring Book.* New York: HarperPerennial, 1985. This book, a favorite of medical students, makes brain anatomy visual from the cellular level on up.

Online resources

Medscape
http://www.medscape.com

This searchable, online index contains abstracts and articles from hundreds of medical journals, as well as original literature reviews and other resources.

PubMed
http://www.ncbi.nlm.nih.gov/PubMed

PubMed is a free interface for searching the MEDLINE medical database, which can help you find out about studies, medications, and more.

Genetic counseling resources

Genetic counselors have special training in helping families understand the implications of having a member diagnosed with a genetic disorder. They can explain whether these disorders will be passed on to a diagnosed person's children, and help you assess associated risks. They can also provide information about genetic testing for other family members.

American Board of Genetic Counseling Inc.
9650 Rockville Pike
Bethesda, MD 20814-3998
(301) 571-1825
Fax: (301) 571-1895
http://www.faseb.org/genetics/abgc/abgcmenu.htm

The ABGC credentials professionals in the field of genetic counseling, and can help you find a reputable member via phone, mail, or its web site.

GeneTests
Children's Hospital and Regional Medical Center
P.O. Box 5371
Seattle, WA 98105-0371
(206) 527-5742
Fax: (206) 527-5743
genetests@genetests.org
http://www.genetests.org

GeneTests is a genetic testing resource funded by the National Library of Medicine of the NIH and Maternal & Child Health Bureau of the HRSA. It provides a list of genetic research and clinical laboratories, description of genetic testing and counseling, and information for genetic professionals.

European Society of Human Genetics
Clinical Genetics Unit
Birmingham Women's Hospital
Birmingham B15 2TG UK
(44) 0-121-623-6820
esgh@esgh.org
http://www.eshg.org

Human Genetics Society of Australasia
Royal Australian College of Physicians
145 Macquarie Street
Sydney, NSW 2000 Australia
(02) 9256-5471
Fax: (02) 9251-8174
hgsa@racp.edu.au
http://www.hgsa.com.au

Healthcare and insurance

Health care and insurance are difficult issues for people with disabilities. The following resources include information about navigating bureaucracies for better care, and obtaining needed services and coverage.

Beckett, Julie. *Health Care Financing: A Guide for Families.* Iowa City, IA: National Maternal and Child Health Resource Center. This overview of the health care financing system includes advocacy strategies for families, and information about public health insurance in the US. Order from: NMCHRC, Law Building, University of Iowa, Iowa City, IA 52242; (319) 335-9073.

Keene, Nancy. *Working with Your Doctor: Getting the Healthcare You Deserve.* Sebastopol, CA: O'Reilly & Associates, 1998. This book walks you through the process of creating a partnership with your healthcare providers in meticulous detail.

Larson, Georgianna, and Judith Kahn. *Special Needs/Special Solutions: How to Get Quality Care for a Child with Special Health Needs.* St. Paul, MN: Life Line Press, 1991.

Neville, Kathy. *Strategic Insurance Negotiation: An Introduction to Basic Skills for Families and Community Mental Health Workers.* Boston, MA: Federation for Children with Special Needs. Single copies of this pamphlet are available at no cost from: CAPP/NPRC Project, Federation for Children with Special Needs, 95 Berkeley Street, Suite 104, Boston, MA 02116.

Insure Kids Now
Children's Heath Insurance Program (CHIPs)
(877) 543-7669
http://www.insurekidsnow.gov

CHIPs is a Federal program that encourages US states to establish health insurance programs for uninsured children, based on Medicaid waivers. This site includes information about and links to state programs.

National Association of Insurance Commissioners (NAIC)
444 National Capitol Street NW, Suite 309
Washington, DC 20001
(202) 624-7790

Call NAIC to locate your state insurance commissioner, who can tell you about health insurance regulations in your state regarding Tourette's syndrome.

Medication and supplement references

There are a number of books available that list actions, side effects, and cautions regarding medications. The biggest and best is the *Physicians Desk Reference* (PDR), but its price is well out of the average person's league. You may be able to find a used but recent copy at a good price, and it is available in most public libraries. The web sites listed below offer much the same information. Some also provide manufacturing information and link to pharmaceutical companies that make specific drugs.

If your child is allergic to food dyes; or to corn, wheat, and other materials used as "fillers" in pills; you should consult directly with the manufacturer of any medications he takes.

Books and newsletters

The British National Formulary (BNF). London: British Medical Association and the Royal Pharmaceutical Society of Great Britain, 1999. This is the standard reference for prescribing and dispensing drugs in the UK, updated twice yearly.

Eades, Mary Dan, MD. *The Doctor's Complete Guide to Vitamins and Minerals.* New York: Dell, 1994.

Gruenwald, Joerg. *Physicians Desk Reference for Herbal Medicines,* Second Edition. Montvale, NJ: Medical Economics Co., 2000.

Preston, John D., John H. O'Neal, and Mary C. Talaga. *Consumer's Guide to Psychiatric Drugs.* Oakland, CA: New Harbinger Publications, 1998.

Silverman, Harold M. (editor). *The Pill Book,* Eighth Edition. New York: Bantam Books, 1998. This is a basic paperback guide to the most commonly used medications in the US.

Sullivan, Donald. *The American Pharmaceutical Association's Guide to Prescription Drugs.* New York: Signet, 1998.

Tyler, Varro E. and Stephen Foster. *Tyler's Honest Herbal: A Sensible Guide to the Use of Herbs and Related Remedies, Fourth Edition.* Binghamton, NY: The Haworth Press, 1999.

Wilens, Timothy E., MD. *Straight Talk About Psychiatric Medications for Kids.* New York: Guilford Press, 1998.

Latitudes
1128 Royal Palm Beach Blvd., #382
Royal Palm Beach, FL 33411
(561) 798-0472
http://www.latitudes.org

This bimonthly newsletter of the Association for Comprehensive NeuroTherapy carries articles on alternative therapies for ADD, Tourette's syndrome and autism.

Online resources

Canadian Drug Product Database
http://www.hc-sc.gc.ca/hpb-dgps/therapeut/htmleng/dpd.html

Dr. Bob's Psychopharmacology Tips
http://www.dr-bob.org

Public Citizen's eLetter on Drugs for Severe Psychiatric Conditions
http://www.citizen.org/eletter/articleindex.htm

This consumer watchdog group's newsletter often breaks stories on dangerous side effects and interactions before the mainstream media. It also includes background info on the drug approval process.

Federal Drug Administration (FDA)
http://www.fda.gov/cder/drug/default.htm

Official US information on new drugs and generic versions of old drugs, FDA warnings and recalls, etc., can be accessed at this web site.

The Internet Drug List
http://www.rxlist.com

MedEc Interactive/PDR.net
http://www.pdrnet.com

This medical info site includes a link to a web-accessible version of the *Physicians Desk Reference* (PDR).

National Center for Complementary and Alternative Medicine
NCCAM Clearinghouse
P.O. Box 8218
Silver Spring, MD 20907-8218
(888) 644-6226
Fax: (301) 495-4957
http://nccam.nih.gov

NCCAM examines claims made about herbal medications, bodywork, acupuncture, and other complementary treatments.

Pharmaceutical Information Network
http://www.pharminfo.com

PharmWeb
http://www.pharmweb.net

RXmed
http://www.rxmed.com

Drug company patient assistance programs

If you do not have health insurance, or your health insurance does not cover prescriptions, you may be eligible to receive some or all of your TS medications at no charge. Most major pharmaceutical companies will accommodate requests for free or reduced price drugs; others may have reimbursement programs.

Check the package inserts for your medications to find out who makes them, and then call the patient assistance program directly. If the manufacturer's name is not listed below, or if you live outside the US, talk to your pharmacist or check one of the pharmaceutical information web sites listed earlier in this appendix for more information.

Pharmaceutical Company	Phone Number
3M Pharmaceuticals	(800) 328-0255
Abbott Labs Patient Assistance Program (includes Survanta)	(800) 922-3255
American Home Products (includes Lederle)	(800) 395-9938
Amgen	(800) 272-9376
Astra-Zeneca (includes Ici-Stuart)	(800) 488-3247
Aventis Pharmaceuticals (includes Rhone-Poulenc Rorer, Hoecht Roussel)	(800) 207-8049
Bayer Indigent Patient Program	(800) 998-9180
Berlex	(800) 423-7539
Boehringer Ingleheim	(203) 798-4131
Bristol Myers Squibb	(800) 736-0003
Genetech	(800) 879-4747
Glaxo Wellcome Inc. (includes Burroughs)	(800) 722-9294
Immunex Corp.	(800) 321-4669
Janssen Pharmaceutica (includes Johnson & Johnson)	(800) 526-7736
Knoll	(800) 526-0710
Lilly Cares Program (Eli Lilly)	(800) 545-6962
Merck National Service Center	(800) 672-6372
Novartis Patient Support Program (includes Sandoz, Ciba-Geigy)	(800) 257-3273
Ortho-McNeil Pharmaceuticals	(800) 682-6532
Pfizer Prescription Assistance Program (includes Parke-Davis, Warner-Lambert)	(800) 646-4455
Pharmacia Inc. (includes Upjohn)	(800) 242-7014
Proctor & Gamble	(800) 448-4878
Roche Labs (includes Syntex)	(800) 285-4484
Roxane Labs	(800) 274-8651

Pharmaceutical Company	Phone Number
Sanofi Winthrop	(800) 446-6267
Schering Labs	(800) 521-7157
Searle	(800) 542-2526
SmithKline Access To Care Program	(800) 546-0420 (patient requests)
Solvay Patient Assistance Program	(800) 256-8918

Mail-order pharmacies

These pharmacies require a valid prescription, and some have other restrictions. When using a mail-order pharmacy outside your country, be sure to check with Customs about paperwork and permissions that may be required to import medication. To find out more about compounding pharmacies that can fill prescriptions by mail, contact the International Association of Compounding Pharmacies at (281) 933-8400, (800) 927-4227, or *http://www.iacprx.org*.

CanadaRx
http://www.canadarx.net

This is a consortium of Canadian pharmacies set up specifically to provide discounted prescriptions to US customers, although Canadians and others can use the service as well. Mail-order arrangements must be made over the Net, or directly through one of the consortium members (their addresses are available on the web site).

CVS ProCare Pharmacy
600 Penn Center Blvd.
Pittsburgh, PA 15235-5810
(800) 238-7828
Fax: (800) 221-0504
http://stadtlander.com

Previously known as Stadtlanders Pharmacy, this firm has developed a stellar reputation in the disability community.

DrugPlace.com (formerly Preferred Prescription Plan)
2201 West Sample Road, Bldg. 9, Suite 1-A
Pompano Beach, FL 33073
(954) 969-1230 or (800) 881-6325
Fax: (800) 881-6990
pharmacy@drugplace.com
http://www.drugplace.com

This site can be accessed in English or Spanish.

Farmacia Rex S.R.L.
Cordoba 2401
Esq. Azcuénaga 1120
Buenos Aires, Argentina
(54-1) 961-0338
Fax: (54-1) 962-0153
http://www.todoservicio.com.ar/farmacia.rex/rexmenu.htm

This firm offers deeply discounted prices, and it will ship items anywhere.

GlobalRx
4024 Carrington Lane
Efland, NC 27243
(919) 304-4278 or (800) 526-6447
Fax: (919) 304-4405
info@aidsdrugs.com
http://globalrx.com

Some drugs carried by GlobalRx may not be sent to US customers. You can access this site in English, French, or Spanish.

Masters Marketing Company, Ltd.
Masters House
5 Sandridge Close
Harrow, Middlesex HA1 1TW UK
(011) 44-181-424-9400
Fax: (011) 44-181-427-1994
mmc@mastersint.com
http://www.mastersmarketing.com

Masters carries a limited selection of European and American pharmaceuticals.

No Frills Pharmacy
1510 Harlan Dr.
Bellevue, NE 68005
(800) 485-7423
Fax: (402) 682-9899
refill@nofrillspharmacy.com
http://www.nofrillspharmacy.com

Peoples Pharmacy
http://www.peoplesrx.com

This Austin, Texas-based chain provides online-only mail-order service, and can compound medications as well.

Pharmacy Direct
3 Coal Street
Silverwater, NSW 2128 Australia
(02) 9648-8888 or (1300) 656-245
Fax: (02) 9648 8999 or (1300) 656 329
pharmacy@pharmacydirect.com.au
http://www.pharmacydirect.com.au

You must have a prescription from an Australian doctor to use this mail-order service.

The Pharmacy Shop
5007 North Central
Phoenix, AZ 85012
(602) 274-9956 or (800) 775-6888
Fax: (602) 241-0104
sales@pharmacyshop.com
http://www.pharmacyshop.com

The Pharmacy Shop is one of the mail-order vendors that will waive your medication co-pay, if you have the right insurance plan.

Victoria Apotheke (Victoria Pharmacy)
C/o Dr. C. Egloff, PhD
P.O. Box CH-8021
Zurich, Switzerland
(01) 211-24-32 (Europe) or (011) 411-211-24-32 (US)
Fax: (01) 221-23-22 (Europe) or (011) 411-221-23-22 (US)
victoriaapotheke@access.ch
http://www.access.ch/victoria_pharmacy

Special education

These books and web sites will help you understand special education law so that you can advocate for your child during the IFSP and IEP process.

Books

Anderson, Winifred, Stephen Chitwood, and Dierdre Hayden. *Negotiating the Special Education Maze: A Guide for Parents and Teachers,* Third Edition. Rockville, MD: Woodbine House, 1997. Well-written and very complete, this new edition includes information on the changes wrought by IDEA '97.

Cutler, Barbara Coyne. *You, Your Child, and "Special" Education: A Guide to Making the System Work.* Baltimore MD: Paul H. Brookes Publishing Co., 1993. An uppity guide to fighting the system on your child's behalf.

Pruitt, Sheryl, and Marilyn Pierce Dornbush. *Teaching the Tiger; A Handbook for Individuals Involved in the Education of Students with Attention Deficit Disorders, Tourette Syndrome, or Obsessive Compulsive Disorder.* Duarte, CA: Hope Press, 1995.

Online resources

Learning Disabilities Online
http://www.ldonline.org

LDOnline covers all aspects of special education and learning difficulties.

Schwab Learning
http://www.schwablearning.org/

The Schwab Learning site features information about learning disabilities, and hands-on educational activities for kids.

The Special Ed Advocate/Wrightslaw
http://www.wrightslaw.com

This site contains the actual text of special education laws, information on the latest court battles, and answers to your special education questions.

Special Education and Disabilities Resources
http://www.educ.drake.edu/rc/sp_ed_top.html

US information and links on special education law, assistive technology, and related topics can be found on this site.

Special-needs parenting

"Bending the Rules: A Guide for Parents of Troubled Children" is a 1996 video that features excellent ideas about handling problem behaviors that are driven by TS or other types of brain dysfunction. It is available through the TSDA, listed earlier in this appendix.

Bruun, Ruth Dowling, MD, et al. *Problem Behaviors and Tourette's Syndrome* (pamphlet.) Bayside, NY: Tourette Syndrome Association Inc., 1993

Budman, Cathy, MD, and Ruth Dowling Bruun, MD. *Tourette Syndrome and Repeated Anger Generated Episodes (RAGE).* Bayside, NY: Tourette Syndrome Association Inc., 1998

Crisis Prevention Institute
3315-K North 124th Street
Brookfield, WI 53005
(262) 783-5787 or (800) 558-8976
http://www.crisisprevention.com

Duke, Marshall P., Stephen Nowicki, Jr., and Elisabeth A. Martin. *Teaching Your Child the Language of Social Success.* Atlanta, GA: Peachtree Publishers Ltd., 1996.

Greene, Ross. *The Explosive Child: A New Approach for Understanding and Parenting Easily Frustrated, "Chronically Inflexible" Children.* New York: HarperCollins, 1998. The title says it all: This may be the best book ever on raising a child with a "difficult" temperament. It's full of parent-tested strategies for defusing behavior problems.

Greenspan, Stanley I., MD, with Jacqueline Salmon. *The Challenging Child.* Reading, MA: Addison-Wesley, 1995. Greenspan explains why some children's neurological makeup predisposes them to having a "challenging" temperament, and offers excellent ideas for turning down the volume of outbursts, anxiety, and other behavior problems.

Greenspan, Stanley I., MD, and Serena Wieder, with Robin Simons. *The Child With Special Needs.* Reading, MA: Addison-Wesley, 1998. This book concentrates on working with developmentally or emotionally challenged children from infancy through school age. Highly recommended, especially if your child has an additional diagnosis of PDD/autism, ADHD, etc.

Greenspan, Stanley I., MD, with Jacqueline Salmon. *Playground Politics: Understanding the Emotional Life of Your School-Age Child.* Reading, MA: Addison-Wesley, 1993. Help for parents of children who "don't fit in."

Kurcinka, Mary Sheedy. *Raising Your Spirited Child.* New York: HarperPerennial, 1991. This book covers handling sensory defensiveness and other contributors to "spirited" behavior.

Marsh, Diane T., Rex M. Dickens, and E. Fuller Torrey. *How to Cope With Mental Illness in Your Family: A Self-Care Guide for Siblings, Offspring, and Parents.* New York: Putnam Publishing Group, 1998.

Meyer, Donald (editor.) *Uncommon Fathers: Reflections on Raising a Child with a Disability.* Rockville, MD: Woodbine House, 1995.

Naseef, Robert A. *Special Children, Challenged Parents: The Struggles and Rewards of Raising a Child with a Disability.* New York: Birch Lane Press, 1997.

Osman, Betty B. *No One to Play With: The Social Side of Learning Disabilities.* New York: Random House, 1982.

Phelan, Thomas W. *1-2-3 Magic: Effective Discipline for Children 2-12.* Glen Ellyn, IL: Child Management Inc., 1996. Phelan has devised a workable system for managing behavior without getting physical, especially for strong-willed kids. Many parents swear by it. Also available on audiotape.

Wollis, Rebecca, and Agnes Hatfield. *When Someone You Love Has a Mental Illness: A Handbook for Family, Friends, and Caregivers.* Los Angeles, CA: J. P. Tarcher, 1992

Sibling issues

In families coping with childhood disability or illness, the non-affected siblings also experience stresses and may require special help. These books and web sites attempt to address sibling issues.

Meyer, Donald, and Patricia Vadasy. *Living with a Brother or Sister with Special Needs.* Seattle, WA: University of Washington Press, 1996.

Meyer, Donald (editor.) *Views from Our Shoes: Growing up with a Brother or Sister with Special Needs.* Rockville, MD: Woodbine House, 1997.

SibShops/Sibling Support Project
Children's Hospital and Medical Center
P.O. Box 5371, CL-09
Seattle, WA 98105
(206) 368-4911
Fax: (206) 368-4816
http://www.chmc.org/departmt/sibsupp/sibshoppage.htm

"SibShops" are special support groups for children dealing with a sibling's disability. This site provides information on SibShops and related topics, and can help you find a SibShop program in your area.

Public mental health agencies

The agencies listed here provide advice and direct services to persons with mental or neurological conditions. Even if you have private health insurance, these agencies offer referrals to community services, specific treatment programs, and other resources.

United States

Alabama

Department of Mental Health and Mental Retardation
RSA Union
100 North Union Street
P.O. Box 30140
Montgomery, AL 36130-1410
(334) 242-3417
Fax: (334) 242-0684
http://www.mh.state.al.us/

Alaska

Alaska Division of Mental Health and Developmental Disabilities
50 Main Street, Room 214
P.O. Box 110620
Juneau, AK 99811-0620
(907) 465-3370
Fax: (907) 465-2668
TDD/TTY (907) 465-2225
http://www.hss.state.ak.us/dmhdd

Arizona

Arizona Department of Health Services
Behavioral Health Services
2122 East Highland
Phoenix, AZ 85016
(602) 381-8999
Fax: (602) 553-9140
http://www.hs.state.az.us/bhs/home.htm

Arkansas

Department of Human Services
Donaghey Plaza West
Slot 3440
P.O. Box 1437
Little Rock, AR 72203-1437
(501) 682-8650
http://www.state.ar.us/dhs

Colorado

Mental Health Services
3824 West Princeton Circle
Denver, CO 80236
(303) 866-7400
Fax: (303) 866-7428
http://www.cdhs.state.co.us/ohr/mhs/index.html

District of Columbia

DC Commission on Mental Health Services
Child Youth Services Administration
2700 Martin Luther King Avenue SE
St. Elizabeth's Hospital, L Bldg.
Washington, DC 20032
(202) 373-7225

Florida

Childrens Medical Services (CMS)
Department of Health and Rehabilitative Services
1311 Winewood Blvd.
Building 5, Room 215
Tallahassee, FL 32301
(904) 488-4257
http://www.doh.state.fl.us/cms/index.html

Georgia

Department of Human Resources
878 Peachtree Street NE, Room 706
Atlanta, GA 30309
(404) 894-6670
http://www2.state.ga.us/Departments/DHR

Hawaii

Department of Human Services
1000 Bishop Street, No. 615
Honolulu, HI 96813
(808) 548-4769
http://www.hawaii.gov/dhs

Idaho

Department of Health and Welfare
450 West State Street
Boise, ID 83720-0036
(208) 334-5500
http://www.state.id.us/dhw/hwgd_www/home.html

Illinois

Department of Mental Health and Developmental Disabilities
402 Stratten Office Building
Springfield, IL 62706
(217) 782-7395
http://www.state.il.us/agency/dhs/mhddfsnp.html

Indiana

Department of Mental Health
117 East Washington Street
Indianapolis, IN 46204-3647

Iowa

Department of Human Services
Hoover State Office Building
Des Moines, IN 50319
(515) 278-2502 or (800) 972-2017
http://www.dhs.state.ia.us

Kansas

Child & Adolescent Mental Health Programs
506 North State Office Building
Topeka, KS 66612
(913) 296-1808

Kentucky

Department of Mental Health and Mental Retardation Services
100 Fair Oaks Lane, Fourth Floor
Frankfort, KY 40621
(502) 564-4527
http://dmhmrs.chr.state.ky.us

Louisiana

Department of Health and Human Resources
1201 Capitol Access Road
P.O. Box 629
Baton Rouge, LA 70821-0629
(504) 342-9500
Fax: (504) 342-5568
http://www.dhh.state.la.us

Maine

Department of Mental Health, Mental Retardation, and Substance Abuse Services
40 State House Station
Augusta, ME 04333-0040
(207) 287-4200
Fax: (207) 287-4268
http://www.state.me.us/dmhmrsa

Maryland

Department of Health and Mental Hygiene
201 West Preston Street
O'Connor Building, Fourth Floor
Baltimore, MD 21201
(410) 767-6860 or (877) 463-3464
http://www.dhmh.state.md.us

Massachusetts

Department of Mental Health
25 Staniford Street
Boston, MA 02210
(617) 727-5600
(617) 727-4350
http://www.state.ma.us/eohhs/agencies/dmh.htm

Minnesota

Children's Mental Health
Minnesota Department of Human Services
444 Lafayette Road
St. Paul, MN 55155
(651) 297-5242

Minnesota Children with Special Health Needs
717 Delaware Street SE
P.O. Box 9441
Minneapolis, MN 55440-9441
(612) 676-5150 or (800) 728-5420
Fax: (612) 676-5442
mcshn@kids.health.state.mn.us
http://www.health.state.mn.us/divs/fh/mcshn/mcshn.html

Mississippi

Department of Mental Health
1101 Robert E. Lee Building
239 North Lamar Street
Jackson, MS 39201
(601) 359-1288
http://www.dmh.state.ms.us

Missouri

Department of Mental Health
1706 East Elm Street
P.O. Box 687
Jefferson City, MO 65102
(573) 751-3070 or (800) 364-9687
dmhmail@mail.state.mo.us
http://www.modmh.state.mo.us

Montana

Department of Public Health and Social Services
P.O. Box 4210
111 Sanders, Room 202
Helena, MT 59604
(406) 444-2995
http://www.dphhs.state.mt.us

Nebraska

Nebraska Health and Human Services
Office of Community Mental Health
P.O. Box 95007
Lincoln, NE 68509
(402) 471-2330
http://www.hhs.state.ne.us/beh/behindex.htm

Nevada

Department of Human Resources
State Capitol Complex
505 East King Street
Carson City, NV 98710
(702) 687-4440
http://www.state.nv.us/hr

New Hampshire

Division of Mental Health and Developmental Services
Department of Health and Welfare
State Office Park South
105 Pleasant Street
Concord, NH 03301
(603) 271-5013

New Jersey

Services for Children With Special Health Care Needs
New Jersey Department of Health and Senior Services
P.O. Box 364
Trenton, NJ 08625
(609) 984-0755
http://www.state.nj.us/health/fhs/schome.htm

New Mexico

Department of Health
1190 South Street Francis Dr.
P.O. Box 26110
Santa Fe, NM 87502-6110
(505) 827-2613
http://www.health.state.nm.us

New York

New York State Office of Mental Health
44 Holland Street
Albany, NY 12229
(518) 473-3456
http://www.omh.state.ny.us

North Carolina

Department of Health and Human Resources
620 North West Street
P.O. Box 26053
Raleigh, NC 27611
(919) 733-6566
http://www.dhhs.state.nc.us

North Dakota

Department of Human Services
State Capitol Building
Bismarck, ND 58505
(701) 224-2970
http://lnotes.state.nd.us/dhs/dhsweb.nsf

Ohio

Ohio Department of Mental Health
State Office Tower
30 East Broad Street, Eighth Floor
Columbus, OH 43266-0315
(614) 466-1483
http://www.mh.state.oh.us

Oklahoma

Oklahoma Department of Mental Health and Substance Abuse Services
1200 NE 13th Street
P.O. Box 53277
Oklahoma City, OK 73152-3277
(405) 522-3908
http://www.odmhsas.org

Oregon

Office of Mental Health Services
Department of Human Resources
2575 Bittern Street NE
Salem, OR 97310
(503) 975-9700
http://omhs.mhd.hr.state.or.us

Pennsylvania

Special Kids Network
Pennsylvania Department of Health
P.O. Box 90
Harrisburg, PA 17108
(800) 986-4550
http://www.health.state.pa.us/php/special.htm

Rhode Island

Department of Mental Health, Retardation, and Hospitals
14 Harrington Road
Cranston, RI 02920-3080
(401) 464-3201
Fax: (401) 462-3204
http://www.mhrh.state.ri.us

South Carolina

Department of Mental Health
2414 Bull Street, Room 304
Columbia, SC 29202
(803) 898-8581
scdmh@yahoo.com
http://www.state.sc.us/dmh

South Dakota

Department of Human Services
East Highway 34, Hillsview Plaza
C/o 500 East Capitol Avenue
Pierre, SD 57501-5070
(605) 733-5990
Fax: (605) 733-5483
http://www.state.sd.us/dhs

Tennessee

Department of Mental Health and Developmental Disabilities
Cordell Hull Building, Third Floor
425 Fifth Avenue North
Nashville, TN 37243
(615) 532-6500
http://www.state.tn.us/mental

Texas

Department of Mental Health and Mental Retardation
909 West 45th Street
P.O. Box 12668-2668
Austin, TX 78711
(512) 454-3761 or (800) 252-8154
http://www.mhmr.state.tx.us

Utah

State Division of Mental Health
Department of Human Services
120 North 200 West, Room 415
Salt Lake City, UT 84145
(801) 538-4270
http://www.hsmh.state.ut.us

Vermont

Department of Developmental and Mental Health Services
103 South Main Street
Weeks Building
Waterbury, VT 05671-1601
(802) 241-2609
Fax: (802) 241-1129
http://www.state.vt.us/dmh

Virginia

Department of Mental Health, Mental Retardation, and Substance Abuse Services
P.O. Box 1797
Richmond, VA 23218-1797
(804) 786-0992
http://www.dmhmrsas.state.va.us/

Washington

Mental Health Division
Health and Rehabilitative Services Administration
P.O. Box 1788, OB-42C
Olympia, WA 98504
(800) 737-0617 or (800) 446-0259 (emergency)
http://www.wa.gov/dshs/hrsa/hrsa2hp.html

West Virginia

Office of Behavioral Health Services
Department of Health and Human Resources
350 Capitol Street, Room 350
Charleston, WV 25301-3702
(304) 558-0298
http://www.wvdhhr.org/bhhf

Wisconsin

Bureau of Community Mental Health
Department of Health and Family Services
1 West Wilson Street, Room 433
P.O. Box 7851
Madison, WI 53707
(608) 261-6746
Fax: (608) 261-6748
http://www.dhfs.state.wi.us/mentalhealth/index.htm

Canada

British Columbia

British Columbia Ministry of Health
Parliament Buildings
Victoria, B.C. V8V 1X4
(250) 952-1742 or (800) 465-4911
http://www.hlth.gov.bc.ca

Manitoba

Manitoba Health
Legislative Building
Winnipeg, Man. R3C 0V8
(204) 786-7101 or (877) 218-0102
http://www.gov.mb.ca/health

New Brunswick

New Brunswick Department of Health and Wellness
P.O. Box 5100
Fredericton, N.B. E3B 5G8
(506) 453-2536
Fax: (506) 444-4697
http://www.gnb.ca/HW-SM/hw/index.htm

Newfoundland and Labrador

Newfoundland and Labrador Department of Health and Community Services
Division of Family and Rehabilitative Services
Confederation Building, West Block
P.O. Box 8700
St. John's, N.F. A1B 4J6
(709) 729-5153
Fax: (709) 729-0583
http://www.gov.nf.ca/health

Nova Scotia

Nova Scotia Department of Health
P.O. Box 488
Halifax, N.S. B3J 2R8
(902) 424-5886 or (800) 565-3611
http://www.gov.ns.ca/health

Prince Edward Island

Prince Edward Island Health and Social Services
Second Floor, Jones Building
11 Kent Street
P.O. Box 2000
Charlottetown, P.E.I. C1A 7N8
(902) 368-4900
Fax: (902) 368-4969
http://www.gov.pe.ca/hss/index.php3

Quebec

Quebec Ministére de la Santé et Services Sociaux
1075 Chemin Sainte-Foy, R-C.
Québec, Québec G1S 2M1
(418) 643-3380 or (800) 707-3380
Fax: (418) 644-4574
http://www.msss.gouv.qc.ca

Saskatchewan

Saskatchewan Health
T.C. Douglas Building
3475 Albert Street
Regina, Sas. S4S 6X6
(306) 787-3475
Fax: (306) 787-3761
http://www.health.gov.sk.ca/

UK

People in England, Scotland, Wales, and Northern Ireland will generally need to be referred to a specialist at a clinic or hospital by their general practitioner.

The National Health Service Confederation
http://www.nhsconfed.net

This site lists all local NHS authorities and boards, as well as specific sites for health care (including mental health services).

Ireland

Eastern Health Board
Canal House, Canal Road
Dublin 6
(01) 406 5600
http://www.erha.ie

Midland Health Board
Arden Road
Tullamore, County Offaly
(0506) 21868
http://www.mhb.ie

Mid-Western Health Board
31-33 Catherine Street
County Limerick
(061) 316655
http://www.mwhb.ie

North-Eastern Health Board
Navane Road
Kells, County Meath
(046) 40341
http://www.nehb.ie

North-Western Health Board
Manorhamilton, County Leitrim
(072) 20400
Fax: (072) 20431
http://www.nwhb.ie

South-Eastern Health Board
Lacken, Dublin Road
County Kilkenny
(056) 51702
http://sehb.ie

Southern Health Board
Aras Slainte, Dennehy's Cross
Wilton Road
Cork, County Cork
(021) 545011
Fax: (021) 545748
http://www.shb.ie

Western Health Board
Merlin Park Regional Hospital
County Galway
(091) 751131

Australia

Australian Capitol Territory

ACT Mental Health Services
Regional Community Mental Health
Belconnen Health Centre
Corner Benjamin Way and Swanson Court, Belconnen
(02) 6205-1110 or (800) 629-354 (crisis)
http://www.health.act.gov.au/mentalhealth/index.htm

New South Wales

NSW Health
73 Miller Street
Sydney, N.S.W. 2060
(02) 9391-9000
Fax: (02) 9391-9101
nswhealth@doh.health.nsw.gov.au
http://www.health.nsw.gov.au

Northern Territory

Northern Territory Health Services
P.O. Box 40596
Casuarina, N.T. 0811
(08) 8999-2400
Fax: (08) 8999-2700
http://www.nt.gov.au/nths

Queensland

Queensland Health
G.P.O. Box 48
Brisbane, Qld. 4001 (07) 323-40111
http://www.health.qld.gov.au

South Australia

Commonwealth Department of Human Services
Disability Services Office
55 Currie Street
Adelaide, S.A. 5000
(08) 8226-6721
Fax: (08) 8237-8000
http://www.dhs.sa.gov.au

Tasmania

Commonwealth Department of Human Services
Child and Family Services
34 Davey Street
Hobart, Tas.
(03) 6233-3185 or (800) 067-415
http://www.dchs.tas.gov.au/home.html

Victoria

Department of Human Services
Disability Programs
Casselden Place
2 Lonsdale Street
G.P.O. Box 9848
Melbourne, Vic. 3001
(03) 9285-8888
http://www.dhs.vic.gov.au

Western Australia

Department of Health and Family Services
Central Park, 12th Floor
152 St. George Terrace
Perth, W.A. 6000
(08) 9346-5111 or (800) 198-008
Fax: (08) 9346-5222
http://www.public.health.wa.gov.au

New Zealand

New Zealand Ministry of Health
133 Molesworth Street
P.O. Box 5013
Wellington, N.Z.
(04) 496-2000
Fax: (04) 496-2340
http://www.moh.govt.nz

Tourette's Syndrome Genetics

GENETICS IS A COMPLICATED TOPIC to explain. The basic building block of our genetic code is deoxyribonucleic acid, or DNA. DNA itself is comprised of just four substances called nucleotides (adenine, thymidine, guanine, and cytosine.) To form DNA, these nucleotides bind to each other in a structure called a double helix, which looks like a ladder that's been twisted into a spiral.

Chromosomes, which are found in every cell and tell each cell how to behave, are made entirely of DNA sequences. Humans normally have 46 chromosomes, including two sex chromosomes. Occasionally, humans have a genetic mutation that results in an extra chromosome, as is the case with Down syndrome.

Each chromosome contains thousands of discrete DNA sequences that cells can convert into instructions. Each of these sequences is called a gene. According to data recently released by the Human Genome Project, there are at least 30,000 different human genes (a genome is one individual's complete set of genes.)

One gene found on a chromosome might include the instructions for making cells in the pancreas that secrete insulin. If there's an error in this sequence—a genetic mutation or difference—these cells may not work properly. As a result, the person who inherits this gene may have diabetes. This will only occur if the gene is expressed, meaning that the DNA "code" is translated to produce a substance called ribonucleic acid (RNA), which can actually carry out activities within a cell.

Many people inherit genetic differences that are not expressed. Something stops the DNA from being translated into RNA. Perhaps a gene inherited from one parent overcomes one inherited from the other parent, as in the case of the "dominant" gene for brown eyes overcoming the gene for blue eyes. Or perhaps there's a bit of code in a gene that only allows it to be expressed under certain circumstances. This is probably why some people in families affected by Tourette's syndrome have TS, while others have OCD (believed by many to be an "alternative" expression of the same genes), and many have no neurological problems at all.

The two genetic differences currently believed to be involved in all or most cases of TS are on chromosomes 4 and 8. They are shown in bold type in the first column of the table that follows. These sites were identified in an extensive study of sibling pairs with Tourette's syndrome.[1]

Four other sites were also identified in the sib-pair study, although the linkage was less certain. These areas of the genome are still being investigated, and may or may not contribute to TS. These are noted in plain text in the first column of the table.

Between 80 and 90 percent of the human genome has now been excluded in the search for "TS genes," allowing researchers to concentrate their attentions on the most likely sites.

Other genetic differences shown in the table below have been found in only a few people with TS, and probably represent unique conditions. Indeed, some of these have been ruled out as "TS genes" by recent genetic studies, although they may contribute to specific individual cases or be part of "TS-like" disorders not yet understood. These differences are listed in the first column below, but are in parentheses.

Genes linked to disorders that occur more often in persons with TS may also play a role in specific cases, and are listed in two separate columns.

As for the other terms used in the table, "translocation" means that genes have switched their usual order. Some genes have been given proper names, such as the "Dopamine receptor 1 gene," while others are named with numbers and letters that describe where on a chromosome they are located. Sometimes these names can be confusing: for example, the gene known as 5-HTT is actually found on chromosome 17—its name stands for serotonin (5-HT) transporter gene.

The Tourette Syndrome Association can provide more information about TS genetics, including a recent booklet, *The Genetics of Tourette Syndrome: Who It Affects and How It Occurs in Families*.

Chromosomes with possible TS-linked genes	Tourette's Syndrome	Obsessive-Compulsive Disorder	Other disorders that may be linked
1	Region identified in sib-pair study (Translocation with 8)		
2			Dyslexia (DYX3)
4	4q: Region encompassing D451644 and D4S1625 identified in sib pair study		
5	(Dopamine receptor 1 gene, 5q31-35)		Autistic-spectrum disorders (5q22.1; duplications)
6	(D6S477)		Autistic-spectrum disorders (Complement C4 protein gene; duplications)
7	(Translocation with 18)		
8	8p: Two regions bounded by D8S1106, D8S1145, and D8S136 (Translocation with 1)		
9			Autistic-spectrum disorders (9q34)
10	Region identified in sib-pair study		
11	(D11S933) (Dopamine receptor 2 gene, 11q22-23)		Alcoholism, ADHD, schizophrenia (Dopamine receptor 2 gene, 11q22-23)
13	Region identified in sib-pair study		
14	(D14S1003)		

Chromosomes with possible TS-linked genes	Tourette's Syndrome	Obsessive-Compulsive Disorder	Other disorders that may be linked
15			Anxiety disorders, autistic-spectrum disorders (GABA receptor genes, 15q11-13, duplications)
17	(Serotonin transporter gene (5-HTT), 17q11.1-q12)	5-HTT gene	Affective disorders/ depression, anxiety disorders, autistic-spectrum disorders (5-HTT)
18	(Translocation with 7)		
19	19p7: Region identified in sib-pair study		
20	(D20S1085)		
21	(D21S1252)		
22		Catechol-O-methyltransferase (COMT) gene	Anxiety disorders Alcoholism, bipolar disorders (COMT gene)
X	(X-linked gene affecting monamine-oxidase [MAO] receptors)	HRAS (Part of the G protein secondary messenger system)	Substance abuse (X-linked gene affecting MAO receptors) Autistic-spectrum disorders (Fragile X, MECP2, HRAS)

Diagnostic Tests for TS and Related Disorders

TOURETTE'S SYNDROME DIAGNOSIS is mostly a matter of observation, collecting data, and matching symptoms seen with established criteria. This process is covered in Chapter 2, *Diagnosis*, along with the criteria most frequently used.

Standardized questionnaires, tests, and instruments designed to measure everything from tic severity to intelligence may also have a place in the diagnostic process, however. This appendix presents several lists of tests that your doctor or diagnostic team may request. Many of these are also used by schools, disability benefits programs, and vocational assessment professionals.

Diagnostic instruments for Tourette's syndrome

Tics can be highly individual, but the vast majority have been experienced and described by other people with TS. These lists have been turned into questionnaires that can both provide objective information about tics and their severity, and serve as a jumping-off point for in-depth personal interviews.

The following is a list of some diagnostic instruments used to evaluate persons who may have TS or a tic disorder:

- Yale Global Tic Severity Scale (YGTSS). This instrument rates current tic severity on multiple points that can be expressed numerically. The YGTSS can also be used retrospectively, to reveal "worst ever" or "typical" tic severity. Results are expressed on a scale from 0 to 50.

- Schedule for Tourette and Other Behavioral Syndromes, Adult-on-Child Version, Revised (STOBS-R). This instrument is used to guide a structured interview covering tics and other TS-related symptoms, including the presence of comorbid disorders. A version for self-reported symptoms is also available for use with adults who have TS.

- Tourette Disorder Scale (TODS). The TODS is primarily a basic screening tool for general practitioners, and can be used like a structured interview guide. You can also find an abbreviated version online at *http://www.tourettehelp.com/pages/patient/check.html*.

- Tourette Syndrome Diagnostic Confidence Index (DCI). A relatively new tool, the TCI was designed by a team of prominent TS experts in concert with the Tourette Syndrome Association. It attempts to measure the lifetime likelihood that a person has TS. It takes the *DSM-IV* criteria and uses them as a guideline for getting information on symptoms that may have appeared over a person's lifespan, improving accuracy. It returns a score ranging from 0 to 100 that measures whether it's likely that a person has TS.

Diagnostic instruments for OCD

Many clinicians automatically check for OCD symptoms whenever someone comes in who has tics. This can be very helpful—obsessions and compulsions are not as visible as tics, but can have more direct impact on a person's ability to function.

Common instruments used include the following:

- Florida Obsessive-Compulsive Inventory (FOCI). This questionnaire rates OCD severity based on a list of common symptoms. Results are expressed as a scale.

- University of Hamburg Obsession-Compulsion Inventory Screening Form. This questionnaire about symptoms is commonly used as a screening instrument for OCD.

- Yale-Brown Obsessive Compulsive Scale (Y-BOCS). The Y-BOCS rates the severity of a patient's obsessive-compulsive symptoms, based on answers to detailed questions. Results are expressed as a scale.

- Children's Yale-Brown Obsessive Compulsive Scale (CY-BOCS). The CY-BOCS is a version of the Y-BOCS developed specifically for children. It rates the severity of OCD symptoms and expresses its results on a scale.

Behavioral, psychiatric, and neuropsychiatric tests

Some of these tests are highly clinical instruments used to tell disorders with similar symptoms apart, or to diagnose disorders like ADHD or developmental delay that may coexist with TS (see Chapter 3, *Related Conditions*). Others are more subjective, and are used by teachers and other non-physicians to rank behavior problems or uncover emotional difficulties.

Like the Rorschach Blot interpretation test, which is rarely used anymore, tests for emotional disturbance that ask people to make a picture and interpret what they've drawn are highly subjective. These so-called projective tests have little use in diagnosing TS, but are sometimes administered anyway, especially in school settings.

No test should ever be used as the sole means of diagnosing or measuring emotional disturbance. The following is a list of tests sometimes used to help the diagnostic team get more information:

- Aberrant Behavior Checklist (ABC). One of the most popular behavioral checklists, the ABC also has a good reputation for accuracy. Versions are available for children and adults. Scores are expressed as scales in the areas of irritability and agitation, lethargy and social withdrawal, stereotypic behavior, hyperactivity and noncompliance, and inappropriate speech.

- Achenbach Child Behavior Checklist (CBC). The CBC is available in versions for girls and boys of various ages. Six different inventories are used, including a parent report, teacher report, youth report (if practical), and structured direct observation report. It looks at the child's behaviors in several areas, including withdrawal, anxiety, etc. The results are classified as clinically significant or normal.

- **Attention Deficit Disorders Evaluation Scale.** Versions of this questionnaire about certain behaviors linked with ADHD are available for parents to fill out at home or in a clinical setting, as well as for direct use with older children and adults. Scores are expressed as a scale.

- **Behavior Assessment System for Children (BASC).** This set of tests includes a Teacher Rating Scale, Parent Rating Scale, and Self-Report of Personality. The BASC attempts to measure both problem and adaptive behaviors, as well as behaviors linked to ADHD. Scores are expressed as a scale keyed to a norm.

- **Conner's Rating Scales (CRS).** Parent and Teacher versions are available of this scale-based test, which is intended to uncover behaviors linked to ADHD, conduct disorders, learning disabilities, psychosomatic complaints, and anxiety, among other conditions. Scores are plotted graphically.

- **Draw-a-Person.** This a projective psychological screening procedure in which the patient is asked to draw three human figures: a man, a woman, and himself. The drawing is then rated on a scale, with differences in ratings according to gender and age. Ratings are subjective interpretations, not objective measures.

- **DuPaul AD/HD Rating Scale.** This instrument rates the severity of ADHD symptoms. Scores are expressed as a scale.

- **House-Tree-Person Projective Drawing Technique.** In this projective test, the patient is asked to draw a house, a tree, and a person, and then is asked a series of questions about these drawings. Sometimes these drawings are separate; sometimes they are done on a single page. Ratings are subjective interpretations, not objective measures.

- **Kinetic Family Drawing System for Family and School.** In this projective test, the patient draws her family or class doing something. Then the patient is asked questions about what's going on in the drawing. Ratings are subjective interpretations, not objective measures.

- **Luria-Nebraska Neuropsychological Battery (LNNB)/Luria-Nebraska Neuropsychological Battery, Children's Revision (LNNB-CR).** The LNNB-CR contains eleven scales with a total of one hundred and forty-nine test items, which are intended to measure Motor Skills, Rhythm, Tactile, Visual, Receptive Speech, Expressive Language, Writing, Reading, Arithmetic, Memory, and Intelligence. Each test item is scored on a scale, and a total scale for all items is also derived. The adult LNNB also tests the maturation level of the frontal lobe tertiary zones.

- **Pediatric Symptom Checklist (PSC).** A simple questionnaire about behavioral symptoms, the PSC is commonly used as a screening tool by pediatricians. Score is expressed as a scale.

- **Psychiatric Assessment Schedule for Adults with Developmental Disability (PAS-ADD).** Used primarily in the UK, this is a self-reporting questionnaire used to assess psychiatric state in people with developmental delay, learning disability, neurobiological disorders, or senility, among other conditions. Score is expressed as a scale.

- Reitan-Indiana Neuropsychological Test Battery (RINTB)/Reitan-Indiana Neuropsychological Test Battery (RINTBC)/Halstead-Reitan Neuropsychological Test Battery for Children (HNTBC). These may be the most widely used neuropsychological tests, and are intended to look for signs of brain damage. The RINTBC contains the following tests: Category, Tactile Performance, Finger Oscillation, Sensory-Perceptual Measures, Aphasia Screening, Grip Strength, Lateral Dominance Examination, Color Form, Progressive Figures, Matching Pictures, Target, Individual Performance, and Marching. The HNTBC adds the Seashore Rhythm Test, Speech Sounds Perception, Finger-Tip Number Writing Perception, and Trail-Making, but omits some other tests. The RINTB is very similar. Results are usually expressed as a scale (the Neuropsychological Deficit Scale or the Halstead Impairment Index). Additional information about right-left dominance or performance patterns may also be derived.

- Vineland Adaptive Behavior Scales. These tests measure personal and social skills from birth to adulthood, using a semi-structured interview with a parent or other caregiver. Versions are available for children of all ages. Social and behavioral maturity in four major areas—communication, daily living skills, socialization, and motor skills—is assessed. Responses are rated on a 100-point scale for each area, and a composite score is also provided. Scores can be translated into developmental or mental ages.

Intelligence, developmental, and academic tests

Some school and medical programs require IQ testing for all newcomers. Don't let these tests or scores give you too much worry: repeated studies have shown that IQs can and do change when they are measured differently, or when a person is taught differently and then re-tested. Some people may find these tests especially difficult for special ed placement. For example, if a person with both TS and OCD is asked to choose between numbered multiple choice answers and the right answer is her "unlucky" number, she may deliberately give an incorrect answer. A person with hand tics may perform poorly at tests of skill and dexterity, such as fitting pegs into a board.

Most IQ tests also carry some cultural, racial, language, and/or gender bias, although testing companies are certainly trying to create better instruments. However, because this bias has inappropriately placed non-handicapped students from ethnic minorities into special education classes in the past, it is no longer legal to use IQ tests alone as an evaluation tool in US schools.

IQ testing has been supplanted in some school districts and other programs by tests that measure adaptive behavior, which can be loosely described as how well and how quickly a person can come up with a solution to a problem and carry it out. These provide a more realistic measure of "intelligence" as most people think of it, as opposed to measuring cultural knowledge.

Developmental tests rank the individual's development against the norm, often resulting in a "mental age" or "developmental age" score. Some of the tests listed in the "Behavior, psychiatric, and neuropsychiatric tests" section in this chapter also chart a patient's developmental stages.

Academic testing is a must during the special education evaluation process. It's also used with adults to provide clues about undiscovered learning disabilities, to design transition programs for teenagers and for adults re-entering the workplace after being disabled, and to design adult learning programs. Some clinicians like to compare the results of various types of tests, a practice that provides a picture of actual achievement against the background of supposed innate capability.

Sometimes a local, state, or national academic test is used to rate a child by grade level instead of one of the commercial tests listed.

Following is a list of some intelligence, developmental, and academic tests in common use:

- **Adaptive Behavior Inventory for Children (ABIC).** This standardized measure of adaptive behavior uses a questionnaire format, with a parent or other caregiver providing the answers. It includes sub-tests called Family, Community, Peer Relations, Nonacademic School Roles, Earner/Consumer, and Self-Maintenance. Used with the WISC-III IQ test and a special grading scale, ABIC is part of the System of Multicultural Pluralistic Assessment used by some districts to make more-sensitive assessments of racial minority children. Results are expressed on a scale.

- **Battelle Developmental Inventory.** This test ranks children's self-adaptive skills (self-feeding, dressing, etc.) as a percentage of his chronological age. The score may be expressed as a percentage, such as "between 40 percent and 55 percent of his/her chronological age," or as a single-number standard deviation.

- **Cattell Scales.** This test rates the person's developmental level. The score is expressed as a Mental Age (MA).

- **Children's Memory Scale (CMS).** The CMS test is intended to provide a complete picture of a child or adolescent's cognitive ability, and is often used with children who have acquired or innate neurological problems. Areas screened in six subtests include verbal and visual memory; short-delay and long-delay memory; recall, recognition, and working memory; learning characteristics; and attentional functions. It rates skills in all areas, and links them to an IQ score.

- **Developmental Assessment Screening Inventory II (DASI-II).** This screening and assessment tool for pre-school children does not rely heavily on verbal or language-based skills. Its scores rate the patient's developmental level.

- **Developmental Profile II.** This developmental skill inventory is for children up to nine years old (or older people whose developmental levels fall within that range) and is based on an interview with a parent or other caregiver. It covers physical, self-help, social-emotional, communication and academic skills. Scores are provided as an individual profile depicting the functional developmental age level in each area.

- **Kaufman Assessment Battery for Children (Kaufman-ABC).** A non-verbal IQ test, the Kaufman-ABC measures cognitive intellectual abilities in children aged 2-and-a-half to 12. It's one of the best tests for use with non-verbal children without significant fine-motor problems. Scaled scores are provided for overall ability (the Mental Processing Composite) and for Simultaneous and Sequential Processing.

- **Learning Potential Assessment Device (LPAD).** This test of cognitive function uses different assumptions from some of the other IQ tests, and was designed for use primarily with learning disabled or developmentally disabled children. It provides several scaled scores, with interesting ideas about interpreting and using them.

- Leiter International Performance Scale - Revised (Leiter-R). This non-verbal IQ test has puzzle-type problems only covering the areas of visual, spatial, and (in a few cases) language-based reasoning. It produces scaled results.

- Peabody Developmental and Motor Scales (PDMS). These tests use activities, such as threading beads or catching a ball, to gauge the level of physical development, as well as motor capabilities and coordination. They can be used to test large groups of children. Scores are expressed on a scale interpreted as an age level, so raw numbers may be followed by notations like "below age level by five percentiles" or "above age level."

- Peabody Individual Achievement Test (PIAT). These short tests measure performance in reading, writing, spelling, and math. Scores are expressed as a grade level.

- Stanford-Binet Intelligence Test Fourth Edition (S-B IV). This intelligence test is sometimes used with young or non-verbal children, although it is not preferred by most clinicians. The score is expressed as an IQ number or as a scale.

- Test of Non-Verbal Intelligence 3 (TONI-3). This short, non-verbal IQ test for children over five presents a series of increasingly difficult problem-solving tasks, such as locating the missing part of a figure. The score is expressed as an IQ number or age equivalent.

- Vineland Adaptive Behavior Scales. A standardized measure of adaptive behavior, the Vineland scale tests problem-solving and cognitive skills. Scores are presented as a scale, IQ-style number, or age equivalent.

- Weschler Preschool and Prima Scale of Intelligence (WPPSI), Weschler Intelligence Scale for Children-Revised (WISC-R), Weschler Intelligence Scale for Children-Third Edition (WISC-III), Weschler Adult Intelligence Scale (WAIS-R). All of the Weschler Scales are intelligence tests that use age-appropriate word-based activities and mechanical, puzzle-like activities to test problem-solving skills. They return scores for verbal IQ and performance IQ, which may be broken down into several categories.

- Wide Range of Assessment Test - Revision 3 (WRAT 3). This standardized test determines academic level in reading, writing, spelling, and math. Scores are expressed as raw numbers or grade level equivalents.

- Woodcock-Johnson Psycho Educational Battery - Revised (WJPEB-R, WJ-R). An individual test of educational achievement in reading, writing, spelling, and math, the WJ-R has many sub-tests that can be given as a group or separately. Standard scores are derived that compare the test-taker against U.S. norms, and that can also be expressed as an age or grade-level equivalency. One popular sub-test, the Scales of Independent Behavior-Revised (SIB-R/Woodcock, Johnson Battery, Part IV) is a standardized measure of adaptive behavior. SIB-R scores are raw numbers similar to IQ scores, but may be shown as a grade or age equivalency.

Notes

Chapter 1: Introduction to Tourette's Syndrome

1. Tanner, Caroline M., and S. M. Goldman. "Epidemiology of Tourette Syndrome," *Neurology Clinics,* 1997. 15: 395–402.

2. Freeman, Roger D., MD, J. E. Connolly, and P. A. Baird. "Tourette's Syndrome: Update." *Canadian Medical Association Journal,* January 15, 1984. 130 (12): 1554–1557.

3. Tourette Syndrome Association, Inc. *Questions and Answers About Tourette Syndrome.* Bayside, NY: Tourette Syndrome Association Inc.

4. Greenberg, B. D. , et al. "Altered Cortical Excitability in Obsessive-Compulsive Disorder." *Neurology,* January 11, 2000. 54 (1): 142–147.

5. Moriarty, J., et al. "Brain Perfusion Abnormalities in Gilles de la Tourette's Syndrome." *British Journal of Psychiatry,* 1995. 167: 249–254.

6. Peterson, B., et al. "Reduced Basal Ganglia Volumes in Tourette's Syndrome Using Three-Dimensional Reconstruction Techniques from Magnetic Resonance Images." *Neurology,* 1993. 43: 941–949.

7. Singer, H. S., et al. "Volumetric MRI Changes in Basal Ganglia of Children with Tourette's Syndrome." *Neurology,* 1993. 43: 950–956.

8. Robinson, D., et al. "Reduced Caudate Nucleus Volume in Obsessive-Compulsive Disorder." *Archives of General Psychiatry,* May 1995. 52: 393–398.

9. Kushner, Howard I., *A Cursing Brain?: The Histories of Tourette Syndrome.* Cambridge, MA: Harvard University Press, 1999: 40–44.

10. Swedo, Susan, MD, and Henrietta Leonard, MD, et al. "Identification of Children with Pediatric Autoimmune Neuropsychiatric Disorders Associated with Streptococcal Infections by a Marker Associated with Rheumatic Fever." *American Journal of Psychiatry,* 1997. 154 (1): 110–112.

11. Murphy, Tanya, MD, W. K. Goodman, et al. "B-Lymphocyte Antigen D8/17: A Peripheral Marker for Childhood-Onset Obsessive-Compulsive Disorder and Tourette's Syndrome?" *American Journal of Psychiatry,* 1997. 154 (3): 402–407.

12. Swedo, op cit.

13. Eric Hollander, et al. "B-Lymphocyte Antigen D8/17 and Repetitive Behaviors in Autism." *American Journal of Psychiatry,* February 1999. 156 (2): 317–320.

14. Kushner, op cit.: 66–81.

15. Beers, Mark H., MD, and Robert Berkow, MD, editors. *The Merck Manual of Diagnosis and Therapy, Seventeenth Edition.* Whitehouse Station, NJ: Merck Research Laboratories, 1999: 1437–1439.

16. Riedel, M., et al. "Lyme Disease Presenting as Tourette's Syndrome." *Lancet,* February 1998. 7: 351 (9100): 418–419e.

17. Turley, J. M. "Tourette-like Disorder After Herpes Encephalitis." *American Journal of Psychiatry,* December 1988. 145 (12): 1604–1605.

18. Tourette Syndrome Association Inc. *The Genetics of Tourette Syndrome: Who it Affects and How It Affects Families.* Tourette Syndrome Association Inc., 2000.

19. Lichter, D. G., et al. "Influence of Family History on Clinical Expression of Tourette's Syndrome." *Neurology,* January 15, 1999. 52 (2): 308–316.

20. Hyde, Thomas M. and Daniel R. Weinberger. "Tourette's Syndrome: A Model Neuropsychiatric Disorder." Grand Rounds at the Clinical Center of the National Institutes of Health. Bethesda, MD: National Institute of Mental Health, 1995.

21. Kushner, op cit.: 119–143.

Chapter 2: Diagnosis

1. American Psychiatric Association. *Diagnostic and Statistical Manual of Mental Disorders, Fourth Edition.* Washington, DC: American Psychiatric Association, 1994.

2. World Health Organization. *International Classification of Diseases 10.* Geneva: World Health Organization, 1992.

3. Swedo, Susan, MD, Henrietta Leonard, MD, et al. "Identification of Children with Pediatric Autoimmune Neuropsychiatric Disorders Associated with Streptococcal Infections by a Marker Associated with Rheumatic Fever." *American Journal of Psychiatry, 1997.* 154 (1): 110–112.

4. Trifiletti, Rosario R., MD, and A. Bandele. "Antibodies to the Calpain-Calpastatin Complex in Patients with Tics, Tourette Syndrome, or Obsessive-Compulsive Disorder." Presented at the 29th National Meeting of the Child Neurology Society. Abstract: *Annals of Neurology,* 2000. 48: 542.

5. Nixon, R. A. "Fodrin Degradation by Calcium-Activated Neutral Proteinase (CANP) in Retinal Ganglion Cell Neurons and Optic Glia: Preferential Localization of CANP Activated in Neurons." *Journal of Neuroscience,* 1996. 6: 1264–1271.

6. Antoine, J. C., and J. Honnorat. "Anti-Neuronal Antibodies and Central Nervous System Diseases: Contribution to Diagnosis and Pathophysiology." *Revue Neurologique,* January 2000.156 (1): 23–33 (article in French).

7. Ho, C. S. et al. "Association of Allergy with Tourette's Syndrome." *Journal of the Formosan Medical Association,* July 1999. 98(7): 492–5.

8. Trifiletti, R. R., and A. M. Packard. "Immune Mechanisms in Pediatric Neuropsychiatric Disorders: Tourette's Syndrome, OCD, and PANDAS." *Child and Adolescent Psychiatric Clinics of North America,* October 1999. 8(4): 767–75.

9. Singer, Harvey S., MD, Joseph D. Giuliano, Aphrodite M. Zimmerman, and John T. Walkup. "Infection: A Stimulus for Tic Disorders." *Pediatric Neurology,* May 2000. 22 (5): 380–383.

10. Rickard, Hugh, "Tics and Fits: The Current Status of Gilles de la Tourette Syndrome and Its Relationship with Epilepsy." *Seizure,* December 1995. 4 (4).

11. Beers, Mark H., MD, and Robert Berkow, MD, editors. *The Merck Manual of Diagnosis and Therapy, Seventeenth Edition.* Whitehouse Station, NJ: Merck Research Laboratories, 1999: 2415.

12. Ibid.

13. Angelini, L., et al. "Tourettism as Clinical Presentation of Huntington's Disease with Onset in Childhood." *Italian Journal of Neurological Science,* December 1998. 19 (6): 383–385.

14. Nemeth, A. H., et al. "Do the Same Genes Predispose to Gilles de la Tourette Syndrome and Dystonia? Report of a New Family and Review of the Literature." *Movement Disorders,* September 1999. 14 (5): 826–831.

15. Rickard, op cit.

16. Kumar, R., and A. E. Lang. "Tourette Syndrome: Secondary Tic Disorders." *Neurologic Clinics,* 1997. 15: 309–331.

17. Riedel, M., et al. "Lyme Disease Presenting as Tourette's Syndrome." *Lancet,* February 1998. 7: 351 (9100): 418–419e.

18. Turley, J. M. "Tourette-like Disorder After Herpes Encephalitis." *American Journal of Psychiatry,* December 1988. 145 (12): 1604–1605.

19. Beers, op cit.: 56–57.

Chapter 3: Related Conditions

1. Robertson, M. M., M. R. Trimble, and A.J. Lees. "The Psychopathology of Gilles de la Tourette Syndrome: A Phenomenological Analysis." *British Journal of Psychiatry,* 1988. 152: 383–390.

2. George, M. S., M. R. Trimble, H. A. Ring, et al. "Obsessions in Obsessive-Compulsive Disorder With and Without Gilles de la Tourette's Syndrome." *American Journal of Psychiatry,* 1993. 150: 93.

3. Schwartz, Jeffrey M., MD, and Beverly Beyette. *Brain Lock: Free Yourself from Obsessive Compulsive Behavior.* New York: ReganBooks/HarperPerennial, 1996: 58–59.

4. Walkup, J. T., L. D. Scahill, and M. A. Riddle. "Disruptive Behaviour, Hyperactivity and Learning Disabilities in Children with Tourette's Syndrome." *Advances in Neurology,* 1995. 65: 259–272.

5. American Psychiatric Association. *Diagnostic and Statistical Manual of Mental Disorders, Fourth Edition.* Washington, DC: American Psychiatric Association, 1994.

6. Coffey, B., J. Frazier, and S. Chen. "Comorbidity, Tourette Syndrome, and Anxiety Disorders." *Advances in Neurology,* 1992. 58: 95.

7. Ho, C. S. et al. "Association of Allergy with Tourette's Syndrome." *Journal of the Formosan Medical Association,* July 1999. 98 (7): 492–5.

8. V. K. Singh, R. Warren, R. Averett, and M. Ghaziuddin. "Circulating Autoantibodies to Neuronal and Glial Filament Proteins in Autism." *Pediatric Neurology,* July 1997. 17 (1): 88–90.

9. Hollander, Eric, et al. "B-Lymphocyte Antigen D8/17 and Repetitive Behaviors in Autism." *American Journal of Psychiatry,* February 1999. 156 (2): 317–320.

10. Baron-Cohen, Simon, et al. "The Prevalence of Gilles de la Tourette Syndrome in Children and Adolescents with Autism: A Large Scale Study." *Psychological Medicine,* September 1999. 29 (5): 1151–1159.

11. Ibid.

12. Simeon, D., Eric Hollander, D. J. Stein, et al. "Body Dysmorphic Disorder in the DSM-IV Field Trial for Obsessive-Compulsive Disorder." *American Journal of Psychiatry,* 1995. 152: 1207–1209.

13. McElroy, S. L., K. A. Phillips, and P. E. Keck. "Obsessive Compulsive Spectrum Disorder." *Journal of Clinical Psychiatry,* 1994. 55 (supplement 10): 33–51.

14. Bruun, Ruth, MD, et al. "Guide to the Diagnosis and Treatment of Tourette Syndrome." Tourette Syndrome Association, 1984: *http://www.mentalhealth.com/book/p40-gtor.html.*

15. Berthier, M. L., J. Kulisevsky, and V. M. Campos. "Bipolar Disorder in Adult Patients with Tourette's Syndrome: a Clinical Study." *Biological Psychiatry,* 1998. 43: 364.

16. Kerbeshian, J., and L. Burd. "Comorbid Down's Syndrome, Tourette Syndrome, and Intellectual Disability: Registry Prevalence and Developmental Course." *Journal of Intellectual Disability Research,* 2000. 44: 60.

17. Kerbeshian, J., R. Severud, L. Burd, and L. Larson. "Peek-a-boo Fragile Site at 16d Associated with Tourette Syndrome, Bipolar Disorder, Autistic Disorder, and Mental Retardation." *American Journal of Medical Genetics,* 2000. 96: 69.

18. Comings, David E., MD, N. Gonzalez, S. Wu, et al. "Studies of the 48 bp Repeat Polymorphism of the DRD4 Gene in Impulsive, Compulsive, Addictive Behaviors: Tourette Syndrome, ADHD, Pathological Gambling, and Substance Abuse." *American Journal of Medical Genetics,* 1999. 88: 358.

19. Porth, Don and Gary Hughes. "Juvenile Firesetting Research Project 2000: An Analysis of Youth Firesetting Behavior." SOS Fires Youth Intervention Programs: *http://www.sosfires.com/sosfires.htm.*

20. Barlow, David H. "Anxiety Disorders, Comorbid Substance Abuse, and Benzodiazepine Discontinuation: Implications for Treatment." National Institute on Drug Abuse: *http://165.112.78.61/pdf/monographs/monograph172/033-051_Barlow.pdf.*

21. Carey, Kate. "Challenges in Assessing Substance Use Patterns in Persons with Comorbid Mental and Addictive Disorders." National Institute on Drug Abuse: *http://165.112.78.61/pdf/monographs/monograph172/016-032_Carey.pdf.*

22. Brown, V. B., et al. "The Dual Crisis: Mental Illness and Substance Abuse." *American Psychologist,* 1989. 44: 565–569.

23. Comings, David E., MD. "Genetic Factors in Substance Abuse Based on Studies of Tourette Syndrome and ADHD Probands and Relatives." *Drug and Alcohol Dependency,* 1994. 35: 1.

24. Barlow, op cit.

25. Muller-Vahl, K. R., et al. "Cannabinoids: Possible Role in Patho-Physiology and Therapy of Gilles de la Tourette Syndrome." *Acta Psychiatrica Scandinavica,* December 1998. 98 (6): 502–506.

26. Comings, op cit.

27. Comings, David E., MD, S. Wu, C. Chiu, et al. "Polygenic Inheritance of Tourette Syndrome, Stuttering, Attention Deficit Hyperactivity, Conduct, and Oppositional Defiant Disorder: the Additive and Subtractive Effect of the Three Dopaminergic Genes—DRD2, D beta H, and DAT1." *American Journal of Medical Genetics,* 1996. 67: 264.

28. Ibid.

29. Herman, B. H., et al. "Role for Opioid Peptides in Self-Injurious Behavior: Dissociation from Autonomic Nervous System Functioning." *Developmental Pharmacology and Therapeutics,* 1989. 12 (2): 81–89.

30. Barnhill, L. Jarrett, MD. "Tourette Syndrome, Self-Injury, and Developmental Disorders." Presentation, 7th Annual Institute on Dual Diagnosis Conference, August 17, 2000. Abstract: *http://www.theraed.com/institute/7th/sessions/barnhill.htm.*

31. McElroy, S. L., K. A. Phillips, and P. E. Keck, Jr. "Obsessive Compulsive Spectrum Disorder." *Journal of Clinical Psychiatry,* October 1994. 55 (supplement): 33–53.

32. Palumbo, D., A. Maughan, Roger Kurlan, MD. "Hypothesis III: Tourette Syndrome Is Only One of Several Causes of a Developmental Basal Ganglia Syndrome." *Archives of Neurology,* 1997. 54: 475–483.

33. Sheppard, D.M., J. L. Bradshaw, R. Purcell, C. Pantelis. "Tourette's and Comorbid Syndromes: Obsessive Compulsive and Attention Deficit Hyperactivity Disorder. A Common Etiology?" *Clinical Psychology Review,* August 1999. 19 (5): 531–552.

Chapter 4: Growing Up with Tourette's Syndrome

1. Walls, Lisa. "Bullying and Sexual Harassment in Schools." Seattle, WA: Committee for Children, 1998: *http://www.cfchildren.org/PUbully.html.*

2. Goleman, D. *Emotional Intelligence.* New York: Bantam Books, 1995: 122.

3. Learning Disabilities Association of America, "Harassment Based on Disability Is Wrong, Illegal." *FYI,* Sept. 13, 2000. Pittsburgh, PA: Learning Disabilities Association of America. 106 (35.)

4. US Supreme Court. *Davis v. Monroe Board of Education, et al.* Washington, DC: US Supreme Court: May 24, 1999: *http://laws.findlaw.com/us/000/97-843.html.*

5. Learning Disabilities Association of America, op cit.

6. Committee for Children. "Steps to Respect: A Bullying Prevention Program." Seattle, WA: Committee for Children, 2000: *http://www.cfchildren.org/str.html.*

7. Budman, Carol L., Ruth Bruun, MD; K. S. Park; and M. E. Olson. "Rage Attacks in Children and Adolescents with Tourette's Disorder: A Pilot Study." *Journal of Clinical Psychiatry,* 1998. 59: 576.

8. Greene, Ross W. *The Explosive Child: A New Approach to Understanding and Parenting Easily Frustrated, "Chronically Inflexible" Children.* New York: HarperCollins, 1998.

Chapter 5: Living with Tourette's Syndrome

1. Pappalardo, John, and James Turner. *Memorandum of the United States as Amicus Curiae in Opposition to Defendant's Motion for Summary Judgment, US District Court, District of Massachusetts, Joanne Cohen v. the trustees of Boston University.* Washington, DC: US Department of Justice, Civil Rights Division, Disability Rights Section, October 7, 1993.

2. Adapted from Hoffman, Barbara, editor, and National Coalition for Cancer Survivors. *A Cancer Survivor's Almanac: Charting Your Journey.* New York: John Wiley & Sons Inc., 1996.

3. Associated Press. "Tourette's Employee Firing Legal." Associated Press, July 21, 2000.

4. Richardson, Morris. "Bag Boy's Case Raises Issues of Free Speech and Disability Rights." *Detroit News,* February 22, 1999.

5. "Employment." *Tourette Syndrome Association Inc. Newsletter,* Summer 1996. Bayside, NY: Tourette Syndrome Association Inc. 24 (1).

6. Lichter, D. G., J. Dmochowski, L. A. Jackson, and K. S. Trinidad. "Influence of Family History on Clinical Expression of Tourette's Syndrome." *Neurology,* January 15, 1999. 52 (2): 308–316.

7. Canadian Press Association, "Driver Trial Causes Problems for Tourette Advocates: Spokeswoman." *Canadian News Digest,* October 19.

8. Budman, Cathy, MD, and Ruth Dowling Bruun, MD. *Tourette Syndrome and Repeated Anger Generated Episodes.* Bayside, NY: Tourette Syndrome Association Inc., 1998.

9. Ibid.

10. Ibid.

11. Tourette Syndrome Association Inc. *Questions and Answers About Tourette Syndrome.* Bayside, NY: Tourette Syndrome Association Inc.

12. Morris, op cit.

13. Chicago Lawyers' Committee for Civil Rights Under Law, Inc. "Tourette's Sufferer Receives $385,000 Payment to Settle Housing Discrimination Case." *National Fair Housing Advocate,* August 17, 2000.

14. Ibid.

15. Comings, David E., MD. *Search for the Tourette Syndrome and Human Behavior Genes.* Duarte, CA: Hope Press, 1996.

16. Ibid.

Chapter 6: Medical Care

1. Kushner, Howard I., *A Cursing Brain?: The Histories of Tourette Syndrome.* Cambridge, MA: Harvard University Press, 1999: 119–133.

2. Ibid.: 134–141.

3. Bruun, Ruth Dowling, MD, and Cathy Budman. "Risperidone as a Treatment for Tourette's Syndrome." *Journal of Clinical Psychiatry,* 1996. 47: 29.

4. Sallee, F. R., R. Kurlan, C. G. Goetz, et al. "Ziprasidone Treatment of Children and Adolescents with Tourette's Syndrome: A Pilot Study." *Journal of the American Academy of Child and Adolescent Psychiatry,* 2000. 39: 292.

5. Awaad, Y. "Tics in Tourette Syndrome: New Treatment Options." *Journal of Child Neurology,* May 1999. 14 (5): 316–319.

6. Salloway, S, C. F. Stewart, and L. Israeli, et al. "Botulinum Toxin for Refractory Vocal Tics." *Movement Disorders,* 1996. 11: 746.

7. Trimble, M. R., R. Whurr, and G. Brookes, et al. "Vocal Tics in Gilles de la Tourette Syndrome Treated with Botulinum Toxin Injections." *Movement Disorders,* 1998. 13: 617.

8. Muller-Vahl, K. R., et al. "Cannabis in Movement Disorders." *Forsch Komplementarmed,* October 1999. 6 (Supplement 3): 23–27.

9. Muller-Vahl, K. R., et al. "Treatment of Tourette's Syndrome with delta-9-tetrahydrocannabinol." *American Journal of Psychiatry,* 1999. 156: 495.

10. Shytle, R. D., A. A. Silver, and P. R. Sanberg. Poster presented at the International Behavioral Neuroscience Society Annual Meeting. Richmond, VA: International Behavioral Neuroscience Society, June 1998.

11. Bonnier, C., M. C. Nassogne, and P. Evrard. "Ketanserin Treatment of Tourette's Syndrome in Children." *American Journal of Psychiatry,* 1999. 156: 1122.

12. Dursun, S. M., and M. A. Reveley. "Differential Effects of Transdermal Nicotine on Microstructured Analyses of Tics in Tourette's Syndrome: An Open Study." *Psychological Medicine,* 1997. 27: 483.

13. Erdmann, R., and U. Schneider. "Nicotine and Tourette's Syndrome." *Psychiatric Praxis,* 1996. 23: 41.

14. Toren, P., N. Laor, D. J. Cohen, L. Wolmer, and A. Weizman. "Ondansetron Treatment in Patients With Tourette's Syndrome." *International Clinical Psychopharmacology,* November 1999. 14 (6): 373–376.

15. DeNoon, Daniel J. "Anti-Nausea Drug Helps Bulemics: Zofran May Break the Binge/Purge Cycle." *WebMD Medical News,* March 2, 2000: *http://my.webmd.com/content/article/1728.55389.*

16. Vandewalle, V., C. van der Linden, H. J. Groenewegen, and J. Caemaert. "Stereotactic Treatment of Gilles de la Tourette Syndrome by High Frequency Stimulation of Thalamus." *Lancet,* 1999. 353 (9154): 724.

17. Tourette Syndrome Association Inc. "PANDAS Update." TSA Medical Letter 2000. Bayside, NY: Tourette Syndrome Association Inc.: 2.

18. Ibid.

19. Ibid.

20. Leckman, James F., Bradley S. Peterson, and David Pauls. "Tic Disorders." *Psychopharmacology: The Fourth Generation of Progress* (online edition). American College of Neuropsychopharmacology, 2000: *http://www.acnp.org/G4/GN401000161.*

21. Ibid.

22. Jenike, Michael, MD. "Neurosurgical Treatment of Obsessive-Compulsive Disorder." *British Psychiatry,* 1998. 173 (supplement 35): 79–90.

23. Jensen, P. S., L. Kettle, M. T. Roper, et al. "Are Stimulants Overprescribed? Treatment of ADHD in Four US Communities." *Journal of the American Academy of Child and Adolescent Psychiatry,* 1999. 38: 797.

24. Jacobvitz, D., L. A. Sroufe, M. Stewart, et al. "Treatment of Attentional and Hyperactivity Problems in Children with Sympathomimetic Drugs: A Comprehensive Review." *Journal of the American Academy of Child and Adolescent Psychiatry,* 1990. 29: 677–88.

25. Biederman, J. "Attention-Deficit/Hyperactivity Disorder: A Life-span Perspective." *Journal of Clinical Psychiatry,* 1998. 59 (Supplement 7): 4–16.

26. Castellanos, F. X. "Stimulants and Tic Disorders: From Dogma to Data." *Archives of General Psychiatry,* 1999. 56 (4): 337.

27. Papolos, Dimitri F. "Facts About Childhood-Onset Bipolar Disorder." Child and Adolescent Bipolar Foundation, 1999: *http://www.bpkids.org/learning/reference/articles/003.htm.*

28. Burton, Thomas M. "Lilly Says Ritalin Alternative Shows Significant Promise: Alternative Treats Disorder Without Stimulants." *Wall Street Journal,* October 26, 2000.

29. Ibid.

30. Spencer, T., J. Biederman, R. Steingard, et al. "Buproprion Exacerbates Tics in Children with Attention-Deficit Hyperactivity Disorder and Tourette's Syndrome." *Journal of the American Academy of Child and Adolescent Psychiatry*, 1993. 32: 211.

31. Zubieta, J. K., and N. E. Alessi. "Acute and Chronic Administration of Trazodone in the Treatment of Disruptive Behavior in Children." *Journal of Psychopharmacology*, 1992. 12: 346–351.

32. Thompson, T., T. Hackenberg, D. Cerutti, D. Baker, and S. Axtell. "Opioid Antagonist Effects on Self-Injury in Adults with Mental Retardation: Response Form and Location as Determinants of Medication Effects." *American Journal of Mental Retardation*, 1994. 99: 85–102.

33. Azar, Beth. "The Body Can Become Addicted to Self-Injury." *APA Monitor*, December 1995.

34. US Food and Drug Administration, Center for Drug Evaluation and Research. "FDA Public Health Advisory: Risk of Drug Interactions with St. John's Wort and Indinavir and Other Drugs": *http://www.fda.gov/cder/drug/advisory/stjwort.htm*.

35. Lerner, Maura. "The Secret Behind Drug Side Effects May Be in Your Genes." *Minneapolis-St. Paul Star Tribune*, November 15, 2000.

36. Ibid.

37. Tollefson, G. D., et al. "Blind, Controlled, Long-Term Study of the Comparative Incidence of Treatment-Emergent Tardive Dyskinesia with Olanzapine or Haloperidol." *American Journal of Psychiatry*, 1997. 154 (9): 1248–1254.

Chapter 7: Other Interventions

1. National Institutes of Health. *Acupuncture*. NIH Consensus Statement, November 1997. 15 (5): 1–34: *http://odp.od.nih.gov/consensus/cons/107/107_statement.htm*.

2. Li, Y., G. Tougas, S. G. Chiverton, and R. H. Hunt. "The Effect of Acupuncture on Gastrointestinal Function and Disorders." *American Journal of Gastroenterology*, 1992. 87 (10): 1372–81.

3. National Institutes of Health, op cit.

4. Yi, Lian-chon, et al. "A Report on the Treatment of 156 Cases of Tourette's Syndrome with Acupuncture." *Zhong Yi Za Zhi (Journal of Chinese Medicine)*, 1993. 7: 423–424.

5. Trotta, Nicolina, DC. "The Response of an Adult Tourette Patient to LIFE Upper Cervical Adjustments." *Chiropractic Research Journal*, 1989. 1 (3).

6. National Council Against Health Fraud. "Homeopathy: A Position Statement by the National Council Against Health Fraud." Loma Linda, CA: National Council Against Health Fraud, 1994: *http://www.skeptic.com/03.1.jarvis-homeo.html*.

7. Baron-Cohen, Simon, et al. "The Prevalence of Gilles de la Tourette Syndrome in Children and Adolescents with Autism: A Large Scale Study." *Psychological Medicine*, September 1999. 29 (5): 1151–1159.

8. Rimland, Bernard. "Vitamin B6 and Magnesium in the Treatment of Autism." San Diego, CA: Autism Research Institute: *http://www.autism.com/ari/editorials/vitb6.html*.

9. Gabrielska, J., J.Oszmianski, R. Zylka, and M. Komorowska. "Antioxidant Activity of Flavones from Scutellaria baicalensis in Lecithin Liposomes." *Zeitschrift für Naturforschung (Journal of Biosciences)*, November–December 1997. 52 (11–12): 817–823.

10. Levine, J. "Controlled Trials of Inositol in Psychiatry." *European Neuropsychopharmacology*, 1997. 7: 147.

11. Ibid.

12. Miller, Lucinda G. "Herbal Medicinals: Selected Clinical Considerations Focusing on Known or Potential Drug-Herb Interactions." *Archives of Internal Medicine*, November 1998. 9; and other sources.

13. Stoll, Andrew L., MD. *Omega-3 Fatty Acid User Guide*. Belmont, MA: McLean Hospital, 1998.

14. Stoll, Andrew L., MD, et al. "Omega-3 Fatty Acids in Bipolar Disorder: A Preliminary Double-blind, Placebo-controlled Trial." *Archives of General Psychiatry*, May 1999. 56(5): 407–412.

15. Stoll, Andrew L., MD. Presentation, San Diego, CA: Defeat Autism Now 2000 conference, September 16, 2000.

16. Burd, L., and J. Kerbeshian. "Treatment-Generated Problems Associated with Behavior Modification in Tourette Disorder" (letter.) *Developmental Medicine and Child Neurology*, 1987. 29: 831–833.

17. Tansey, M. A. "A Simple and a Complex Tic (Gilles de la Tourette's Syndrome): Their Response to EEG Sensorimotor Rhythm Biofeedback Training." *International Journal of Psychophysiology*, July 1986. 4 (2): 91–97.

18. Trajanovic, N. N., C. M. Shapiro, and Paul Sandor, MD. "REM Sleep Behaviour Disorder in Patients with Tourette's Syndrome." *Sleep Research,* 1997. 26: 524.

19. Grimaldi, Bonnie, BSMT. "Bonnie's Supplements and Diet." Columbus, OH: Bonnie Grimaldi, October 11, 1999: *http://hometown.aol.com/bonniegr/BONNIE_1.HTM.*

20. Knivsberg, Ann-Mari, Karl Reichelt, and Magne Nodland. "A Survey of Dietary Intervention in Autism." Presentation, Durham, UK: 10th Annual Durham International Research Conference on Autism, April 8, 1999.

Chapter 8: School Issues

1. Office of Special Education and Rehabilitation. *Twentieth Annual Report to Congress on the Implementation of the Individuals with Disabilities Education Act.* Washington, DC: US Department of Education, Office of Special Education and Rehabilitation, March 12, 1999: *http://www.ed.gov/offices/OSERS/OSEP/OSEP98AnlRpt.*

2. Singer, H. S., et al. "Learning Difficulties in Children With Tourette Syndrome." *Journal of Child Neurology,* 1995.

3. Jewers, Robin, OTM. "Characteristics of Handwriting in the Child with Tourette Syndrome." *MovemenTS.* Manitoba, Canada: Manitoba Society for Tourette Syndrome, Winter 1998.

4. St. Louis, K. O., and F. L. Myers. "Management of Cluttering and Related Fluency Disorders." In R. Curlee and G. Siegel (Eds.) *Nature and Treatment of Stuttering: New Directions.* New York: Allyn and Bacon, 1997: 313–332.

5. US Department of Education. *Individuals with Disabilities Education Act of 1997.* Washington, DC: US Department of Education, Office of Special Education and Rehabilitation, March 1999.

6. W. B., et al. v. Matula, et al. US Court of Appeals for the Third Circuit, October 17, 1995: *http://www.tourettesyndrome.net/CourtCases/matula.htm.*

Chapter 9: Healthcare and Insurance

1. Consumers for Quality Care, "HMO Arbitration Abuse Report." May 11, 2000: *http://www.consumerwatchdog.com/healthcare.*

2. National Technical Assistance Center of Welfare Reform/Welfare Policy Clearinghouse. "Welfare Reform and Disability": *http://www.welfare-policy.org/weldisab.htm.*

Appendix B

1. The Tourette Syndrome International Consortium for Genetics. "A Complete Genome Screen in Sib Pairs Affected by Gilles de la Tourette Syndrome." *American Journal of Human Genetics* 1999. 65: 1428–1436.

Index

"Bending the Rules" video, 79
Beneficiary Advisory Services, New Zealand, 307
Benzodiazepine, 165
Beta carotene, 192
Bifodobacterium bifidum, 198
Biofeedback, 174
    neurobiofeedback, 203–204
Biotin, 197
Bipolar disorders, 56–58
    behavioral side effects (BSEs) with, 160–161
    cyclothymic disorder, 57
    resources on, 334–335
    substance abuse and, 59–60
Bite guards, 158
Biting, 105
Bitter melon, 197
Black cohosh, 209
Black current seed oil, 194
Blood flow in brain, 11
Blood pressure, 191
Blood tests, 121–124
    understanding results, 122–124
B-lymphocyte antigen D8/17, 15
BOCES Tourette's syndrome program, 250
Body dysmorphic disorder (BDD), 56, 105–106
    resources on, 335
Bodywork, 205
Books
    medical resources, 338
    medication information, 341
    on parenting skills, 347–348
    on St. John's wort, 175
    on special education, 346
    on TS, 69–70, 323–324
Borage oil, 189, 194
Boston University, 93–94
Botox, 139
Bradyphrenia, 162
Brain, 8. *See also* Encephalitis
    misfirings of, 10–11
Brain scans, 10–11
Brain surgery, 19
Breastfeeding. *See* Pregnancy
Breathing exercises, 112
Brewer's yeast, 176
Bruun, Ruth, 313–314
Bruxism, 157
Buddy system, 202
Bulimia, 106
    ondansetron for, 141
Bullying, 69–71
    provocative victims, 71
    school policies, 70
Buproprion. *See* Wellbutrin
Burning, 105

Burning behavior, 62
BuSpar, 156
    sexual response and, 161–162
Buspirone. *See* BuSpar
Butterfly needles, 121
B vitamins, 187. *See also* specific types
    Brewer's yeast, 176
    sleep disorders and, 208

C

Caffeine, 210
Calcium, 193
Calpain, 36
Calpastatin, 36
Canada
    healthcare in, 301–303
    mental health support, 318
    public mental health agencies, 359–361
    school issues in, 265–266
    support groups in, 316
    treatment centers in, 330
Canadian Human Rights Act, 97
Canadian Mental Health Association, 318
Cannabinoids, 139–140
Cannabis indica, 139–140
Cannabis sativa, 139–140
Caprylic acid, 198
Caramel color, 210
Carbamazepine, 42, 127
Carbon dioxide inhalation, 19, 112
Case management, 274
Catapres. *See* Clonidine
Cat's claw, 193
Cattell Scales, 372
Caudate nucleus, 10
CBC (complete blood cell) count, 123–124
Celexa, 143, 144
    for obsessive-compulsive disorder (OCD), 145
Center for Computer Redistribution, 311
Center Watch, 310
Central nervous system (CNS), 11
    nicotine and, 140–141
Centrax, 156
Centrelink Web site, Australia, 306
Cerebral palsy, 39
    Medicaid waivers, 294
Certified Medication Aide (CMA) license, 224
Chamomile, 208
Charter schools, 248–249
Checklist of symptoms, 33
Child abuse, 34
    sexual child abuse, 3
Child and Family Services (CFS), 294
    TANF applications, 299
Child development issues, 73–74

504 plans, 229–231
  legal actions, 262
  socialization goals, 229–231
Flaxseed oil, 194
Flexibility skills, 203
Florida Obsessive-Compulsive Inventory (FOCI), 49, 369
Fluoxetine hydrochloride. *See* Prozac
Fluphenazine, 136
Fluvoxamine maleate. *See* Luvox
Folic acid, 187
  Dilantin and, 189
Food and Drug Administration (FDA), 175
Food dyes, 210
Food stamps, 299
Foreign language information, 324–325
Formularies, 116, 282–283
French language information, 325
Freud, Sigmund, 3, 33
Friends, 170
Full-body tics, 218
Full integration, 243
Functional behavior assessment (FBA), 226–227
Functional intervention plan (FIP), 226–227
Functional magnetic resonance imaging (fMRI), 11

G

GABA (gaba-amino butyric acid), 209
Gambling, pathological, 58
Gammalinolenic acid (GLA), 194
Garlic, 198
GEDs (Graduate Equivalency Diplomas), 270
  homeschooling programs, 255
  programs to achieve, 259–260
Gender, xiv
  pyromania, 59
  Rett syndrome, 55
Generic interactions, 118
Genetics, 17. *See also* Chromosomes
  appendix information on, 365–367
  autism and, 54
  counseling resources, 339–340
  differences, 16–18
  dystonia musculorum deformans, 40
  Huntington's chorea, 40
  hyperekplexia, 41
  Lesch-Neyhan syndrome, 41
  neuroacanthocytosis, 43
The Genetics of Tourette Syndrome: Who It Affects and How it Occurs in Families, 366
Geodon, 128
GGT (gamma glutamyl transpeptidase), 123
Gingko biloba, 186
  cautions, 189
  immune system support, 192

Gingseng cautions, 189
Glial cells, 11–14
Glucosamine, 186
Glutathione, 175, 176
  immune system support, 192
Gluten, 210
Goldenseal, 197
Google, 120
Grapefruit juice, drug interactions, 159
Grape seed extract. *See* Proanthocyanidins (OPCs)
Greene, Ross, 77, 200
Grievances to health insurance, 286
Grimaldi, Bonnie, 187, 210
Group A beta-hemolytic streptococcus (GABHS) bacteria, 14
Guanfacine, 114, 138–139
  for Attention Deficit Hyperactivity Disorder (ADHD), 155
  benefits of, 131
  vitamin B3 and, 191
Guilt, 19–20
  rage behaviors and, 103

H

Habitat for Humanity, 300
Habit reversal, 200–202
Habitrol, 140
Hair-pulling. *See* Trichotillomania
Haldol, 3, 42, 99, 113, 129, 132
  liquid form, 119
  as older medication, 116
  side effects of, 113
  tardive dyskinesia (TD) and, 164
Haloperidol. *See* Haldol
Harassment
  disability harassment, 71–72
  workplace harassment, 99
Harris, Eric, 227
Hate speech, 109
Hawaii, medicaid in, 292
Hawking, Steven, 69
Head-banging, 62
Head injuries, 40–41
Healthcare, 273–274. *See also* Health insurance
  in Australia, 305–306
  in Canada, 301–303
  change, advocating for, 311
  clinical trials, 310
  discounts for, 311
  in Ireland, 340
  local health plans, 296–297
  in New Zealand, 306–307
  private health care, 275–276
  private-pay arrangements, 307–308
  public healthcare, 291–298

Healthcare *(continued)*
    resource information, 340–341
    state health plans, 296–297
    in United Kingdom, 303–304
Health Care Flex spending Account (FSA), 300
Health insurance, 25, 275–285. *See also* HMOs
            (health maintenance organizations)
    alternatives to, 307–311
    appealing denial of claim, 287–290
    arbitrating claims, 290
    change, advocating for, 311
    COBRA plans, 280–281
    compassionate care exception, 291
    decision-making on, 276–280
    denial of care, fighting, 285–290
    denial of coverage, 280–281
    employer-provided, 279–280
    grievances, 286
    legal actions, 290
    mental health carve-outs, 278
    for new treatments, 291
    in New Zealand, 307
    point-of-service (POS) options, 278
    pre-existing conditions, 278
    preferred provider organizations (PPOs), 276–277
    questions to ask, 277–280
    resource information, 340–341
    workplace issues, 96
Health Law Project, 295
Heart palpitations, 162
Hemp, 139–140
Hemp seed oil, 194
Herbal PDR, 190
Herbal remedies. *See also* Herbal supplements
    antibiotics, herbal, 196–197
    in Chinese medicine, 182–183
    naturopathy and, 180
    orthomolecular medicine, 181
    sleep aids, 208
Herbal supplements
    interactions with, 159
    medications interacting with, 118
    neurotransmitter production and, 14
Heredity. *See* Genetics
Herpes virus, 16
    tics and, 44
Hiccups, 43
Higher education programs, 93–94, 272–273
History of TS, 2–3
Hitting, 105
HIV, 16
HMOs (health maintenance organizations), 25.
        See also Health insurance
    appealing denial of claim, 287–290

documentation for, 283
emergency room treatment, 167
formularies, 116, 282–283
formulary, 116
gag orders, 278
grievances, 286
hospital admissions, 168
managing with, 281–285
master policy document, 281–282
medication choices, 116
National Committee for Quality Assurance
        (NCQA), 277–278
referrals, 29–30, 283
tips for dealing with, 284–285
Home and Community-Based Services (1915(c))
        waivers, 294
Homebound instruction, 252–254
Homeopathy, 180
Homeschooling, 254–255
    in United Kingdom, 267
Hops, 209
Hormones, 11
    medications affecting, 14
Hospitals. *See also* Psychiatric facilities
    education, hospital-based, 252
    financial arrangements with, 308
    problems with, 171–173
    treatment in, 165–168
House-Tree-Person Projective Drawing Technique,
        370
Human Genome Project, 17
Humor, 68
    relationships and, 102
    as social skill, 203
Humulus lupulus, 209
Huntington's chorea, 40
Hydrastis canadensis, 197
Hydrotherapy, 180
Hyperactivity. *See* Attention Deficit Hyperactivity
        Disorder (ADHD)
Hyperekplexia, 41
Hyperkinesia, 162
Hyperlexia, 54
Hypervitaminosis, 191
Hypnosis, 19, 112
Hypomania, 56–58

I

Ibuprofen interactions, 117, 150
Ignorance about TS, 91
Immobilizing child, 80
Immune system, 14–16. *See also* Autoimmune
        disorders
    antioxidants, 191–193